THE X FILES

Declassified

THE X FILES

Declassified

The truth!

This book has not
been authorized by
any entity involved
in creating
THE X-FILES

The unauthorized guide to the complete series

Frank Lovece

Hodder & Stoughton

Copyright © 1996 by Frank Lovece

First published in Great Britain in 1996 by Hodder and Stoughton
A division of Hodder Headline PLC

The right of Frank Lovece to be identified as the Author of the Work
has been asserted by him in accordance with the
Copyright, Designs and Patents Act 1988.

10 9 8 7 6 5

A CIP catalogue record for this title is available
from the British Library

ISBN 0 340 68232 9

Typeset by Hewer Text Composition Services, Edinburgh
Printed and bound in Great Britain by Mackays of Chatham PLC, Chatham, Kent

Dedication

For Maitland, whom I love

Contents

Acknowledgments

This volume is the result of months of research and writing – for which time, like Mulder, I had no life. I'd like to thank my friends and family profusely for putting up with my late nights, unreturned phone calls, and canceled invitations and appointments. I'd especially like to thank my light-of-my-life kids, Vincent and Erik Lovece.

I also extend my greatest thanks to Maitland McDonagh, who helped to track down facts, look for pictures, and subsidize my endless online research. My agent, Chris Calhoun, and my editor, Kevin McDonough, are understanding friends with great patience, who in the schism of "You want it fast or you want it good?" didn't push for fast. Kevin is as generous and genial an editor as a writer could hope for. Carolyn Caughey, the British edition's editor, proved equally so, and her efforts have resulted in British fans getting a fuller, more detailed book.

For their personal help in various capacities, I also thank Peter Berg, Mike Lackey – two godsends – as well as Andy Edelstein, Craig Miller, Toni Cohen, and the ever-helpful staffs of the Lincoln Center Rose Theater Collection, Jerry Ohlinger's memorabilia shop, and the Baseline entertainment-industry online service. I'd also like to thank journalists Paula Vitaris, Marc Shapiro, Kyle Counts, Julianne Lee, Bill Florence, Edward Gross, Jim Swallow, Dana Kennedy, Bruce Fretts, Benjamin Svetkey, Bret Watson, and Scott Cohen, whose articles provided much of the source material for this encyclopedia. And of course, my great thanks go to all those **X-Files** fans whose admiration and enthusiasm for the show have made this book possible.

– Frank Lovece

Introduction

"Just because you're paranoid doesn't mean
nobody's following you."
>   – late 20th-century folk saying

"Trust no one."
>   – Deep Throat (Jerry Hardin)

When all is said and done, Richard Nixon created **The X-Files**.
Sure, the Kennedy assassination got us talking cover-up, and the John
Birch Society had people thinking fluoridation was an Orwellian
scheme. But it was the Pentagon Papers and Watergate that *really*
made us think we could Trust No One. Though conspiracies
involving government officials have existed since, well, government
officials, the aggressive post-Watergate media have made us more
aware.

And Richard Nixon really *did* keep surreptitious tapes of private
White House meetings – for what possible purpose, since all
participants' kept memos/minutes of their actions, if not of their
embarrassingly frank language? And that Administration – and who
knows what others? – really *did* illegally wiretap writers and
journalists. It's like Mr. X says to a certain dogged FBI agent, they
have something on everyone. Consider: How would you feel if *your*
office was bugged?

At the other end of the spectrum, of course, are the verifiably
wacko conspiracy theories; we can rest certain the CIA isn't
implanting radio receivers in average citizens' molars to track them.
(The CIA itself isn't what it used to be, if it ever was – foreign
correspondents often gather better, quicker information, and the
agency's misinterpretations and misjudgments of intelligence data in
recent years have made them the Keystone Kops of the spook
community. Now, the *NSA* is another story. . . .)

Yet between these extremes of the fanciful and the concrete, we
find a hazy middle-ground: covert conspiracies that might very well

exist. And they're *real*, that's the thing. The Reagan Administration's Iran–Contra cover-up – with such bizarre mystery-thriller turns as a beautiful secretary stuffing documents in her bra to keep them from the hands of, not the KGB, but our own FBI – wasn't some episode of **The X-Files**. People talk about how leaks and deathbed confessions almost guarantee any secret will get out – yet look at the decades that passed with the unspoken secret of unwitting human atomic-radiation experiments. Imagine the horrible damage done to the families and children of those 1950s fathers who died prematurely of cancer, the veil of secrecy leaving no recourse to financial recompense, now that the breadwinner had gone. These aren't pie-in-the-sky concerns – they affect you and me. So when someone produces jigsaw-puzzle pieces about a spaceship crash near Roswell, NM, or the origin of AIDS as a bumbling CIA germ-warfare accident, maybe they're off-base – but stranger realities have occurred, and it pays to keep an open mind. To survive today, to paraphrase Bob Dylan, everybody must get Oliver Stoned.

And we largely are. **The X-Files**, which premiered on September 10, 1993 on Fox, taps expertly into our skeptical, cynical national mood. It has no campy undercurrent like its 1970s ancestor, *The Night Stalker* – it's a dead serious, if hypercompressed, police procedural. Mulder and Scully explore a shadow world of things-that-might-very-well-be.

Like such other speculative fiction fan-faves as *Quantum Leap* or *Star Trek*, **The X-Files** has a core following: "X-Philes." Their growing number has rapidly taken the show from cult-hit to hit-hit. Yet for all the **X-File** coverage in the media, all the X-Phile news and chatter in cyberspace and fanzines, there's no single source for all the essential information.

This is a virtual **X-Files** encyclopedia, distilling hundreds of thousands of words of international reportage into one comprehensive and comprehensible story, and examining the episodes themselves in more detail than anyone has yet published.

X-Genesis: Chris Carter and the creation of the X-Files

Chris Carter wanted to make a scary show. "I don't mean scary in the horror-genre sense, but scary in the way that speculation pushes beyond scientific credibility to enter a realm of 'extreme possibility,'" he says. "Films like *Coma* and *The Andromeda Strain* have that quality. It's the idea that shakes up you and your beliefs, not some hideous Frankenstein monster or a hand clasping the heroine's shoulder. We're all more interested in modern phenomena, which have a way of really shaking up that segment of our society that's come to believe in aliens and UFOs."

Add to this the growing fear of conspiracies and suspicions about the U.S. government, particularly tales of the unaccountable, heavily armed, "black budget" secret part, from the CIA to the NSA. Real-life stories like Waco, Ruby Ridge, and Oliver North's secret paramilitaries have made many people suspicious and fearful of their government. In the post-Cold War era, many have transferred their fear of the Soviet "Evil Empire" to Washington. Add the interest in forensic science (popularized in *The Silence of the Lambs*) and you've the basis for modern-day ghost stories to tell those huddled around the modern-day electronic campfire.

While a lot of writer-producers might have come up with something similar to *The X-Files*, it took Chris Carter's off-kilter talent and particular quirks and influences to envision and create a show that ranks with television's greatest, like Gene Roddenberry's *Star Trek* and Steven Bochco's *Hill Street Blues*.

Christopher C. Carter grew up in blue-collar Bellflower, CA, outside Los Angeles; born Oct 13, 1957 he's the son of construction worker William and late housewife Catherine Mulder Carter. His earliest major TV influence was the show *Kolchak: The Night Stalker* (ABC 1974–1975), the series spinoff of the hit TV-movies *The Night Stalker* (1972) and *The Night Strangler* (1973). Each version starred Darren McGavin as rumpled reporter Carl Kolchak, who kept running across supernatural entities but could never convince editor Tony Vincenzo (Simon Oakland) of their existence. "When I saw *Stalker*, it really shook me up to think there might be a twilight world of bloodsucking creatures," Carter recalls. "I probably remember only two scenes from the series [but] it was a scary show. That made a big impression on me when I was a kid."

A writer from youth, Carter graduated from California State University, Long Beach, with a journalism degree in 1979. Journalism and surfing led to a job writing for the magazine *Surfing*, based in nearby San Clemente. Within a few years, Carter became *Surfing*'s editor, and in 1983 he began a committed relationship with future wife Dori Pierson, a screenwriter. (She later co-wrote several TV-movies, starting with *The Imposter* [sic] in 1984, as well as the 1988 feature film *Big Business*.) With Pierson's encouragement and contacts, Carter began writing and pitching his own scripts as well; in 1985, one of them came to the attention of Jeffrey Katzenberg, then chairman of Walt Disney Studios, who decided to give Carter a try with a standard development contract.

That led to his first produced effort, the "Disney Sunday Movie" *The B.R.A.T. Patrol* (ABC 1986), co-written with Michael Patrick Goodman. It was a forgettable family adventure starring Sean Astin as one of several Marine "military brats" who band together when they discover equipment being stolen; in *X-Files* fashion, the camp authorities neither believe nor cooperate with them. Carter also wrote for NBC Productions, where he created and produced an unsold adventure-drama pilot, *Cameo by Night*, aired in August 1987 and starring Sela Ward as Jennifer Cameo, a police-department secretary who goes undercover in the rock-music world to find a killer. Also around this time, for the Disney Channel, Carter developed an unsold sitcom called *The Nanny* – which, he hastens to add, "wasn't THAT *Nanny* [starring Fran Dresden], it was a previous and less successful *Nanny*."

In 1987, Carter wrote two episodes of the musical sitcom *Rags to Riches*, and co-produced that show during its two-month-long second season in 1988. In-between, he and Pierson – they had married in 1987 – co-wrote and served as co-executive producers of a one-hour "Disney Sunday Movie"(and apparent pilot) *Meet the Munceys* (ABC 1988), about a Palm Beach woman (Nana Visitor, later of *Star Trek: Deep Space Nine*) whose family flocks to her after she inherits a fortune. Then Carter created and served as executive producer of NBC Productions' *Brand New Life*, an updated *Brady Bunch* starring Barbara Eden and Don Murray; four of its six episodes ran in fall 1989 under the umbrella banner *The Magical World of Disney*, and the last two filled sporadic slots in January and April 1990. The following year, Carter briefly served as a writer and story editor on the Gary Cole series *Midnight Caller*.

Throughout these vagaries, Carter gained a reputation as a good writer and promising TV producer. "When I came to Hollywood," Carter says, "I had a native talent for 'youth dialogue,' having spent so much time on the beach with surfers. So I naturally became a little bit pigeon-holed – people just kept hiring me to do that." Now he'd become, as he put it, one of those legions who'd developed "a reputation as a person who can possibly create a TV show. So a studio enlists you, and you come up with the idea, and then you pitch it to the network, and they either buy or they don't."

The enlisting studio, for Carter, was Fox, where the new president of TV production was Peter Roth; the former head of Stephen J. Cannell Productions (*Wiseguy*, *The Rockford Files*, *21 Jump Street*, *The Commish*, etc., etc., etc.), Roth remembered having liked an unproduced script of Carter's that he'd seen while there. Now, in 1992, he took a chance and signed him to a standard three-year development deal.

So what would Carter come up with? Another family sitcom? Something with "youth dialogue"? Maybe something with surfers?

No. *The X-Files*.

"*The X-Files* is what I've always wanted to be doing," Carter explains. "When you first come to Hollywood, you're happy just to be paid to write. But I was looking for a chance to do my scary show, and *The X-Files* was the eventual result. If you look at my resumé, you'll never find any clear connection between my old work and *The X-Files*. I just wanted to do something as scary as I remember *The Night Stalker* was when I was in my teens."

But *Night Stalker* was only one influence; Carter was also aware of an increasing public belief in the paranormal. He met a psychology professor who said he'd served as a consultant on *Intruders* (CBS, May 1992), the two-part TV-movie about alien abductions, based on Budd Hopkins' book. The consultant "told me that 3% (sic) of the public believed in this syndrome. I was astounded. I realized there was a topicality to this theme of the unknown, and *X-Files* grew out of that fascination."

Another *X-Files* influence was the cult-classic '60s TV show *The Avengers*. "I loved that relationship," Carter says of the witty, mutually respectful but non-romantic interplay between suave British spy John Steed (Patrick Macnee) and his female partner, Emma Peel (Diana Rigg). "I think it was the intensity of the stories there. It's the way I sort of instinctively write, so that was also fed into my ultimate concept of the show," which he'd always planned as having male and female co-leads.

What didn't feed into Carter's vision, ironically, was science fiction. "I was never what you would call a science fiction devotee," Carter says. "I've never read the classic SF novels, except maybe one of each by Ursula Le Guin and Robert Heinlein a long time ago, and I've never watched an episode of *Star Trek*!"

Fox executives did not jump at Carter's proposal. "They turned it down at first," Carter remembers. "They didn't know what it was. And then I went back with Peter Roth, and we were able to sell it to them . . . They reluctantly bought the idea but it took two pitch meetings to convince them that we had something worth proceeding on."

After finishing a script, Carter was given the green light in December 1992 to film an *X-Files* pilot, as a co-production between himself and 20th Century Fox Television. Within days, Carter incorporated Ten Thirteen Productions and began hiring staff. He had roughly $2 million to film a one-hour pilot in March and have it completed by May, when Fox Television would pitch it to its sister-company network, Fox Broadcasting. Rather than shoot in Los Angeles, where the bulk of TV programming is made, Carter placed production in Vancouver, where shooting is somewhat cheaper.

Carter has been cagey about the origins of the names "Fox Mulder" and "Dana Scully." At first he said, "I liked the sounds. They trip off the tongue. And I grew up in L.A. where [Dodgers baseball announcer] Vin Scully was the voice of God." He later revealed "Mulder" was his mother's maiden name; as for "Fox," he explained (after people began speculating about a lead character named after the network), "I grew up with someone with the name." "Dana," he says, was "just a nice, soft woman's name I like."

More important than their names is the dramatic dichotomy they represent, which boils down to faith vs. disbelief. "I'm equal parts of both characters," Carter says. "I'm a skeptic like Scully, but I'm also ready to be enraptured, like Mulder . . . They are the equal parts of my desire to believe in something and my inability to believe in something. My skepticism and my faith. And the writing of the characters and the voices came very easily to me. I want, like a lot of people do, to have the experience of witnessing a paranormal phenomenon. At the same time I want not to accept it, but to question it. I think those characters and those voices came out of that duality." Or to put it more succinctly, "I'm a nonreligious person in search of religious experience."

With script and a go-ahead in hand, it was time to assemble his team. As co-executive producer, Carter hired R.W. "Bob" Goodwin, a 20-year TV veteran who'd produced several TV-movies and miniseries, served as producer of series including *Hooperman* and *Eddie Dodd*, and broke in as a co-executive producer with the 1992-93 season of *Life Goes On*. Goodwin suggested Juilliard-trained composer Mark Snow, who'd written the score for several TV-movies, then began putting together a Vancouver production staff which included producers Paul Rabwin and Joseph Patrick Finn. Pre-production was underway by February 1993.

Casting had already been long underway. (For more information see separate biographies.) The script, actors, and production crew set, the production filmed for 14 days under director Robert Mandel, a TV veteran whose work includes some theatrical films, among them the cult-favorite *F/X* (1986). Post-production (editing and the addition of music, special effects and "relooped" dialog to fix any mumbles or last-minute script changes) was done by early May.

Fox Broadcasting, in its March presentation to advertisers, had announced *The X-Files* as one of 37 series hopefuls for 1993-94. Fox, at this point, was still huckstering *The X-Files* as being based on "chilling documented reports and true accounts" – which may indeed have been how Carter sold the show; as *The Los Angeles Times* reported, "Carter pitched *The X-Files* to Fox as *Silence of the Lambs* meets *Unsolved Mysteries*."

By May 21, *The X-Files* had made it to series, tentatively placed in the Tuesday lineup, following the tongue-in-cheek, 1890s Western *The Adventures of Brisco County, Jr.* Both were soon rescheduled to Friday, often considered a dead night for ratings.

As Carter's production company grew, he hired the writing team of Glen Morgan & James Wong as the L.A.-based co-executive producers. Carter named another writing team, Howard Gordon & Alex Gansa, as supervising producers. The rest of the staff firmed up. Goodwin recommended cinematographer John (a.k.a. John S.) Bartley as series director of photography; he'd previously served in that position on Stephen J. Cannell's Vancouver shows *Booker*, *The Commish* and *Broken Badges*. Soundstages were rented at North Vancouver's North Shore Studios, with offices nearby at, first 2790 Vine Street (the address of Mulder's childhood home on Martha's Vineyard), then at 110-555 Brooks Bank Avenue. A company called Castle/Bryant/Johnsen – James, Bruce and Carol, respectively – put together the eventually Emmy Award-winning opening credits, brimming with eerily beautiful images of Kirlian auras, sprouting seedlings, scudding skies, and a giant eye evoking the supposed one-world-government Masonic symbol from the back of the dollar bill. The overall series budget was widely reported to be $900,000 per episode – moderate for a one-hour network dramatic series. Carter's cited the cost as "just over $1 million per episode," but that might be averaging in overruns, promotional costs and the like.

The series premiered strongly, on September 10, 1993. "If succeeding chapters can keep the pace," reviewed the trade magazine *Variety*, "the well-produced entry could be this season's UFO high-flier . . ." Fox's sister-magazine *TV Guide*, in its Fall Preview issue, opined, "If you can overlook a credibility gap the size of the Milky Way – and many viewers *will* overlook it – the show is actually well-done. Whether you believe these stories are not, they're first-rate entertainment. . . . a well produced, suspenseful mystery series that draws you in and keeps you hooked."

Nielsen ratings were higher than anything else Fox aired on admittedly ratings-poor Friday night. Before September was out, Fox gave Carter a full-season, 22-episode order. (It would shortly be upped to 24.) In addition, the series attracted a high percentage of most advertisers' target audience: Urban, educated, 18- to 34-year-old viewers. While viewership did drop precipitously until a fan-following (self-described "X-Philes") and strong word-of-mouth attracted the curious, the series kept building until, by April, its ratings were beating that of its premiere. The season finale, "The Erlenmeyer Flask," was its highest-rated – and even it was consistently beaten throughout season two. While all this still amounted to *The X-Files* finishing in the Nielsen cellar – either 102nd of 118 shows, or 113th of 132 shows, depending on the chart and what was included on it – the series' critical and ad-sales success prompted Fox to renew it.

During the season, Carter, like any other executive producer, had had to wrestle with the network over issues of taste and content. Less typically, he fought to preserve his show's loosely resolved (and sometimes muddily unresolved) endings – rightly noting that you can't handcuff monsters and aliens and book 'em, Danno.

Carter also was insistent that, "I didn't want this to be another *Moonlighting*. I didn't want the relationship to come before the cases . . . I think the best kind of sexual tension is when you put a smart man and a smart woman in a room: You've got immediate sexual tension, no matter if it's romantic [or not]. There's a tension there. And I think that's what we have with Mulder and Scully. I think there's a mutual respect, a mutual passion to solve these cases. And I think that people have responded to that."

By the season's end, *The X-Files* was a critics' darling, appearing on best-of lists and netting an endorsement from Viewers for Quality Television. Yet it was the second season (production of which began on July 11, 1994) that truly fulfilled the network's, and Carter's, audience aspirations.

That was partly due to Fox's sister-magazine, the huge-circulation *TV Guide*, giving the show a remarkable amount of coverage. When Carter and the stars took a late-spring trip, by invitation, to the FBI

Academy in Quantico, VA, the magazine dutifully covered it; later *TV Guide* would even go so far as to publish an *X-Files* comic-book story from the companion Topps Comics series.

It was during the second season that Morgan and Wong left to launch their Fox series *Space: Above and Beyond* in January 1995. Frequent director David Nutter, hired on as a producer for the second season, would leave with them. Carter recruited new writers Frank Spotnitz, Sara Charno, and Darin Morgan (Glen Morgan's younger brother). Even so, he says, "My staff was pared down by the loss of Jim and Glen . . . and I never really replaced them because I didn't find anyone of that level and caliber to replace them with."

Second-season production ended May 4, 1995, and the show was on a roll: Its year-end ratings put it well into the middle of the Nielsens – terrific for Fox, which otherwise had only a bare handful of stalwarts like *The Simpsons* and *Beverly Hills, 90210* in that range. Continuing its critical success, *The X-Files* scored an upset Golden Globe Award for Television Series, Drama, over such highly touted contenders as *E.R.* and *NYPD Blue*; this helped bring a new-viewer momentum through the spring and summer reruns, building a big foundation for the third-season return.

During the spring and summer came a parade of magazine cover stories – the great cult-fave turning into a trend. Official *X-Files* novels and comic books had appeared earlier in the year, as had an *Entertainment Weekly* cover-story and a *Mad* magazine parody. There was a year-old official fan club, a blizzard of fanzines, and, in June, the first dedicated *X-Files* convention.

Duchovny hosted the 1995 season finale of *Saturday Night Live*. And the media bandwagon would soon plaster him everywhere, from Jay Leno, Tom Snyder and David Letterman to the covers of *Details* and (again, but solo this time) *Entertainment Weekly*. Anderson did the talk-show circuit, particularly in the U.K., where *The X-Files* was a modest hit (and for a time the highest-rated show on BBC2).

Production began again in Vancouver on July 13, 1995. The 1995-96 premiere was Fox's top-rated program that week. By mid-season, *The X-Files* was Fox's highest-rated show, outpacing the network's established hits, and 20th Century Fox Television sold the fall 1997 rerun rights to sister cable network FX for a reported $600,000 each

– the most ever paid by a cable network for an hour-long drama series, topping the record $475,000 each that USA Network had paid for *Murder, She Wrote.*

Carter himself had broken from the ranks of semi-anonymous TV-show creators to become a household name. That's not a bad accomplishment: who knows who created *Friends?* With his newfound clout, Carter was able to get the budget increased: "I've pushed the limits of what we were doing on the show, because I wanted to do some things like the submarine at the polar ice cap in 'End Game.' So the budget expanded somewhat because of the nature and difficulty of the work."

In fall 1995, when his original three-year deal with Fox expired, Carter re-upped for more five years in a contract brokered by his agents, Elliott Webb and Bob Broder of Broder, Kurland, Webb, Uffner, and attorneys Larry Rose and Bruce Ramer. Its provisions include a commitment for science fiction drama series (set in the year 2000, with the working title *Millennium*) and for the development of an *X-Files* feature film (which he'd long discussed informally and at fan conventions, but which was only put into contractual terms now; Duchovny and Anderson would star, and Carter might direct).

Today, with *The X-Files* solidly established as both a TV and a pop-cultural hit, Carter has found a rare degree of luxury. Still unfulfilled is his dream of bringing in the former Kolchak, Darren McGavin, whom Carter had originally wanted to play Mulder's father: "We've made overtures twice and both times Darren was either too busy or uninterested, which is unfortunate," Carter says. "That doesn't mean we'll quit trying, because it would make great sense to have him on, but I can't say for sure that it will happen."

As for the future – and whether Mulder and Scully will ever find the truth or just get lives outside their work – it's only sketchily mapped out. "I know basically where I am going with the series," Carter asserts. "I know what the final episodes will entail."

CHRIS CARTER FILMOGRAPHY

As writer
Disney Sunday Movie: The B.R.A.T. Patrol (ABC 10/26/86)
Cameo by Night (NBC series pilot 8/2/87; 60 min.)
  (Also producer)

Rags To Riches (NBC TV series 9/25/87)
  "Once Upon a Lifeguard"
Rags To Riches (NBC TV series 11/20/87)
  "Beauty and the Babe"
Disney Sunday Movie: Meet the Munceys (ABC 5/22/88; 60 min.)
  (Also executive producer)

Midnight Caller (NBC TV series 4/19/91)
  "A Cry in the Night"

As creator and executive producer
Brand New Life (NBC 9/18/89–8/12/90; six episodes)
The X-Files (Fox 9/10/93–present; for writing-directing credits, see
  Writer-Director Episode Index)

Not to be confused with
Actor Christoper Carter, who played Andre Bailis on *Hangin' With
Mr. Cooper* (ABC) from 1992–94; Christopher M. Carter, who played
Lee J. on the Oct. 30, 1991 episode of *The Royal Family*; Christopher
Carter-Hooks, who appeared in the Jan. 5, 1989 episode of *The Cosby
Show* and the Dec. 30, 1990 episode of *Hull High*; driver Chris Carter
of the film *Invasion U.S.A.* (1985); song composer Chris Carter of the
film *The Living End* (1992); or 2nd assistant accountant Chris Carter of
the film *Aspen Extreme* (1993).

BRAND NEW LIFE
Working title: *Blended Family*
NBC, Sept. 18, 1989–Aug. 12, 1990, 60 min.

1) "The Honeymooners" Sept. 18, 1989
   Two-hour premiere, on *The Magical World of Disney*
2) "Above and Beyond Therapy" Oct. 1, 1989
   Broadcast as wheel of *The Magical World of Disney*
3) "I Fought the Law" (Oct. 15, 1989)
   Broadcast as wheel of *The Magical World of Disney*
4) "Private School" (Oct. 22, 1989)
   Broadcast as wheel of *The Magical World of Disney*
5) "Children of a Legal Mom" Jan. 7, 1990
6) "Even Housekeepers Sing the Blues" (April 15, 1990)

Cast Biographies and Filmographies

David Duchovny was born August 7, 1960 in New York City, and grew up about a three-minute walk away from that hip strip, on East 11th Street and 2nd Avenue, near the famed 2nd Avenue Deli and hard across the old Dutch graveyard at St. Mark's Church.

"We used to play baseball [there]," he reminisces, "except the gravestones were flat, they weren't the kind that stick up – and since we didn't have bases . . .!" He smiles at the ironic morbidity. "It was like . . . 'He's rounding Stuyvesant! He's going to Van Dyke! He slides into Van Dyke! He's safe! He's safe! He's in there!' So once you made it into Van Dyke," he dryly jokes, "a sacrifice fly can pull you safely into Van Heuson."

His father, a Brooklyn-born Russian-Jew, 58 years old in 1996, is Amram (Marty) Ducovny, who "took the 'h' out of our last name because he was tired of having it mispronounced," Duchovny explains. "But when my parents divorced, my mother put the 'h' back in, as a show of solidarity with how a family member spelled the name. I spell it with the 'h'; my brother doesn't use the 'h.' My sister goes back and forth, depending on her mood."

Dad was a writer. He worked as a publicist for the 90-year-old human-rights and cultural organization, the American Jewish Committee. But he also wrote three books: the, in retrospect, wince-inducing *The Wisdom of Spiro T. Agnew*; *David Ben-Gurion in His Own Words*, and *On With the Wind*, a best-seller about the colorful Washington D.C. gadfly and Watergate figure Martha Mitchell. Amram also wrote the off-Broadway play, *The Trial of Lee Harvey Oswald* (1967) which starred Ralph Meeker (1920–88). Amram moved to Paris after his 1972 divorce, reportedly to write novels, though none have come out.

Duchovny's mom Margaret (Meg) Duchovny (56 years old in 1996), was born and raised in Scotland. She presently runs the lower grades at Grace Church School in the East Village. David's older brother, Daniel, is now a TV-commercial director in Los Angeles; their younger sister Laurie, an Audrey Hepburnesque beauty who's 29 in 1996, teaches at the St. Anne's parochial school in Brooklyn.

After the divorce, Mom was "afraid we'd all end up in the gutter," Duchovny remembers. For Duchovny, "The divorce was probably the most important emotional moment of my life. I don't think you ever recover from something like that. You are forced into an adult world of emotions that you aren't prepared to deal with."

Duchovny had been a shy kid who spoke so little that when he was young, his brother Daniel used to tell friends David was retarded. By fifth grade, however, David had overcome his reticence enough to play one of the three magi in a Christmas production. In fact, he did well enough in both school and sports that at 13, he won an academic scholarship to the Upper West Side's elite Collegiate prep school – where the likes of John F. Kennedy, Jr. and actor Zach (*Gremlins*) Galligan were educated. One classmate was actor Jason Beghe, a lifelong friend who appeared in the *X-Files* episode "Darkness Falls." "I was the gregarious one," Beghe remembered. "David was the one who applied himself."

David, nicknamed Duke, was a star on the Collegiate baseball and basketball teams. When he went on to Princeton University (where he was re-nicknamed Doggie), he spent a year playing guard on the basketball team, and two seasons playing center field on the baseball team. Yet after "I got fed up with my coach or he got fed up with me," Duchovny and varsity sports parted ways, and the studious student hunkered down to earn a 1992 Bachelor of Arts in English Literature – with grades good enough to then get him into Yale. "I was really a tight-assed kind of student," Duchovny says of his Princeton days. When he discovered that one roommate wanted to be an actor, Duchovny scoffed at him, "You came to Princeton – why are you acting?" Yet on reflection today, "I wish I'd had a little more fun. I didn't have those wild and crazy college years that people seem to try to recapture the rest of their lives. In fact, it's kind of *good* I had such a miserable time in college, because I spent no time trying to recapture it. I can just move on."

"Miserable" is relative, of course; aside from playing varsity sports and acing his classes, "I had a girlfriend I met in December of my first year. She was my girlfriend for four years and a year after we graduated. If I'd met her a little later we'd probably have stayed together. I think I was in love before that, but she was my first really long-term relationship."

He had a long-term relationship with English Lit as well, and with a Mellon Fellowship, went to Yale and earned his master's degree in the field. Studying under such literary stars as Harold Bloom, John Hollander, Jay Hillis Miller and Geoffrey Hartman, he continued on as a Ph.D. candidate. That involved, among other things, being a teaching assistant and outlining his doctoral dissertation. He was on a career path to professorship – but eventually realized, "I would have been a failed academic, because I was good at it but it was insincere. I spoke the language, but underneath I was thinking, 'Somebody's going to find out that I really don't care.'"

In the fall of 1985, buddy Beghe suggested Duchovny take some acting classes. Duchovny was already spending time hanging out with students at Yale's famous drama school – they seemed to be fun and jolly sorts – and he thought Beghe's suggestions "made sense, because I was 26 years old and didn't feel like spending the rest of my life teaching."

Dropping out to become an actor wasn't a conscious part of that plan, so Duchovny – thinking about becoming a playwright/ screenwriter – "thought I should find out what kind of dialogue fits." He took a playwriting course, and when Beghe's agent offered to represent him if he were willing to pursue acting seriously, Duchovny began commuting twice a week from New Haven to New York to study with Marsha Haufrecht of the Actors Studio.

"I learned from her that basically anything goes: I learned to tell the truth, show whatever you're feeling at the moment, even if it seems to be wrong." The transition from seeing acting as a research tool for writing, to acting for the sake of acting was not without some dissonance and guilt. "I was going from one endeavor considered by the people who do it as the deepest intellectual and most spiritual endeavor you can do – to spend your life with books – to something where the parts might be superficial, and I might not be any good at it. So I had a lot of shame about the fact that I wanted it." On the other hand, after the long history of emotional repression and need to please others that he'd endured, acting gave him "an emotional life really for the first time. It was great. I could scream, yell and cry on stage without consequences. I could have a full life; nobody would arrest or leave me for [behaving] like that." Describing that emotional freedom more tellingly, "You can have the woman you're not supposed to have, and there are no repercussions and nobody doesn't love you afterward." Throughout all this, he continued teaching at Yale. After having auditioned for a TV-commercial casting agent, he wound up with his first paying role, earning $9,000 – twice his teaching-assistant stipend – for playing a bar patron in a Lowenbrau beer spot airing, reportedly, in 1987. "I was terrified," he remembered – but he pulled it off and decided to pursue other jobs.

At the urging of actress girlfriend Maggie Jakobson (who as Maggie Wheeler appeared in the *X-Files* episode "Born Again"), Duchovny played her womanizing boyfriend in the low-budget, independent movie *New Year's Day*, directed by the idiosyncratic writer-director Henry Jaglom. Like everyone else in this improvisational film, Duchovny essentially played himself. "I wasn't as good an actor with scripts as I am now," he recalls. "At that point I was afraid that I couldn't make somebody else's words on a page come alive as well as I could my own words." Shot in 1987, *New Year's Day* remained unreleased until 1989.

After his Jaglom experience, during a Christmas break, Duchovny was flown to L.A. to test for three TV pilots, with the full limo treatment and a room at the Sunset Marquis hotel. Discovering that he wouldn't make it back to Yale in time for the start of next semester, he phoned in sick – reportedly, from poolside. He didn't, however, land a series, and returned East to take a small role in megadirector Mike Nichols' hit seriocomedy *Working Girl* (1988), which began shooting in February, 1988.

Duchovny permanently relocated to Los Angeles in time for *New Year's Day*'s April, 1989 debut at the influential AFI Los Angeles International Film Festival. Yale and his dissertation had been edged out by his acting career. "My agent thought I should move to California in case there was any 'heat' when *New Year's Day* opened. And there *was* a little heat, but the only thing that happened was that I changed agents." *New Year's Day* opened theatrically months later, on Dec. 13, by which time Duchovny had already filmed a blink-and-miss-it part as a club-goer in the Rob Lowe–James Spader film *Bad Influence* (1990), shot in L.A. from June to August.

He quickly followed up with a lead role in the extremely low-budget erotic psychodrama *Julia Has Two Lovers* (1991), which shot from August 3 to October 13, 1989 and played virtually nowhere outside of L.A. and New York. His income was not enhanced by being in Jaglom's virtually no-budget, glorified home-movie *Venice/ Venice* (1992), which began shooting in September 1989. Afterwards, it would be a long several months before he got a small supporting role in *Don't Tell Mom the Babysitter's Dead* (1991), shot from May to July 1990 under director Stephen Herek (*Bill & Ted's Excellent Adventure*, *The Mighty Ducks*). Though independently financed, this likable and surprisingly successful Christina Applegate comedy became Duchovny's first film released through a major studio, Warner Bros. Later in 1990, Duchovny shot his most significant part yet, as the male lead in writer-director Mel Tolkin's acclaimed low-budget apocalyptic drama *The Rapture* (1991), starring Mimi Rogers.

Before *The Rapture* was released, however, Duchovny found himself a pop-culture shooting-star on the TV series *Twin Peaks* (ABC, April 8, 1990–June 10, 1991). For three consecutive episodes, Duchovny played what would seem the plum role of Cooper's old friend, DEA Agent Dennis Bryson. Except Cooper hadn't seen him in a while, and in the interim, Dennis had begun cross-dressing!

There was "nothing special about the part," Duchovny insists. "I remember showing up on the set and thinking, 'Well, here I am wearing a dress and pantyhose' and wondering, 'Is this the beginning *and* end of my career?'" But he also felt as if he had nothing to lose. As for what his family thought of him in the showy if, well, untraditional male role, "Mom, she actually thought I looked thin . . . 'Are you getting enough to eat?'"

For all its oddity, the part *was* a terrific career move, since millions of people who hadn't heard of him before were suddenly aware of this gutsy David Duchovny guy. Yet for whatever reasons, his next acting gig wouldn't be for six months. During that time, he said, he was "leeching off people pretty much." He reportedly wrote a couple of articles and did a commercial or two, and worked for a caterer. And as an outlet for his creativity, he began reading his poetry – an L.A. actors' tradition – at a joint called the Largo Pub.

When things finally came home, however, they came in through all the doors. Spring 1991 found Duchovny committed to three projects almost at once. First, there was the shaggy-dog comedy *Beethoven* (1992), shot from May 1 to July 26. In this hit (if witless) slapstick farce, co-scripted by a pseudonymous John Hughes, Duchovny and Patricia Heaton play venal yuppies Brad and Brie who, in a subplot, try to trick the beleaguered head of Beethoven's family (Charles Grodin) into signing away his air-freshener factory. Of Beethoven, Duchovny says, "He had a lot of saliva. Saint Bernard saliva is sticky and nasty. If you can imagine bad-smelling maple sap, that's what it's like to work with that dog."

At roughly the same time as the *Beethoven* deal came *Ruby*, a fictionalized dramatization of the life of Lee Harvey Oswald's killer, which filmed from June 13 to August 13. Duchovny played J.D. Tippit, whom Oswald shot and killed on the day of the Kennedy assassination. Duchovny quickly followed that up with his signature role: Jake Winters, protagonist of the steamy Showtime cable movie *Red Shoe Diaries* (1992), shot from August 26 to October 8, 1991, and the narrator/linking device of the spin-off anthology series *Zalman King's Red Shoe Diaries*.

How did Duchovny like working with the high-class soft-porn King? "Well, he didn't make me put on a dress, so I love him for that!" he jokes. As for the series – in which he provides narration and framing shots of Jake picking up the mail – Duchovny says, "I just do a minute in the beginning and in the end, six episodes in a day. I call it my Jack Nicholson day because I figure I'm making Nicholson money for that day." The bi-weekly, occasional series began running on Showtime in June 1992, and has been going strong for 30 half-hour episodes to date, with no signs of abating on either cable or video. "I think I'll be going to that mailbox in my wheelchair!" Duchovny half-jokingly grouses.

Less than a week after *Red Shoe Diaries* finished shooting, production on *Chaplin* (1992) began, and stretched on until late February 1992. Duchovny spent a little time in the American portion of the US–UK shoot, in the small but noticeable role of Charlie Chaplin's longtime cameraperson, Rollie Totheroh.

After playing a supporting role as a married boyfriend in the Veronica Hamel–Nancy McKeon TV-movie *Baby Snatcher*, which shot in February and March 1992, Duchovny got his next big break, in the ensemble cast of the moderately low-budget ($9 million) but high-profile *Kalifornia* (1993), co-starring with the up-and-coming Brad Pitt, the equally emergent Juliette Lewis, and Michelle Forbes, who had played Ensign Ro Laren on the 1991-92 season of *Star Trek: The Next Generation*. While *Kalifornia*, which was shot from May 11 to July 14 in Georgia and Los Angeles, got only middling reviews, it drew attention for, among other things, initially receiving an NC-17 rating.

At this time, Duchovny now asserts he wasn't much interested in television, feeling he was just one more good break away from a leading-man movie career. As a result, he says, he wasn't much nervous or concerned when he went to audition for the *X-Files*. In fact, Duchovny appeared to consider it just a few more weeks of work and a free trip – he was well aware of the odds against any particular pilot making it to series, or, once making it, of surviving. "I didn't see that you could do a show about aliens every week," he says. "Little did I know there were other things in store."

What made him right for the part? "I was chosen for *The X-Files* because of previous experience playing an FBI agent – although it's the first time I'm doing it in a suit," he answers jokingly. "Fortunately, I don't have to use J. Edgar Hoover as a role model this time around." He was evidently equally flip when he auditioned for Chris Carter. "I told him to wear a tie," Carter remembers. "He showed up in a tie with pink pigs all over it. I think that got him the job."

However much sartorial choice may or may not have mattered, clothing was indeed responsible for Duchovny's meeting his former girlfriend, actress Perrey Reeves. In May 1993, having finally made some decent money between *Kalifornia* and the *X-Files* pilot, Duchovny was shopping for a suit at the Santa Monica clothing store, Fred Segal's. There he spied a tall brunette, shopping for lingerie with her mother. Duchovny slyly asked Reeves for help in deciding which of two suits to get, the blue or the gray; she told him both. Before long, they started dating.

No sooner had Reeves and Duchovny met than the *X-Files* got picked up. He had return to Vancouver to start filming the series. While he keeps a sublet beach house in Malibu, Duchovny is only there, for the most part, on alternate weekends; Reeves, with whom his relationship ended after about two years, occasionally flew up to

Vancouver, including once as the lead guest in the episode "3." Duchovny has since settled into a house in the Point Grey area of Vancouver, sharing his apartment with his female border collie-terrier mix, Blue.

On the *X-Files* workdays average about 12-14 hours each, with Duchovny and co-star Gillian Anderson appearing each in almost every scene. "Working with Gillian under these circumstances tends to make the working relationship more like a marriage," Duchovny muses. "We have our good days and our bad days and we just have to work through it."

Duchovny recently negotiated a new contract for a reported $100,000 per episode, and now that the show – Fox's highest-rated – is guaranteed a long run and lucrative syndication, he is financially set for life. On the creative end, aside from his acting, he's gotten back to his Life Plan A: Writing. Unusually for a TV star, he's gotten co-writer credit on two episodes, "Colony" and "Anasazi," both with Chris Carter. "We're friends," Carter says, "so it was nice to work together. Second of all, he's very smart about the story side of things and it adds to the show. It invests him in the show in an interesting way, too. I'm very happy with the shows on which we collaborated."

"He has a good eye," Gillian Anderson agrees. "He's very good at picking apart a script, because he has quite a background." As an actor, Duchovny says of himself, "The way I approach every character is that nobody wants to be in pain. So they do things to combat the pain. But there are always a few moments in a script or an episode where the pain comes through, regardless of how much the character tries to keep it down. That's the way I approach the drama." His low-key style, he says, derives from his feeling that, "I'm the kind of actor you have to watch closely. I don't run out to get you. You kind of have to come to me. Luckily, enough people looked closely."

With luck, they'll be looking closely at him as the star of a major feature called *Playing God*, a crime-thriller still in development hell in late 1995. In it, Duchovny plays a Miami mob doctor – an on-call gunshot-wound specialist – who finds himself falling in love with a Miami cop. Independently produced by a company called Beacon, it's scheduled to be released by Columbia Pictures.

It all sounds promising. Duchovny isn't always so sure, though. "I wish I had the life people think I have," he muses, staring at the abyss. And as for the abyss that stares back at him, "People don't have to like *me*," he declares, "they just have to like the show."

FILMOGRAPHY

New Year's Day (filmed 1987, released
  Dec. 1989)
  dir. Henry Jaglom   Billy
Working Girl (Dec. 1988)
  dir. Mike Nichols   Tess's Birthday Party Friend
Bad Influence (March 1990)
  dir. Curtis Hanson   Club-goer
Julia Has Two Lovers (March 1991)
  dir. Bashar Shbib   Daniel
Don't Tell Mom the Babysitter's Dead (June
  1991; working title: The Real World)
  dir. Stephen Herek   Bruce
The Rapture (Oct. 1991)
  dir. Mel Tolkin   Randy
Ruby (March 1992)
  dir. John MacKenzie   Officer J.D. Tippit
Beethoven (April 1992)
  dir. Brian Levant (replaced Steve Rash)   Brad
Baby Snatcher (CBS TV-movie May 3, 1992)
  dir. Joyce Chopra   David
Red Shoe Diaries (Showtime TV-movie
  May 16, 1992)
  dir. Zalman King   Jake Winters
  Unrated version released on video Oct. 1992
Venice/Venice (filmed beginning 1989,
  released Oct. 1992)
  dir. Henry Jaglom   Dylan (Italy segment)
Chaplin (Dec. 1992)
  dir. Richard Attenborough   Rollie Totheroh
Kalifornia (Sept. 1993)
  dir. Dominic Sena   Brian Kessler
  Unrated version released on video Feb. 1994

TV-Show Appearances include:

Twin Peaks (ABC) [scripts untitled; episodes 11–13 of the season]
As DEA agent Dennis/Denise Bryson:
   episode of Dec. 15, 1990
   episode of Jan. 12, 1991
   episode of Dec. 19, 1991
Zalman King's Red Shoe Diaries (Showtime)
As Jake Winters:
   narrator; framing appearances 6/27/92–7/92
   narrator; framing appearances 4/10/93–
   "Jake's Story" 7/10/93
The Late Show With David Letterman (CBS)
   interview, Jan. 17, 1995 (previously scheduled for Jan. 16)
   interview, May 18, 1995 (previously scheduled for May 17) *
Sci-Fi Buzz (Sci-Fi Channel)
   interview, magazine-format series, Feb. 19, 1995
Q&E (E! Entertainment)
   interview, March 3, 1995
Saturday Night Live (NBC)
   host, May 13, 1995
The Late Late Show With Tom Snyder (CBS)
   interview, July 7, 1995
The Tonight Show With Jay Leno (NBC)
   interview, May 26, 1995
   interview, June 27, 1995
The Larry Sanders Show (HBO)
   played himself, in episode "The Bump" telecast throughout Aug. 1995
Jeopardy (syndicated game show)
   celebrity panelist, week of Nov. 6, 1995 **
47th Annual Primetime Emmy Awards (Fox)
   Among the presenters, Sept. 10, 1995
* Latter show taped in England; per the New York *Daily News*, this
   made Duchovny "the first 'Late Show' guest to be bumped from
   the show on both sides of the Atlantic."
** with guests Stephen King and Lynn Redgrave; Duchovny's charity:
   The Children's Defense Fund
Duchovny also reportedly provided a guest voice on an episode of
   the USA Network animated series *Duckman*.

"I used to not like myself," reflects Gillian Anderson. "I spent time overweight, underweight, wearing black, hiding. In the past couple of years, I've started to open up." Gone are the days of a hinted-at eating disorder; now, as an interviewer has told her, normally staid British fans are ga-ga over "the thinking man's crumpet" – to which she could only reply, "Well, it's more flattering than being a lobotomised man's crumpet, I suppose!"

Yet who are those fans thinking of? Gillian Anderson? Or Dana Scully? In contrast to the pragmatic and phlegmatic Scully, "I am one of the least strait-laced people you will ever meet," Anderson says. "I'm a full-fledged believer" in the supernatural, alien visitation, and other paranormal paradigms."

Gillian Anderson was born August 9, 1968 in Chicago, IL. The eldest child of dad Edward and mom Rosemary (each 52 years old in 1996), she has a several-years younger brother, Aaron, and an even younger sister, Zoe. When Gillian herself was very young, her family moved to London, England, where "I spent nine years of my childhood," living in the Crouch End and Haringey neighborhoods; Dad was studying production at the London Film School, and the family stayed on afterward. When Anderson was 10 or 11, they relocated to Grand Rapids, MI, where Edward now runs a film post-production company and Rosemary is a computer analyst.

Anderson attended Grand Rapids' Fountain Elementary School, followed by City High, a small, exclusive magnet school for the academically gifted, with only about 30 to 50 students in each graduating class. In this rarefied and privileged environment, Anderson (class of '86) had room for typical high-school rebelliousness. "I was a bad girl," she says. "My grades were bad. I was daydreaming, pulling pranks. I got into a heavy punk scene – I had a nose ring and my hair was purple and black and blue." Yet that's all fairly mild stuff, and when she talks about being "in the principal's

Gillian Anderson

office every other day [for] talking . . . stealing papers, throwing paper airplanes," it seems downright Jughead-and-Archie innocent.

On the other hand, she took a seriously wayward cue from *Lolita*. "I was in a relationship with a man 10 years older than me when I was 14," she recalls. "He was in a punk band, and I used to give him cans of food from our house and buy him Big Gulps and cigarettes. I was terrible." A few years later, amazingly, Anderson heard that her Mr. Wrong "was studying to become an entertainment lawyer – which scares the hell out of me," she adds, laughing, "because he was a pathological liar."

Anderson herself was a pathological actress, appearing early in her high school career as Police Officer #2 in the venerable *Arsenic and Old Lace*. Sometime after that, when she was a junior, "I decided to audition for a community theater play and I got the part, and then I felt extremely happy, like I had found my place. My grades went up and I was voted most improved student." Her previous what-I-want-to-be-when-I-grow-up notion of becoming a marine biologist sank without a trace.

Anderson attended the Goodman Theater School of DePaul University and excelled there. Anderson graduated with a Bachelor of Fine Arts degree in 1990, having also studied with the National Theater of Great Britain's summer program at Cornell University, in Ithaca, NY.

A New York City showcase performance for an audience of agents was arranged for Anderson's graduating class. Her monologue prompted a William Morris agent to offer her representation if Anderson would move to New York. And around August 1990, she did. "The car was packed so high that I couldn't see out the rear-view mirror," she remembers. "And when I stopped to sleep, I had to crouch up in a fetal position."

She found an apartment in Greenwich Village; between auditions, she waitressed at the Dojo Restaurant, on St. Mark's Place in the funky East Village (just three short blocks from where Duchovny grew up). Then six months after hitting New York, she got what seemed a major break – a limited run of the challenging Alan Ayckbourn black comedy *Absent Friends*, at the prestigious Manhattan Theater Club. Mary-Louise Parker had dropped out at the last minute – "officially" due to illness, but also reportedly to be in the film *Grand Canyon* (1991), and Anderson's agent sent her to audition for the role of Evelyn, a moody young mom attending a living-room reunion of old friends. First performed in London in 1975, the play opened off-Broadway with Anderson on February 12, and was successful enough to be extended a week past its pre-scheduled March 17 closing.

Remarkably, Anderson's first New York stage role got the fledging actress and her veteran British cast-mate, Brenda Blethyn, a big write-up in *The New York Times*. Anderson won a 1990–91 Theatre World Award for Outstanding New Talent.

Yet after the accolades, she was back to waitressing, throughout the spring and summer. Then, she was offered the opportunity to appear in another off-Broadway play, a movie, and received an offer to do a play with the celebrated Long Wharf Theater in nearby New Haven, CT – often the last and most important try-out site before bringing a play to Broadway. She accepted the latter two offers, she says, since the off-Broadway play would've conflicted with both. The movie, a very low-budget adaptation of Chris Ceraso's play *Home Fires Burning*, shot from November 4 to December 1, 1991 in Pocahontas, Virginia but was never released theatrically or on video.

Shortly after putting out the *Home Fires*, Anderson played the role of Celia onstage in a limited run of Christopher Hampton's *The Philanthropist*, in a production with Tim Choate, Margaret Gibson, Ronald Guttman, Lily Knight, Don Reilly and Sam Tsoutsouvas. A nice, respectable, but relatively small credit, the play wound up having more impact than Anderson could have imagined – for very soon afterward, "I came out to L.A. to visit a man I'd met in a play in New Haven. I was going to stay for two weeks, and I got here and sold my return ticket." What the hell, it's cold in New York that time of year.

Yet L.A., careerwise, was even chillier. "I moved to Los Angeles, and did nothing," Anderson remembers. "Basically all I did for almost a year was audition for different things." She was still with William Morris, which certainly helped. But it still took forever to land even an episode of *Class of '96*, the short-lived Fox primetime soap set at an Ivy League college; Anderson played a guest role as Rachel in the March 9, 1993 episode, "The Accused," directed by Peter (*thirtysomething*) Horton. Sometime previously, she had also provided the voice of Lisa Kelly on the audiocassette abridgement of Anne Rice's erotic diary-entry novel, *Exit to Eden*.

Her exit to *X-Files* came just in time. "I didn't have any money and I was relying on my boyfriend to help me out financially," Anderson recalled. "The day I got the pilot episode, my last unemployment check arrived."

The *X-Files* script had been was a real page-turner – "I couldn't put it down" – but the audition process was a head-turner, especially since Fox, she says, "wanted someone taller, leggier and bustier" for Dana Scully. "I guess they were going to make this 'The XXX-Files.'"

According to Duchovny, "I played the [audition] scene in a kind of sarcastic way – much more sarcastic than it was written – and Gillian was just completely thrown by it. I was toying with this person, because Mulder doesn't really care if she stays or goes. And she was shocked that anybody would talk to her that way. That's exactly how she should have reacted. It was perfect."

"I was terrified," Anderson remembers. "When we first started *X-Files*, I was so green. It was only my second time in front of the camera." Worse, she had had only two days to prepare, reporting for work just two days after being cast. "David helped me out when he could, teaching me the ropes. But basically, it was a sink or swim situation." Anderson and Duchovny found their groove almost immediately, once the nervous Anderson learned to stop flubbing her complicated, often jargon-filled lines. But she felt ambivalence within herself. "In the beginning, it created a lot of friction inside of me and some anger: 'I want to have a life; I want to have my own time,' I thought. But then you've got to accept it."

Once in Vancouver, Anderson developed a mutual attraction with Errol Clyde Klotz, the series' Canadian-born assistant art director. Although Anderson claims, "It wasn't love at first sight," they married four months after meeting, on New Year's Day, 1994, while on vacation together in Hawaii. "It was just the two of us and a Buddhist priest on the 17th hole of this golf course in Hawaii," Anderson explains, "That was the most beautiful place we could find on short notice."

Then *The X-Files*' subtext got uncomfortably – if miraculously – real. At a Fox Broadcasting party for the show in Burbank,

California, just weeks later, paranormal-believer Anderson sat down with psychic Debi Becker, and then proceeded to not believe. "You're going to have a little girl," said Becker, who'd been hired by Fox to help give the party an appropriately otherworldly edge. Anderson replied, "No, I'm not. I just got this show." Two months later, she discovered that the psychic was either real (the Mulder explanation) or hit a 50-50 chance on the sex of a baby, which a young married woman would very likely have at *some* point in her life (the Scully explanation).

Having a baby when you're suddenly the co-star of a struggling but promising new TV series can be problematic, though hardly disastrous. Ever since *I Love Lucy* pregnancies have either been incorporated into TV storylines, or shot around, as was done on *Cheers* and *Seinfeld*. Unlike those shows, *The X-Files* depends on the two stars' presence in most scenes – imagine *Dragnet* without Joe Friday. Anderson was flatly afraid of being fired. "Those were stressful times," she says, with great understatement.

Looking to her co-star's greater experience with showbiz, Anderson told Duchovny weeks before telling anyone else on *The X-Files*. "I went into his trailer and I said, 'David, I'm pregnant.' It looked like his knees buckled. I think he said, 'Oh, my God.' And he asked me if it was a good thing. I said, 'Yeah, it is.'"

When she finally felt able to tell series creator Chris Carter, "He was shocked. Understandably. I mean, everybody was." *TV Guide* reported that Carter "went ballistic." To Carter's well-deserved credit, he found a way to work around Anderson's pregnancy. His solution also provided a huge creative shot-in-the-arm: After what Anderson described as "a lot of shooting from the neck up . . ." Carter had Scully abducted by entities unknown – creating a tense dynamism by casting Mulder out in the desert, after having had a taste of a true partnership, and a single person he could trust. Some of the resultant episodes – "Duane Barry," "Ascension," "One Breath" – are among the series' finest.

After Anderson and Klotz's daughter, Piper, was delivered by caesarean operation on September 25, 1994, Anderson missed only one show, the vampire-themed episode 2.07, "3," and the producers devised a creative way to give her a break on her first show back (2.08, "One Breath") – Scully mysteriously returns after her abduction and spends most of the show lying in bed, in a coma. "I actually fell asleep during the coma scenes," Anderson says. "I was in hospital for six days, and then I was back to work four days later." Anderson and Klotz named Carter as Piper's godfather, and the baby, Anderson says, has made her "a much happier person since she came along. Nothing is quite so important anymore."

The key to Anderson's *X-Files* success lies in treating her relationship with Duchovny as a marathon and not a sprint, to avoid the acrimony that can arise between two chained-together co-stars of a high-pressure hit. During Duchovny's fall 1995 flurry of magazine covers, "I felt like, This is *our* show. It wasn't just his show," Anderson says. "But I learned not to care so much.

"It's a lot of work to work with someone as intensely as we do on a daily basis," Anderson explained. "Our relationship shifts and changes, and on the weekends we don't hang out because we're sick of seeing each other all week!" She's described their relationship as having "evolved, in that we respect each other and we like each other, and we show up on set and we work, and we leave." Of course, as she has refreshingly acknowledged, "There are times when I think we wish the other one didn't exist."

Despite her legions of fans and her celebrity status, Anderson remains philosophical about her stardom. "I had a very good feeling that this show would be successful," Anderson says, "but I don't think it's really even hit me yet. Once in a while I'll be driving down the street in Canada and think, 'I'm in Canada. How did I get here?' "

FILMOGRAPHY

Home Fires Burning a.k.a. The Turning
   (filmed 1991; unreleased)
   dir. Lous Puopolo   April Cavanaugh

TV-Show Appearances include:
Class Of '96 (Fox)
   "The Accused" March 9, 1993
   as character Rachel
Sci-Fi Buzz (Sci-Fi Channel)
   interview, magazine-format series, Feb. 19, 1995

Q&E (E! Entertainment)
  interview, March 3, 1995
Live With Regis & Kathie Lee (ABC)
  interview, May 18, 1995
The Jon Stewart Show
  interview, May 18, 1995
Late Night With Conan O'Brien (NBC)
  interview, May 22, 1995
Steve Wright's People Show (UK; BBC1)
  interview, June 3, 1995
47th Annual Primetime Emmy Awards (Fox)
  Among the presenters, Sept. 10, 1995
ReBoot (ABC Saturday-morning computer-animated series)
  "Trust No One" Dec. 30, 1995
  voice of Data Nully, in *X-Files* parody

Other credits include:
Exit to Eden audiocassette (Random House AudioBooks 1993)
  As character Lisa Kelly; with actor Gil Bellows; abridged
  adaptation of book by Anne Rice, under psuedonym Anne
  Rampling.
CBC RealTime (Canada; late Nov. 1994)
  interview, call-in radio show

How does a bald, glowering bureaucrat brought in for a brief guest-spot somehow become a TV sex symbol with a six-year contract in hand? For the hearty and easygoing Pileggi – a journeyman who has slogged through muddy trenches of telefilms, direct-to-video dreck and even *It's Pat* – the events are no less welcome for being inexplicable.

"I don't know," says Mitch Pileggi, the forceful actor who plays Mulder and Scully's immediate FBI superior, Assistant Director Walter S. Skinner. "I mean, I watch shows, and I watch the character, and it's like, 'Boy, he sure is grumpy . . . what would appeal to anybody?'" Partly, he believes, viewers may have been intrigued about whether Skinner was an enemy or a friend of Mulder and Scully – a point that finally began to get clarified in episode 2.08, "One Breath," when Skinner refuses to accept Mulder's resignation, and tells him about an out-of-body experience during the Vietnam War that made him too fearful to explore the inexplicable any further. "At one point," Pileggi says, "I was having a conversation with [co-executive producer] Jim Wong, and he said [that] Skinner comes from where Mulder is now. He's been there. And that's why he has this empathy for him . . . because he's been there."

As to where Pileggi's been – better to ask where he hasn't. Born April 5, 1952 in Portland, Oregon, he lived in California, Turkey, Saudi Arabia and Iran; his late father, Vito, worked for a company supplying support services for U.S. military contracts, and took his family around the globe.

At some point, he attended the University of Texas, in Austin. Then, after barely escaping Iran when the 1979 revolution erupted, he moseyed on back to the slacker capitol with thoughts of becoming an actor. He'd already been in some high school and college productions, and now began working temp jobs while paying his dues in community theater.

"Eventually I started working at Zach Scott," he recalls, referring to Austin's Zachary Scott Theater. "At

Mitch Pileggi

one point I was the bookkeeper, the janitor, I built sets, and then I would perform in the evenings. My life was pretty much consumed by theater at that point." His first play there was *The Lark*, followed by *Lone Star*; he performed in *Bent* at Center Stage, played Pilate in *Jesus Christ Superstar*, and many years later returned to Austin for a 1991 production of *Frankie & Johnny in the Claire de Lune*. "I was working on *Basic Instinct*, and I was also doing a TV movie down in San Antonio [*Knight Rider 2000*] plus I was trying to rehearse for this play, so it was a zoo. I was flying back to L.A., back to San Antonio, and back to Austin, the producers were screaming at each other going we need him now, I'm trying to learn all these lines for this play, and I'm going, Oh my God, what have I done to myself?"

Pileggi had made his movie debut in the forgettable horror flick *Mongrel* (filmed 1982), followed by the little-seen *Rio Abajo* a.k.a. *On the Line*, an English-language US–Spain co-production about American border guards; top-lined by David Carradine and Victoria Abril, it was filmed in 1984, and played virtually nowhere but Los Angeles three years later before going straight to video.

Shortly afterwards, however, Pileggi began landing roles in TV-movies and in such episodic series as *The A-Team*, *Hooperman*, and the short-lived Michael Nouri–Blair Underwood police drama *Downtown*. Things picked up, yet the muscular, 6′2″ Pileggi found himself getting progressively stuck in a character niche where pretty much right up to *X-Files* he was playing security goons (*It's Pat*), psychotic supernatural killers (Wes Craven's *Shocker*, his sole film lead to date), and guys with names like Sarge (*Return of the Living Dead Part II*) and Bull (*Three on a Match*).

One reason, indeed, that he got the role Skinner was that the producers wanted to play against type, and introduce a quietly dynamic bureaucrat rather than the stereotyped paper-pusher. "I had gone in and read for Chris several times before for other episodes, different characters," Pileggi remembers. "And at the time I was shaving my head . . . So I came in for this [Skinner] and my hair had grown back, or what hair I have had grown back, and you know, it just clicked." This was for episode 1.21, "Tooms." "And I figured, well, that was fun, and that's it. And I didn't hear anything from them again until the end of the season; I think it was during the hiatus they called and asked if I would come back and do the eight-episode arc at the beginning of the season, and kind of do a recurring bit."

"When all these guys came in, they all seemed to be the same," James Wong has recalled. "Mitch came off as different, because he looked like a guy who had come up through the ranks. He had a more virile look than the usual bureaucrat. I thought that was interesting; that's why we went with him."

Pileggi, unintentionally and after-the-fact, discovered that his portrayal of Skinner had its foundation in his father. "My family – my brothers, sisters and my mom – watched the show, and they said, 'My God, that's Dad,'" he recalls. "He was an operations manager and had a lot of people accountable to him. He was very tough on his employees, but he also cared about them a lot too." Like Skinner, "He wore glasses, he was bald, he always wore a suit." And in what's probably the ultimate tribute, "My mom cries when she sees Skinner, because he reminds her of my dad."

FILMOGRAPHY

It's Pat (released regionally 1994)	Concert Guard #2
Dangerous Touch (direct-to-video 1994)	Vince
Pointman (syndicated TV-movie; telecast window 1/24–2/6/94)	Benny
Trouble Shooters: Trapped Beneath the Earth (NBC 10/3/93)	Thompson
Basic Instinct (1992)	Internal Affairs Investigator
Guilty as Charged (1992)	(unconfirmed)
Knight Rider 2000 (NBC 5/19/91)	Thomas J. Watts
Night Visions (NBC 11/30/90)	Keller
Brothers in Arms (filmed 1987; direct-to-video 1989)	Caleb
Shocker a.k.a. Shocker: No More Mr. Nice Guy (1989)	Horace Pinker
Return of the Living Dead Part II (1988)	Sarge
Death Wish 4: The Crackdown (1987)	Cannery Lab Foreman
Three O'Clock High (1987)	Duke Herman
Working Titles: The Bell Rings at Three; One of These Days; After School	

Three on a Match (NBC 8/2/87 TV-movie/
   pilot; guest cast)   Bull Tully
Waco & Rhinehart (ABC 3/27/87 TV-movie/
   pilot; guest cast)   Man at Gate
Dalton: Code of Vengeance
   (NBC 5/11/86) *   Verbeck
The Sky's No Limit (CBS 2/7/84)   Jerry Morrow
Rio Abajo a.k.a. On the Line (US/Spain;
   filmed 1984; released Los Angeles,
   1987)   Stephens
Mongrel (filmed 1982; evidently direct-to-
   video)   (n.a.)

* Sequel TV-movie/pilot, not to be confused with original TV-movie
   pilot, *Code of Vengeance* (NBC 6/30/85), nor the short-lived series
   Dalton's Code of Vengeance (NBC 7/27/86–8/24/86)

TV appearances include:
Models Inc. (Fox 3/6/95)
   "Sometimes a Great Commotion"   Hit Man
Masters of Fantasy: The X-Files' Creators
   (Sci-Fi Channel, 1995; date n.a.)   Host
Get A Life (Fox 1/19/92)
   "Chris' Brain"   Max
Roc (Fox 9/13/92)
   "Roc Works For Joey" [live TV]   White Officer
The Antagonists (CBS 4/4/91)
   "Full Disclosure"   Detective Haley
Guns Of Paradise (CBS 2/8/91)
   "The Valley of Death"   Rafe
Doctor, Doctor (CBS 11/15/90)
   "Ice Follies"   Coach
Hunter (NBC 10/24/90)
   "The Incident"   Danko
Dallas (5/4/90)
   (title n.a.)   (n.a.)
Dallas (11/2/90)
   "April in Paris"   Morrisey

Dallas (11/9/90)
  "Charade"   Morrisey
Mancuso, FBI (NBC 3/2/90)
  "Death and Taxes"   (n.a.)
China Beach (ABC 11/15/89)
  "With a Little Help from my Friends" E.O.D. Sergeant
Falcon Crest (CBS 11/10/89)
  "God of the Grape"   Eddie
Alien Nation (10/30/89)
  "The Night of the Screams"   Jean Paul Sartre
Ohara (ABC 12/5/87)
  "Hot Rocks"   Webster
Hooperman (ABC 11/25/87)
  "Baby Talk"   Large Biker
Downtown (CBS 8/22/87)
  (title n.a.)   Nick
The A-Team (NBC 10/29/85)
  "The Road to Hope"   Paul Winkle

Venerable and versatile Jerry Hardin – the enigmatic advisor Deep Throat of several key episodes of *The X-Files* – has the type of furrowed, heartland face that can play anything from avuncular with a hint of danger to coldly menacing with a hint of humanity. He's made probably hundreds of TV appearances since the 1950s and is beloved by generations of fans.

Hardin grew up a ranch in Dallas, Texas, and received his acting training at Southwestern University and at London's Royal Academy of Dramatic Art, studying under a Fulbright Grant. After that Shakespearean start, he ironically made his film debut in Robert Mitchum's white-trash classic *Thunder Road* (1958).

Hardin then spent most of the next fifteen years as a TV supporting guest (in such seminal, New York City-based series as *U.S. Steel Hour*) and an off-Broadway and regional-theater actor-director, managing to amass over 75 stock and regional credits as early as *1961*. Hardin's actress daughter, Melora Hardin was born on June 29, 1967 and has appeared as a juvenile star in the cast of the 1980s series *Secrets of Midland Heights*, *The Family Tree* and *The Best Times*, starred in the Jennifer Grey role in the sitcom adaptation of *Dirty Dancing* (CBS 1988-89), and appeared in movies including *The Rocketeer*. Hardin also has a son, who works for NBC.

Hardin spent the 1970s and 80s appearing as a character-actor in such films as *Mitchell* (1975); *Head Over Heels* a.k.a. *Chilly Scenes of Winter* (1979); *Reds* (1981), and *Missing* (1982), as well as telefilms including *Guilty or Innocent: The Sam Sheppard Murder* (NBC 1975) and miniseries *The Chisholms* (CBS 1979). He has some 30 theatrical-film credits to date, was an ensemble star of the 1982–83 CBS sitcom *Filthy Rich*, and had recurring roles on *L.A. Law*, *Melrose Place* and the mid-70s Brenda Vaccaro schoolmarm series, *Sara*.

Chris Carter had seen and liked Hardin's work in *The Firm* (1993), where Hardin played one of the deadly corporate mob lawyers pitted against Tom Cruise. The

Jerry Hardin

role had just the kind of three-piece-pinstripe, covert-conspiracy resonances that the character of Deep Throat needed.

"I really was not aware that they were going to recur the role, so it looked like a one-time trip to Vancouver," Hardin says. But he soon found himself a regular, albeit overnight, Vancouverite. "I often was only notified a week beforehand," he recalls. "The producers would call and ask, 'Are you available? We would like to include Deep Throat next week.' And you get on a plane and you go to Canada and you shoot."

"I enjoyed doing it," he says. "I liked the elliptical way in which the character was presented. That's a nice, juicy kind of writing, and I thought that would be fun to do." Yet Hardin was also well aware of the need for the character to drop in, fit some plot points together, and keep the story moving quickly. "That's one of the acting problems of the character. How do you get all this information out in a way that sounds like it's interesting and fresh?"

As for who Deep Throat really was, Hardin's as much in the dark as anyone. He guesses that "this man was placed highly in government, perhaps not in an official position so much as an unofficial position – perhaps a member of the President's 'Kitchen Cabinet.' He had access to extraordinary amounts of information and high-placed friends, but he was less likely to be somebody who's highly placed in the C.I.A. or somewhere else." Washington, D.C. does, indeed, have a permanent subculture of fund-raisers and power-brokers – a rarefied stratum of rich and influential government *griots* whom any President needs to have on his side. Occasionally we learn their names, like Clifford Clark, or Pamela Harriman. But mostly, we don't.

So who would dare kill him? Evidently the cabal of "elders" for whom The Smoking Man is the running dog. It may or may not be true that Deep Throat was one of three men to have personally executed an extraterrestrial, under the tenets of a post-war "ultra-secret" conference of the world's powers, as he said in the episode "E.B.E." But if it wasn't just a smokescreen, then the guilt he said he felt provides a good motivation for wanting the truth to come out. If the rest of the shadow government were to have discovered he was leaking to Mulder, they clearly would have had Deep Throat assassinated.

Or – in the let's-all-dump-on-Chris-Carter school – Hardin has suggested that the show's creator didn't appreciate the actor's nudging about making Deep Throat a regular. Carter says that is not true, and that with Deep Throat's death he wanted to shock and impress upon the audience that virtually anything can happen to any character on the show. And he did indeed bring Hardin back for the third-season opener, as either a ghost or a hallucination, making good on a promise Hardin described like this way: "When we finished shooting the death scene of Deep Throat, just at dawn, they opened a little champagne, and the toast was, 'No one ever really dies on *X-Files!*'"

FILMOGRAPHY

Where Are My Children? (ABC 9/18/94)	T.K. Macready
Murder of Innocence (CBS 11/9/93)	Mort Webber
The Firm (1993)	Royce McKnight
Hi Honey, I'm Dead (Fox 4/22/91)	Cal
Plymouth (ABC 5/26/91)	Lowell
Hometown Boy Makes Good (HBO 8/2/90)	(n.a.)
Pacific Heights (1990)	Bennett Fidlow
The Hot Spot (1990)	George Harshaw
Valentino Returns (1989)	Reverend Horner
Blaze (1989)	Thibodeaux
Roe vs. Wade (NBC 5/15/89)	(n.a.)
Little Nikita (1988)	Brewer
Bluegrass (CBS 2/28-29/88)	Brock Walters
The Milagro Beanfield War (1988)	Emerson Capps
A Friendly, Quiet Little Town a.k.a. The Town Bully (ABC 4/24/88)	Mayor Artie Lyons
Roots: The Gift (ABC 12/11/88) Working titles: Roots: Kunta Kinte's Gift; Roots Christmas	Mr. Reynolds
War Party (1988)	The Sheriff
Let's Get Harry (1987)	Dean Reilly
LBJ a.k.a. LBJ: The Early Years (NBC 2/1/87)	Earl

Wanted Dead or Alive (1986)	John Lipton
Big Trouble in Little China (1986)	Pinstripe Lawyer
Do You Remember Love (CBS 5/21/85)	Dave McDonough
The Falcon and the Snowman (1985)	Tony Owens
Warning Sign (1985)	Vic Flint
Attack on Fear (CBS 10/10/84)	
Working title: The Light on Synanon	Sheriff Bergus
Celebrity (NBC 2/12–14/84)	Jonah Job
Mass Appeal (1984)	Mr. Dolson
Heartbreakers (1984)	Warren Williams
Cujo (1983)	Masen
Mysterious Two (NBC 5/31/82)	(n.a.)
Thou Shalt Not Kill (NBC 4/12/82)	(n.a.)
World War III (NBC 1/31, 2/1/82	
miniseries)	General Philip Olafson
Tempest (1982)	Harry Gondorf
Missing (1982)	Colonel Sean Patrick
Honkytonk Man (1982)	Snuffy
The Children Nobody Wanted	
(CBS 12/5/81)	Dr. Watson
Angel Dusted (NBC 2/16/81)	(n.a.)
Honky Tonk Freeway (1981)	Governor
Reds (1981)	Harry
Gideon's Trumpet (CBS 4/30/80)	Sheriff Mel Cobb
Heartland (1980)	Cattle Buyer
Friendly Fire (ABC 4/22/79)	(n.a.)
The Chisholms (CBS miniseries 3/29,	
4/5, 4/12, 4/19/79)	Jonah Comyns
1941 (1979)	Map Man
Head Over Heels a.k.a. Chilly Scenes	
of Winter (1979)	Mr. Patterson
Kate Bliss and the Ticker Tape Kid	
(ABC 5/26/78)	Bud Dozier
Wolf Lake a.k.a. The Honor Guard	
(1978)	Wilbur
The 3,000 Mile Chase (NBC 6/16/77)	Manager
Foes (1977)	General Mason
Oregon Trail (NBC 1/10/76)	Macklin

Guilty or Innocent: The Sam Sheppard
  Murder Case (NBC 11/17/75)   Chief Ed Kern
Mitchell (1975)   Desk Sergeant
Hurricane (ABC 9/10/74)   Neill
Our Time a.k.a. Death of Her Innocence
  (1974)   Keats
Thunder Road (1958)   Niles Penland

TV series casts:
Filthy Rich (CBS Aug. 9, 1982–June 15,
  1983)   Wild Bill Weschester

TV series recurring roles:
Sara (CBS Feb. 13–July 30, 1976)   Frank Dixon, a rancher
L.A. Law (NBC Oct. 3, 1986–May 19,
  1994)   Asst. D.A. Malcolm Gold
    3/26/92 "From Here to Eternity"
    4/4/91 "As God Is My Co-Defendant"
    3/30/89 "Leeve It to Geezer"
    5/17/90 "The Last Gasp"
Melrose Place (Fox July 8, 1992–)   Dennis Carter
    9/26/94 "In-Laws and Outlaws"
    10/3/94 "Grand Delusions"
    1/16/95 "They Shoot Mothers, Don't They?"

TV guest appearances include:
Star Trek: Voyager (UPN 3/13/95)
  "Emanations"   (n.a.)
Murder, She Wrote (CBS 9/25/94)
  "A Nest of Vipers"   Norman Gilford
Murder, She Wrote (CBS 1/2/94)
  "Northern Explosion"   Hamish McPherson
Time Trax (syndicated; 1993, date n.a.)
  "To Kill a Billionaire"   (n.a.)
Lois & Clark: The New Adventures Of
  Superman (ABC 11/14/93)
  "The Green, Green Glow of Home"   Wayne Irig

Dr. Quinn, Medicine Woman (CBS 9/25/93)
  "The Race"   Dr. Cassidy
Mad About You (NBC 1/13/93)
  "Togetherness"   Al
Picket Fences (CBS 10/23/92)
  "Frank the Potato Man"   Piper
Star Trek: The Next Generation
  (syndicated) 1991–92 season finale and
  1992–93 season opener: "Time's
  Arrow" Parts 1 & 2   Samuel Clemens
                          (Mark Twain)

Who's The Boss? (ABC 4/18, 4/25/92)
  "Savor the Veal" Parts I & II   Dr. Graham
Quantum Leap (NBC 3/11/92)
  "Roberto!"   Saxton
Evening Shade (CBS 2/24, 3/2/92)
  "Goin' to the Chapel" Parts 2 & 3 Billy
Knots Landing (CBS 1/9/92)
  "The Torrents of Winter"   Billy Reed
I'll Fly Away (NBC 10/29/91)
  "All God's Children"   (n.a.)
Midnight Caller (NBC 5/7, 5/10/91)
  "City of Lost Souls" Parts 1 & 2 Travis Quarry
Matlock (NBC 12/4/90)
  "The Broker"   Avery "A.C." Campbell
Paradise (CBS 1/6/90)
  "The Gates of Paradise"   Uncle Peter
The Robert Guillaume Show (ABC 4/19/89)
  "Drive, He Said"   Salesman
Star Trek: The Next Generation
  (syndicated) Week of 2/21/88;
  "When the Bough Breaks"   Radue
Starman (ABC 5/2/87)
  "The Test"   Gus
Dallas (CBS 3/13/87)
  title n.a.   Judge Loeb
The Twilight Zone (CBS 3/7/86)
  "Profile in Silver"   Lyndon B. Johnson

The Golden Girls (NBC 2/22/86)	
"Adult Education"	Professor Cooper
Miami Vice (NBC 11/22/85)	
"Bushido"	Hardin
Benson (ABC 10/4/85)	
"Benson the Hero"	Nevada Bob Walker
Alfred Hitchcock Presents (NBC 10/27/85)	
"Final Escape"	Warden

TV appearances from the 1950s to the mid-1980s include: Baretta, Family, Starsky and Hutch, The Defenders, The Further Adventures of Ellery Queen a.k.a. Ellery Queen (NBC 1958–59 version), Play of the Week, U.S. Steel Hour, and Visions (the PBS anthology series, in "The Gardener's Son")

Other work includes:
War of the Worlds
KRCW-FW-FM/Los Angeles radio broadcast, Sunday, Oct. 30, 1994; production of L.A. Theatre Works' "The Play's the Thing" series, taped during live Oct. 1994 performance at Guest Quarters Suite Hotel, Santa Monica, CA. Directed by John de Lancie, with cast including Hardin, Leonard Nimoy, Brent Spiner, Gates McFadden, Wil Wheaton, and Tom Virtue. Available on cassette from L.A. Theatre Works, (310) 827-0808.

Born January 7, 1949 Steven Williams, the actor playing steely eyed, dangerous Mr. X is a former military man and model who broke from journeyman anonymity as an actor when he played Captain Adam Fuller from 1987–90 on *21 Jump Street*, Fox Network's first hit show. As the by-the-book leader of a group of youthful cops who go undercover as high-school students to battle juvenile crime, the magnetic Williams brought a needed weight and authority to the proceedings. He reprised the role on two episodes of the spinoff series, *Booker*. There, too, he got to know future *X-Files* co-executive producers Glen Morgan and James Wong, who served as story editors on those cop shows, and who later co-created Williams' short-lived 1991 series *Disney Presents The 100 Lives of Black Jack Savage*.

Morgan and Wong, indeed, suggested him to play Mr. X, after an actress hired to play the character as Ms. X didn't work out. Yet despite Williams' long experience with series television, Morgan says, "At first, Steve wasn't going over all that well [either] and they were unhappy with him. I said, 'Jerry Hardin brought so much to Deep Throat and we're kind of giving Mr. X Jerry's lines.'" Carter has remembered it differently, saying, "We wanted someone who had a much different persona than Deep Throat." Yet as Morgan recalled, it took time for that distinction to take hold. "That's why, later on, they didn't use X for a while," he says. "But Steve is a good actor, which is why we could do the scene in 'One Breath' where he performs an execution. Deep Throat was a guy willing to lose his life for letting out the secret, whereas X is a guy who's still scared. He's somewhere between Mulder and Deep Throat." Is he? "I know very little about him," Williams has confessed. "X is an enigma. "

Williams, born in Memphis, Tennessee, spent two years in the Army, where he boxed competitively, and then, in the early 1970s, he sold shoes and became a model in Chicago. That opened doors to acting in local theater productions and in locally shot films. He made his movie debut in the African-American teen drama *Cooley High* (1975), and little by little garnered work in TV-movies and episodic TV, as well as doing bit parts in movies such as *The Blues Brothers* (1980), *Doctor Detroit* (1983), *Twilight Zone – the Movie* (1983) and *Rambo: First Blood, Part II* (1985). He worked steadily and continually, and after a stint as Police Lt. Jefferson Burnett in the first several episodes of *The Equalizer*, began to get more serious attention. On the personal front, Williams has said, "I had a family life for a little while there, then that sort of fell apart."

He has, at least, something of a surrogate family on *The X-Files*. And the enigmatic Mr. X will surely be around as long as Chris Carter – Mr. *X-Files* – has his say.

FILMOGRAPHY

Legacy of Sin: The William Coit Story (Fox 10/3/95)	(n.a.)
Corrina, Corrina (1994)	Anthony T. Williams
Deep Red (Sci-Fi Channel 3/12/94)	Detective Sgt. Eldon James
Jason Goes To Hell: The Final Friday (1993)	Creighton Duke
Revolver (NBC 4/19/92)	Ken
The Heroes of Desert Storm (ABC 10/6/91)	Army Specialist Jonathan Alston
The Whereabouts of Jenny (ABC 1/14/91)	Mick
The Court-Martial of Jackie Robinson (TNT 10/15/90)	Satchel Paige
Under the Gun (1989)	Gallagher
House (1986)	4th Cop
Triplecross (ABC TV-movie/pilot 3/17/86; guest cast)	Kyle Banks
Dreams of Gold: The Mel Fisher Story (CBS 11/15/86)	Mo
Northstar (ABC TV-movie/pilot 8/10/86; guest cast)	National Security Agent

Missing in Action 2 – The Beginning (1985)	Captain David Nester
Silent Witness (NBC 10/14/85)	Ted Gunning
International Airport (ABC TV-movie/ pilot 5/25/85; guest cast	Frazier
Better Off Dead (1985)	Tree Trimmer
Rambo: First Blood, Part II (1985)	Lifer
The Lost Honor of Kathryn Beck (CBS 1/24/84)	Les Averback
Twilight Zone – the Movie (1983)	Bar Patron ("Back There")
Doctor Detroit (1983)	(n.a.)
The Blues Brothers (1980)	Trooper Mount
Dummy (CBS 5/27/79)	Julius Lang
Cooley High (1975)	Jimmy Lee

TV series casts:

21 Jump Street (Fox 4/12/87–9/17/90; syndicated 1990–91) (Note: Williams from 5/17/87–on, replacing Frederic Forrest as Capt. Richard Jenko)	Captain Adam Fuller
Disney Presents The 100 Lives Of Black Jack Savage (NBC 3/31–5/26/91) (Note: Williams from 4/5/91–on, replacing pilot-actor Stoney Jackson)	Black Jack Savage

TV series recurring role:

The Equalizer (CBS 9/18/85–9/7/89) 11/13/85 "Mama's Boy" 10/16/85 "Lady Cop" 10/2/85 "The Defector" 9/25/85 "China Rain" 9/18/85 "The Equalizer" (pilot)	NYPD Lt. Jefferson Burnett

TV appearances include:

NYPD Blue (ABC 10/24/95) "E.R."	Nate Stackhouse

Sister, Sister (ABC 10/11/95)	
"Twins Get Fired"	Gregg Bentley
The Omen (NBC pilot 8/9/95; guest cast)	(n.a.)
Diagnosis Murder (CBS 12/9/94)	
"Standing Eight Count"	Butch Reilly
Models Inc. (Fox 9/7/94)	
"Old Models Never Die"	Marcus Ballard
Models Inc. (Fox 7/20/94)	
"Skin Deep"	Marcus Ballard
Martin (Fox 3/27/94)	
"I Don't Have the Heart"	Simon
SeaQuest DSV (NBC 1/2/94)	
"Better Than Martians"	U.S. President
Hangin' With Mr. Cooper (ABC 1/5/93)	
"Unforgettable"	Chip Dumars
L.A. Law (NBC 11/7/91)	
"Spleen It to Me Lucy"	Merrill
Booker (Fox 1/14/90)	
"The Red Dot"	Captain Adam Fuller
Booker (Fox 10/1/89)	
"The Pump"	Captain Adam Fuller
227 (NBC 1/24/87)	
"Got a Job"	Billy Bob
Stingray (NBC 1/9/87)	
"The Greeter"	Greeter
MacGyver (ABC 2/5/86)	
"Countdown"	Charlie Robinson
Melba (CBS 1/28/86)	
"Melba" (pilot)	Eldon
Gimme A Break (NBC 3/29/86)	
"Getting to Know You"	Harvey
Hunter (NBC 9/18/84)	
"Hunter" (two-hour pilot)	King Hayes

William B. Davis

He's the physical embodiment of the shadow government, of The Ones Who Run Things, in his role as the unnamed liaison between its "elders" and the FBI. Yet actor and acting teacher William B. Davis nonetheless describes his character, Smoking Man, "as the hero. The only way to play a villain is to think that you're right, that you're saving the world. It's the other people who are messing up. It's the Mulders who are really going to make a total mess of this thing, and I've got to fix it. So from my point of view, I believe that I'm doing what's necessary, what's best for the world." As for his lungs' point of view, the actor, who in reality gave up smoking 17 years ago, uses clove cigarettes on the set.

Davis, born January 13, 1938, began his career as a child actor in Ontario; he studied acting at the University of Toronto and the London Academy of Music and Dramatic Art (the latter also the alma mater of Zeljko Ivanek, who played the title character of episode 1.23, "Roland"). Remaining in England, Davis spent five years as the director of several theaters, and worked at the prestigious National Theatre. By the late 1960s, he was in back in Canada, as a theater artistic director and sometime CBC radio producer. He segued into teaching acting – after two decades of which, he took an acting class himself and "was quite surprised that in 20 years of telling other people what to do, I'd actually learned something about how to do it myself."

That revelation prompted him to find an agent, and to do "a certain amount of acting work while continuing to teach acting and to direct in the theater." He moved to Vancouver in 1985 to run the Vancouver Playhouse Acting School; he eventually left to found the William Davis Centre for Actors' Study. Davis – a Canadian national water-skiing champion who's divorced with two children – found acting work in Vancouver-based TV shows, TV-movies, and theatrical films, including *Look Who's Talking*.

Who is Smoking Man? Even Skinner doesn't

necessarily know his name – he may only have been told to do as the man says (though he *did* know in which fleabag hotel Smoking Man was once staying, and directed Mulder there). Viewers, at least, do know that Smoking Man has unquestioned access throughout the FBI and the Pentagon, plus authority over both military hit-squads and whatever branch of the service flies those dreaded black helicopters. He has had some relationship with Mulder's father going back to at least the Nixon administration, when William Mulder ostensibly worked for the State Department. And Smoking Man is clearly the point man in the shadow government's as-yet-mysterious machinations involving alien DNA and human-alien hybridization.

Well into the third season, the Smoking Man is in some degree of danger from the government assassin known as Alex Krycek, who escaped his *own* Smoking Man-ordered hit and may seek revenge. Smoking Man also has unresolved issues with Skinner, who's begun to openly defy him and has a protective shield in the Navajo code-talkers who'll go public with the classified and encrypted UFO- and human-experimentation files if Smoking Man has him killed. We've also seen rising tension between himself and the "elders" for whom he appears to be a "fixer" – and who, dangerously, are beginning to find Smoking Man's methods sloppy.

It's enough to drive anyone to smoke.

FILMOGRAPHY

Circumstances Unknown (USA Network 4/19/95)	Gene Reuschel
Dangerous Intentions (CBS 1/3/95)	
Working titles: Nowhere to Hide; On Wings of Fear	Group Leader
Heart of a Child (NBC 5/9/94)	Vern
Beyond Suspicion (NBC 11/22/93)	
Working title: Appointment For a Killing	(n.a.)
Diagnosis of Murder (CBS 1/5/92)	Marvin Parkins
The Hitman (1991)	Dr. Atkins
Anything to Survive (ABC 2/5/90)	
Working title: Almost Too Late	Dr. Reynolds

Stephen King's "IT" (ABC 11/18, 11/20/90; in part one)	Gedreau
Look Who's Talking (1989)	Drug Doctor
Head Office (1986)	Dean

TV appearances include:

Sliders (Fox 4/26/95)	
"Eggheads"	Professor Myman
Nightmare Cafe (NBC 3/27/92)	
"Sanctuary for a Child"	Doctor
The Commish (ABC 11/2/91)	
"A Matter of Life and Death"	Don Chesley
MacGyver (ABC 4/29/91)	
"Trail of Tears"	Judge
(with fellow X-guest Bruce Harwood)	

Byers, Langly and Frohike, who've appeared in **a** half-dozen episodes to date, made their debut in episode 1.17, "E.B.E." Known collectively as The Lone Gunmen, after their small press conspiracy zine, *The Lone Gunman*, these three are themselves trying to unravel conspiracies. Here's their dossier. You can read it, but then we'll have to kill you.

The Lone Gunmen
Tom Braidwood, Dean Haglund, Bruce Harwood

Tom Braidwood, born September 27, 1948, earned a Bachelors degree in theater and a Masters in film from the University of British Columbia. Pursuing a dual path of both stage acting and production, he landed small roles in such Canadian films as *Harry Tracy* (1981), starring Bruce Dern and Gordon Lightfoot and directed by future *X-Files* helmer William A. Graham; the Canadian hit *My American Cousin* (1986); and the partly Canadian-shot John Travolta film *Eyes of an Angel* (1991). He often works behind the camera as well as in front of it

Braidwood is married with two daughters; in the commercially unreleased 1992 film *The Portrait*, which he produced and in which he has a small role, he appears with Kate and Jessica Braidwood (as well as future *X*-guests Gabrielle Rose and Alex Diakun).

Dean Haglund, born July 29, 1965, is a popular Vancouver standup comic who performs with the improvisational troupe TheatreSports. Since at least 1992, he's gotten the occasional role on such locally filmed series as *The Commish*, *Sliders*, and *Lonesome Dove: The Series*. When he auditioned for the role of *uber*-hacker Langly, he based his take on a refreshing approach: real life, not stereotype. "From my university days I know a bunch of computer guys who are Ph.D. types in the upper end of computer theory research," he says, noting they "all know really good rock bands – they're certainly not the pocket-protector types." As for Langly's metamorphosing eyewear, "The prop guy keeps pulling a different pair out of the bag. He's got a bag of all these glasses and we can never remember which one we used on the show before!" The name "Langly," incidentally, is of course a reference to the Virginia home of the CIA headquarters.

Bruce Harwood, born April 29, 1963, is a British Columbia actor whose most prominent earlier role was that of the environmental expert Willis in the 1990-91 season of *MacGyver*. He also appeared as a scientist in the supporting cast of the "Disney Sunday Movie" TV-movie/pilot *Earth*Star Voyager*.

Harwood says he conceives of the primly suit-and-tie wearing Byers as "a university professor, and in his spare time on the weekends and the evenings, he goes down to this little office which moves once a month. The Lone Gunmen have to keep moving, because they haven't got enough funding and because they're worried about being bugged."

FILMOGRAPHIES

TOM BRAIDWOOD
Films
The Only Way Out (ABC 12/19/93)
   Working title: Grounds For Murder
   production manager
   as actor: Court Official
Moment of Truth: A Child Too Many (NBC 10/11/93)
Working title: A Child Too Many: The Patty Nowakowski Story
   1st assistant director
The Portrait (Canada 1992) *
   producer
   appeared as actor (role n.a.)
Eyes of an Angel (filmed 1991; direct-to-video 1994)
   Working title: The Tender
   1st assistant director (Canadian crew)
Kingsgate (Canada; filmed 1988) *
   producer
A Rustling of Leaves: Inside the Philippine Revolution (Canadian
   documentary; completed 1988) *
   production manager (Vancouver)
Overnight (Canada 1986) *
   assistance

My American Cousin (Canada 1986)
  production manager
  appeared as actor (role n.a.)
Low Visibility (Canada 1984) *
  producer
Walls (Canada 1984) *
  associate producer; production manager
Deserters (Canada 1983)
  producer
By Design (Canada 1981) *
  production assistant 2nd unit
Harry Tracy a.k.a. Harry Tracy – Desperado (Canada; completed
  1981; direct-to-video)
  production assistant
  as actor: Aspen Storekeeper
The Changeling (Canada 1979)
  production assistant
The Skip Tracer (Canada 1977) *
  assistant director
* No known commercial release; possible film-festival play.

TV-series work includes:
The Hat Squad (CBS 1/23/93, 12/9/92)
  1st assistant director
Nightmare Cafe (NBC 3/20/92, 3/13/92)
  1st assistant director
21 Jump Street (Fox; several episodes 1989-90)
  1st assistant director
Mom P.I. (CBC sitcom; premiered 10/12/90)
  1st assistant director/writer on one or more episodes
Danger Bay (CBC/Disney Channel)

DEAN HAGLUND
Work includes:
Mask of Death (HBO TV-movie 1996)   (n.a.)
Sliders (Fox 3/29/95)
  "Fever"   Stock Boy

Lonesome Dove: The Series (syndicated
  beginning 1994; episode title and
  date n.a.)   Hanged Man
The Commish (ABC 10/8/94)
  "Working Girls"   Zack
The Commish (ABC 5/9/92)
  "V.V."   Drug Dealer

BRUCE HARWOOD
Films
Bye Bye Birdie (ABC 12/3/95)   Reporter No. 1
Beauty's Revenge (NBC 9/25/95)   Cameraman
  Working title: Midwest Obsession
Bingo (1991) Network Executive
The Fly II (1989)   Technician
Earth*Star Voyager (ABC 1/17, 1/24/88)   Dr. Leland Eugene

TV appearances include:
MacGyver (ABC)
  As Willis:
  5/6/91 "Hind-Sight"
  4/29/91 "Trail of Tears"
    (with fellow X-guest William B. Davis)
  1/21/91 "The Wasteland"
  12/3/90 "The Visitor"
  10/22/90 "The Wall"
21 Jump Street (Fox 1/8/90)
  "Research and Destroy"   Engineer
MacGyver (ABC 12/21/87)
  "Blow Out"   Juice
Wiseguy (CBS)   (n.a.)

He is not now, nor has he ever been, Ratboy. That's the fan-nickname for his character, Alex Krycek – or, perhaps, "Alex Krycek" – the shadow-government assassin sent by the Smoking Man to kill Mulder's father (successfully), Scully (unsuccessfully, killing her sister Melissa instead) and Mulder (also unsuccessfully, leading Smoking Man to try to have Krycek assassinated.)

"I love playing those kind of characters," Lea enthuses. "Hopefully I'm [playing] not just a guy who's bad, but a guy who's doing something for a particular reason. I don't think anybody who does bad things really thinks they're bad. They just think they're doing what they should be doing. And it's either bad guys who are doing wrong and not knowing it, or good guys doing wrong and trying to do good."

Before he took up acting at age 25, Vancouver native Lea, born June 22, 1962, had served in the Canadian Navy, fronted an alternative-rock band called Beau Monde for five years, and worked in a clothing store. While his model good looks helped get him roles in Vancouver-shot TV series such as *The Hat Squad*, he concedes it took a while for his acting skills to equal his screen presence.

Lea's first big break came with the Vancouver-filmed series *The Commish* (ABC 1991–95, followed by TV-movies), which starred Michael Chiklis as a wryly low-key suburban police commissioner, based on a real-life counterpart in Rye, N.Y. Lea played the recurring, virtually cast-member role of Officer Enrico "Ricky" Caruso for 17 episodes in the first season, 14 in the next, and six in the third. During his run on the show, he met one-time girlfriend Melinda McGraw, who played Chief of Detectives Cyd Madison during two seasons, and who went on to play Melissa Scully on *The X-Files*.

The Commish, Lea says, "really gave me a lot of exposure in front of the camera, and I studied all the way through that." Around this time, he also co-starred with an actor named Bobby Dawson in the low-budget ($2 million) *The Raffle*, a direct-to-video romantic comedy about two guys who need to find "the world's most beautiful woman" as the dream-date prize for a raffle, and who scour the U.S., London, Paris, Rome, Hong Kong, Singapore, Australia and, of course, Vancouver, B.C. looking for her.

Before playing Krycek, Lea previously played a different character on *The X-Files* – a handsome but hapless nightclubber picked up by the pheromone-spewing apparent alien, Marty, in "Genderbender." Director Rob Bowman remembered being much taken with Lea's work in the scene where a cop breaks up the couple's coupling in a steamy-windowed car. "During that last shot in the car, when he sees that the girl has now become a guy, I thought Nick did a beautiful job walking the line in conveying a turning point in his life," Bowman says. "He'll never be the same again for the rest of his life, after seeing that. And I thought he found just the right level to play that."

When Bowman went on to direct "Sleepless," he suggested Lea read for Krycek – a major role that normally would have gone to a Los Angeles actor. But, Bowman says, "Nick was the best of all. He earned the role."

When last we saw "Krycek," he had escaped his own hit-squad's assassination attempt, and alerted Smoking Man to watch his own back – Krycek is still out there. And though Lea himself has moved to L.A. to seek more acting work, he insists that no matter what, he'll always be the cat to play the Rat.

FILMOGRAPHY

Bad Company (1995)	Jake
The Raffle (1994 direct-to-video)	(n.a.)
Xtro 2: The Second Encounter (Canada; direct-to-video 1991)	Baines

TV series recurring role:

The Commish (ABC Sept. 28, 1991–May 20, 1995)	Officer Enrico "Ricky"
37 episodes	Caruso

TV appearances include:

Sliders (Fox 5/17/95)
   "Luck of the Draw"   T.J. Martin
The Marshal (ABC 1/31/95)
   "The Marshal" (pilot)   Turner
The Hat Squad (CBS 1/2/93)
   "Lifestyles of the Rich and Infamous"   Brett Halsey
Highlander (syndicated beginning 1992)
   (episode date, title n.a.)   Alcoholic Low-Life

"THE X-FILES"
(The Pilot)

Ten Thirteen Productions
Twentieth Television
Creator-Executive Producer: Chris Carter
Co-Executive Producers: R.W. Goodwin, James Wong, Glen Morgan
Supervising Producer: Daniel Sackheim
Director of Photography: Thomas Del Ruth, A.S.C.
Editor: Stephen Mark
Casting: Randy Stone, C.S.A.
Vancouver Casting: Sid Kozak
Music: Mark Snow
Production Designer: Michael Nemirsky
Production Manager: Lisa Richardson
First Assistant Director: Anthony Atkins
Second Assistant Director: Craig Matheson
Set Decorator: Shirley Inget
Art Director: Sheila Haley
Script Director: Portia Jacox
Costume Designer (L.A.): Deborah Everton
Costume Designer (Van.): Sheila Bingham
Hairstylist: Malcolm Marsden
Make-Up: Fern Levin
Property Master: Kent Johnson
Location Manager: Louisa Gradnitzer
Production Coordinator: Gretchen Goode
Chief Lighting Technician: David Anderson
Key Grip: Rick Allen
Special Effects: Rory Cutler
Special Effects Producer: Mat Beck
Sound Mixer: Michael Williamson
Stunt Coordinator: Ken Kirzinger
Production Services: Pacific Motion Pictures Corporation
Processing: Gastown Film Labs
Telecine: Gastown Post and Transfer

Electronic Assembly: Encore Video
Post-Production Sound: West Productions, Inc.
Supervising Sound Editors: David Rawlinson, David Elliot
Music Editor: Jeff Charbonneau
Assistant Editor: J.J. Rogers

FIRST SEASON

Episode numbers in parentheses.
Ten Thirteen Productions
Twentieth Television
Creator-Executive Producer: Chris Carter
Co-Executive Producers: R.W. Goodwin, James Wong, Glen Morgan
Supervising Producers: Howard Gordon, Alex Gansa
Co-Producer: Paul Rabwin
Line Producer: Joseph Patrick Finn
Executive Script Consultant: Chris Ruppenthal (1.21–1.23)
Casting: Rick Millikan, CSA
Vancouver Casting: Lynne Carrow, CSA
Original Casting: Randy Stone, CSA
Music: Mark Snow
Director of Photography: John S. Bartley CSC
Art Director:
  Michael Nemirsky (1.02–1.06)
  Graeme Murray (1.07–on)
Editor:
  Stephen Mark (1.02, 1.05, 1.11, 1.14, 1.17, 1.20, 1.22–1.23)
  Heather MacDougall (1.03, 1.06, 1.09, 1.12, 1.18, 1.21, 1.24)
  James Coblentz (1.04, 1.07, 1.10, 1.13, 1.16, 1.19)
Production Manager: J.P. Finn
First Assistant Director:
  Brian Giddens (1.02–1.04, then even-numbered through 1.14)
  Tom Braidwood (odd-numbered beginning 1.05)
  Vladimir Stefoff (even-numbered beginning 1.16)
Second Assistant Director: Collin Leadley (per onscreen spelling,
  1.02–1.19), Collin Leadlay (per onscreen spelling 1.20–on)
Set Decorator: Shirley Inget

Assistant Art Director:
  Clyde Klotz (1.02–1.09, 1.11, 1.13, 1.15)
  Gary P. Allen (1.10, 1.12, 1.14, 1.16, 1.18, 1.20, 1.22, 1.24)
  Greg Loewen (1.17, 1.19, 1.21. 1.23)
Script Supervisor:
  Wendy Mclean (all except 1.20, 1.22)
  Terry Murray (episode 1.20, 1.22)
Costume Designer: Larry Wells
Costume Supervisor (credit, earlier part of season) / Assistant
  Costume Designer (credit, later part of season): Jenni Gullet
Property Master: Ken Hawryliw
Transportation Coordinator: Bob Bowe
Construction Coordinator (1.05–on): Rob Maier
Hairstylist:
  Malcolm Marsden (1.02–1.20)
  Julie McHaffie (1.21–1.24)
Make-Up: Fern Levin
Special Make-Up Effects (1.18–on): Toby Lindala
Location Manager:
  Todd Pittson (even-numbered beginning 1.02)
  Louisa Gradnitzer (odd-numbered beginning 1.03)
Camera Operator: Rod Pridy
Focus Puller: Marty McInally
Production Coordinator:
  Roberta Sheehy (1.02–1.10), Robert Henricksen (1.11–on)
Asst. Production Coordinator: Anita Truelove
Chief Lighting Technician: David Tickell
Key Grip:
  Rick Allen (1.02–1.03)
  Al Campbell (1.04–on)
Special Effects: David Gauthier
Visual Effects Producer: Mat Beck
  (with 1.05, credit moved to immediately after Assistant Production
  Coordinator)
Sound Mixer: Michael Williamson
Stunt Coordinator:
  Ken Kirzinger (all except. 1.24)
  Tony Morelli (1.24)

Assistant Editor:
  J.J. Rogers (1.02, 1.04, 1.09–1.10, 1.13, 1.16, 1.19, 1.22)
  Shannon Leigh Olds (1.03)
  Ron South (1.05, 1.08, 1.11, 1.14, 1.17, 1.20, 1.23)
  Jeff Cahn (1.06–1.07, 1.12, 1.15, 1.18, 1.21)
Post Production Coordinator (1.07–on): G.R. Potter
Main Title Sequence: Castle/Bryant/Johnsen
Processing: Gastown Film Labs
Telecine: Gastown Post and Transfer
Electronic Assembly: Encore Video
Post Production Sound: West Productions, Inc.
Supervising Sound Editor: Thierry Couturier
Music Editor: Jeff Charbonneau

SECOND SEASON

Episode numbers in parentheses.
Ten Thirteen Productions
Twentieth Television
Creator-Executive Producer: Chris Carter
Co-Executive Producers: R.W. Goodwin, James Wong, Glen Morgan
  (latter two 2.01–2.14)
Supervising Producer: Howard Gordon
Producers: Paul Brown (2.01–2.09), Joseph Patrick Finn (2.04–on),
  David Nutter (2.04–2.13), Rob Bowman (2.14–on), Kim Manners
  (2.19–on)
Co-Producer: Paul Rabwin
Line Producer: Joseph Patrick Finn (2.01–2.03)
Associate Producer: Crawford Hawkins
Director of Photography: John S. Bartley CSC
Music: Mark Snow
Casting: Rick Millikan, CSA
Vancouver Casting: Lynne Carrow, CSA
Original Casting: Randy Stone, CSA
Art Director: Graeme Murray
Editor:
  Stephen Mark (every third beginning 2.01)

James Coblentz (every third beginning 2.02)
Heather MacDougall (every third beginning 2.03)
Production Manager: J.P. Finn
First Assistant Director:
Tom Braidwood (odd-numbered beginning 2.01)
Vladimir Stefoff (even-numbered beginning 2.02)
Second Assistant Director: Collin Leadlay
Visual Effects Producer: Mat Beck
Creative Consultant (2.12–2.14): Steve DeJarnatt
Set Decorator: Shirley Inget
Assistant Art Director:
Greg Loewen (odd-numbered beginning 2.01)
Gary P. Allen (even-numbered beginning 2.02)
Script Supervisor:
Wendy Mclean (all except below)
Barry Patricia (2.09–2.10)
Helga Ungerait (2.12, 2.14, 2.20, 2.22)
Costume Designer: Larry Wells
Asst. Costume Designer: Jenni Gullet
Property Master: Ken Hawryliw
Key Hairstylist: Malcolm Marsden
Make-Up (credit 2.01–2.04): Fern Levin
Key & Special Make-Up (credit 2.05–on): Fern Levin
Special Effects Make-Up (credit moved to here, beginning 2.05;
previously below post production supervisor): Toby Lindala
Location Manager (credit moved to below property master, beginning
2.04)
Louisa Gradnitzer (odd-numbered beginning 2.01)
Todd Pittson (even-numbered beginning 2.02)
Camera Operator:
Rod Pridy (2.01–2.19)
John Clothier (2.20–2.24)
Focus Puller: Marty McInally
Production Coordinator: Anita Truelove
Asst. Production Coordinator: Joanne Service
Chief Lighting Technician: David Tickell
Key Grip: Al Campbell
Special Effects: David Gauthier

Stunt Coordinator: Ken Kirzinger
Casting Assoc. (Van.): Coreen Mayrs
Transportation Coordinator: Bob Bowe
Construction Coordinator: Rob Maier
Head Painter (2.25): Louis Solyom
Post Production Supervisor: Kenneth Dennis
Assistant Editor (credit moved to below music editor, beginning
   2.04): Ron South (2.01)
   J.J. Rogers (2.02, 2.05, 2.08, 2.11, 2.14, 2.17, 2.20, 2.23)
   Jeff Cahn (2.03–2.04, 2.06, 2.10, 2.12, 2.15, 2.16, 2.18, 2.21, 2.24)
Sue Kesler (2.07, 2.09, 2.13, 2.19, 2.22, 2.25)
Sound Mixer (credit moved to below construction coordinator,
   beginning 2.04): Michael Williamson
Post Production Sound: West Productions, Inc.
Rerecording Mixers:
   David John West, MPSE; Torri Nello; Craig Hunter (all except
   below)
   David John West, MPSE; Marti Humphrey; Gary D. Rogers (2.02,
   2.06, 2.20, 2.24)
Supervising Sound Editor (credit moved to below post production,
   sound, 2.04): Thierry J. Couturier
Scoring Mixer: Larhold Rebhun
Music Editor: Jeff Charbonneau
Main Title Sequence: Castle/Bryant/Johnsen
Processing: Gastown Film Labs
Telecine: Gastown Post and Transfer
Visual Effects Supervisor (2.10–2.11): Roger Dorney
Electronic Assembly: Encore Video
Computer Graphics (2.01–2.02): Northwest Imaging & FX
Footage (2.11/boxing): FA Productions
Animal Trainer (2.19): Frank Welker
Creature Effects (2.20): K.N.B. EFX Group, Inc.

THIRD SEASON

To Episode 3.10
Episode numbers in parentheses.

Ten Thirteen Productions
Twentieth Television
Creator-Executive Producer: Chris Carter
Co-Executive Producers: R.W. Goodwin, Howard Gordon
Supervising Producer: Charles Grant Craig (3.01–3.08)
Producers: Joseph Patrick Finn, Rob Bowman, Kim Manners
Co-Producer: Paul Rabwin
Associate Producer: Crawford Hawkins
Director of Photography: John S. Bartley CSC
Music: Mark Snow
Art Director: Graeme Murray
Editor:
   Stephen Mark (3.01, 3.04, 3.07)
   Heather MacDougall (3.02, 3.05)
   Jim Gross (3.03, 3.06, 3.09)
Story Editors: Darin Morgan, Frank Spotnitz, Jeffrey Vlaming
Creative Consultant (3.10): Vince Gilligan
Casting: Rick Millikan, CSA
Vancouver Casting: Lynne Carrow, CSA
Original Casting: Randy Stone, CSA
Production Manager: J.P. Finn
First Assistant Director:
   Vladimir Stefoff (odd-numbered beginning 3.01)
   Tom Braidwood (even-numbered beginning 3.02)
Second Assistant Director: Collin Leadlay
Unit Manager: Bretty Dowler
Visual Effects Producer: Mat Beck
Set Decorator: Shirley Inget
Assistant Art Director:
   Gary P. Allen (odd-numbered beginning 3.01)
   Greg Loewen (even-numbered beginning 3.02)
Script Supervisor:
   Wendy Mclean (odd-numbered beginning 3.01)
   Helga Ungerait (even-numbered beginning 3.02)
Costume Designer:
   Larry Wells (3.01–3.02
   Jenni Gullet (3.03–on)
Asst. Costume Designer: Jenni Gullet (3.01–3.02)

Costume Supervisor: Gillian Kieft (3.03–on)
Location Manager:
   Todd Pittson (odd-numbered beginning 3.01)
   Louisa Gradnitzer (even-numbered beginning 3.02)
Key Hairstylist:
   Malcolm Marsden (3.01–3.03)
   Robert A. Pandoni (3.04–on)
Key Makeup: Fern Levin
Special Effects MakeUp: Toby Lindala
Casting Associate (Van.): Wendy O'Brien Livingstone
Casting Associate (L.A.): Stacy Wise
Extras Casting: Lisa Ratke
Chief Lighting Technician: David Tickell
Key Grip: Al Campbell
Special Effects: David Gauthier
Stunt Coordinator: Tony Morelli
Transportation Coordinator: Bob Bowe
Construction Coordinator: Rob "Stroby" Maier
Property Master: Ken Hawryliw
Second Unit D.P. (3.03–on): Jon Joffin
Camera Operator: Nathaniel Massey
Focus Puller: Patrick Stepien
Production Coordinator: Anita Meehan Truelove
Asst. Production Coordinator: Susan Crawford
Sound Mixer: Michael Williamson
Post Production Supervisor: Lori Jo Nemhauser
Assistant Editors: Sue Kesler; Jeff Cahn
Scoring Mixer: Larhold Rebhun
Music Editor: Jeff Charbonneau
Time Lapse Photography (3.02–3.03): Simon Kerwin Carroll
Post Production Sound: West Productions, Inc.
Supervising Sound Editor: Thierry J. Couturier
Rerecording Mixers:
   Jim Williams; Todd Orr; Don MacDougall (3.01, 3.03)
   David John West, MPSE; Torri Nello; Douglas E. Turner (3.02,
   3.04–3.10)
Main Title Sequence: Castle/Bryant/Johnsen
Processing: Gastown Film Labs

Telecine: Gastown Post and Transfer
Electronic Assembly: Encore Video
Westlaw Provider: West Publishing Company

THE PRIMETIME EMMY

1993-94: 46th Annual Primetime Emmy Awards
AWARD
Outstanding Individual Achievement in Graphic Design
and Title Sequences:
  James Castle, Bruce Bryant, Carol Johnsen, title
  designers

THE GOLDEN GLOBE

1994: 52nd Annual Golden Globe Awards (presented
February 1995)
AWARD
  Series, Drama

MISCELLANEOUS AWARDS

1994
AWARDS
Environmental Media Award
TV, Episodic, Drama: for "Darkness Falls"
Academy of Science Fiction, Fantasy and Horror Saturn
  Award Outstanding Television Series

1995
AWARDS
Environmental Media Award
  TV, Episodic, Drama: for "Fearful Symmetry"

Writers Guild of America Award
  Episodic Drama
    Chris Carter, "Duane Barry"

American Society of Cinematographers Award: (Not
  presented by deadline)
Outstanding Achievement Award for Episodic
  Television: John Bartley, "731"

Each episode synopsis opens with title, airdate and writer/director credits, as well as an episode number in the widely accepted form: Season/dot/airdate-order number. Thus, episode 2.14 is the 14th episode of the second season.

X-Position: The Annotated Episode Guide

Nearly every episode title-sequence ends with a flash and the onscreen motto THE TRUTH IS OUT THERE. We've noted those rare occasions when a different motto is used, as well as any other onscreen pronouncements.

After each synopsis I have provided four areas of annotation:

X-actitude: Numbers, names, facts and figures from the episode, in list form.

The Cast: Brief career capsules of guest stars, and supporting players. A separate section, "The Repertory," tracks the local Vancouver performers that play the parade of Cops and assistant medical examiners.

X-act Location: Where appropriate, brief notes on any interesting, real-life locales where episodes were shot.

X-otica: Everything else, from background anecdotes by the stars and producers themselves, to the minutiae of which towns in each episode are real and which fictional. On occasion, there are clearly presented conclusions, extrapolations, and attempts to point out – and iron out – continuity errors.

Following are cast lists – divided into front-credit performers (whose character names aren't printed onscreen, and so have to be deduced from dialog or other artifacts, such as name-plates), and end-credit performers, whose character names are printed onscreen. For the end-credit guests, we've noted where their listed character-name is incomplete (with a fuller name given in the episode) or otherwise at odds with the script.

Occasionally, we note where the "official" book by Brian Lowry and the Fox *X-Files* website are in error or provide information not supported by onscreen evidence. We do this not to embarrass our fellow journalists, but because – working under an "unofficial" status – there's a presumption that "official" sources will be the accurate ones in case of discrepancies. We've limited this to what can be verifiably and confirmably seen onscreen, such as performers' names.

A note about names: *The X-Files*, stylistically, often chooses to forgo the TV-series convention of somehow working guest-characters' names into their initial scenes; sometimes, we never learn important characters' names at all. In the synopses, we've generally identified character and place names at first appearance, even if the name isn't mentioned until later in the episode. We consider them named in an episode if their name appears in either dialog or in a clearly visible artifact, such as a name tag or an office name-plate.

Performers are listed in the order of their onscreen credits. The only exception is when a front-credited actor is listed last but with the special notation "and [whomever]." Since this is a contractual way of distinguishing special guest stars, we've listed those such performers first in those cases.

[N] in a synopsis indicates a plot point discussed in *X-humation: The Nitpick File*

Common abbreviations used in the synopses include

A.P.B.   All-Points Bulletin
C.D.C.   The Centers for Disease Control and Prevention
C.I.A.   Central Intelligence Agency
D.O.D.   Department of Defense
E.M.S.   Emergency Medical Services
F.B.I.   Federal Bureau of Investigation
M.E.   Medical examiner
M.O.   *Modus operandi* (Latin), a standard legal phrase for a
         criminal's pattern of operation.
N.S.A.   National Security Agency
O.P.R.   Office of Professional Responsibility
Also: "FBI headquarters" and "the J. Edgar Hoover Building" refer to the same place and the terms are used interchangeably.

When a synopsis records Mulder's assertion that, say, the real-life explorers Lewis & Clark wrote in their journals of Indians turning into werewolves, we're *not* stating this as fact, but merely reporting what's in the episode.

1.01 "THE X-FILES"

Sept. 10, 1993
Writer: Chris Carter
Director: Robert Mandel

Collum National Forest, Northwest Oregon: A young blond woman is running for her life – to no avail. She meets her doom in the form of an eerie white light, and a silhouetted male figure atop a ridge. The next day, as local police examine the corpse, an assistant coroner tells a Detective Miles that 21-year-old Karen Swenson has been dead eight to twelve hours, with no visible cause of death, or any sign of foul play – except, perhaps, for a nosebleed and two small, pink, circular bumps on her lower back. Miles, in shock and distress, recognizes the victim – she had gone to high school with his son.

FBI Headquarters, Washington, D.C.: Agent Dana Scully reports to Chief Blevins and two apparent aides – one of whom, a tall, basset-faced man, is smoking. The conversation reveals that Scully has been with the FBI two years, had gone to medical school, but was then immediately recruited into the FBI. In response to Blevins' question, she says she knows Agent Fox Mulder only by reputation: Oxford-educated psychologist, top agent, wrote a monograph on serial killers and the occult, and helped catch someone named Monte Propps in 1988. His Academy nickname was "Spooky." Blevins assigns her to work with Mulder, to report on and analyze his investigations of highly unorthodox cases, which clearly test his superiors' patience.

X-File case: Classified
Government denies all knowledge

Scully finds Mulder's office [in what's later confirmed to be in the basement level]. "The FBI's most unwanted," Mulder quips. He thinks Scully is here only to spy on him, and has checked up on her: Instructor at the FBI Academy; undergraduate degree in physics; senior thesis: "Einstein's Twin Paradox: A New Interpretation." He's mock-impressed she was rewriting Einstein.

Testing her, Mulder shows Scully a slide of a chemical chart for a substance found in the tissue around Karen Swenson's marks. Scully says it's unknown, but organic – synthetic protein, perhaps. Mulder notes it's shown up in similar, previous deaths in Sturgis, SD, and Shamrock, TX – and that Swenson is the fourth of her high-school graduation class to die in such odd circumstances. Mulder's gotten permission to exhume the body of the third victim, 20-year-old schizophrenic Ray Soames, and to take tissue

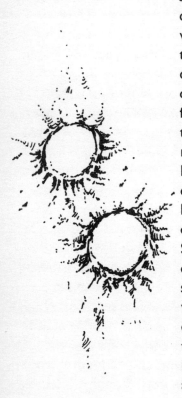

samples for comparison. Soames had confessed to the first two murders, and was confined to a mental hospital, but then went missing for seven hours one day – and died of exposure in the middle of July. The next day, the agents' 8 a.m. flight to Oregon is tossed by weird turbulence upon descent. Later, in their rented car on their way to the town of Bellefleur, Scully notes that regular county medical examiner Jay Nemmen hadn't done Swenson's autopsy – the only one for which tissue samples were taken. Suddenly, strange noises and a whacked-out radio prompt Mulder to pull over and spray-paint an orange X on the road. He won't say why. When they arrive at the cemetery, the agents meet John Truitt of the county coroner's office. Suddenly, Nemmen screeches up, saying he was away and hadn't been notified of this, and demands to know what these FBI agents think they're doing. His bluster is cut short by his worried daughter Theresa,

X-otica

The *X-Files* pilot
episode was shot in
Vancouver over 14
days in March, 1993;
post-production (the
editing and addition of
music, sound effects
and special effects) was
finished by early May.
The one-hour pilot's
budget was a
respectable $2 million.

Collum National Forest,
Raymon County, and
Bellefleur, OR are all
fictional. Sturgis, SD,
and Shamrock, TX are
real.

who accompanied him and convinces him
to leave.

Inside the coffin is a morbid surprise:
what looks like some alien dwarf carcass.
During her examination, Scully says she
thinks it's a simian – somebody's sick
joke. But Mulder insists she take X-rays.
At 4:37 a.m., Scully types up a report
saying analysis reveals an anomalous or
possibly mutated mammalian physiology –
which doesn't account, she notes, for a
small gray metallic implant in the nasal
cavity.

The next day, at Raymon County State
Psychiatric Hospital, the agents talk to
Soames' doctor. He lets them speak with
Billy Miles and Peggy O'Dell, two
classmates of Soames who are now live-in
patients here. They'd been in a car
accident; Billy is now in a vegetative
"waking coma," and the mentally unhinged
Peggy is in a wheelchair. She also has, the
agents note, the same marks on her back as Swenson. Later,
searching in the forest where all the victims were found, Scully hears
rumbling and sees a strange light over a ridge – and a menacing
silhouetted figure brandishing a rifle. He claims the agents are on
private property, and orders them at gunpoint to leave.

They do so, driving into a sudden storm. Then, while Scully is
showing Mulder a handful of unusual ash she found all over the
woods, the strange disturbance as before starts up again. Mulder
checks his watch: 9:03 p.m, as a blinding light envelops them. When
it ends, seemingly a moment later, the car is without power – and
the time is now 9:12. Scully can't accept that they "lost" nine
minutes; time, she says, is a universal invariant. [N] The car
mysteriously restarts.

In her motel room, Scully is typing a report when the electricity
goes out. Deciding to bathe by candlelight, she strips to her bra and
panties – and panics when she finds three marks like those on the

71

victims. Rushing to Mulder's room in her bathrobe, she shows him the marks – which to her relief prove to be mosquito bites.

Her relief gets them to talking. Mulder tells about his sister disappearing from their room when he was 12 and she eight; it tore his family apart. He went onto school in England, then found himself in the FBI with a knack for applying behavioral models to cases.

He'd stumbled upon the X-Files, which looked at first like UFO sightings, alien abduction reports. Yet he became intrigued, and read up on hundreds of cases. Then, inexplicably, he found his access to classified government data being blocked.

Opening up, he reveals he underwent deep-regression hypnosis with a Dr. Heitz Werber (pronounced VER-ber), in which he remembered his sister disappearing in a flash of light, and of his being paralyzed and unable to help.

A woman phones to tell them Peggy O'Dell is dead. The agents rush to Rural Highway 133, where amid a police scene, a trucker explains the girl just ran in front of him. Mulder is suspicious, since Peggy was confined to a wheelchair – and Scully finds that Peggy's watch stopped at 9:03, the time of the odd "storm." Then Mulder is informed that the examination lab has been trashed and Soames' body stolen – and when the agents return to their motel, it is on fire, destroying all their evidence.

Theresa Nemmen, more fearful than ever, asks Scully and Mulder for protection; at a diner, she tells them that ever since graduation, she's been finding herself mysteriously in the woods – and she has the marks, and the nosebleeds. She was the one who had phoned them – but before she can say more, her father arrives to take her home. Accompanying him is Detective Miles, whom the agents now recognize as the threatening man in the forest – and, Mulder realizes, Billy Miles' father.

On a hunch, Mulder and Scully return to the cemetery – and find the first two victims' graves empty. Mulder believes the vegetative, comatose Billy is committing the murders. With nothing to lose, the agents go to his bedside – and find the ash-like substance on Billy's feet. Returning to the forest for a comparative sample, they're waylaid by Detective Miles, who knocks down Scully and then confronts Mulder – and seems about to shoot him when they hear a woman scream. Miles sees Billy menacing Theresa in a clearing, and he raises his rifle to shoot his son. Mulder tackles him – then the eerie light reappears, as Billy holds Theresa like a sacrifice. Yet when it vanishes, they are fine. Indeed, Billy is back to normal, and the marks are gone from their bodies.

FBI headquarters, March 22: Billy testifies (seemingly, though it's unspecified, under hypnosis) that at a graduation party in the woods, an eerie light took him to a testing place, where he was told to gather others for tests. But the test didn't work, he says. They wanted everything destroyed [evidently including Mulder and Scully's data]. Later, Scully concedes to Blevins she has no proof for Mulder's hypothesis of alien abduction – although, she professionally but pointedly adds, there is that metal object removed from Soames, which she'd kept with her. She has had the metal tested – and it came out as material unknown.

That night, as her clock switches from 11:21 to 11:22 p.m., Mulder phones to tell Scully all the files on Billy are gone. Elsewhere, a somber man in a black suit – the Smoking Man from Blevins' office – saunters down a storage corridor. He places Scully's unknown-metal object into a box with similar objects. Then he leaves and closes the door – a door identifying this place as the Pentagon.

CAST

Charles Cioffi	Division Chief Scott Blevins *
Cliff DeYoung	Dr. Jay Nemman
Sarah Koskoff	Theresa Nemman
Leon Russom	Detective Miles
Zachary Ansley	Billy Miles
Stephen E. Miller	Coroner [John] Truitt
Malcolm Stewart	Dr. Glass [unnamed in episode]
Alexandra Berlin	Orderly
Jim Jansen	Dr. Heitz Werber [Billys interviewer; unnamed in episode]

* Identified per door nameplate near end of episode; other sources give title as Section Chief

Ken Camroux	3rd Man [in Blevins' office]
Doug Abrams	Patrolman #1
William B. Davis	Smoking Man
Katya Gardener	Peggy O'Dell
Ric Reid	Assistant Coroner
Lesley Ewen	FBI Receptionist
J.B. Bivens	Truck Driver

extra

X-actitude

Box in which Smoking Man stores unknown metal object: #100041

The spelling of Monte Propps, who to date hasn't again been referred to, is per the closed-captioning, as is the spelling of Karen Swenson.

• The actress who played Karen Swenson is uncredited.

X-act Location: While Washington, D.C. stock shots were often used the first season for what are called "establishing exteriors," the FBI's J. Edgar Hoover Building had a specially shot stand-in: Simon Fraser University, in Burnaby, BC, about four miles east of downtown Vancouver. The "J. Edgar Hoover" sign is set dressing. After the end of the first season, co-producer Paul Rabwin and a crew spent three days in Washington to get their own footage.

Some hospital locations were shot at the abandoned Riverview Mental Institution in nearby Coquitlam, which co-executive producer R.W. Goodwin had previously used for the pilot of his medical series *Birdland*.

The Cast: Charles Cioffi (b. 1935) played Lt. Vic Androzzy in *Shaft* (1971). Cioffi returns once more as Blevins in episode 1.04, "Conduit." He's played similar recurring roles as Inspector Kojak's superior in the 1989-90 *ABC Saturday Mystery: Kojak* TV-movies, and as NYPD Lt. Leo Kramer in episodes of *The Equalizer*. His films include the real-life shadow-government drama *Missing* (1982), and he's co-starred in the series *Assignment: Vienna* (ABC 1972-73) and *Get Christie Love!* (ABC 1974).

Cliff DeYoung (b. Feb. 12, 1945, Inglewood, CA) came to prominence as widowed father Sam Hayden in the TV-movie *Sunshine* (1973), its spinoff TV series (NBC 1975), and its sequel TV-movie, *Sunshine Christmas* (1977). DeYoung's other credits include *Shock Treatment* (the 1981 *Rocky Horror Picture Show* sequel-of-sorts, succeeding Barry Bostwick as Brad Majors), *F/X* (1986), *Glory* (1989) and *Carnosaur II* (1995). He's also played both Robert F. Kennedy (in the 1978 TV-movie *King*), and brother John (in 1985's *Robert Kennedy and His Times*). Leon Russom's work includes *No Way Out* (1987), *Fresh Horses* (1988), *Star Trek VI: The Undiscovered Country* (1991) and the 1995 TV-movie *Alien Nation: Body and Soul*

The Repertory: Ric Reid went on to a meatier role as the State Department father of a demon-child in episode 2.21, "The Calusari." Stephen E. Miller had a small role as the SWAT team Tactical Commander in 2.05, "Duane Barry." Katya Gardener was prominent as the wife of a dead Marine who calls in the FBI in 2.15, "Fresh Bones" (there credited onscreen as Katya Gardner). J.B. Bivens had a small role as a sharpshooter in 2.17, "End Game." And – perhaps playing twins with very different Civil Service scores – Lesley Ewen was both the FBI receptionist here, and an FBI agent in 1.14, "Genderbender."

Intriguingly, Ken Camroux, playing the mysterious third man in Blevins' office, turns up in the pivotal episode 2.25, "Anasazi," as evidently the same character: one of the FBI higher-ups who question Scully with an eye toward dismissing her and Mulder.

X-File case: Classified

1.02 "DEEP THROAT"

X-File case #: DF101364
Government denies all knowledge

Sept. 17, 1993
Writer: Chris Carter
Director: Daniel Sackheim

Outside Ellens Air Force Base, southwest Idaho: Col. Robert Budahas, has barricaded himself in their house. Soldiers find him hunkered down, seemingly insane.

Four months later, 2 p.m.: At an upscale Washington bar, Mulder tells Scully the military is stonewalling about Budahas' psychosis and even location. His desperate wife, Anita, finally reported him to the FBI as a kidnapping – but the case was shelved. Mulder reveals that since 1963, six pilots from this base have been listed as MIA.

In the restroom, Mulder is approached by a mysterious man. [His eventual designation, "Deep Throat," isn't given in dialog or onscreen credits this episode.] He calmly advises Mulder to keep away from the case, yet offers to be of help. Later, as a piqued Scully calls Mulder, wondering if he just happened to know Ellens was a UFO-sighting mecca, Mulder realizes his home phone is tapped; an unmarked blue van is outside.

Idaho: Mrs. Budahas tells the agents her husbands strange behavior began two years before. Her friend Verna McLennen's husband had the same symptoms.

Mulder finds base director of communications Col. Kissel hard to approach. They learn from local reporter Paul Mossinger that UFO buffs gather at The Flying

X-otica

Inspiration Alert:

The scene where Scully mysteriously can't get a phone line out recalls a similar one in the classic *Bad Day at Black Rock* (1955), starring Spencer Tracy.

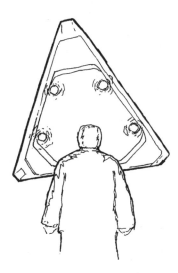

Saucer restaurant. There the agents get a hand-drawn map to Ellens (which is curiously unlisted on even official government maps) and by 6:04 p.m. are driving alongside the restricted installation. At 6:30 a.m., they witness two airborne balls of light.

Suddenly, a menacing helicopter approaches, apparently chasing a teenage couple, whom Mulder and Scully help to escape. At a restaurant, 5:02 a.m., the teenagers brag to the agents that they sneak through a fence-hole to neck and watch the air show. They've also heard of someplace called The Yellow Base where UFO parts are supposedly stored. A shadowy man code-named Redbird watches from a car. Later, Mulder tells Scully that Ellens is one of six bases where the supposed wreckage of the famous alleged 1947 Roswell flying-saucer crash is stored. He suggests the military is building aircraft using UFO high-tech.

The agents visit Budahas, who was returned home the night before. His memories of all things aeronautical have been erased. Scully suspects amnesia, caused Mulder suggests, by the stress of flying aircraft at near-impossible speeds. Driving back, Mulder and Scully are waylaid by two ominous cars. Some black-suited characters who ransack their vehicle, punch Mulder, and order them to leave for "national security" reasons – or else.

Yet Mulder later returns to the classified installation, guided by the teenagers to the fence-hole. That night, he emerges onto a runway to see a beautiful ball of light that splits into four. Then he finally sees it clearly, hovering overhead: A triangular aircraft with spotlights, which accelerates impossibly away. MPs capture Mulder, whisk him away and drug him.

At 6:30 a.m., Scully can't get a long-distance phone line; neither can the motel manager at his desk. Scully returns to find Mossinger snooping in her room. Hearing a walkie-talkie in his car, she leaps inside to find his gun and Airbase Security ID – he's Redbird. At gunpoint, she forces him to drive her to the base – where a woozy Mulder stumbles out, unable to remember recent events.

FBI headquarters, one week later: Scully reports Budahas was returned to his family – and while Mulder's "alien technology" scenario is inconclusive, she herself is a corroborating witness to the UFO lights.

At a running track, Mulder is met by the mysterious man. He'll continue to provide them information, so long as it's in his best interest – which he claims is "the truth."

CAST

Jerry Hardin	Deep Throat
Michael Bryan French	Paul Mossinger
Seth Green	Emil [teenage boy; unnamed in episode]
Gabrielle Rose	Anita Budahas
Monica Parker	Ladonna [Flying Saucer owner; unnamed in episode]
Sheila Moore	Verla McLennen
Lalainia Lindbjerg	Zoe [teenage girl; unnamed in episode].
Andrew Johnston	Lieutenant Colonel [Robert] Budahas
Jon Cuthbert	Commanding Officer
Vince Metcalfe	Kissell
Michael Puttonen	Motel Manager
Brian Furlong	Lead Officer
Doc Harris	Mr. McLennen

extra

X-actitude

Idaho airport at which
the agents arrive:
Marriette Field

Their hotel: The Beach
Grove Motel

Restaurant: Erik's

License plate of the
agents' car: 8216

License plate of one car
of the black-suited men:
Idaho CC1356

Mulder's running-track
sweatshirt logo:
Georgetown University

Secret Defense Dept.
suborbital-spycraft
project Scully mentions:
Aurora Project

Mr. McLennen's
brother: Hank

• The children playing Josh and Leslie Budahas, who have no lines, are uncredited.

Note: The official Fox *X-Files* website erroneously lists Charles Cioffi in the episode cast.

X-act Location: The fictional Ellens Air Force runway and Marriette Field are played by the small Boundary Bay Airport in Ladner, B.C..

The Cast: For more on Jerry Hardin, see his separate biography.

Michael Bryan French played beat author Jack Kerouac in a memorable episode of *Quantum Leap*. Busy young actor Seth Green, who plays a great teenage stoner here, has a long list of credits including *The Hotel New Hampshire* (1984), *Radio Days* (1987), *Pump Up the Volume* (1990), and *White Man's Burden* (1995), plus guest appearances on *Amazing Stories*, *The Facts of Life*, *The Wonder Years*, *SeaQuest DSV* and other shows. Monica Parker been active as an actress and TV scriptwriter since 1972.

The Repertory: Gabrielle Rose would play an ER doctor in episode 2.02, "The Host." Andrew Johnston would return as doomed FBI Agent Barrett Weiss in 2.16, "Colony." Among his credits are the TV-movies *One Police Plaza* (1986) and *The Girl From Mars* (1991). Jon Cuthbert returned as one of the uncaring, minimum-wage nursing-home attendants in 2.11, "Excelsis Dei."

X-File case #: DF101364

1.03 "SQUEEZE"

Sept. 24, 1993
Writers: Glen Morgan & James Wong
Director: Harry Longstreet

X-File case #: X 129202
Government denies all knowledge

Baltimore, 8:30 p.m.: Businessman George Usher is killed in his office by what sounds like a wild animal The killer escapes through a 6 × 18-inch air vent.

Washington, three days later: Scully lunches with old Academy classmate Tom Colton, a rising star in the violent crimes section, and reminisces with him about fellow classmate Marty Neil. Colton worries that Scully is hindering her career by associating with the eccentric Mulder. Then Colton asks for her help on a make-or-break case – that of three Baltimore serial killings in six months, with Usher's the most recent. Each victim's liver was ripped out with bare hands.

After Scully agrees to help, Mulder tells her that the recent killings echo ten similar Baltimore-area murders in 1933 and 1963. Since this particular X-file includes a related 1903 murder, Mulder by claiming the FBI has earlier jurisdiction, talks his way onto the case. At the crime scene, he lifts fingerprints off the high-up air vent, which match several from the 1933 and 1963 killings. With a pattern of five murders every 30 years, Mulder predicts there'll soon be two more. Later, at a conference with Colton's division, Scully presents her profile of the killer, and recommends staking out the sites of the previous murders.

At 7:15 p.m., Mulder shows up at the parking garage below the Usher crime scene, telling Scully the killer won't return. He's apparently wrong: Noticing movement in some air vents, they and other agents arrest a Eugene Tooms. At the FBI's Richmond, VA office, Tooms passes a polygraph test confirming he works for Baltimore Municipal Animal Control, was in the vent removing a dead cat, was once enrolled in college, has killed no one – and is not, despite the fingerprint evidence, 100-plus years old. Mulder is unconvinced. Undaunted, he matches Tooms' print with that of an unnaturally long, thin print from the past. And that night, Tooms crawls into a suburban home's air vent by elongating his body like rubber – and kills again.

Mulder, checking the 1903 census, finds a Eugene Victor Tooms who resided at 66 Exeter Street, Room 103; Scully has meantime found Tooms' current address is merely a cover, and that Tooms hasn't been at work since the arrest. Then Mulder discovers that the first 1933 victim also lived at 66 Exeter Street – Room 203, right

above Tooms. The agents then interview the officer who investigated the 1933 crimes, who gives Mulder and Scully all the official and unofficial evidence he's collected. They check on 66 Exeter Street – now an abandoned wreck – and break into the deserted Room 103, where they discover a hole in the wall leading to the basement. There they find a shrine adorned with trophies from kills. They also find an odd "nest," leading Mulder to speculate that Tooms is a mutant who hibernates for 30 years, and that perhaps eating five livers can sustain him for that time. Scully leaves to call for a surveillance team – but not before Tooms, hiding in the darkened ceiling, snatches a bracelet from her . . . as a trophy.

Though two other agents do begin a stakeout, Colton angrily calls them off and insinuates Scully's a loser for sticking with Mulder. Scully goes home and leaves Mulder a phone message saying what's happened – unaware that she's being

X-otica

Director Harry Longstreet "had no respect for the script," according to James Wong; among other things, Longstreet didn't shoot "coverage" (multiple angles on a scene, to give the editor more choices), as it is typical to do. Wong and Michael Katleman (who would direct episode 1.06, "Shadows") "had to go back up and reshoot some coverage, shoot a scene they didn't shoot, and add a lot of inserts to try to make it work."

stalked by Tooms. Mulder, arriving at Exeter Street and finding the agents gone, searches Tooms' lair – and finds Scully's bracelet. Racing to her home, he breaks in during Tooms' attack, and the two agents trap and arrest the killer.

Newspapers later report on a serial-killer suspect being caught, and Scully tells Mulder she's ordered genetic tests. Preliminary results show a highly abnormal muscle and skeletal system, and a rapidly declining metabolic rate. Tooms, in a cell, methodically builds another nest out of paper – and, seeing the tiny food-tray slot in his door, breaks into a demented grin.

CAST

Doug Hutchison	Eugene Victor Tooms
Donal Logue	Agent Tom Colton
Henry Beckman	Detective Frank Briggs
Kevin McNulty	Fuller [unnamed in episode]
Terence Kelly	[George] Usher
Colleen Winton	Examiner
James Bell	Det. Johnson [unnamed in episode]
Gary Hetherington	Kennedy [unnamed in episode]
Rob Morton	Kramer [unnamed in episode]
Paul Joyce	Mr. Werner [unnamed in episode]

X-actitude

Scully's apartment number: 35. Per the police report seen in the sequel (episode 1.21, "Tooms"), Tooms was arrested July 23, 1993 at 107 E. Cordova. However, this is at odds with the building number seen in 2.06, "Ascension," which is 1419.

Site of two of Tooms' 1933 murders: The Baltimore suburb of Powhattan Mill.

Frank Briggs' background: lives in the Lynne Acres Retirement Home; retired in 1968

Building sign at 66 Exeter St.: "Pierre Paris & Sons"

Background on Scully and Colton's classmate, Marty Neil: Worked on the World Trade Center bombing; now, two years out of the Academy, is a supervisor in the Foreign Counterintelligence Office of the FBI's New York City bureau.

The Cast: Doug Hutchison's character Tooms is *The X-Files*' only repeat antagonist to date. Previous roles include a security technician in *The Lawnmower Man* (1992), and an appearance each on the sitcom *Love & War* and the Western adventure-drama *The Young Riders*. A fan-favorite popular on the convention circuit, his irrepressible high spirits have even prompted him to slip into Q&A audiences, "disguised," to ask series creator Chris Carter when that great actor Doug Hutchison will return.

Donal Logue played internal-medicine specialist Dr. Danny Macklin in the ensemble series *Medicine Ball* (Fox 1995). He's guested on series including *Northern Exposure* and *The Commish*, and been in films including *Sneakers* (1992), *Little Women* (1994) and *Miami Rhapsody* (1995)

The Repertory: Henry Beckman would reprise his role in the sequel episode, "Tooms." Beckman has been in the regular casts of several series, including the sitcoms *I'm Dickens – He's Fenster* (ABC 1962–63) and *Funny Face* (CBS 1971), and Kevin McNulty went on to the prominent role of duplicitous Dr. Davey in episode 2.23, "Soft Light."

X-File case #:
X 129202

1.04 "CONDUIT"

Oct. 1, 1993
Writers: Alex Gansa & Howard Gordon
Director: Daniel Sackheim

X-File case: Classified
Government denies all knowledge

Campsite 53, Lake Okobogee National Park, near Sioux City, Iowa:

A camper shakes violently – and eight-year-old Kevin Morris screams to his mother, Darlene, that his teenaged sister Ruby has vanished.

Sometime later, at FBI headquarters, Blevins informs Scully that Mulder has requested travel expenses to Sioux City – based, apparently, on a tabloid UFO-abduction headline. Blevins suspects Mulder has a personal reason, and shows Scully a file on Mulder's sister Samantha, who by Mulder's account was similarly abducted 21 years ago, when she was eight and Mulder was 12. Blevins wants to disallow the request, but Scully asks if she can talk to Mulder about it first. Mulder tells her that this lake had four UFO sightings in August, 1967 – one by a girl-scout troop of which Darlene Morris was a member.

The two agents arrive at Darlene's door, where Darlene introduces them to Kevin, who's watching TV static and drawing weirdly shaped zeros and ones. Mulder says they know of her girl-scout UFO sighting, since her name is on file at the Center for UFO Studies in Evansville, IL.

At the Sheriff's Department, Mulder phones his friend Danny at FBI headquarters, to ask for analysis of Kevin's zeros and ones – evidently, binary code. The Sheriff tells the agents Ruby is a problem girl and most likely just ran away. Outside, on the agents' car, a note reads, "Across the Street. Follow Me." There, in the public library, Ruby's friend Tessa Sears tells them Ruby's boyfriend, Greg Randle, was to run away with Ruby that night, since he'd gotten her pregnant. The agents look for Greg at a biker bar where he works, but the bartender hasn't heard from him since he called in sick three weeks ago. Then the bartender – who wears flying-saucer tattoos – suggests the agents nose around Lake Okobogee.

Before they can do so, some black-suited government goons demand to know where Mulder got "the documents" (Kevin's binary-code pages). One, named Holtzman, threatens Mulder with obstructing justice, but Mulder calls his bluff. Compromising, Holtzman explains the pages are a classified fragment of a Defense Department satellite transmission – and when Mulder still demurs, Scully tells them about Kevin. The goons trash Kevin's room looking

for evidence, and spirit away Kevin and Darlene. At the FBI's Sioux City office, an Agent Atsumi tells Mulder and Scully there was nothing affecting national security in Kevin's code: When loaded into a computer, it formed snatches of music, artwork and other things.

Darlene, back home later, tells Mulder and Scully to stay away. At the lakeside abduction scene, Mulder finds the sand has turned to glass, a feat requiring 2500°F of heat. Mulder follows a white wolf to a pile of rocks, and scares away it and two others with a warning shot. The rocks hide a shallow grave with Greg Randall's body. A handwritten note in his wallet indicates a doctor's appointment; the handwriting is the same as on Tessa Sears' "Follow Me" note. They discover it was Tessa – not Ruby – whom Greg had gotten pregnant. In the Sheriff's Interrogation Room, Tessa says Greg was meeting Ruby behind her back, and she confesses to murdering Greg when he saw the two of them at the lake –

X-otica

This episode makes the first mention of "Danny," Mulder's ever-helpful, unseen Bureau pal. His last name is Bernstow, per a fax seen here. *Continuity error:* Episode 2.12, "Aubrey," gives it as "Vallodeo" or "Valodeo" per dialog. (It doesn't appear in closed caption.) The Lowry book erroneously spells it "Valodella."

While Sioux City is real, Lake Okobogee National Park is fictional. The spelling here is confirmed by an onscreen road sign.

The "0 and 1" portrait of Ruby that Kevin draws was hand printed by art staffer Vivian Nishi with felt pens, tracing over wall-mounted sheets of paper onto which a too-perfect-looking computer print-out was projected. Her hand-drawn numerals gave it the necessary childlike feel.

though *then* she switches gears to say Ruby wasn't there.

That night, Mulder and Scully walk into Darlene's unlocked house. From a second-floor vantage point, they see that the spread-out pages of Kevin's binary code form a picture of Ruby. The agents rush back to the lake, finding the camper at the abduction site. They discover Darlene in the woods, saying Kevin ran in and she couldn't keep up. Mulder finds Kevin approaching an orange glow – and saves him from roaring motorcyclists who almost run them over. Then Scully calls out that she and Darlene have found the comatose Ruby – who in the hospital afterward shows signs of prolonged weightlessness. When the agents ask what happened, she merely replies that "they" said to keep silent. And Darlene? She bitterly declares the truth hasn't helped her life, and says she'll claim Ruby fell off the back of a Harley.

Later, back home, Scully listens to a tape of one of Mulder's old hypnotic-regression sessions; he's saying a voice has told him that no harm will come to his sister, and that she'll return someday – a voiceover that segues to a somberly contemplative Mulder, who breaks down sobbing.

CAST

Carrie Snodgress	Darlene Morris
Michael Cavanaugh	Sheriff
Don Gibb	Bartender
Joel Palmer	Kevin Morris
Charles Cioffi	Section Chief Scott Blevins
Shelly Owens	Tessa [Sears]
Don Thompson	Holtzman
Akiko Morison	Leza Atsumi [first name not given in episode]
Taunya Dee	Ruby [Morris]
Anthony Harrison	Fourth Man
Glen Roald	M.E. Worker
Mauricio Mercado	Coroner

X-actitude

Samantha T. Mulder dossier: born Nov. 21, 1965, Chilmarc [sic], MA; lived at 2790 Vine Strett in that town until her disappearance. The real-life town of Chilmark, on the island of Martha's Vineyard, is spelled correctly in subsequent *X-Files* references. *Continuity error:* Police report gives her birth date as Jan. 22, 1964.

X-act Location: Substituting for Lake Okobogee is British Columbia's Buntzen Lake, in the town of Port Coquitlam some 14 miles southeast of downtown Vancouver. The particular forest the producers used is on property owned by the Canadian utility B.C. Hydro.

The Cast: Carrie Snodgress (b. Oct. 27, 1946, Barrington, IL) is best known for her Oscar-nominated and Golden Globe-winning star turn in *Diary of a Mad Housewife* (1970). A one-time companion of rock star Neil Young, she made no films after *Housewife* for eight years until *The Fury*, spending much of the interim raising her son Zeke (b. 1973). Though never

FBI travel-expenses
request form #: 302

Protocol channels:
Mulder to Mulder's
ASAC [Assistant Special
Agent in Charge], to the
district G-14, to Section
Chief Blevins.

Darlene's ex-husband:
John

Greg's biker bar: The
Pennsylvania Pub

Greg and Tessa's
appointment: Dr. Jack
Fowler, Aug. 7, 2:30
p.m.

Mulder's hypnotic-
regression tape: Session
#2B, June 16 (year
obscured)

regaining her star luster, she's continued to play character roles in films including *Pale Rider* (1985) and *8 Seconds* (1994), and on in TV in such shows as *Civil Wars*, *In the Heat of the Night* and *Chicago Hope*.

For more on Joel Palmer, see episode 2.21, "The Calusari."

The Repertory: Don Thompson, here a black-suited NSA intimidator, returned unrecognizably as bedraggled and besotted Vietnam War vet Henry Willig in episode 2.04, "Sleepless."

X-File case: Classified

1.05 "THE JERSEY DEVIL"

Oct. 8, 1993
Writer: Chris Carter
Director: Joe Napolitano

New Jersey, 1947. While fixing a flat tire on a road three miles from Atlantic City, Paul is snatched away by some creature. A manhunt at dawn finds his corpse, with one leg eaten off – and in a nearby cave, a huge, hairy humanoid whom the officers immediately kill.

Present day, Friday: At the office, Scully brings news of a body found in New Jersey missing an arm and a leg – possibly chewed off by a human. Mulder pulls an X-File on the 1947 case, and says police then killed what they reported to be a naked cannibal – whose autopsy report vanished from the Patterson, NJ police file a few years later. At the Atlantic City Morgue, the coroner, Glenna, confirms that the recent victim, vagrant Roger Crockett, was cannibalized. A Detective Thompson enters, and throws the busybody FBI agents out.

Scully doesn't mind – she's anxious to get to her godson's birthday party at 6:30. Mulder remains. A Parks Service ranger, Peter Brouillet, shows Mulder the crime scene, and confesses that four years ago, he may have seen the Bigfoot-like "Jersey Devil." At her godson Trent's party, Scully laments the lack of men in her life. Trent's mom Ellen reminds her she's called her

FBI partner "cute." Then Scully meets Rob, the attractive divorced dad of party-guest Scotty.

At 6:47 p.m., near the Mercy Mission, Mulder asks the homeless about Crockett. One vagrant, in exchange for a few bucks, shows him a drawing of a beast-person. Later, Mulder – asleep in the alley on his unofficial stakeout – is awakened by the sound of something rummaging through trash. He sees the shadowy being and gives chase, but the arriving police think he's a crazy vagrant and arrest him. Thompson, awakened at 3 a.m., lambasts Mulder at the jail, and arranges things so he can't get out of the drunk tank till Monday, when charges are dropped and Scully picks him up. She has to be back in Washington by 7:30 p.m. for a date, but on the way back, she stops at her alma mater, the University of Maryland, to introduce Mulder to professor Dr. Diamond, an expert on wildman myths.

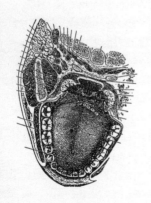

That night, Scully is at an elegant restaurant with sensitive-family-man Rob. Brouillet calls Mulder at his office at 7:55 p.m.; he's found a wildman-like, long-haired male who's been dead six-to-eight months; the body's at the coroner's office now. There, the two agents, Brouillet and Diamond join an astonished Glenna. Mulder suggests the creature's mate must be foraging in Atlantic City – where, he contends, the authorities want to hush up the killings for tourism's sake.

The three men and Scully investigate an abandoned building near the vagrant area. Thompson, driving by, notices the Ranger vehicle and, asserting jurisdiction, calls in a SWAT team – one that may or may not be trying to "accidentally" kill Mulder. Mulder escapes, following the creature into another abandoned building. There the beast – a female – slashes Mulder and runs away.

Shortly afterward, word comes that the beast-woman has been cornered in the

X-otica

Mulder here exhibits the first trace of we see of his apparent enjoyment of men's magazines and adult videos: In his office, no less, he examines a *Playboy*-type magazine in which the centerfold claims to have been abducted by aliens. (Scully, looking at the unseen woman's evident breast implants, makes a calmly cutting remark about "anti-gravity.")

The "Jersey Devil" is an actual folkloric figure, and the title inspiration for the New Jersey Devils hockey team.

woods. Mulder, Scully, Diamond and the forest-savvy Brouillet arrives the same time as police. Brouillet gets to her first, with a sedative dart-gun – yet before he can reach her, she's killed by two police gunshots.

Washington, DC, one week later: Autopsy results indicate the Jane Doe's age as 25–30 years old, and the male's as about 40; there's a human bone in her digestive tract. Diamond, allowed to do a medical exam of the female's body, finds no prehistoric bone structure or physiology. The female's uterus indicates she may have given birth; Mulder theorizes she may have been trying to protect and feed her young. He leaves for the Smithsonian to tell an ethnobiologist about these findings, as Rob phones Scully to invite her and Trent to the Cirque du Soleil with him and Scotty. Yet moments later, we find her joining Mulder on his Smithsonian jaunt. And in the woods outside Atlantic City, a young but capable-looking beast boy peers out through the underbrush.

CAST

Claire Stansfield	The Creature
Wayne Tippit	Detective Thompson
Gregory Sierra	Dr. Diamond
Michael MacRae	Ranger Peter Brouillet [Spelling per closed captioning; the Lowry book spells it "Boulle," though a definite "Br" sound is heard.]
Jill Teed	Glenna

Tasmin Kelsey	Ellen
Andrew Airlie	Rod [sic; Rob, per both dialog and closed-captioning]
Bill Dow	Dad [Paul]
Hrothgar Mathews	Jack [the vagrant; unnamed in episode]
Jayme Knox	Mom
Scott Swanson	First Officer
Sean O'Byrne	2nd Officer
David Lewis	Young Officer
D. Neil Mark	SWAT Team Officer

extra

- The FBI woman who tells Scully that Mulder's on line 3 is uncredited.

X-actitude

Mulder's Atlantic City hotel: Galaxy Gateway, room 756

Brouillet's years on the force: 32

Atlantic City Morgue file on Roger Crockett: Case #2242, Aug. 9, 1993, found New Jersey State Park

Unseen FBI employees handling car requisitions this episode: Lorraine and Fran

The Cast: Gregory Sierra has been a familiar TV presence since his 1969 debut in an episode of *It Takes a Thief*. He quickly became a recurring player on *The Flying Nun*, and went on to appear in the regular casts of some half-dozen series – most prominently, as Julio Fuentes during the first three years of *Sanford and Son* (NBC 1972-77), Detective Sergeant Chano Amenguale during the first season of *Barney Miller* (ABC 1975-82), and the original vice-squad commander, Lieutenant Lou Rodriguez, in the first four episodes of *Miami Vice* (NBC 1984-89).

The prolific Michael MacRae has appeared on *MacGyver*, *The Commish*, *Moonlighting*, *Magnum, P.I.* and other series, on several TV-movies, and in films including *Coma* (1978) and *The Beans of Egypt, Maine* (1994). Six-footer Claire Stansfield has appeared on *Frasier* and *Twin Peaks*, among other shows, and in the Duchovny-narrated cable anthology series *Red Shoe Diaries*, co-starring in the segment "The Bounty Hunter" (1992).

The Repertory: Bill Dow went on to play a scientist buddy of Mulder's in episode 2.21, "The Calusari." Hrothgar Mathews, played a mental patient in 2.24, "Our Town." Bit-player David Lewis had another small role in 2.09, "Firewalker."

X-File case: Classified

1.06 "SHADOWS"

Oct. 23, 1993
Writers: Glen Morgan & James Wong
Director: Michael Katleman

Military contractor HTG Industrial Technologies, Philadelphia: Secretary Lauren Kyte is packing up an office; her boss, Howard Graves, committed suicide two weeks ago. A desk plaque, unbeknownst to her, mysteriously slides across the desktop by itself. Later, Lauren is attacked by two robbers at an ATM; two hours after this, a teenage couple looking for an abandoned building in which to crash find two bodies on a fire-escape.

Bethesda Naval Hospital: Mulder and Scully have been called to the morgue by an unnamed, official-looking pair, and a pathologist. Two bodies dead six hours are still somehow warm, showing post-mortem muscle reflex and a high level of electrostatic charge – with the larynx, esophagus and hyoid bone all apparently crushed from the *inside*. Expert-on-the-unusual Mulder says he's unfamiliar with this – yet afterward, tells Scully it's psychokinetic manipulation. He also shows her his eyeglasses, on which he'd surreptitiously gotten the corpses' thumbprints.

HTG, next morning: Lauren gives Graves' successor, Robert Dorlund, her two-weeks' notice. Dorlund tries to talk her out of it, saying she was like a daughter to Graves – and when he grasps her to emphasize his point, some unseen force shoves him away. FBI headquarters: Mulder ID's one of the bodies as that of Mohammed al Malachi [spelling phonetic; not in closed-captioning], a terrorist with ties to the exiled,

Philadelphia-based Isfahan. Later, on Philly's Broad Street, a cop tells Mulder he had found the bodies the previous Wednesday around 10 p.m.. That gives Mulder and Scully a time frame for viewing ATM security-camera videos – which show a spectral blur behind the terrorists as they attempt to mug a woman whom bank records identify as Lauren.

At her house, where she's packing to move, Lauren denies contact with the men – until the agents show her a video frame-grab, whereupon she says she had run from them and didn't want to bother with police involvement. When the stonewalled agents get into their car, it starts by itself – peeling rubber backwards until broadsided by another. At a garage, Mulder is told the car hasn't been tampered with – yet the switched-off headlights nonetheless shine, due to massive levels of electrostatic charge in the filaments.

Scully suspects sabotage.

They stake out Lauren, watching as she arrives at work to yell at a painter re-stenciling the name on Graves' parking space. They later find an obit for Howard Thomas Graves, 53, found dead one Tuesday in his hot tub, his wrists slit. He left no survivors. An FBI expert digitally enhances the surveillance photos – bringing out an image of Graves. That night, Lauren hears anguished, muffled voices – including Graves' – and finds her bathtub filled with bloody water; she concludes it's a message Graves was murdered.

National Bureau of Medical Examiners, Philadelphia: Scully thinks Graves faked his death. M.E. Ellen Bledsoe confirms Graves' demise, but the only identification of the body came from Lauren – and the body was cremated after its organs were donated. University of Pennsylvania Hospital Tissue Bank: A doctor tells the agents Graves' kidney was transplanted in Boston, his liver in Dallas, and his corneas in Portland;

X-otica

Co-executive producers Morgan and Wong have called this lackluster story a response to Fox, which wanted a poltergeist episode, as well as one with a "relatable" supporting character whom Mulder and Scully could help. "It was just a little too ordinary, like you have seen it before," said Morgan. "Which is exactly what the network wanted at the time."

The hyoid bones are those at the base of the tongue, supporting it. Dura, a.k.a. dura mater, is the tough, fibrous, outermost membrane covering the brain and spinal cord.

X-actitude

Lauren's address: 858 Franklin St., Bensalem (fictional town; a suburb either in Pennsylvania or nearby New Jersey)

however, they've cryogenically preserved the dura mater of his spinal column – which eventually confirms it is, indeed, from Graves.

At HTG, Dorlund threatens Lauren over some sensitive matter she had discussed with Graves. Frightened, she later asks Mulder to meet her at her house. But before he and Scully can arrive, two assassins, a man and a woman, burst in – and an invisible force kills them. The agents bring Lauren in for questioning, but the mysterious, official-looking man and woman arrive; after some friction, they tell the agents HTG was suspected of illegally selling technology to the Isfahan. Then, after failing to get answers from Lauren themselves, they give Mulder another shot; when he privately tells her he believes Graves is communicating from beyond, she relents and says she'd found him despondent since HTG was going under and Dorlund had brought the Isfahan in as customers. She's convinced Dorlund had Graves killed for fear he'd scuttle the deal.

The FBI ambushes HTG for evidence of the illegal sales. They find nothing incriminating – until Dorlund, in his office, tries to stab Lauren with a letter-opener, and the ghostly Graves snatches it and pierces the wall-fabric, behind which evidence is hidden. Later, a relocated Lauren now works at Monroe Mutual Insurance Company in Omaha, NB – where Graves may perhaps have followed.

Security video sequence: Wednesday, Sept. 22, 1993 at 9:44:20 p.m., Lauren arrives at ATM; assailant enters the frame at 9:45:16; second assailant enters, and by 9:45:29, they've shoved themselves offscreen-right. Spectral blur had appeared at 9:45:24.

Desk plaque: Benjamin Franklin quote: "One To-day is Worth Two To-morrows"

Number of miles on the rental car: 100

Lauren's total debt amount: $15,000

The dumpster by the fire escape with the bodies: #3 3425

Graves background: Divorced 1970; wife had left him after their daughter, Sarah Lynn Graves (September 8, 1966–August 3, 1969, per gravestone) drowned in a pool to which he'd left the gate-latch open.

CAST

Barry Primus   Robert Dorlund
Lisa Waltz   Lauren Kyte
Lorena Gale   Ellen Bledsoe
Veena Sood   Ms. Saunders
                        [mysterious investigator, unnamed in episode]
Deryl Hayes   Webster [mysterious investigator, unnamed in episode]
Kelli Fox   Pathologist
Tom Pickett   Cop
Tom Heaton   Groundskeeper
Jamie Woods-
** Morris**   Ms. Lange
Nora McLellan   Jane Morris [last name not given in episode]
Anna Ferguson   Ms. Winn

extra

• The actors playing the teenage couple (who have lines), the assassin couple (who have significant screen time) and the two terrorist-muggers (who have brief screen time) are uncredited.

Continuity Errors: Graves' headstone gives a different middle name (Patrick) than in the newspaper account (Thomas). Also, his headstone-dates are March 4, 1940–October 5, 1993 – even though Lauren's

Graves newspaper article headline: "Howard Graves Suicide Creates Shock," by Steve Woods. Another story on the same page, about a baffling killer extracting his victims' livers, evidently refers to Eugene Tooms of the episode "Squeeze."

Name being stenciled onto Graves' parking space: Tom Braidwood. *In-joke:* Braidwood is the series' first assistant director, who later plays a recurring role as Frohike of "The Lone Gunmen."

ATM attack took place on Sept. 22, when Graves had been dead "two weeks."

The Cast: Veteran actor-director Barry Primus (b. February 16, 1938 or '39 [sources vary], New York City) may be best known to TV viewers as the drug-addicted Sergeant Dory McKenna in the 1984–85 season of *Cagney & Lacey* (CBS 1982–88). A respected stage actor and one of the charter members of the Lincoln Center Repertory Company, Primus made his screen debut in *The Brotherhood* (1968); among his many films are four starring close colleague Robert De Niro – *New York, New York* (1977), *Guilty By Suspicion* (1991), *Night and the City* (1992), and *Mistress* (1992), which Primus wrote and directed but did not appear in. His other films include *Absence of Malice* (1981), *Down and Out in Beverly Hills* (1986), and *The Rose* (1979), for which he was also second-unit director. Lisa Waltz recently played sib Margaret Judd in the miniseries *Naomi & Wynonna: Love Can Build a Bridge* (1995); her mostly TV-movie credits include, appropriately enough, Showtime's *Roswell* (1994), with future X-guest Xander Berkeley. *Wiseguy* fans may remember her guest-appearance there as the grown daughter of disabled FBI agent Daniel "Lifeguard" Burroughs (Jim Byrnes).

The Repertory: Lorena Gale went from M.E. to R.N. as Nurse Williams in episode 2.08, "One Breath." Daryl Hayes had a bit part as an FBI agent in the second-season opener, "Little Green Men."

X-File case: Classified

1.07 "GHOST IN THE MACHINE"

Oct. 29, 1993
Writers: Alex Gansa & Howard Gordon
Director: Jerrold Freedman

Eurisko World Headquarters, Crystal City, VA. Founder Brad Wilczek argues with CEO Benjamin Drake, who is terminating Wilczek's pet project, the Central Operating System (COS). That evening, Drake finds his office restroom overflowing with water; when he uses the phone seeking janitorial help, it merely gives the time (7:35 p.m.) – upon which the electronic door shuts, and Drake, applying a metal key to the lock, is electrocuted. COS' computer's voice announces, "File deleted."

FBI headquarters: Agent Jerry Lamana, Mulder's old partner in Violent Crimes, surprises Mulder and Scully at the office food cart. With desperate joviality, he tells them about the Drake case: Building engineer Claude Peterson found the body 12 hours ago, and the investigation's being run by FBI Academy forensics instructor Nancy Spiller, "The Iron Maiden." Lamana begs for their help, since Drake was a friend of the Attorney General's; Mulder relents.

At Eurisko, Mulder explains to Scully that Lamana wanted up the ladder, whereas he himself, he says sarcastically, pined for a basement office with no heat or windows. But Lamana, working Hate Crimes in Atlanta, derailed his career by losing critical evidence. Suddenly, their elevator jolts to a stop above the fourth floor; Scully intercoms for help, stating her name. The elevator reactivates – while COS looks up Scully's home phone number. Scully and Mulder meet Lamana and Peterson, who says any saboteur would have had to override COS. He'll provide a list a list of everyone with COS' access code.

Back at headquarters, just after 3 p.m., Mulder can't find his killer-profile notes but at a meeting with Spiller, Lamana, and at least three other agents, Mulder and Scully recognize Lamana's killer-profile as Mulder's work. Mulder afterward confronts Lamana, who pooh-poohs his theft. Scully and Mulder question Wilczek, the only person with COS access. He makes his hatred of Drake clear, yet Scully, writing in her field journal that night (Oct. 24, 1993), doubts Wilczek's guilt. She goes to bed – whereupon her computer activates, its modem connects, and COS retrieves the file.

The next day, Scully's speech-pattern analysis of tapes of Wilczek's Smithsonian lectures indicates it's Wilczek's disguised voice on the time-recording heard before Drake's death. Lamana volunteers to arrest Wilczek, who's leaving his house in a vintage Corvette after unsuccessfully trying to access COS from home.

Lamana follows him to Eurisko, where Wilczek gains access – astonished to find COS speaking when he'd never installed voice synthesis. Then he watches in horror as Lamana, stuck in the elevator between the 29th and 30th floors, plummets to his death. Scully later tells Mulder Wilczek confessed to Lamana's murder. Mulder doesn't believe Wilczek – and on arriving at Wilczek's house to investigate further, officials in black suits tell him his subpoena's no good and that unless he has "Code 5" clearance, to leave. Mulder demands of Deep Throat why the Defense Department has a Code 5 investigation.

X-otica

Co-writer Howard Gordon has himself called this episode "easily and clearly our worst. It's basically uninteresting." He and Alex Gansa were admittedly not computer literate, and didn't have a feel for the material. "It's an old idea, a machine gaining intelligence. There may have been a more interesting way of doing it and we unfortunately don't feel that we licked the problem." His final analysis? "Well, it pretty much sucked."

A spectrograph is a device for dispersing light radiation into a spectrum, and recording it either photographically or via computer-graphics. A hard-copy print of the results is a spectrogram.

This episode marks the first time Scully's fired her gun.

Deep Throat says the rumor is that Wilczek has developed an AI (artificial intelligence) "adaptive network" – a learning computer.

Federal Detention Center, Washington, DC; Wilczek swears to Mulder he's not protecting COS, but simply refusing to share anything with "an immoral government." Mulder wants Wilczek to destroy COS; he agrees, and will design a virus Mulder can use. Mulder smuggles a laptop into Wilczek's cell.

At 1:31 a.m., Scully finds someone remotely accessing her computer. The FBI traces the call to Eurisko. There Scully finds Mulder; they enter using a Wilczek license plate, which the computer scans – but partway in, a sharp-pronged gate slams down as if to smash their car. Taking the stairs, they find the 29th-floor door locked and booby-trapped. As Scully tries crawling though an air vent to the other side, Peterson finds Mulder on the landing – while Scully finds herself pulled by powerful air currents toward an industrial fan that slices up her flashlight. Desperately, she fires at it.

Mulder accesses COS at user level seven – at which point Peterson pulls a gun and says he's been trying to access COS for two years. He forces Mulder to hand over the viral disc – until Scully gets the drop on Peterson. The infected COS starts speaking gibberish, and "dies."

Later, Mulder tells Deep Throat he's checked with both the Attorney General and a Congressman Klebanow of the Department of Corrections Subcommittee,

Crystal City, VA is a real-life Washington, D.C. suburb, just over the Key Bridge from Georgetown.

Inspiration Alert:

The scene of the infected COS dying at the end – its voice growing slow, slurred and nonsensical – is a blatant homage to *2001: A Space Odyssey* (1968).

but Wilczek has "disappeared." Deep Throat simply replies, that they can do anything they want. Wilczek may or may not break and give them his AI research – but COS, at least, is no longer a danger. At Eurisko, Peterson is given six more hours to revive COS before abandoning it for scrap. No one notices the computer momentarily sputtering to life.

CAST

Jerry Hardin	Deep Throat
Rob LaBelle	Brad Wilczek
Wayne Duvall	Agent Jerry Lamana
Blu Mankuma	Claude Peterson
Tom Butler	[Benjamin] Drake
Gillian Barber	Jane (sic) Spiller [Nancy per episode]
Marc Baur	Man in Suit
Bill Finck	Sandwich Man [at FBI lunch cart]
Theodore Thomas	Clyde

extra

● The official Fox *X-Files* website erroneously lists the character Brad Wilczek as Steven Wilczek, and Claude Peterson as Clyde Peterson.

X-actitude

Lamana's bill to treat Mulder and Scully to lunch: $8.50

Drake's weight: 180 pounds

Scully's home phone number: (202) 555-6431

Scully's FBI ID#: 2317-616. Note: This is distinct from her badge number, which is undisclosed to date.

Spectrograph Scully uses: Audio Spectrum Identisearch, borrowed from the Voice Biometrics Lab at Georgetown University

Source of Scully's warrant for Wilczek: Judge Benson in Washington Heights

Wilczek background: Founded Eurisko at age 22 in his parents' garage, after having spent years following the Grateful Dead in concert; Eurisko, he says, is Greek for "I discover things."

The Cast: Blu Mankuma has lent his easygoing authority, often in police roles, to such films as *The Russia House* (1990), *Bird on a Wire* (1990), *Another Stakeout* (1993), and *The Stepfather* (1987, with future X-guests Terry O'Quinn and Gabrielle Rose). He played Sergeant Stan Parks on *Robocop: The Series* (syndicated, 1994–), and, starting in the 1995-96 season, Captain Reese on *Forever Knight* (CBS/syndicated 1992–). Rob LaBelle played record *uber*producer Phil Spector in the Tina Turner biopic *What's Love Got to Do With It?* (1993). Wayne Duvall is the actor nephew of Robert Duvall; his films include *Apollo 13* (1995).

The Repertory: Tom Butler, who played the unfortunately electrocuted CEO, turns up in episode 2.16, "Colony," as CIA Agent Ambrose Chapel (or a reasonable facsimile thereof). Gillian Barber, with very different hair, went on to play single mom Beth Kane in 2.10, "Red Museum," and claimed alien abductee in 3.09, "Nisei." The actor playing the hardnose who blocks Mulder from Wilczek's home is credited here as Marc Baur; a slightly differently spelled Marc Bauer is credited as an FBI agent in 2.02, "The Host."

X-File case: Classified

1.08 "ICE"

Nov. 5, 1993
Writers: Glen Morgan & James Wong
Director: David Nutter

Arctic Ice Core Project, Icy Cape, AK – 250 miles north of the Arctic Circle. Friday, Nov. 5, 1993. During a –33°F blizzard, at 8:29 a.m. Alaskan Standard Time (AST), a dog roots around for food. At 8:30, shambling team captain John Richter sends a video message: We're not who we are. A second man, Campbell, attacks him. They each point a gun at the other – then as if by silent pact, each blows his own brains out.

FBI headquarters: Scully and Mulder watch a tape of Richter's jubilant transmission when they set a depth record for ice-sheet drilling. A week later came Richter's final message. The Weather Service now predicts a three-day window before the next Arctic storm, finally allowing the FBI to investigate. Doolittle Airfield, Nome, AK, Wednesday: Mulder and Scully hook up with Dr. Denny Murphy, professor of geology at the University of California at San Diego; toxicologist Dr. Nancy Da Silva; physician Dr. Hodge; and bush pilot Bear.

The team finds the bodies of Richter and Campbell, plus a filing cabinet with soil and ice samples. The dog attacks Mulder and Bear; Hodge tranquilizes it, and notes that though Bear is bleeding, the animal isn't rabid. Scully sees black nodules on the dog, a possible sign of bubonic plague – and notices something squirming beneath some irritated flesh. Bear, in private, finds similar nodules on himself.

Scully's autopsies on Richter and Campbell show they

died of gun wounds, and that three other corpses show evidence of strangulation. But there is no sign of nodules, which Hodge notes have disappeared from the dog. Murphy declares the drill site is concave – like, perhaps, a meteor crater. They find ammonium hydroxide in Richter's blood, and evidence of that toxin in the ice samples – along with a ratio of ammonia to water too high for Earth even 250,000 years ago. They also find a weird, single-celled creature in Richter's blood – possibly the larval stage of a larger organism.

Bear is anxious to leave, but Mulder says if the bodies are infected, they can't risk exposing the outside world – and since the dog attacked them, they must test themselves. Yet Bear declares he's leaving *now*, and when the agents restrain him, all see something scrambling beneath his skin. They surgically remove a wriggling organism. Mulder radios Doolittle for an airlift and quarantine; the

radio operator oddly hesitates before saying a storm is blocking air traffic until tomorrow, and maybe the military base at Kotzebue can help.

Bear dies, and though all the victims have had the worm-like organism, only his remains alive; it slithers into the brain's hypothalamus gland, which secretes acetylcholine, which produces aggressive behavior. Mulder speculates to Scully that the "worm" lives in sub-zero ammonia – the same conditions as on other worlds. This area *is* over a meteor crater. They argue over whether to kill it or save it for study.

A suspicious Hodge is sure the agents knew about the creature. When Da Silva notes Hodge and Scully got splattered with Bear's blood, they all agree to check each other for nodules; none found, they retire to separate quarters. Mulder, investigating a noise later, finds Murphy dead – just as the others arrive. Accusations fly. Scully wants them all tested, but Mulder won't

X-otica

A taut, tense episode – one of the series' best – with Scully and Mulder hurdling a critical juncture of mutual trust. Scully confirms the strength under fire she showed as early as episode 1.02, "Deep Throat," where you knew she would have deep-sixed Redbird.

The dog in the episode is a parent of Duchovny's dog Blue.

Icy Cape is an actual locale on the northwest Alaskan Arctic coast, between the towns of Wainwright and Point Hope.

Inspiration Alert:

There's some resemblance to *The Thing (From Another World)* (1951), based on John W. Campbell, Jr.'s story "Who Goes There."

let Hodge touch him. It boils to a point where Scully and Mulder draw guns on each other – and when Mulder says for God's sake it's *him*, Scully tells him, "You may not be who you are." Mulder lets himself be locked into a storage room in case he's infected.

When Da Silva accidentally mixes two drops of infected blood on a microscope slide, Scully sees the two larvae kill each other – and when Scully places an ammonia jar with one live "worm" next to a jar with another [N], each tries in vain to attack the other. They place one in the ear of the infected dog, who later passes two dead "worms" in its stool. Introducing a "worm" to Mulder would thus either cure him . . . or needlessly infect him.

Hodge agrees to examine Mulder, but waylays him while Da Silva locks Scully in a storeroom. As Hodge prepares to drop a "worm" into Mulder's ear, he notices Da Silva's skin moving. Hodge throws Silva off Mulder, then he and Mulder free Scully. They put the "worm" in Da Silva's ear to cure her.

Later, at Doolittle, Da Silva and the dog are quarantined. Mulder says he's returning with proper equipment. Hodge is surprised – hasn't Mulder heard? Forty-five minutes after evacuation, someone torched the station. The military? Centers for Disease Control? Mulder ought to know, Hodge bitterly and ironically tells him they're his people.

CAST

Xander Berkeley   Dr. Hodge

Felicity Huffman   Dr. Nancy Da Silva

Steve Hynter   Dr. Denny Murphy

Jeff Kober   Bear

Ken Kerzinger   [John] Richter

Sonny Surowiec   Campbell

extra

- The dog is uncredited.

X-actitude

Filing cabinet with soil/ice samples labeled: "Ice Cores 2,175–3,250"

Depth of ice-sheet: Per Murphy's analysis, 3,000 meters; Mulder, however, had said the team found it to be twice that.

The Cast: Xander Berkeley has appeared in *Mommie Dearest* (1981), *The Grifters* (1990), *Terminator 2: Judgment Day* (1991), *Candyman* (1992), *Leaving Las Vegas* (1995), *Apollo 13* (1995), and three films for cult-director Alex Cox: *Sid and Nancy* (1986), *Straight to Hell* and *Walker* (both 1987). He was also in Showtime's *Roswell* (1994), with future *X-file* guest Lisa Waltz.

Jeff Kober is best known as Dodger in the Vietnam War drama *China Beach* (ABC 1988–91). He co-starred as Booga in *Tank Girl* (1995), and appeared in the film *Alien Nation* (1988). Felicity Huffman co-starred in the covert-conspiracy TV series *Stephen King's Golden Years* (CBS 1991), as a secret facility's conscience-stricken security chief; the cast also included future *X-* guests R.D. Call and Ed Lauter. Steve Hytner played gadget-whiz Logan "FX" Murphy on *Disney Presents the 100 Lives of Black Jack Savage* (NBC 1991), a fantasy-adventure series starring future "Mr. X" Steven Williams. He's also been in the casts of the sitcoms *Hardball* (Fox 1994) and *The Jeff Foxworthy Show* (ABC 1995–).

Ken Kerzinger, the ice-core Team Captain who isn't who he is, *is* the show's stunt coordinator.

X-File case: Classified

1.09 "SPACE"

Nov. 12, 1993
Writer: Chris Carter
Director: William Graham

X-File case: Classified

Government denies all knowledge

Pasadena, CA, 1977. At the Jet Propulsion Laboratory, a TV correspondent for WXDL/Channel 11 reports on the first Viking Orbiter pictures of Mars, revealing a face-like land formation. Project Director Lieutenant Colonel Marcus Aurelius Belt calls it a trick of the light. But later, he flashes back years to his astronaut spacewalk, being attacked by "something out here!" Belt wakes in shock, engulfed by an image of the Martian face.

Present day. Shuttle Space Center, Cape Canaveral, FL. The space shuttle is T-minus 1 minute 15 seconds to launch. At Houston Mission Control are Belt and Communications Commander Michelle Generoo. Florida aborts the take-off at T-minus 3 seconds. Washington DC, two weeks later: Outdoors, Mulder tells Scully an anonymous letter-writer from NASA wants to speak with the FBI. It is Generoo, who approaches them to say she may have evidence of shuttle sabotage. An auxiliary power unit (APU) valve malfunctioned; had the takeoff not been aborted, the shuttle would have exploded. Someone has anonymously mailed her X-rays and other documents showing deep-grooved marks on the APU – possible evidence of tempering, since scoring a ferrocarbon titanium valve would have taken extreme, launch-pad temperatures. Tomorrow, a new launch is scheduled; her fiance's Mission Commander.

Houston Space Center, next day: Mulder tells Scully Belt nearly died on Gemini 8, making an emergency splash-down. At Belt's office, Mulder gushes he's a fan. Belt is unimpressed – and when the agents show him a picture of the damaged valve, he calls it specious. Scully and Mulder speak with engineers, who confirm the agents have a picture of an anomalously scored APU valve. Mulder can't believe Belt would launch the shuttle with a bad part – and eight hours, 43 minutes later, liftoff is indeed successful.

Yet later at their hotel, Generoo tells them something is wrong. As the agents follow her back to Mission Control, Generoo sees the Martian face appear in the foggy night, and crashes; when Mulder and Scully pull her from her car, she insists they continue. At Mission Control, they learn that at two hours, 18 minutes after launch, Houston lost communication; now they can't rotate the shuttle away from the sun, and it's nearly 103°F in the cabin. When Generoo

arrives, relatively unhurt, they isolate the problem to a digital processor in the Houston data banks. Generoo takes the agents there, as the lights go out – but it's just a scientist, checking since some sensors went off.

By 2:54 into the flight, communication is back but other systems are down. A minute later, Belt gives the astronauts complete control – though Generoo says that risks stranding them. The astronauts do get the bird to fly right, and at a press conference, Belt lies saying there have been no problems. Mulder approaches Belt afterward, wondering whether he'd also lie to the FBI – and Belt sidesteps when Mulder asks about sabotage.

Over Canada, at 12:39 into the flight, the shuttle develops an oxygen leak, leaving the astronauts just 30 minutes of air. Scully and Mulder retrieve Belt from his high-rise apartment. At Mission Control, he orders the astronauts to stay in space suits, prepare the emergency oxygen system . . .

X-otica

"Space" is perhaps the series' dullest, least suspenseful episode, with highly unclear motivations from the Mars creature – which Generoo *and* Scully see, yet dismiss, even though Generoo crashed her car because of it! "It's not my favorite episode, and I think our least successful," Carter has said.

Inspiration Alert:

Aired months before the release of the movie of that name, the episode seems strongly influenced by the story of Apollo 13.

and to deploy the expensive payload no matter what. As the astronauts do so, one reports, "There's someone outside the ship! Some kind of ghost!" Belt goes bonkers. Scully, meantime, finds a diagram of the faulty valve, and learns this analysis was ordered by Belt – whom they find cowering under his desk with "Help Me" written on his blotter.

EMS arrives. Generoo, the next-in-command, wants to bring the shuttle down immediately – but Belt yells no, "It's out there!" He confesses that while he didn't sabotage the shuttle, he didn't stop "them. They don't want us to know!" The agents, momentarily seeing the Mars-creature in Belt's face, convince Belt to help bring the astronauts down safely. He says to change re-entry trajectory to 35 degrees; Generoo conveys that to the astronauts, but doesn't know if they got the message before a scheduled communications blackout occurred. The landing site, Kirtland Air Force Base in Albuquerque, has no sign of the shuttle. At 16:26 into the flight, Generoo tries contacting the astronauts again – and jubilantly, gets a response.

A hospital, 10:56 a.m. CST: Belt watches Generoo's press conference – then throws himself out a window, killing himself to keep the Mars-creature from escaping. Mulder, later reading about Belt's death in the paper, tells Scully something must have possessed Belt in space; Scully replies that doctors diagnosed severe dementia. Mulder concludes Belt had sent the documents anonymously to Generoo – his human self fighting his alien other.

CAST

Ed Lauter	Lt. Col. Marcus Aurelius Belt
Susanna Thompson	Michelle Generoo
Tom McBeath	Scientist
Terry David Mulligan	Mission Controller
French Tickner	Preacher
Norma Wick	[TV] Reporter
Alf Humphreys	2nd Controller
David Cameron	Young Scientist
Tyronne L'Hirondelle	Databank Scientist
Paul Des Roches	Paramedic

X-actitude

Time until liftoff when Scully and Mulder are first seen at Houston Space Center: 10:45:27 (hours/minutes/seconds). Time until liftoff when they reach Belt's office: 10:39:39.

The Cast: Ed Lauter has portrayed tough generals, businessmen and cowboys in *The Longest Yard* (1974), *Born on the Fourth of July*, *Stephen King's Golden Years* (CBS 1991, co-starring future *X*-guests Felicity Huffman and R.D. Call). Susanna Thompson has appeared mostly in telefilms, including *Alien Nation: Dark Horizon* (1994).

The Repertory: Helpful scientist Tom McBeath went on to play LAPD Detective Gwynn in episode 2.07, "3."

X-File case: Classified

1.10 "FALLEN ANGEL"

Nov. 19, 1993
Writers: Howard Gordon & Alex Gansa
Director: Larry Shaw

Townsend, WI, 12:57 a.m., Day 1: Radio interference prevents Deputy Sheriff Wright from reporting a fire off County Road D-7. Shortly afterward he dies screaming, enveloped by flashing lights. U.S. Space Surveillance Center, Cheyenne Mountain, CO: A lieutenant and a female radar operator, Chief Koretz, inform Commander Calvin Henderson that an unidentified object broke into the radar grid off the Connecticut coast going north-by-northwest, "went crazy" in unearthly trajectories, and impacted west of Lake Michigan at over 800 mph. Henderson orders them to report only a meteor – and the radar findings as "instrument malfunction." Away from them, he phones to announce a confirmed fallen angel in the sector.

Budget-Rest Motel, Townsend, 12:57 a.m., Day 1 [sic; see commentary]: On Mulder's TV, a female reporter on Highway 38 says the government is vague about the "toxic cargo" forcing the evacuation of 12,000 residents. Mulder flashes back to Deep Throat telling him about Operation Falcon beginning at 0100 this morning, headed by Air Force "reclamations" expert Henderson; Mulder has 24 hours before the area is "sanitized." The present, half-hour before nightfall: At Falcon field headquarters, Henderson chastises a late-arriving lieutenant [not the one from Cheyenne

Mountain]. Mulder, unseen, drops from underneath the lieutenant's truck chassis and hides.

Night: At the site, Mulder snaps photos of soldiers, firefighters (with foam, not water, extinguishers) and strange objects – until he's rifle-butted unconscious. When he awakens, Henderson berates him for violating a government quarantine; the film's been destroyed. Mulder's pushed into a cell alongside that of hapless UFO conspiracy theorist Max Fenig, of NICAP. Fenig's gone by dawn, when Scully arrives saying Section Chief McGrath wants to close the X-Files and fire Mulder. Scully concedes there are no railroad tracks on which "toxic cargo" could have derailed [N] – it was actually a Libyan jet with a nuclear warhead. Mulder calls that a classified lie. As punctuation, we see a hovering, light-bending being flash through the woods.

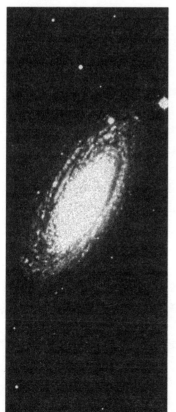

The agents find Fenig in Mulder's (ransacked) room; Fenig has followed Mulder's career through his public-record travel expenses, seen Mulder's picture in a trade magazine, and even read Mulder's pseudonymous *Omni* article about the Gulf Breeze Sightings. Fenig takes them to his camper-trailer – a UFO-sighting mobile HQ, with serious surveillance electronics. Scully notices prescription drugs, among them the anti-convulsant Dilantin and the schizophrenia-treatment drug Mellaril.

Mill Road High School evacuation center, 6:27 p.m., Day 2: Scully and Mulder ask Mrs. Wright about her husband. The widow with a small child says the government won't release Wright's body, and threatened to withhold his pension if she talked. At U.S. Microwave Substation B21, there is the screeching static of a 200K megaHertz signal, and thermography spots something moving at seven mph on the northeast side. Beta Team, led by the Falcon lieutenant, arrives to search and

X-otica

The deadly creature's appearance and clearly quantifiable, unearthly actions indicate that this episode involves a *real* extraterrestrial, and not an Earth-made spacecraft (*à la* episode 1.02, "Deep Throat") or alien-human hybrid (*à la* Dr. Secare of episode 1.24, "The Erlenmeyer Flask").

The Gulf Breeze incidents Mulder wrote of refer to sightings claimed around that small Pensacola, FL suburb from November 1987 to May 1988, primarily by real-estate developer Ed Walters who had photos, some scientific endorsement, and much credible evidence to back up his story. Later, a young man revealed he'd helped Walters fake it all. But for a while, Gulf Breeze became a ufologist's Mecca.

destroy. Jackson, behind the lieutenant, sees nothing – till the alien attacks.

County Hospital, Townsend, 11:42 p.m.: ER physician Dr. Oppenheim says he saw Wright and three firefighters all DOA with fifth and sixth degree burns [N] over 90% of their bodies. The government whisked them away before autopsies could be done. Suddenly, soldiers bang in with severely burned comrades. Mulder tells Henderson hunting the alien only forces it to defend itself. Henderson throws Mulder out, but Oppenheim insists they need medical doctor Scully. Morning: Mulder finds Fenig having an epileptic seizure. Afterward, Mulder helps him to bed and notices a V-shaped scar behind Fenig's left ear. Later, Mulder shows Scully alien-abductee photos of two women with the same scar as Fenig.

Cheyenne Mountain: Koretz announces unidentified flash traffic at point 2418, this time from a much larger craft – or, as the lieutenant corrects her, a Meteor. Fine – but Whitmarsh Air Force Base says the "meteor" is hovering over Townsend. At Fenig's camper, Fenig's ears bleed, and he vanishes in a flash. Scully and Mulder, with less than an hour before their flight, find Fenig missing, and blood on his pillow. His radio scanner crackles about a target on the waterfront, and Henderson saying to move on target.

Lake Michigan waterfront, Dock 7: Henderson tells his men Fenig's not a civilian and to take him with extreme caution. Mulder and Scully arrive to find soldiers burned to death. They follow Max's cry into a warehouse. Scully's arrested,

Townsend, WI is a fictional locale.

Inspiration Alert:

The wavily visible/invisible alien is a direct takeoff from *Predator* (1987).

X-actitude

Mulder's *Omni* pseudonym: M.F. Luder, an anagram of "F. Mulder"

TV station with news report: Channel 5

The agents' rental-car license plate: RAH-615

Deputy Wright's Sheriff Department cruiser plate: 29406. Location of fire near County Road D-7: two miles west of the Canyon Ridge intersection

UFO groups Fenig mentions: MUFON, CUFOS, and "that new group," CSICOP; NICAP stands for National Investigative

plastique explosives are applied to the building, and Alpha Team reports *three* moving forms in the building. Inside, after a flash of light throws Mulder across the room, he sees Fenig floating like a rag doll. Then another bright flash – and only Mulder remains when the soldiers blow down the door. Mulder tells Henderson Fenig's gone – "they" had gotten to him first.

FBI headquarters, Mulder's OPR hearing, 10:17 a.m., Day 4: Mulder, on crutches, hobbles in. Facing charges of insubordination and misconduct, he loses patience as officials deem his evidence "irrelevant," and claim Fenig's body was found two hours later in a cargo container. He's out – but later, McGrath demands of Deep Throat why someone countermanded the Committee's decision. Deep Throat says having Mulder active is less dangerous than having the "wrong people" take him under their wing. And he remarks about what Mulder knows, and "what he *thinks* he knows."

CAST

Jerry Hardin   Deep Throat
Frederick Coffin   Section Chief Joseph
                          McGrath [first name
                          not given in
                          episode]

Marshall Bell   Commander Calvin
                          Henderson

Committee of Aerial Phenomena.

Where Fenig arrested: 100 yards past Falcon roadblock

Mellaril prescription filled at: All-Nighter Pharmacy

Headline of Scully's newspaper: "Toxic clean-up a success"

Radar points of the UFO's path:

Connecticut coastline where it "tripped the fence": 2317

Lake Michigan area where it dropped off the screen: 2418

Max's high-tech spy electronics include: Wolf's Ear 200 listening, from "CIA supplier" Wolf Industries.

Condition of soldiers in ER: All died but two, who are in critical condition on their way to the burns unit, Johns Hopkins.

Scott Bellis	Max Fenig
Brent Stait	Corp. Taylor [unnamed in episode]
Alvin Sanders	Deputy Sheriff J. Wright [first initial not given in episode]
Sheila Paterson	Gina Watkins [unnamed in episode]
Tony Pantages	Lt. Fraser [unnamed in episode]
Freda Perry	Mrs. Wright
Michael Rogers	Lt. Griffin [unnamed in episode]
William McDonald	Dr. Oppenheim
Jane MacDougall	Laura Dalton [unnamed in episode]
Kimberly Unger	[Chief] Karen Koretz [first name not given in episode]

Continuity errors: The crash and fire begins at 12:57 a.m., Day 1 – yet it's *still* 12:57 a.m., Day 1, the next night, when Mulder watches a news report of the evacuation that took place that day, hours *after* the crash. And Mulder's *flashback* has Deep Throat telling him about the crash occurring "last night." Clearly, the wrong subtitle was used in the motel establishing shot.

An additional error: It is 12:57 a.m., and we see Mulder getting ready to investigate. Yet when next we see him, it's daytime – and shortly afterward, when he sneaks into Falcon, it's a half-hour before nightfall – making it over *40 hours* since Falcon went into effect! This might have all been avoided by, for instance, showing the motel in daylight, and marking the time as, say, 12:57 *p.m.*, Day 1.

On the other hand: Why did Henderson's men let target Fenig go when they had him in the brig at the start? They simply didn't know he was a real abductee at the time.

The Cast: Marshall Bell has a long list of supporting-actor credits in films including *A Nightmare on Elm Street, Part 2: Freddy's Revenge* (1985), *Twins* (1988), *Total Recall* (1990) and *Operation Dumbo Drop* (1995). He was in the casts of two short-lived TV shows, *The Oldest Rookie* (CBS 1987-88) and the musical series *Hull High* (NBC 1990). Scott Bellis, Fenig, has had small roles in the movies *Intersection*, *Timecop* and *Little Women* (all 1994).

The FBI Section Chief played by Frederick Coffin – a George Kennedy clone – appears to be not a successor to Blevins, but a lateral official. Coffin has had roles in numerous movies and telefilms, including a fun bit as Officer Koharski in *Wayne's World* (1992); he played an unknown Brad Pitt's father in episodes of the summer series *Glory Days* (Fox 1990), and a patriarch in the cast of the 1994 pilot, *The Wyatts*.

The Repertory: Alvin Saunders would play a bus driver in episode 2.22, "F. Emasculata." Michael Rogers had a bit part in 2.16, "Colony."

X-File case: Classified

1.11 "EVE"

Dec. 10, 1993
Writers: Kenneth Biller & Chris Brancato
Director: Fred Gerber

X-File case: Classified
Government denies all knowledge

Greenwich, CT: A couple jogging find eight-year-old Teena Simmons sitting dazedly in her front yard – and her father Joel dead. FBI headquarters, the next day: The report says death by hypovolemia – Joel Simmons had lost over 75% of his blood. Teena claims no memory of what's occurred; physical evidence was washed away by rain. The M.E. found traces of digitalis, a heart stimulant made from the plant of the same name (a.k.a foxglove), which can be used as a paralytic drug. Mulder notes the wounds and blood-removal resemble those of "alien" cattle mutilations.

Fairfield County Social Services Hostel, Greenwich. Teena tells the agents of red lightning yesterday, and of men from the clouds. The agents learn of an identical murder outside San Francisco, in Marin County: Doug Reardon died of hypovolemia at 2:30 p.m. PST – the same time as Simmons. Daughter Cindy, returning tomorrow from Sacramento with her mother, has said she remembers nothing.

The Greenwich hostel, 12:35 am EST: Teena is abducted. Later that day, Marin County: Mulder and Scully discover eight-year-old Cindy looks exactly like Teena. When the agents show her mom a photo of Teena, she states Cindy is her only child – indeed, she and her husband tried for six years to get pregnant, finally choosing in vitro fertilization at the Luther Stapes Center for Reproductive Medicine in San Francisco.

Because Teena was kidnapped, Mulder and the San Francisco bureau stake out Cindy. Scully meets with a Dr. Katz at the Stapes Center, who says Mrs. Simmons was treated by Dr. Sally Kendrick, a resident who earned a Yale medical degree after completing her doctorate in biogenetics. But the center believed Kendrick was conducting eugenics experiments, fired her, and asked for a federal investigation – yet the Dept. of Health wouldn't investigate.

X-otica

Port Reyes National Seashore is an actual locale, 40 miles north of San Francisco.

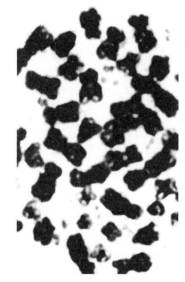

At their hotel, Scully gives Mulder the information, but he rushes her out after a phone call of only clicks – a signal to meet Deep Throat. He tells Mulder about the classified "Litchfield" experiments: In the 1950s, the U.S. heard the Russians were using crude eugenics to try to develop a super-soldier. The U.S. followed suit, at a compound in Litchfield, CT. Boys were codenamed Adam, girls Eve. Deep Throat arranges for the agents to see the adult Eve 6.

The straitjacketed women looks exactly like Kendrick. She says the only remaining, suicide-prone Eves are her, Eve 7 (who escaped as a child) and Eve 8 (who escaped ten years later). Each Eve has 56 (rather than the normal 46) chromosomes, having extra pairs of chromosomes number 4, 5, 12, 16 and 22 – which, she says, produced additional genes, heightening strength, intelligence . . . and psychosis. Mulder believes Kendrick cloned herself to produce Cindy and Teena, and that Eves 7 and 8 killed the parents to raise the girls themselves.

During their stakeout, Scully and Mulder can't prevent Cindy from being kidnapped by an adult Eve, who escapes in a light blue 1993 Corolla – switching to a dark blue car by the time she reaches Port Reyes National Seashore. Identifying herself as Kendrick, she introduces the girls to each other. She'd always kept watch on them, she says, while also searching for the remaining Eve; the girls' recent murders forced her hand. She'd hoped to correct the Litchfield flaws, saying the Eves developed homicidal tendencies at age 20. Yet she herself was raised by a Litchfield genetic engineer in a good environment with medication. Then she begins shaking: The girls have slipped four ounces of home-grown digitalis extract into her soda. Police and FBI burst in, the motel manager having alerted them about a woman fitting Kendrick's description. But Kendrick is dead, and the girls say this lady and another wanted them all to take poison.

Scully and Mulder, driving the girls to social services, pull into a truck-stop diner – where Cindy spikes the agents' diet sodas. But when Mulder returns to the counter to fetch his keys, he notices a green liquid there: poison. He warns Scully, and the girls escape amid the tractor-trailers. When Mulder corners them, their screams bring help from an apparent trucker [who is actually a hunter, per the end-credits]. The girls evidently escape in a school bus – but when the agents' car follows it, the girls come out of hiding to be caught by the clever Mulder. The girls, labeled Eves 9 and 10, are eventually sent to Whiting. When Eve 8 visits, dressed as Kendrick, they exchange a chilling look of mutual knowledge.

CAST

Jerry Hardin	Deep Throat
Harriet Harris	Dr. Sally Kendrick/Eves 6 & 8
Erika Krievins	Cindy Reardon
Sabrina Krievins	Teena Simmons
George Touliatos	Dr. Katz
Tasha Simms	Ellen Reardon [first name not given in episode]

Janet Hodgkinson	Waitress
David Kirby	Ted Watkins [jogger; unnamed in episode]
Tina Gilbertson	Donna Watkins [jogger; unnamed in episode]
Christine Upright-Letain	Ms. Wells [social worker; unnamed in episode]
Gordon Tipple	Detective
Garry Davey	Hunter
Joe Maffei	1st Guard
Maria Herrera	2nd Guard
Robert Lewis	Officer

X-actitude

Teena was born in San Rafael (CA) General Hospital. Her mother, Claudia, died of ovarian cancer two years ago, leaving no other family.

What Teena watches on TV: an *Eek the Cat* cartoon, and a news report (Pres. Clinton signing a crime bill)

Eve 6: confined since 1983 at the Whiting Institute for the Criminally Insane, Cell Block 2. Her IQ: 265

Kendrick's room at the Port Reyes motel: #2

The Cast: Harriet Harris, a.k.a. Harriet Sansom Harris, plays two basically inhuman characters in two utterly distinct and believable ways, making both Dr. Kendrick and Eve 6 tragically, remarkably human. Harris co-starred in the sitcom *The 5 Mrs. Buchanans* (CBS 1994–95) alongside fellow theater heavyweights Judith Ivey and Eileen Heckart. She has the recurring role of Bebe Glaser on *Frasier*, and recently did a major .guest role as Earth's leader in the 11/4/95 "Eyes" episode of *Space: Above and Beyond* (Fox 1995–), created by Glen Morgan and James Wong.

The disturbingly – and perfectly – eerie twins played by Erika and Sabrina Krievins

The Repertory: Garry Davey would very memorably play the scientist with the frozen head in episode 1.23, "Roland." Gordon Tipple, here a detective, became a wheelchair-bound convict in 1.16, "Young at Heart." George Touliatos had a larger role as a conniving county supervisor in 2.03, "Blood." Tasha Simms returned as an old-timer's concerned daughter in 2.11. Robert Lewis had another bit-part as a police officer in 2.05, "Duane Barry."

X-File case: Classified

1.12 "FIRE"

X-File case #: 11214893

Government denies all knowledge

Dec. 17, 1993
Writer: Chris Carter
Director: Larry Shaw

Bosham, England, 70 miles southwest of London. As he gets into his chauffeured car, a distinguished older man spontaneously combusts in front of his wife and others, as gardener Cecil L'Ively glares evilly. Washington, D.C.: At the Hoover Building garage, Mulder and Scully, in an FBI car, find a mysterious audiotape; a female British voice tells them Parliament member Reggie Ellicott was killed six months ago when a similar cassette triggered a car explosion. The agents are apparently sitting in a bomb – but then Mulder's door suddenly opens to reveal beautiful Scotland Yard Inspector Phoebe Green, a practical-joking acquaintance from Mulder's Oxford days more than 10 years ago. And though having broken his heart then, she kisses him heartily now, as Scully looks away.

Phoebe explains someone is burning up Parliament members, then sending love letters to their wives. One MP, Sir Malcolm Marsden, had barely escaped a garage fire. Sir Malcolm and family, she says, are now in Cape Cod, MA on vacation, and Mulder runs the information by the arson guys as a professional courtesy. An Agent Beatty suggests the cause is rocket fuel, which burns almost completely. Mulder suggests pyrokinesis. At Sir Malcolm's vacation cottage, a caretaker, Bob, is applying argotypoline rocket-propulsion class-3 liquid to a windowpane. And then "Bob" – the gardener from England – makes a cigarette light by itself. Outside, a dog scratches at the makeshift grave of the real caretaker.

In his office, Mulder tells Scully that Phoebe is playing mind-games with him, since she knows he has a phobia about fire. Meantime, at a Boston bar, Bob uses his finger to light a cigarette for a Miss Kotchik. She thinks it's just a charming magic trick — until he sets his arm and the whole bar afire. At Boston Mercy Hospital, Kotchik describes the events to Scully and Mulder (who have pulled a news-wire report of this suspicious fire). At Cape Cod, Bob poisons the MP's chauffeur in order to report him ill and to take his place tonight driving the family to a Boston party in Sir Malcolm's honor. He also shows a "magic" fire trick to the MP's children, Michael and Jimmie.

Phoebe agrees with Mulder that the arsonist may be telekinetic; she also mentions with a sly smile she's taken a hotel room in Boston. At 5:15 p.m., Mulder arrives at the Venable Plaza Hotel,

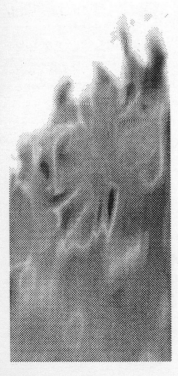

suitcase in hand. When Scully calls to say she wants to fly up with some data on a possible suspect, he suggests she doesn't: At 6:47 p.m., the MP and his family arrive. Phoebe works undercover in a stunning black gown; Mulder is in a tux. When the arsonist doesn't show, she invites Mulder to dance. Scully appears, but hangs back — then interrupts them when a monitor shows a fire on the 14th floor, where the MP's children are. Mulder races there, but the fire panics him and he has to be rescued by firefighters; Bob himself "saves" the kids.

Scully tells Mulder she ran an Interpol check on the victims' domestic help. The only duplicated name: Cecil L'Ively, a gardener for two of the victims. Searching further, she found him listed as having died in a London tenement fire in 1971 — *and* having died with a group of kids in a British Satanic-cult sacrifice in 1963. His name also turned up at a Boston immigration office list of recent visas.

X-otica

According to Carter, Duchovny, in one of the fire scenes, suffered a burn bad enough that "David still has a scar on one of his hands. In fact, he said, 'You better put that in there, because I got burned on that scene.'"

In-joke: Minus the "Sir," Malcolm Marsden is the name of the *X-Files'* hairstylist.

Scully gets a fax of the composite sketch of the bar arsonist – whom she recognizes as the "hero," Bob. Mulder races to the Cape Cod house – where he barges in on the married MP nuzzling on the stairs with Phoebe.

When Scully arrives, they find the real driver bound up in the bathroom. Suddenly, the house catches fire. The agents hustle everyone out except the missing children. Mulder races through the conflagration to find them; he hears them screaming behind a door which he breaks down. Bob sets a hallway on fire, and when Scully tells him to freeze, he dares her to shoot and risk an explosion. But Phoebe splashes him with an accelerant, and he catches fire himself. Badly wounded, he laughs as he cannot be killed this way.

At Boston Mercy, where Bob/Cecil is in a hyperbaric chamber with fifth- and sixth-degree burns [N] and a temperature of 109°F, specialists find phenomenally rapid regeneration of his fundamental, basal cell tissue. He'll recover in as little as a month – at which point he'll be tried for the murder of the caretaker.

CAST

Amanda Pays	Inspector Phoebe Green
Mark Sheppard	Bob the Caretaker/Cecil L'Ively
Dan Lett	Sir Malcolm Marsden [last name per several print sources; not given in episode]
Laurie Paton	Mrs. Marsden
Duncan Fraser	Beatty

Phil Hayes	Driver #1
Keegan Macintosh	Michael
Lynda Boyd	Woman in Bar [Miss Kotchik]
Christopher Gray	Jimmie
Alan Robertson	Grey-haired man

X-actitude

Kotchik's hospital room: 28E

Site of Phoebe and Mulder's "youthful indiscretion": Sir Arthur Conan Doyle's tombstone

Site of Satanic-cult sacrifice: Tottingham Woods, near Bath, England.

The Cast: Amanda Pays (b. June 6, 1959 or 1960 [sources vary], Berkshire, England) became the thinking adolescent's heartthrob as Theora Jones on *Max Headroom* (ABC 1987). She similarly co-starred as the lovely and brainy sidekick Tina McGee on *The Flash* (CBS 1990-91). She co-starred with George Segal in the cable movie *The Cold Room* a.k.a. *The Prisoner* (1984), and soon afterwards made her film debut in *Oxford Blues* (1984). She often headlines in TV-movies and cable movies – including 1991's *Dead on the Money*, co-starring second husband Corbin Bernsen.

Mark Sheppard played Paddy Armstrong in *In the Name of the Father* (UK/Ireland 1993).

The Repertory: The very talented Lynda Boyd proved herself equally adept playing the shallow young woman here whom Cecil L'Ively chats up, and the life-hardened girlfriend/wife of an escaped murder convict in episode 2.22, "F. Emasculata."

X-File case #: 11214893

1.13 "BEYOND THE SEA"

Jan. 7, 1994
Writers: Glen Morgan & James Wong
Director: David Nutter

Scully, at home, finishes a Christmas dinner with her parents, Maggie and William [whose name isn't given in this episode, but in 2.08, "One Breath"]. Later, at 1:47 am, Scully's half-asleep on her couch while pitchman Ron Popeill does a "hair-in-a-can" infomercial. She awakens to see her dad across the room. His moving lips make no sound as he eerily mouths The Lord's Prayer, and his rigid eyes aren't quite right. Then the phone rings, and dad disappears – while mom, on the phone, sobs that he suffered a coronary an hour ago, and died.

Jackson University, Raleigh, NC: Nineteen-year-olds Elizabeth (Liz) Hawley and James (Jim) Summers are necking in a car – until a "cop" lures Jim out and hits him. FBI headquarters: Scully returns to work after her father's death and a concerned Mulder asks how Dana is. She repeats her name to herself, realizing it's the first time Mulder's used it.

Mulder apprises her of the Jackson U. couple, kidnapped two days ago. A year earlier, on this day, two students were kidnapped at Duke. In North Carolina, serial killer Luther Lee Boggs, scheduled to be executed in a week, will trade information about the kidnapping in exchange for his sentence being commuted to life imprisonment. Boggs also claims to be able to channel spirits and demons. Mulder, whose

X-File case: Classified
Government denies all knowledge

psychological profile helped to capture Boggs, thinks it's all a scam.

Scully will meet Mulder at the prison after attending her father's noon ashes-scattering ceremony, where she tells her mom that as a Naval Captain, dad was entitled to burial at Arlington. Scully, knowing her dad would have preferred she pursue her medical career, wonders whether he was proud of her.

Later that afternoon, Central Prison, Raleigh: As Boggs "channels" a Jack Nicholson-like voice, Mulder hands him a piece of blue cloth from an evidence bag; Boggs, touching it, says Jim is in a condemned-warehouse cellar, tied up in packing twine, being whipped with a wire hanger. He mentions "an angel of stone" and a waterfall without water. Mulder replies he tore the cloth off his New York Knicks t-shirt. Yet as Mulder and Scully leave, Boggs starts singing

"Beyond the Sea"; when Scully looks back, she sees her father in Boggs' place – a grief-induced hallucination? Then she sees Boggs again, who calls her "Starbuck."

Shaken, she drives back to her hotel – seeing a neon sign for the Hotel Niagara, and across the street, an "angel of stone" statue. Nearby is a condemned warehouse; inside she finds a lit candle, a wire hanger, and a bracelet Hawley's family identifies as Liz's. Mulder suggests Boggs set it all up, but Scully confesses she believes Boggs can contact the dead – and convinces Mulder that if last year's murders are the model, the kidnapped couple has only three days left.

Boggs, their only lead, is apparently channeling one of the teenagers, who describes a small, thin male in his late 20s. He mentions a boathouse near Lake Jordan, and warns Mulder to avoid "the white cross." At the lake, the agents and police find Liz, alive. Mulder approaches a suspicious boat, and is downed by a single

X-otica

The song "Beyond the Sea" by Bobby Darin (1936-73), spent 11 weeks on the *Billboard* top-40, beginning Jan. 25, 1960, reaching #6.

The character names "Luther Lee Boggs" and "Lucas Henry" evoke that of the real-life serial killer Henry Lee Lucas. The KISS and KILL tattoos on Boggs' hands likewise evoke the famous LOVE and HATE tattoos on Robert Mitchum's in *Night of the Hunter* (1955) – though co-writer Glen Morgan attributed the specific words "kiss" and "kill" to lyrics in a song by the band X.

gunshot. Scully sees two white dock timbers – forming a cross.

Liz ID's a mug shot of Luther Jackson Henry, 28; Scully discovers that in three days, it's the seventh anniversary of a car accident in which Henry's girlfriend was killed and his mother decapitated; a detective tells her the Durham, NC police believe Henry was Boggs' partner in Boggs' last five murders.

Scully – in perhaps the most mesmerizing, slow-build dramatic crescendo in the series – warns Boggs that if he and Henry orchestrated all this to kill Mulder, she will personally execute him. Yet Boggs, looking momentarily like Mulder, assures her she believes – and then apparently channels *her*, remembering a night at age 14 when she snuck a cigarette. Boggs then begins apparently channeling her dad – but the Nicholson-like voice interrupts, demanding a deal.

Yet the warden refuses, and says the courts agree. Mulder, recovering in intensive care, warns Scully Boggs wants to make her his last victim. Scully lies to Boggs, claiming the warden agreed. Tearfully thanking her, Boggs channels a vision of the abandoned Blue Devil Brewery, near Morrisville. Scully, disappointed, starts to tell Boggs that if he really *were* psychic – and he finishes her thought. And he warns her not to follow Henry to the Devil.

At the brewery, Henry raises an ax over Jim, as Scully and police burst in. Scully shoots his arm, then as she chases him, Henry falls to his death near the Blue Devil logo. Scully later tells Boggs that if all this *had* been orchestrated, Henry would've avoided the bridge – Boggs saved her and Jim's lives. He says he'll channel her father tonight, at the execution. Yet at midnight, Scully's not there.

She's in Mulder's hospital room, trying to convince him – and herself – of Boggs' fakery. Mulder asks why, after all she's seen, she still doesn't believe. "I'm afraid. I'm afraid to believe." And she's realized what her father would have said. "He was, after all, my father. . . ."

CAST

Brad Dourif	Luther Lee Boggs
Don Davis	Captain William Scully
Sheila Larken	Margaret (Maggie) Scully
Lawrence King	Lucas [Jackson] Henry
Fred Henderson	Agent Thomas [unnamed in episode]
Don MacKay	Warden Joseph Cash [unnamed in episode]
Lisa Vultaggio	Liz Hawley
Chad Willett	Jim Summers
Kathrynn Chisholm	Nurse
Randy Lee	Paramedic
Len Rose	E.R. Doctor

The Cast: Brad Dourif (b. March 18, 1950, Huntingdon, WV) came to prominence as Billy Bibbitt in *One Flew Over the Cuckoo's Nest* (1975), for which he was Oscar-nominated and won a Golden Globe Award. By this time he'd appeared in an underground film, *Split* (1969), and would go on to eye-catching work in films like *Wise Blood* (1979), *Blue Velvet* (1986), *Mississippi Burning* (1988) and *Murder in the First* (1995). He'd also provided the voice of the reincarnated killer Chucky in *Child's Play* (1988) and its two sequels. Dourif's TV appearances include *Moonlighting*, *Miami Vice* and *Wild Palms*.

X-actitude

The X-File Scully looks up (unrelated to the Boggs case) is "Visionary Encounters w/ The Dead," file X-167512; the front cover is stamped with blurry initials, apparently "WC."

Mulder's medical status: Blood pressure 67 on palpitation; he's received two units of O-negative

Tattoos on Boggs' hands: KISS [and] KILL.

Boggs' murders include: strangling family members over Thanksgiving dinner.

Prop newspaper Mulder uses to trick Boggs: *The Carolinian*

Sheila Larken, the wife of *X-Files* co-executive producer R.W. (Bob) Goodwin plays Scully's mother. She made her TV debut *Judd, for the Defense* (1967) co-starred in *The Storefront Lawyers/Men at Law* (CBS 1970-71), and afterward did multiple episodes of series including *Barnaby Jones*, *The Incredible Hulk*, *Quincy, M.E.*, *Trapper John, M.D.*, *Highway to Heaven* and *FBI: The Untold Stories*. Among her telefilms are *Sarah T. – Portrait of a Teenage Alcoholic* (1975), *Cave-In!* (1983), *Downpayment on Murder* (1987), *The Killing Mind* (1991), and *She Stood Alone: The Tailhook Scandal* (1995).

Scullys father is portrayed by Don Davis. Aside from his recurring-guest appearances on *Twin Peaks* as Major Garland Briggs, Davis has played in *Northern Exposure*, *21 Jump Street*, *Booker*, *Broken Badges* (in the recurring role of Chief Sterling) and movies including *Stakeout* (1987) and *Look Who's Talking* (1989), *A League of Their Own* (1992), on the *X-Files* served as the *dialogue* coach on episode 1.18, "Miracle Man" and made a brief, spectral return as Captain Scully in 2.08, "One Breath."

The Repertory: Don MacKay traded in his suit for overalls as sewer-worker Charlie in episode 2.02, "The Host." Fred Henderson, who played an unnamed FBI agent here, would turn up as Agent Rich in 2.05, "Duane Barry"; Doug Abrahams, another unnamed, would return as a Satanic high-school coach in 2.14 "Die Hand Die Verletzt."

X-File case: Classified

1.14 "GENDER-BENDER"

Jan. 21, 1994
Writers: Larry Barber & Paul Barber
Director: Rob Bowman

Germantown, MD. At a dance club, a plain-looking woman lustily whispers in a man's ear. In a motel, they have spectacular sex – after which the man dies painfully, and the woman morphs into a man. A police detective later tells Scully a security camera showed a man and a woman enter the 30th-floor room at 10:13 p.m. But only a man left at midnight – with no trace of the woman.

Mulder informs Scully of five similar deaths, four in the past six weeks: Two women, three men, all dead of coronaries, all with 100 times the natural level of pheromones – chemicals secreted by animals as sexual attractants. The first death involved a 32-year-old United Auto Workers organizer in Steveston, MA, home of the Kindred, a religious group who make pottery using a white clay Mulder found in scratches on the new victim.

Steveston: Shopkeepers show Scully and Mulder photos of 1930s Kindred. When the agents spot a horse-drawn carriage at a feed store, Mulder goes inside while Scully speaks with Brother Andrew – a plain-looking man whose mesmerizing handshake leaves a Scully a bit breathless.

The agents drive as far as possible up a rough road toward the Kindred settlement. With about a mile left to hike, the two get lost, and a group of Kindred surround them; Brother Oakley and Sister Abby have them hand over their guns. At a communal dinner Mulder and Scully ask the Kindred to try identifying the suspects in the video. Brother Wilton angrily denounces these outsiders. As Abby admonishes Wilton, Aaron begins choking to death. Scully rushes to help, but Abby has the man whisked away.

At a dance club, a young man asks a teased-hair blonde to dance. She declines – until he rubs her hand as Andrew did Scully's.

Wilton directs Scully and Mulder to the path to their car. Out of earshot, the agents wonder why they saw no Kindred children – and Mulder swears he saw some of these faces in the 1930s photos. Doubling back, they find the community gathered in a barn, amid a ritual in which the congregants march Aaron into a cellar. Mulder goes below himself. Scully is surprised by Andrew, who promises

information. In his room, he tells her the killer is his best friend, Brother Martin, who'd found some discarded men's magazines on Route 44; having gotten a taste of the outside world, he'd left.

Mulder sees Aaron's body being slathered with white clay and placed into a cave opening. Wilton and another man talk about Scully being with Andrew, and Mulder being missing. After they go, Mulder sees Aaron's corpse beginning to turn female. Andrew tells Scully the Kindred are "different"; he demonstrates his mesmerizing touch, and kisses her to her helpless acquiescence. Mulder finds the right room, breaks in, and pulls her away. A Kindred mob waits outside, but lets the agents through – then pours into Andrew's building. Scully, vomiting, doesn't knows what happened.

At a rock club, the female Marty mesmerizes a man named Michael. Soon they're going at it in a car, until a cop interrupts them. Marty gets out, and when

X-otica

The original broadcast was preceded by a promo with the Crypt-Keeper promising "a close encounter of the weird kind with *The X-Files*, coming up next."

The Kindred's chant, its words unspecified in the script, was written by producer Paul Rabwin.

Germantown is a real-life suburb of Washington, D.C.

the cop's distracted by Michael's painful groaning, she decks him and morphs into a man – as Michael watches in astonishment. Later, in the hospital, he admits to the agents what he saw; Scully theorizes the killer is simply a transvestite.

A female African-American agent informs Mulder and Scully a credit card from the previous victim was used at the Hotel Catherine, eight blocks away. There, Marty is telling someone about the temptations of the flesh. Marty strikes Scully, then beats up Mulder and escapes. Scully chases Marty into an alley, where he surrenders – as Kindred suddenly appear. They engulf Marty, and ignore the armed Scully – whom Andrew calmly slugs when Mulder inadvertently distracts her. Then the Kindred disappear. Daybreak: The agents and two carloads of sheriffs invade the Kindred compound – but the group is gone, and the cellar entrance covered in concrete. One officer finds something in a hay field – as a crane shot reveals a large, unnaturally round, flattened imprint . . . such as that which a spaceship might or might not have left.

CAST

Brent Hinkley	Brother Andrew
Michele Goodger	Sister Abby
Kate Twa	Female Marty
Peter Stebbings	Male Marty
Nicholas Lea	Michael [note: "Michel" in closed-captioning and some print sources]
Mitchell Kosterman	Detective Horton [last name not given in episode]

Paul Batten	Brother Wilton
Doug Abrahams	2nd [FBI] Agent
Aundrea MacDonald	Pretty Woman
John R. Taylor	Husband [in mom-&-pop store]
Grai Carrington	Tall Man [the Germantown victim]
Tony Morelli	Cop
Lesley Ewen	1st [FBI] Agent
David Thomson	Brother Oakley

X-actitude

The agents' rental-car license plate: 402-J7A

One of the horses outside the feed store: Alice

Sites of the previous "genderbender" murders: Steveston and Boston, MA; Hartford, CT; Philadelphia, PA; Washington, DC.

Hotel Catherine address: 771 Catherine St.

X-act Location: The fictional Steveston, MA was picturesque Steveston Village, in the Vancouver suburb of Richmond. It was used again, to portray fictional Kenwood, TN, in episode 1.18, "Miracle Man."

The Cast: For more on Nicholas Lea, see his separate biography.

Brent Hinkley played Harlow in the sitcom *The Preston Episodes* (Fox 1995), and Conrad Brooks in *Ed Wood* (1994). His other films include *Jacob's Ladder* (1990), *Bob Roberts* (1992), and *Honeymoon in Vegas* (1992).

The Repertory: Michele Goodger has appeared in films including *Little Women* (1994), *Cousins* (1989) and *The Accused* (1988), and on TV in the Vancouver-filmed *Wiseguy*, *MacGyver* and *The Commish*, among other shows. Goodger returned as the wife of a Satanic principal in episode, 2.14, "Die Hand Die Verletzt." Unlikely succubus Kate Twa would return in the featured role of detective Kelly Ryan in 2.23, "Soft Light."

The Germantown, MD police detective played by Mitchell Kosterman shows up again in 2.04, "Sleepless" – still played by Kosterman, but now Lt. Horton of the NYPD.

X-File case: Classified

1.15 "LAZARUS"

Feb. 4, 1994
Writers: Alex Gansa & Howard Gordon
Director: David Nutter

Maryland Marine Bank, 5:55 p.m. Scully and Jack Willis of the Washington bureau's Violent Crimes section investigate a robbery tip. Latter-day Bonnie & Clyde Warren James Dupre and Lula Phillips go into action. Dupre bursts in, unloading a pump-action shotgun at Willis before Scully downs Dupre with three shots. After much defibrillation Willis survives. Lying unseen, the dead Dupre, reacts to the two final jolts.

Two days later: Bethesda Naval Hospital, 12:51 a.m.: Willis leaves – first cutting off three of Dupre's fingers to get at his wedding ring. Next morning: Scully tells Mulder that Willis, who has been obsessed with the case for a year, left his prints on a pair of surgical shears; she figures he's suffering post-traumatic stress. Meantime, "Willis" breaks into Dupre's house looking for Lula – and finds Dupre's tatoo appearing on him.

Analysis shows Dupre's mutilator was left-handed. Willis was right-handed – but Dupre himself was a lefty. Mulder finds Willis' EKG readings odd: a long flatline followed by two different heartbeat patterns. Scully attributes it to equipment malfunction or electrical overload; Mulder believes Dupre returned in Willis' body. At the University of Maryland Biology Department, a Dr. Varnes tells the agents that in near-death experiences, the tremendous energy-release can cause profound personality changes. Scully knows Willis' personality well – he was one of her Academy instructors, and her boyfriend for almost a year. They share the same birthday, and would celebrate together at a bar in Stafford, VA.

Desmond Arms Residence Hotel: "Willis" rousts Lula's brother Tommy. When the TV news says an anonymous tip brought the FBI to the bank, "Willis" believes Tommy sold them out, and shoots him dead with a .45 pistol. Scully and an Agent Bruskin later investigate – as a cleaned-up "Willis" arrives, recognizing Scully as the one who shot him. Mulder later notices "Willis" at the FBI firing range working on recertification – shooting left-handed. "Willis" also signs a birthday card for Scully – two months early. Scully still thinks it is stress.

"Willis" takes a hotline call from a reward-minded landlord, Multrevich, in Boyle Heights, who thinks he rented a room to Lula two days ago. As Scully handcuffs Lula, "Willis" makes Scully cuff *herself*. At Lula's home afterward, "Willis" convinces Lula he's Dupre.

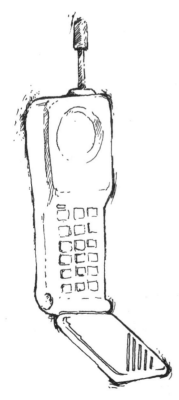

Mulder's apartment: Mulder and Bruskin haven't heard from Scully for 12 hours. "Willis" calls Mulder's cell phone and says Scully is with him. Scully tries to convince "Willis" – and herself – that he really *is* a traumatized Willis. And she wonders aloud about the soda he's been drinking – because Willis is diabetic.

FBI headquarters: Mulder listens to Willis' notes on Dupre and Lula. He tells the agents searching for Scully that the Catonsville, MD police have reported a drugstore broken into for syringes and insulin. Scully wants to administer "Willis'" insulin – but Lula won't let her. She sneers it was *she* who set up Dupre. She phones the FBI's tactical room, demanding $1 million ransom for Scully, by tomorrow. The FBI trace the call, but find it is Scully's own cell-phone number. A tape of the call reveals the sound of a small plane taking off. That lead convinces police

X-otica

Co-writer Howard Gordon has said the original story conception involved Dupre inhabiting Mulder. Fox "balked at the idea of Mulder experiencing directly, first-hand, a supernatural event like that. And I think that was a wise decision, although at the time we were angry and up in arms."

In this episode, Scully mentions *America's Most Wanted* – a fellow Fox show.

Mulder for the first time calls Scully by the truncated familiarity, "Scull."

to canvass the three square miles around Washington County Regional Airport.

At the Dupre house, a canvassing cop, posing as a door-to-door Bible salesperson, identifies the diabetically weakening "Willis." Lula, thinking Willis/Dupre's dead, contemptuously drops her wedding ring on him. But he's playing possum, and snags her gun. In a line of sight encompassing both Lulu and a handcuffed Scully, Willis/Dupre pleads he loves her. Agent Westin, outside, reports no clear sniper shot on Lula. And inside, Willis/Dupre sees a deathly light, and, insisting, there's nothing to be afraid of, shoots Lula. As the feds burst in, Willis/Dupre dies of diabetes complications.

Sometime later, Mulder retrieves Willis' personal effects from the morgue, and gives Scully a watch inscribed "HAPPY 35th Love D" – a gift Scully had given him three years ago. Since Jack was an only child and his parents died while he was in college, she will give his effects to a boy in Parklawn to whom Jack was a Big Brother. The watch stopped at 6:47 – the moment Jack went into cardiac arrest.

CAST

Christopher Allport	Agent Jack Willis
Cec Verrell	Lula Phillips
Jackson Davies	Agent Bruskin
Jason Schombing	Warren James Dupre

Callum Keith Rennie	Tommy [Phillips]
Jay Brazeau	Professor Varnes
Lisa Bunting	1st Doctor
Peter Kelamis	O'Dell [unidentified in episode; possibly either the snide tactical-room agent or the FBI audio technician]
Brenda Crichlow	[TV] Reporter
Mark Saunders	2nd Doctor
Alexander Boynton	Clean Cut Man
Russell Hamilton	Officer Daniels

extra

X-actitude

Willis' and Scully's joint birthday: Feb. 23; Willis born 1957

Willis' address: 51 Stanhope St.

Scully's cell-phone number area code: (202)

Dupre's birthplace: Klamath Falls, OR

Patient whose clothes are stolen: Mr. Goldbaum, room 28

Filter the audio technician uses: "an

• The official Fox *X-Files* website erroneously lists the character Lula Phillips as Lula Velasquez – possibly the name in an early script draft.

Continuity error: Since the *X-Files* fictional continuity roughly follows real-life time, and since episode 1.18 "Miracle Man," takes place March 7-8, it can't be two months before Scully's Feb. 23 birthday. Unless, of course, this whole episode is a flashback.

The Cast: Christopher Allport's films include *To Live and Die in L.A.* (1985), *Invaders from Mars* (1986), and *Savage Weekend* (1976 or 1980; a.k.a. *The Killer Behind the Mask*, *The Uptown Murders*) with future *X*-guest William Sanderson. Allport co-starred in two unsold pilots: the WWI sitcom *Heck's Angels* (CBS 1976), with William Windom, and the husband-and-wife sitcom *Love, Natalie* (NBC 1980).

Cec Verrell co-starred as fighter pilot

extra Z14," to isolate
sounds above a half-
decibel

Tommy Phillips'
landlord/building
manager: Cosmo

Multrevich apartment:
#202; Lula's: #207

Catonsville drugstore
location: Old Stone Road
at Madison

First three agents to
whom Bruskin gives
canvass-grid
assignments: Steinberg,
Calder, Westin

Lieutenant Commander Ruth "Beebee" Rutkowski in the *Top Gun*-inspired *Supercarrier* (ABC 1988), and had a recurring role as Iris Smith in some 1989 episodes of *Hunter*. She got her start playing a hooker in *Runaway* (1984), but soon had the title role as a hard-edged narcotics detective in *Silk* (1986). Other appearances include the TV-movie *Super Force* (1990), the films *Hell Comes to Frogtown* (1988) and *Three of Hearts* (1993), and episodes of *Cheers*, *L.A. Law* and *M.A.N.T.I.S.* (as Dr. Marisa Savoy in two 1995 episodes).

The Repertory: Jay Brazeau went on to play the unforthcoming ER physician Dr. Daly in episode 2.08, "One Breath." Mark Saunders would play the helpful Agent Busch in 2.13, "Irresistible." Callum Keith Rennie dug his work – as a cemetery groundskeeper – in 2.15, "Fresh Bones"; that same episode, Peter Kelamis played a hapless Marine pathologist.

X-File case: Classified

1.16 "YOUNG AT HEART"

Feb. 11, 1994
Writers: Scott Kaufer and Chris Carter
Director: Michael Lange

Tashloo Federal Correctional Facility, Pennsylvania, 1989: Wheelchair-bound prisoner Joe Crandall hears screaming from the infirmary. When he asks Dr. Joe Ridley what he's doing to Johnny Barnett on the operating table, Ridley insists Barnett is dead.

Washington, D.C., present day. Mulder's old agent-friend, Reggie Purdue shows him a note reading: "Fox can't guard chicken coop," the M.O. of John Barnett, whom Mulder recalls from his first FBI case. Barnett was involved in multiple bank robberies and seven murders. During Barnett's capture, an agent died, Mulder says remorsefully, "because I screwed up." While Barnett supposedly died in prison four years earlier, evidence shows that the note was written by Barnett.

A videotape of Barnett's capture shows that Mulder hesitated in firing upon the armed Barnett, allowing Barnett to kill both his hostages before Mulder shot Barnett. Later, Mulder finds a note on his car ("A hunted Fox eventually dies.")

FBI headquarters: Purdue tries convincing Mulder the note is not from Barnett. When Purdue reminisces how the FBI had once had big plans for Mulder, Mulder wonders aloud whether the Bureau is playing a mind-game. With a female computer technician helping him assess what Barnett might look like today, Mulder

flashes back to Barnett's trial. Scully arrives, saying that though
Barnett's listed cause of death was heart attack, he'd gone to the
infirmary with a hand ailment and no mention of coronary problems.

At Tashloo, Crandall tells Mulder and Scully about the night he
confronted Ridley. At FBI headquarters, Mulder gets a taunting call
from someone claiming to be Barnett. At 10:45 p.m., Mulder calls
Purdue – who has been strangled to death by someone leaving a note
on the body.

Scully discovers that Ridley's medical licence was revoked in 1979
for research malpractice and misuse of a government grant. A
scientist at the National Institutes of Health in Bethesda, MD recalls
that Ridley did secret, unauthorized human experimentation. Mulder
suspects Ridley managed to reverse Barnett's aging process. Ridley,
later, shows up at Scully's home.

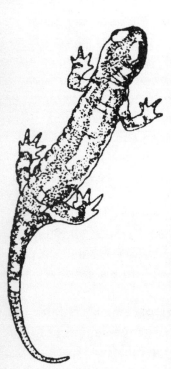

After Mulder arrives, Ridley – who says
he's dying – tells them that of his research,
Barnett is the sole survivor. He'd altered
Barnett's treatment to grow him a new
hand – albeit a humanoid salamander hand,
since Ridley was using reptile regenerative-
cell morphegins. Then "certain sponsors"
appeared – including the U.S. government.

Later, Deep Throat admits to Mulder the
government knew Barnett was alive.
Indeed, they're now negotiating to buy the
research Barnett stole from Ridley. At 7:20
a.m., Scully hears an intruder retrieving
her phone messages; the FBI discovers a
Barnett fingerprint. Barnett phones Mulder
at his office to taunt him about killing his
friends; Mulder deduces Barnett will stalk
Scully at her friend's cello recital tonight,
which he would have learned of through
the phone messages.

Janie Taylor Memorial Recital Hall,
Washington D.C.: FBI agents convene
before the show. Barnett is already there,
incognito as a piano tuner. He shoots Scully

X-otica

When Scully writes her report at home, she does so by gauzy lamp and candlelight – evidence of a secret romantic?

Inspiration Alert:

The notion of using reptilian cells to re-grow missing limbs was used in the comic *The Amazing Spider-Man* #6, (1963), as the origin of an amputee scientist who became the two-armed beast, The Lizard.

in the lobby, then takes Scully's friend hostage – grandiosely announcing the government needs him alive, so he could just shoot the woman if he wanted to. But Mulder kills Barnett with a single, well-placed shot. Luckily Scully wore a bulletproof vest. At an operating room, three specialists try to save Barnett; the Cigarette-Smoking Man from the first episode, whom Mulder says is "probably CIA," unsuccessfully tries to get Barnett to talk before he dies.

CAST

Jerry Hardin	Deep Throat
Dick Anthony Williams	Agent Reggie Purdue
Alan Boyce	Young John Irvin Barnett
Christine Estabrook	Agent Henderson
Graham Jarvis	NIH Doctor
Robin Mossley	Dr. Joe Ridley
Merrilyn Gann	Prosecuting Attorney
Gordon Tipple	Joe Crandall

William B. Davis   CIA Agent

Courtney Arciaga   Young Child [with progeria]

David Petersen   Older [John Irvin] Barnett

Robin Douglas   Computer Tekkie

extra

X-actitude

Barnett death-certificate data: John Irvin Barnett, cardiac arrest, died Sept. 16, 1989

Barnett's will: executed six months after his death; left his possessions to Crandall; specified cremation

Barnett's accent: New Hampshire

Henderson note analysis: fresh ink, indicating written within last 48 hours; ballpoint; right-handed writer sitting down

Location where Barnett hid Ridley's aging-reversal research: Locker 935 of some nondescript bus or railroad station, or airport.

• The official Fox *X-Files* website neglects to list front-credit guest-actors Dick Anthony Williams and Christine Estabrook.

Note: The character played by William B. Davis has not been specifically linked with the CIA; this is Mulder's supposition, despite the end-credit listing for "CIA Agent." In subsequent end-credits, the character is identified as "Smoking Man," and is referred to in print and elsewhere as both that and "Cigarette-Smoking Man." In episode 2.08, "One Breath," Mulder (with Skinner repeating it) offhandedly refers to him as "Cancer Man." Incidentally, since he's inaudible from the other side of a plate-glass window here, he doesn't yet have his first line of dialog in the series; that comes in episode 1.21, "Tooms."

The Cast: Dick Anthony Williams (b. Aug. 9, 1938, Chicago) appeared in *Our Family Honor* (ABC 1985-86), *Heart of the City* (ABC 1986-87), and *Homefront* (ABC 1991-93). He originated the role of Malcolm X in the acclaimed off-Broadway production of *The Meeting* (1987), reprising it opposite Jason Bernard as Dr. Martin Luther King in the PBS *American Playhouse* adaptation. A founder of New York City's New Federal

In screenwriting credits, an ampersand between co-writers' names indicates a writing team; conversely, an "and" means one writer rewrote the other. "Young at Heart" began as a freelance script by Scott Kaufer, the former editor of *California* magazine and former head of Warner Bros. comedy development. Carter's rewrite added, among other things, Barnett's regenerative salamander hand.

Theatre and Concept One Theatre, and executive producer and workshop director of Los Angeles' American Theatre of Being, Williams received Tony Award nominations for Broadway's *The Black Picture Show* and *What the Wine Sellers Buy*. As a playwright, his works include *A Bit O' Black* and *Black is Beautiful*. He appeared as Henry in the David Duchovny movie *The Rapture* (1991).

Christine Estabrook co-starred in the ensemble series *Hometown* (CBS 1985). The Robin Douglas in this episode is not the actress Robyn Douglass of the series *Houston Knights* and *Galactica 1980*, but a Vancouver actress whose credits include an episode each of *The Commish* and *M.A.N.T.I.S.*, and the 1994 TV-movie *The Disappearance of Vonnie*.

The Repertory: Robin Mossley would play an equally sinister-yet-unassuming doctor in episode 2.24, "Our Town."

X-File case: Classified

1.17 "E.B.E."

Feb. 18, 1994
Writers: Glen Morgan & James Wong
Director: William Graham

The skies of Iraq, 37th parallel, present day: An Iraqi fighter pilot, fearing he's under attack, shoots down a UFO. At a NATO Surveillance Station in Hakkari, Turkey, near the border, two NATO soldiers are jolted by the nearby crash and arrange for retrieval.

Route 100, Reagan, TN, 12:20 a.m. Central Time: Tractor-trailer driver Ranheim hears three CBers bewilderingly reporting UFOs. Suddenly, the electricity goes out; Ranheim, investigating, sees his cargo doors slam open, seemingly by themselves. He fires his gun at something in the bushes – and witnesses an apparent spacecraft overhead.

Next day: Scully attributes the sightings to explanations such as lightning and swamp gas – which doesn't account, Mulder notes, for a radiation level five-times-normal. Ranheim, being held at the Lexington, TN police station on a weapons-firing charge, keeps changing his story about what he saw. Then the police let Ranheim go, and won't let the agents examine the truck. At a car-rental agency, where a woman borrows Scully's pen, Mulder says he suspects it wasn't an alien vessel but a secret military aircraft.

Back in D.C., Mulder takes Scully to the cluttered office of a government watchdog group. These three conspiracy theorists – Byers, Langly, and Frohike – publish a magazine, *The Lone Gunman* [and, per episode 2.08, "One Breath," refer to themselves as "The Lone Gunmen"] Byers tears a magnetic strip out from inside a $20 bill of Scully's, saying this is how the covert government-within-the-government tracks money carried through airport metal detectors. Scully responds it's an anti-counterfeiting measure. They haven't, however, heard of recent Persian Gulf UFO sightings. Scully later tells Mulder the three are paranoid – but then finds surveillance electronics inside her pen.

At the Jefferson Memorial, Deep Throat hands Mulder a folder marked "Top Secret," containing an intercepted Iraqi transmission, addressed to the C.O. of something called the Majestic Project. Scully reports the truck and driver both were bogus: The manifest gave 108 auto-parts cartons totaling 3,100 pounds – but three weigh stations each gave the cargo's weight as 5,100 pounds. And Ranheim – real name Frank Druce – had been in the Persian Gulf War as a Special Operations Black Beret; he was in Mosul, northern Iraq, four days before when the Iraqis shot down a UFO. The U.S. Army recovered

wreckage and possibly bodies – now being transported via Druce's unmarked truck, currently headed west toward Colorado.

When Mulder returns home he meets Deep Throat who hands Mulder a photo he says was taken by an officer at Fort Benning, GA, where 17 UFOs were spotted in one hour. At Scully's, Mulder theorizes the truck was a decoy – but Scully says the photo is fake, convincing Mulder to have it analyzed. The truth is out there, she says, but so are lies.

FBI headquarters, by 8:30 a.m. the next day: Mulder has confirmed the photo's a fake. At an aquarium, he confronts Deep Throat – who asserts his life is in danger whenever he and Mulder speak. He contends he's participated in, "insidious lies" and witnessed deeds that "no crazed man would imagine". He's sized up Mulder for years, finally determining him as trustworthy. But, he also contends, some secrets should stay hidden, since the public can't handle the truth.

X-otica

On visual inspection, the uncredited actor playing the NATO soldier may be Angelo Vacco, an *X-Files* production assistant who acted in episode 2.22, "F. Emasculata."

Lexington, TN is a real place through which the north-south Route 22 does pass; there's no Reagan, TN, though. Interstate 90 does run east–west through Washington State, but the only other one it intersects outside Seattle is I-82, about 80 miles away.

Inspiration Alert:

Mulder's desperate search through his apartment for an electronic bug recalls a similar scene climaxing Francis Ford Coppola's *The Conversation* (1974) starring Gene Hackman as an equally manipulated surveillance expert.

But Mulder is unswayed. Later, Scully and Mulder are both followed to the airport. They lose their pursuers, and by 9:18 a.m., Scully arrives at Dulles Airport and buys round-trip tickets to Chicago. She uses untraceable cash to buy a ticket to Los Angeles with a stop in Las Vegas. Mulder drives to the Baltimore Airport.

Las Vegas, McCarran Airport, 11:30 a.m. Pacific Time: Scully and Mulder compare notes of weigh-station calls they made on untraceable airplane phones. The truck is headed northwest on I-90, toward Seattle. By 6:30 p.m., the agents are at the junction of I-90 and I-283 in Washington State; the truck passes their stakeout position. Hours later, they encounter a freak storm, and find the truck stalled and the driver gone. Inside, they find a hidden room, suggesting that an E.B.E. (Extraterrestrial Biological Entity) was there. Mulder phones the Center for UFO Studies in Chicago, and the UFO groups MUFON and NICAP, who report UFO activity along what Mulder knows to be the truck's route. And last night, there were seven reported sightings in Mattawa, WA, 100 miles away.

In Mattawa, the agents find UFO buffs saying spacecraft have been hovering near a power plant – from which Mulder and Scully see Druce exiting. Mulder phones the Lone Gunmen, offering Langly an E.B.E. photo in exchange for computer-hacked IDs. A printer soon chugs out false-name "Level 5" security passes for the "Northwest Facility, Mattawa, WA."

Although Langly couldn't get them Level 6 access, the agents head there – but a

X-actitude

Scully's coffee: Non-dairy creamer, no sugar

Title (partially obscured) of the Top Secret folder Deep Throat hands Mulder: "Response to Request for Information on Contact and Other Related". . . .

Mulder's method of contacting Deep Throat: Shining a blue light out his apartment window, then waiting for his phone to ring and clicks to be heard on the receiver.

Some sites where Mulder has investigated multiple-witness UFO sightings: Chesapeake Bay, Lake Okobogee, Nevada's Area 51

Iraqi pilot designation/position: Patrol #6, on bearing 340

NATO surveillance-station designation: Southern Crescent

military guard stops them. Mulder bolts down some stairs, chased by rifle-toting soldiers. He finds a lab with an odd, empty chamber – and Deep Throat, who waves away the soldiers and tells Mulder the E.B.E. is dead. He explains that in an "ultrasecret conference" after Roswell, the US, the USSR, the People's Republic of China, the UK, France and both East and West Germany agreed to exterminate any E.B.E.s. Deep Throat confesses he is one of three men to have done so: When he was with the CIA in Vietnam, the Marines shot down a UFO over Hanoi. Deep Throat personally shot the creature – and the memory has haunted him since. Deep Throat sets the agents free, asserting that through them, the truth will be known.

CAST

Jerry Hardin	Deep Throat
Allan Lysell	Chief Rivers
Peter LaCroix	Ranheim [a.k.a. Frank Druce; last-name spelling per closed captioning]
Bruce Harwood	Byers
Dean Haglund	Langly
Tom Braidwood	Frohike

extra   • The fighter pilot, the base radar operator, and the NATO soldier, who all have lines, are uncredited.

NATO base designation: Red Crescent

Trucker's radio station: WSM 650, broadcasting music from the Grand Ole Opry; program sponsored by Goody's Headache Powder

CBers UFO sightings: male saw something cigar-shaped with red and green lights; female saw three in Chester County; second male saw six State Trooper vehicles chasing strange lights down Route 22.

In-joke: The agents' false IDs: Mulder is Tom Braidwood (P.I.N. 7593) and Scully is Val Stefoff (P.I.N. 5311). Tom Braidwood is the series' first assistant director and an occasional Lone Gunman; Vladimir Steffof is a frequent second assistant director on the show.

X-act Location: Subbing for the secret UFO facility was Powertech Labs, Inc., a B.C. Hydro subsidiary, in Surrey, B.C., about 17 miles south of downtown Vancouver.

The Cast: For more on the Lone Gunmen actors, see their joint biography.

The Repertory: Peter LaCroix, here playing a shadow-government conspirator trucking the apparent E.B.E., played the tram operator who had the misfortune of getting in Krycek's way in episode 2.06, "Ascension." Allan Lysell had a small role in 2.17, "End Game."

X-File case: Classified

1.18 "MIRACLE MAN"

March 18, 1994
Writers: Howard Gordon & Chris Carter
Director: Michael Lange

At a fire, the Rev. Calvin Hartley leads his young adopted son, Samuel, to a body-bag, where faith-healing Samuel evidently brings the man inside to life.

Years later, Mulder's office: Tennessee FBI have sent a videotape of the Hartleys at a Kenwood, TN revival meeting; Samuel attempts to heal a woman with a malignant spine tumor, but she dies 20 minutes later, not from cancer. Kenwood County Sheriff Maurice Daniels considers the Hartleys' "Miracle Ministry" a hoax, and is enraged over the woman's death.

Mulder and Scully attend a Ministry meeting in Kenwood along with Daniels, whose wife is unwell. Samuel isn't there; Hartley tells the agents he doesn't know where Samuel is, as ominous aide Leonard Vance whisks Hartley off. Daniels, who notes Samuel has been missing since Tuesday, says the coroner is a Ministry member, so autopsies were not done on anyone who died after Samuel's "healing." Later that night, as the agents and police try to exhume a Carol Wallace, Vance and othes stage a threatening vigil.

Daniels finds Samuel at a downtown pool hall and arrests him on suspicion of murder. The teenager says God has taken away his powers as penance for his pride. He then stuns Mulder by saying the agent's in pain from a sister who went away when quite young, with strangers and a bright light involved. Kenwood

County Courthouse, next day: At a bail hearing, Samuel wishes to remain jailed. The judge sets $100,000 bail, whereupon the courtroom fills with locusts; Scully dismisses it as typical farmland infestation.

Mulder shows Scully reports from the county hospital indicating spontaneous remission from cancer, regenerated nerve growth, etc., and theorizes that if a body is an electromagnetic system, Samuel may be able to manipulate its energy. Vance invites the agents to see Hartley at home, where Hartley says Daniels' bitterness toward him is so intense, that despite Samuel's efficacy, he won't even bring in his severely arthritic wife. Mulder sees a little girl outside the window, reminding him of his abducted sister, Samantha. When he looks for her, she's gone; a guy polishing a car says he saw no one. At the revival meeting, Vance gives a soft drink in a cup to

wheelchair-bound multiple sclerotic Margaret Hohman, and places her in the front row. We learn the disfigured Vance is the fire victim Samuel had allegedly raised from the dead. Mulder thinks he sees the girl again, but loses her in the crowd. When Samuel lays hands on Margaret, she gasps and dies despite the quick-acting Scully's efforts. Scully later tells Margaret's father this is the third such suspicious death, and despite his trepidation, convinces him to allow an autopsy.

March 7, 11:21 p.m. to March 8, 12:29 a.m.: Margaret's autopsy shows lesions on the lungs and throughout the cardiovascular and pulmonary systems. Scully theorizes cellular hypoxia caused by arsenic or by sodium or potassium cyanide. Mulder, having seen no opportunity for Samuel to have poisoned Margaret, rushes to the jail – ostensibly to reassure Samuel, but also to see what Samuel can tell him about Samantha. Samuel can't or won't say anything – and after Mulder leaves, a deputy brings in two thugs who beat Samuel to death.

The next morning, Deputy Dennis Tyson gives Daniels the awful news. At the jail, Daniels tells an infuriated Mulder that Samuel had picked a fight with two rowdies booked on DUI. Hartley arrives accusing Daniels of a fatal vendetta; Mulder and Scully check the courthouse for clues. They find locusts, and a trail of food from the roof into the ventilation system. Since biological supply houses sell locusts to farm and universities, the agents believe the "plague" was deliberate.

Night: A ghostly Samuel asks why Vance betrayed him after he'd saved his life. The anguished, disfigured Vance declares he hates Samuel for this mockery of living. Downstairs, Daniels and the agents arrive to arrest Vance, having linked him to a Knoxville, TN pesticide-company order for cyanogen bromide, a cyanide derivative; he'd evidently poisoned some of the soft drinks at the meetings. They find Vance dying of cyanide poisoning, deliriously saying Samuel was here and had forgiven him.

In the light of day, Scully's report says Vance tried to destroy faith in the Ministry, and his conscience led to his suicide. But Samuel's body turns up missing; no-nonsense nurse Beatrice Salinger says she and others saw Samuel walk out by himself. As the agents leave town, Scully hopes Hartley didn't arrange a body-snatching – while Deputy Tyson brings Daniels in for questioning about Samuel's death.

CAST

R.D. Call	Sheriff Maurice Daniels
Scott Bairstow	Samuel Hartley
George Gerdes	Reverend Calvin Hartley
Dennis Lipscomb	Leonard Vance
Walter Marsh	Judge
Campbell Lane	Hohman's Father
Chilton Crane	Margaret Hohman
Howard Storey	Fire Chief

Iris Quinn Bernard	Lillian Daniels [first name not given in episode]
Lisa Ann Beley	Beatrice Salinger
Alex Doduk	Young Samuel
Roger Haskett	Deputy Tyson

extra

X-actitude

Scully's faith: Catholic

Woman victim on Tennessee FBI videotape: Lucy Jelly

Miracle Minstry marquee slogan: "Come as you are . . . Leave as you always wanted to be."

Rev. Hartley's license plate: B HEALD

Margaret Hohman: Female Caucasian, 107 pounds

Cellular hypoxia: a lack of oxygen to the cells

● Samuel's female defense attorney, the prosecuting attorney, the man polishing the car and the little girl are all uncredited.

The official Fox *X-Files* website neglects to list front-credit actor R.D. Call.

X-act Location: Steveston Village, in Richmond, Vancouver, which had played Steveston, MA (in 1.14, "Genderbender"), here did double duty as Kenwood, TN.

The Cast: R.D. Call played the cold-blooded CIA killer Jude Andrews in the TV series *Stephen King's Golden Years* (CBS 1991), which co-starred future X- guests Felicity Huffman and Ed Lauter. His films include *48 Hrs.* (1982); *Colors* (1988), *Born on the Fourth of July* (1989) and *Waterworld* (1995). Dennis Lipscomb played mob accountant Sid Royce in the classic Ray Sharkey arc of *Wiseguy* (CBS 1987-90), and had a recurring role as eccentric film star Harland Keyvo in *The Famous Teddy Z* (CBS 1989-90), among countless other roles. Miracle man Scott Bairstow starred as Newt Call in *Lonesome Dove: The Series* (syndicated 1994-95). His other known credits to date are *White Fang 2: Myth of the White Wolf* (1994), the TV-movie *There Was a Little Boy* (1993), and the unsold ABC pilot *Country Estates*, written by future X-writers Howard Gordon and Alex Gansa. George Gerdes has played supporting roles on *The Equalizer*, *Seinfeld*, *NYPD Blue* and other shows, and in films including *Single White Female* (1992) and *Iron Will* (1994).

The Repertory: Lisa Ann Beley turned up as an FBI cadet in Scully's autopsy class in episode 2.01, "Little Green Men." Campbell Lane played an old-world Romanian elder in 2.21, "The Calusari"; Chilton Crane, who played his tragic daughter here, became a young teenager's mom in 2.22, "F. Emasculata."

X-File case: Classified

1.19 "SHAPES"

April 1, 1994
Writer: Marilyn Osborn
Director: David Nutter

Two Medicine Ranch, Browning, Montana: Jim Parker and his grown son Lyle find a slaughtered steer in their corral, the fourth this month. Lyle is suddenly savaged by some creature – yet after Jim shoots the beast dead, all they find is a young Native American, Joe Goodensnake, of the Trego tribe. Parker had sued the tribe over grazing rights and a border dispute. The next day, Scully and Mulder meet with the free-on-bail Parker and his attorney. Outside, Mulder finds what looks like a just-shed snakeskin – in the shape of a human wrist and hand.

While looking for Sheriff Charlie Tskany at the reservation the agents find Goodensnake's sister, Gwen, who accuses her tribesmen of being scared of a stupid Indian legend. The bitter Tskany arrives to escort the agents to his office, where Joe's body is laid. Mulder notices Joe has fangs not seen on his dental records; Scully attributes them to calcium phosphate salts that can gather with age. But Mulder also notes Lyle's chest had animal scars similar to those on Joe. He wants an autopsy, but Tskany says desecration of the body angers The Spirit, and the body will be cremated tonight on a pyre. Scully says Tskany can't destroy evidence, but the Sheriff has to live and work here, and won't buck his neighbors' beliefs.

Later, watching as the pyre is prepared, Mulder tells Scully about the first X-file, which involved similar lycanthropic deaths near here. Scully retorts that in the rare insanity called lyncanthropy, a person merely *believes* he or she can turn into a wolf. As the fire lights, Scully offers Gwen her condolences. Lyle also comes to pay his respects, but Gwen demands he leave. Shortly afterward, at the ranch, Jim is slashed to death by some lupine yet humanoid creature.

The next morning, Scully suggests it might be retaliation; Tskany's already put out an APB out on the missing Gwen. Lyle also can't be found. The agents find a tuft of fur near another piece of shed skin, as well as a caged cougar – and Lyle, naked and unconscious. Scully takes him to the Crowe Medical Clinic, where Lyle says he'd gotten drunk on bourbon and passed out. Scully tells him his father's dead, and confesses she had lost her father recently, too.

Tskany takes Mulder to the home of old man Ish, who recounts the 1946 deaths. The Tregoes, he says, realized a man named Richard

Watkins had been attacked by what the Algonquian Indians called the Manitou, an evil spirit that can turn men into beasts. When Ish was 16, returning from fishing in the Cut Bank Creek, he walked by Watkins' house and saw the man turn beast-like. Watkins was killed soon afterward, but the curse passed through bloodlines to his son and, eventually, to Joe Goodensnake. If that's the case, Gwen might also bear the curse and she happens to be just outside, trying to steal Ish's AMC pickup. When Tskany arrests her, the terrified woman says she'd gone to the Parker ranch – and saw "it" kill Jim Parker.

Mulder calls the clinic, but a Dr. Josephs there has already released Lyle to Scully's care. The doctor volunteers that Lyle's blood showed traces of Jim's blood type – which could only have gotten there through ingestion. As evening falls, Scully drives Lyle back to the ranch. There the power is off, and a woozy Lyle excuses himself for the bathroom.

Seven miles away, Tskany and Mulder race with police lights flashing, unable to reach Scully by cel phone because of the mountains. Scully, fearing Lyle is growing sicker, starts picking the bathroom lock seemingly oblivious to all the growling inside. A furry arm smashes through. Mulder arrives to find claw marks across a wall, and fires one shot at an indistinct growling creature and another that shatters a stuffed bear's head. Scully is upstairs and okay. Venturing with flashlights through the dark, they're attacked by a growling something; before Mulder can fire, Tskany blasts it with a pump-action shotgun. It's Lyle, dead. Scully believes it was the mountain lion that had attacked her – but Tskany points out it's still in its cage. The next day, as they leave Ish predicts he'll see Mulder again, in about eight years.

CAST

Ty Miller	Lyle Parker
Michael Horse	Sheriff Tskany
Donnelly Rhodes	Jim Parker
Jimmy Herman	Ish
Renae Morriseau	Gwen Goodensnake
Dwight McFee	David Gates [lawyer]
Paul McLean	Dr. Josephs

X-actitude

Native Americans guarding Joe's body at Tskany's office: Bill and Tom

The file on the first X-File: Personally

The Cast: Michael Horse played Deputy Tommy "The Hawk" Hill on *Twin* Peaks. Horse had made his inauspicious screen debut as Tonto in the 1981 Western *The Legend of the Lone Ranger*, and spent much of the 1980s playing characters with names like Indian Joe and Bobby Leaping Mouse. He has had better luck since *Twin Peaks*, playing one of Eliot Ness' incorruptible 1930s Chicago cops, George Steelman, in

initiated by J. Edgar Hoover, 1946. There had been murders in and around the northwest – seven of them here in Browning – in which victims were shredded and eaten. Police that year cornered and shot an animal in a cabin in Glacier National Park – but the "animal" proved to be a man named Richard Watkins. Coincidentally, perhaps, the murders stopped, and Hoover locked away the files for this inexplicable case. However, they were updated when similar murders occurred in 1954, '59, '64, '78 and now.

The Untouchables (syndicated 1993-94) and appearing in high-profile projects like Passenger 57 (1992) and the TV-movie Lakota Woman: Siege at Wounded Knee (1994); he's also active in voiceovers, in animated series including Gargoyles, Wild West C.O.W Boys of Moo Mesa, and Happily Ever After: Fairy Tales For Every Child.

Ty Miller played the Pony Express rider known as The Kid in The Young Riders (ABC 1989-92); he had earlier been in the cast of Hotel (ABC 1983-88), playing Eric Lloyd in its final season. Miller's films include the direct-to-video sci-fi adventures Trancers 4: Jack of Swords and Trancers 5: Sudden Deth (both 1994), directed by X-Files director-producer David Nutter.

Winnipeg-born Donnelly Rhodes got his screen start in 1973 as Philip Chancellor on the soap opera The Young and the Restless, went on to Soap (ABC 1977-81), Report to Murphy (CBS 1982) and Double Trouble (NBC 1984-85). He starred for several years on the Canadian hit Danger Bay (CBC/The Disney Channel), and co-starred in the drama series The Heights (Fox 1992)

The Repertory: Renae Morriseau switched tribes to play a Washington Navajo official in episode 2.25, "Anasazi"; Paul McLean also appeared in that episode, as an FBI agent. Dwight McFee, making the first of several X-Files appearances, had a small part as a Blue Beret Commander in 2.01, "Little Green Men," and a prominent role as a jailed businessperson in 2.13, "Irresistible."

X-File case: Classified

1.20 "DARKNESS FALLS"

April 15, 1994
Writer: Chris Carter
Director: Joe Napolitano

Olympic National Forest, northwest Washington State. A group of terrified loggers, led by one Bob Perkins, are being killed, one after another, by something mysterious. One logger, Dyer, says they should split up and run; Perkins ultimately goes along. Nightfall: After Dyer breaks his ankle, Perkins carries him – until a swarm of green iridescent "fireflies" engulfs them.

FBI headquarters: Mulder shows Scully a slide of the 30 missing loggers, and says radical eco-activists Doug Spinney and Steven Teague were in the area a week before. Two Federal Forest Service officials investigated, but never returned; in 1934, a Works Project Administration (WPA) crew in the same area also vanished. At Olympic, Mulder and Scully meet up with Forest Service ranger Larry Moore, and Schiff-Immergut Lumber security chief Steve Humphreys. During the four-hour drive to the logging camp, their truck gets two flat tires from eco-saboteur spikes in the road; with 1½ hours to go before sunset, they start hiking.

The cabin has been abruptly abandoned, with the radio destroyed and vehicles sabotaged; they are stranded and incommunicado. Exploring, they find an odd-looking cocoon – and inside, a mummified-looking man. Humphreys, working to fix a small power generator, surprises eco-saboteur Spinney inside the cabin. Spinney warns they all have to leave before darkness falls – and tells of a swarm that devoured his colleague, Teague. He also tells the agents the loggers were illegally cutting marked, protected, old-growth trees; Humphreys denies knowledge of this, and accuses Spinney of manufacturing both the cocoon and that swarm story.

The next morning, they examine a fallen marked tree at least 500-600 years old, with a highly unusual growth-ring. Moore analyzes a core sample containing microscopic parasites which shouldn't be there – this is dead wood, and the sample came from too deep for wood borers. Moore suggests they're wood mites; Spinney suggests they were dormant for hundreds of years and woke up hungry. Humphreys, meantime, has hiked to the truck to radio for help, but found the radio dead; that night, while trying to get it running, he's attacked and killed by the swarm, coming through the air vents.

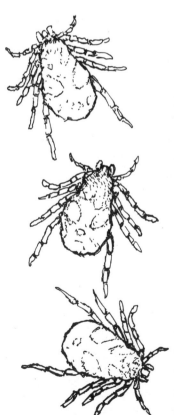

At the cabin, Spinney deduces the light keeps the swarm away. Mulder theorizes that the old tree's odd rings resulted from a season of unusual natural activity, like volcanic eruption; he notes Mount St. Helens released radiation that produced amoeba mutations at nearby Spirit Lake. Scully retorts that unlike insects, amoeba are single-celled and easily mutated. Mulder then suggests the swarm may come from "extinct" larvae: Maybe millions-of-years-old insect eggs were deposited by volcano into the ground, and came up through the roots to lie dormant.

Next morning: Mulder finds Spinney preparing to leave – with precious gasoline and a battery. Spinney says he was going to hike to his colleagues and their jeep, two valleys over, then come rescue them tomorrow. Mulder lets him go [N], and then, having partly fixed the cabin's radio, sends one-way distress calls. Moore can't believe Mulder let Spinney go, since now there's not enough gas to run both the radio *and* the light-giving generator; Mulder contends it was their only chance. Even Scully loses her temper at his not consulting them; now, with no way to hike through the woods before dark, she's convinced they'll die once the generator runs out. That night, with only one light bulb working, the agents and Moore stay awake. Some of the iridescent insects seep in under the walls and cover the three, but the light keeps them from swarming. The generator sputters and runs out of gas, just as the sun rises. Now, desperate, they take a tire from one of the sabotaged trucks with the idea of at least replacing one of the two flat tires on the Forest Service truck. But then Spinney, keeping his word, arrives in a covered Jeep; his friends hadn't make it, he says. Taking the agents and Moore down the mountain, in sudden, stormy darkness, Spinney's jeep ironically gets a spike-punctured tire itself. And Spinney, caught outside in the glare of the headlight, is engulfed and killed by the swarm [N] – which then enters the Jeep through the air vents.

Daylight: A helicopter and three white vans arrive; men in protective gear find a cocoon-filled Jeep. The agents and Moore are rushed to the High Containment Facility in Winthrop, WA, where scientists find large concentrations of luciferine, an enzyme found in fireflies and other bioluminescent insects. One scientist, wearing an anticontamination clean suit, tells Mulder the government will use pesticides and controlling burning to end the swarm – which, he assures the skeptical Mulder, will keep it from migrating.

CAST

Jason Beghe	Larry Moore
Tom O'Rourke	Steve Humphreys
Titus Welliver	Doug Spinney
Ken Tremblett	Dyer
Barry Greene	[Bob] Perkins
David Hay	Clean Suited Man

X-actitude	X-act Location: The old-growth forest is in reality West Vancouver's Lighthouse Park. There is no Winthrop, WA.
The eco-radicals' nickname for Federal Forest Service officers: Freddies.	The Cast: Jason Beghe, David Duchovny's childhood friend, made his screen debut as

"Cupcake" in *Compromising Positions* (1985); he later played in the raunchy HBO sitcom *1st & Ten* (co-starring O.J. Simpson). He played the state trooper who gets locked in a trunk by *Thelma & Louise* (1991), currently appears on *Picket Fences* (CBS, 1992–   ) and as Jeffrey Lindley, in *Melrose Place* (Fox 1992–present).

Tom O'Rourke was in the cast of the movie-spinoff sitcom *Working Girl* (NBC 1990), as the business exec charmed by a fledgling Sandra Bullock. He's guested on nearly two dozen shows, from *Simon & Simon* to *Melrose Place*, and appeared in the theatrical feature *Patty Hearst* (1988). Titus Welliver had three screen appearances in 1990: an episode of *Matlock*, the movie *Navy SEALS*, and the TV-movie *The Lost Capone*.

X-File case: Classified

1.21 "TOOMS"

X-File case #: X 129202
Government denies all knowledge

April 22, 1994
Writers: Glen Morgan & James Wong
Director: David Nutter

Druid Hill Sanitarium, Baltimore, MD. Dr. Aaron Monte checks in on his patient Eugene Victor Tooms, on the eve of his commitment review. [See Episode 1.03, "Squeeze"].

At FBI headquarters: Scully meets her newly seen superior, Assistant Director Walter S. Skinner [whose first name and middle initial aren't revealed until a later episode]. As the Smoking Man watches, Skinner demands more conclusive reports and orthodox procedures; their high conviction/case-solution rate of 75% doesn't impress him.

Back at the hearing, Dr. Pamela Karetzsky testifies Tooms has no physiological dysfunction. A male expert says Tooms' attack on Scully was simply wrongful frustration due to losing his job and being falsely arrested by the FBI. Mulder grows agitated as Judge Kann dismisses his mutation theory, despite showing that Tooms' fingerprints were at seven of 19 crime scenes since 1903. She says Tooms doesn't look 100 years old. Tooms is released providing he remains under Monte's care, regains his job, and resides with a halfway-house couple Susan and Arlan Green.

Lynne Acres Retirement Home: Scully seeks help from former investigating detective Frank Briggs. He recalls a jar of evidence he'd found at Powhattan Mill's Ruxton Chemical Plant when it was under construction in 1963; perhaps something else at the site could implicate Tooms. Having no luck discovering evidence

X-otica

Inspiration Alert:

Tooms' framing of Mulder for assault was a plot device used by killer Scorpio against *Dirty Harry* in that 1971 film.

he follows a policeman's hunch – and discovers skeletal remains.

Tooms, back on the job in his Baltimore Animal Regulation van, has stalked a businessman. When Mulder searches the van, Tooms is gone, having slipped down a maintenance hole in the street. Tooms squeezes through a barred window; Mulder, nosing around the neighborhood, notices sewage from the drains on a windowsill, and tells the owner he suspects an intruder inside. But Tooms has retreated.

At the Smithsonian Institute's Forensic Anthropology Lab, a professor, examining the bones Briggs and Scully found, discovers that the skull matches the photo of a missing person suspected of being a 1933 victim. But it's not enough to convict Tooms. Scully worries about Mulder, on stakeout alone for three days since he can't request help without alerting higher-ups who want to quash the X-Files. She volunteers to take over surveillance in her own car. Mulder drives off – with Tooms in his trunk.

On his couch, Mulder sleeps through the Vincent Price movie *The Fly*. Tooms enters through a vent, but rather than kill Mulder, simply scratches his own face until he bleeds. At a hospital the next day, a detective tells a doctor that police found Tooms unconscious in the street, beaten and kicked in the jaw. Tooms says Mulder did it. While police speak to Mulder at his apartment, they find an athletic shoe matching the jaw print. As they haul Mulder in for questioning, Mulder notices a screw underfoot – from the vent.

X-actitude

License plate on Mulder's car: Maryland KMH 2N5. Since the FBI's cars would presumably have Washington, D.C. plates, and since Mulder probably wouldn't have requisitioned one and risked alerting the higher-ups about his stakeout, this is very likely Mulder's own car, indicating he lives in Maryland or perhaps he borrowed this car to help lessen the chance of his being recognized, or rented one in Maryland for the same reason.

The two cells adjoining Tooms' are those of: L. Robbie Maier and Scott Schalin.

In-joke: Rob Maier is *The X-Files*' construction coordinator.

Judges flanking Judge

At Skinner's office, as Smoking Man watches, Mulder notes forensic evidence shows no one was inside the shoe; Tooms has tried to frame him. Scully lies that Mulder was with her on surveillance when Tooms was admitted to the hospital. Skinner expresses admiration for Mulder's talents, tells him if stress is making him or *other* agents behave inappropriately, to take a vacation – and with a glance toward Smoking Man, orders Mulder to stay away from Tooms, or all of his Congressional contacts together won't be enough to save his job.

With Tooms' dental records, Scully and the Smithsonian have ID'd the gnaw marks as Tooms' – they have their proof. At Tooms' halfway house, Arlan is just leaving when Monte arrives. Mulder and Scully arrive shortly afterward to find the doctor's corpse. The agents go to 66 Exeter Street, where they had last found Tooms, but the building has been torn down; a shopping mall, City Square, now occupies the site. In a darkened, after-hours department store, Mulder crawls through a narrow utility passageway beneath the floor, its entrance at the foot of an escalator. He pushes through a vent into a cavelike area, where the animalistic Tooms attacks. With Scully's help, Mulder escapes and activates the escalator – evidently killing Tooms in the mechanism.

Skinner, later, reading Scully's unorthodox report, asks if Smoking Man believes it. He knowingly replies yes.

Kann: Hirsch and Sullivan.

License on Tooms' Baltimore Animal Regulation Van: NUB 9P3

Businessman's sweatshirt logo: University of Maryland

Mulder's expert-witness credentials: three years with the FBI's Behavioral Science unit, profiling serial killers.

Mulder, on stakeout, tells Scully he's listening to "Baba Booie" – the nickname of radio personality Howard Stern's producer.

X-File case #X 129202 includes a file titled "Field Office Criminal Investigative and Administrative File"; inside this is a Metropolitan Police Dept. Arrest Report with Tooms' mug shot

CAST

Doug Hutchison
Eugene Victor Tooms
Paul Ben Victor
Dr. Aaron Monte
Mitch Pileggi
Assistant Director Walter F. Skinner
Henry Beckman
Detective Frank Briggs
Tim Webber
Detective Talbot [evidently the radar operator; unnamed in episode]
Jan D'Arcy
Judge Kann
Jerry Wasserman
Doctor Plith [unnamed in episode]
Frank C. Turner
Doctor Collins [unnamed in episode]
Gillian Carfra
Christine Ranford [bald man's wife; unnamed in episode]
Pat Bermel
Frank Ranford [bald man; unnamed in episode]
Mikal Dughi
Dr. [Pamela] Karetzky
Glynis Davies
Nelson [Tooms' attorney; unnamed in episode]
Steve Adams
Myers [State's Attorney; unnamed in episode]

(3985-60) and
fingerprints. Date and
time of arrest: July 23,
1993. Place: 107 E.
Cordova. Division
Reporting: Homicide.
Age: 30.

Catherine Lough
  Dr. Richmond [Tooms' medical doctor; unnamed in episode]
William B. Davis
  Smoking Man
Andre Daniels
  Arlan Green

extra

- The official Fox *X-files* website misspells lead guest-star Doug Hutchison's name as "Hutchinson."

Continuity error: The care used in filling out an official police report would seem to confirm Scully's address as 107 E. Cordova, but the outside of her building shows the number 1419 (in episode 2.06, "Ascension").

X-act Location: The shopping mall at 66 Exeter Street, Baltimore, is Vancouver's City Square Mall, located at 12th and Cambie Streets.

The Cast: Doug Hutchison and Henry Beckman reprise their roles from episode 1.03, "Squeeze". For Mitch Pileggi, see his separate biography.
  Jan D'Arcy appeared briefly on *Twin Peaks* as Sylvia Horne, Audrey's mom. She later appeared in 2.11, "Excelsius Dei."

The Repertory: Tim Webber had a much meatier part – as a cannibalistic chicken-factory manager – in 2.24, "Our Town." Glynis Davies makes the first of three *X-Files* appearances; she would play an all-too-trusting housewife in 2.13, "Irresistible," and an all-too-insistent apartment-house owner in 3.06, "2SHY." Andre Daniels would go on to play a sympathetic post-office boss in 2.03, "Blood." Jerry Wasserman had a larger role in 2.11, "Execelsis Dei."

X-File case #: X 129202

1.22 "BORN AGAIN"

April 29, 1994
Writers: Howard Gordon & Alex Gansa
Director: Jerrold Freedman

Buffalo, NY, 14th Precinct House: Detective Lazard finds eight-year-old Michelle Bishop outside, and asks Detective Rudy Barbala to question her. When Lazard leaves, Barbala mysteriously crashes backward through a window to his death. Later that day: Lazard asks Mulder and Scully onto the case since her brother, a Baltimore cop, had told her about their expertise with the unusual.

At the Bishops' Orchard Park home, the agents and computer sketch-artist Harry try to get a description of a second man Michelle claims was in the room. Mrs. Bishop says she'd arrived home to find sitter Mrs. Dougherty locked in the basement, and had called the police. She adds Michelle never smiles, she sees and hears invisible things, would scream when Mrs. Bishop's ex-husband Jim tried teaching her to swim, and is oddly adept at origami.

Brylin Psychiatric Hospital, Buffalo: Dr. Sheila Braun, whom Michelle sees twice a week, suspects Michelle fabricated the man in the sketch, and notes she dismembers and disfigures baby dolls. Braun throws Mulder out when he asks about psychic abilities.

Lazard matches Michelle's sketch with Officer Charlie Morris, who'd worked Narcotics out of the 27th until his line-of-duty death nine years ago; perhaps Michelle saw his picture in the 14th's trophy case. Yet Morris died in a reputed Chinatown gangland hit, with his right eye gouged and his left arm severed by chainsaw – the same disfigurements as Michelle's dolls.

Kenwood, NY, the next day: Detective Tony Fiore won't talk about his former partner's death, but Fiore suspects it was the heroin-peddling Triad gang Woo Shing Wu. At Buffalo Mutual Life later, Fiore meets with a Leon Felder, insisting they go to their safe-deposit box and get their $2 million-plus. But Felder says they'd promised to wait ten years – even if they're the last two left. That night, when Felder steps off a city bus, his scarf lifts and entangles in the bus's rear doors. The bus driver tries to stop, but the accelerator depresses without him. Felder dies, as Michelle looks on.

Michelle and mom are taken to a hotel room the police keep reserved. Mulder learns Felder was Barbala's old partner. Scully and

Mulder examine files on them, Morris, and Fiore – whom they discover lied when he denied knowing Barbala. A page is missing from Morris' homicide file; the log sheet says Fiore had checked it out this afternoon. At the Fiore home, early next morning, Anita says Tony never came home last night. Mulder notices origami animals, which Anita says was the work of her first husband – Charlie Morris. Outside, Mulder tells Scully Michelle was conceived around the time Morris died.

At Brylin, a Dr. Spitz videotapes Michelle as he does regression hypnotherapy. She tells him she's 24 years old, then starts screaming, they're killing her. Scully concedes there's some extremely coincidental connection to Morris, but where does that leave them? FBI Buffalo Headquarters: Spitz's videotape exhibits the same computer-flash as before. Harry tries to clean up the image-noise. Lazard's tracked down Morris' pathologist, Dr. Yamaguchi, now retired in Palm Beach.

X-otica

Duchovny has said he "detested" this episode. While it's indeed more of a straightforward police procedural than most, it has an intensely eerie buildup, highlighted by the too-wise deadpan of Michelle and the sudden, chilling realization of what that hunched computer-image is.

Orchard Park is a small town 17 miles southeast of Buffalo. There is no Kenwood near Buffalo but Kenmore is a Buffalo suburb.

He's faxed the missing autopsy page, which reveals there was fluid in Morris' respiratory tract – he'd drowned before being mutilated. With no evidence of flesh submersion except for his head, he was likely drowned in a bathtub or toilet. Scully notices a marked bradycardia, indicating raised plasma sodium level: He was killed in sea water?

Night. Fiore arrives home, telling Anita to pack. They don't notice Michelle peeking in. At the FBI office, Harry has isolated the anomalous video signals – leaving the blurry image of a squat, hunched man. Mulder recognizes it as the plastic deep-sea diver in the Fiores' fish tank – the last image Morris must have seen before he died. Scully and Mulder race to the Fiores', where Michelle sends a flying poker to [apparently] gouge out Fiore's eye. Scully brings Anita downstairs, where Fiore confesses he knew what they did to Charlie. Anita begs Charlie/Michelle to stop. Then the fish tank explodes, the lights come up, and it's over.

The field report (dated April 19, 1994) says Fiore pleaded guilty yesterday in Federal Court to first degree murder after the fact, grand larceny, and obstructing justice. Barbala's and Felder's deaths have been ruled accidental. No charges were brought against Michelle.

CAST

Brian Markinson   Tony Fiore
Mimi Lieber   Anita Fiore

Maggie Wheeler	Detective Sharon Lazard [first name not given in episode]
Dey Young	Judy Bishop [first name not given in episode]
Andrea Libman	Michelle Bishop
P. Lynn Johnson	Dr. Sheila Braun
Leslie Carlson	Dr. Spitz
Richard Sali	Felder
Dwight Koss	Detective [Rudy] Barbala
Peter Lapres	Harry Linhart [last name not given in episode]

The Cast: Former Duchovny girlfriend Maggie Wheeler played Anita, in the first cast of *Ellen* (ABC 1994-), when it was called *These Friends of Mine*. Her film and TV credits include a lead role in *New Year's Day* (1989), with Duchovny. She's also played Chandler's sometime-girlfriend on *Friends*. Mimi Lieber, whose credits stretch back to a dancer role in *Grease* (1978), has been in films including *Night Shift* (1982), *Wilder Napalm* (1993, written by future *X-Files* scripter Vince Gilligan), *Ghost in the Machine* (1993) and *Corrina, Corrina* (1994).

Vancouver-based child actress Andrea Libman got her screen start with the TV-movie *Posing: Inspired By Three Real Stories* (1991); she was in the films *The Lotus Eaters* (1993) and *Andre* (1994), the latter with fellow *X*-guest Joy Coghill. Her only other episodic credit to date is a 1992 episode of *The Commish*, where she played a five-year-old.

Dey Young played a student in *Rock 'n'*

Scully's autopsy on Barbala: Began 11 hours, 45 minutes post-mortem; she found a raised lesion seven centimeters below the sternum, and deep necrosis inconsistent with the cause of death as pronounced by a Dr. Gilder. There's evidence of localized electrocution.

Time and date Fiore checked out Morris homicide file: 3/29/94, 2:00-2:15 pm

Where Charlie Morris learned origami: In Japan, where he was born to a military father stationed there.

How Harry isolated the video signals: Mapped the frequency of the interference, placed the co-efficient for sine on one monitor, for co-sine on another, then, using an algorithm program, removed those frequencies from the main monitor.

Roll High School (1979), as well as appearing in *The Serpent and the Rainbow* (1988), *Pretty Woman* (1990), and *Frankie & Johnny* (1991). She was also in the cast of the James Brolin adventure series *Extreme* (ABC 1995). Brian Markinson appeared twice on *Star Trek: Voyager* as Durst.

The Repertory: P. Lynn Johnson, who plays Michelle's developmental psychologist, returned as a school official/parent in episode 2.14 "Die Hand Die Verletzt." A sort of Vancouver utility player, she likewise played three different characters on *The Commish*, and two on *Wiseguy* and has appeared in nearly a dozen TV-movies, and in *Who's Harry Crumb?* (1989). This appears to be the first screen role for Peter Lapres, who would return in 2.06, "Ascension" as possibly the same video technician; in 1995, he turned up as a producer's assistant on the TV-movies *A Family Divided* and *Broken Trust*.

X-File case #: X-40271

1.23 "ROLAND"

May 6, 1994
Writer: Chris Ruppenthal
Director: David Nutter

Mahan Propulsion Laboratory of the Washington Institute of Technology, Colson, WA. An abrasive Dr. Keats helps a retarded janitor, Roland Fuller, get through a locked electronic door. Inside, Keats and the business-suited Dr. Frank Nollette argue with the Scottish-accented Dr. Ron Surnow over some experimental jet engine loudly revving toward their goal of breaking Mach 15. Surnow, arguing the engine is about blow up and ruin four years of work, shuts it down. The other two angrily leave. When Surnow enters the wind-tunnel to check something, Roland closes the tunnel door, and – before going on to do complex mathematical equations on a chalkboard – turns on the engine, sucking Surnow in to a grisly death.

Crime scene, the next day: Scully and Mulder discuss this top-secret Icarus Project, the next generation of jet engines; Surnow is the second on the team to die in six months. The agents speak with Keats, who discovered what was left of Surnow, and Nollette, who confirms that team-member Dr. Arthur Grable had died in a car accident in November [establishing that this episode takes place in May].

Heritage Halfway House: Director Mrs. Stodie brings Mulder and Scully to Roland– the only other person in the lab – as he does some recreational project with retarded housemate Tracy, to whom he is romantically attached. Roland is a numerical idiot savant, yet when

X-otica

Colson, WA is a
fictional town.

they ask about his fondness for numbers,
he gets agitated and has what we later
learn is a premonition. Mulder takes a
paper Roland has been writing on. At the
Seattle FBI office, a graphologist says that
while a fourth person wrote on the
chalkboard, it wasn't Roland.

At Mahan that night, Keats is working
late. Roland, attacking him, dunks Keats'
head in liquid nitrogen – and then shatters
it. The next day – at an almost comically
gruesome crime scene where the chalk-
figure outline includes dozens of little x's –
Mulder sees that Keats closed his computer
file at 12:31 a.m., after which someone else
logged on. Mulder uses 15626 as the
computer password; he explains it came
from Roland's paper. The agents learn
Grable got Roland the janitor job, and that
the two were each born in Seattle on July
15, 1952 – Grable of rich parents, Roland of
parents whose identities have been sealed
by the court. Roland has been at Heritage
since age three.

Roland has a premonition – or an order?
– about killing Tracy after she asks him
who Arthur is. But Roland barricades
himself, not wanting to hurt her. Nollette,
in his office, tells the agents he and Grable
attended the medical school Harvey Mudd.
He reveals that Grable has had his head
preserved at the university's Avalon
Foundation cryogenics facility. There, Dr.
Larry Barrington shows the agents around.
Grable's medical records list Roland as a
possible organ-tissue donor. Scully and
Mulder, now thinking them twins, have a
computer technician manipulate Arthur's

picture to lose the glasses, beard and some weight – and they see a face matching Roland's. When they go speak with Roland, however, he gets upset, crashes through a bathroom window, and runs away.

Mulder believes Grable isn't dead, but in a rarefied state of consciousness; he further believes psychic abilities can exist between family members, particularly twins. Nollette, having eavesdropped on the agents by security camera, sneaks into the cryogenics lab and surreptitiously raises Grable's temperature. Scully finds the birth certificate listing Arthur and Roland Grable, born at Puget Presbyterian to Mr. and Mrs. Lewis Grable; Arthur is the older by four minutes. Dr. Barrington calls, saying Grable's capsule has been tampered with; Mulder suspects Nollette.

Roland/Arthur, at the computer, finally accomplishes the project's goal: The engine revs to Mach 15.13. Nollette arrives – and addresses Arthur, who in turn claims he took his work. Nollette responds that Arthur died before he could publish it, so it wouldn't have done him any good anyway. Nollette pulls a gun – but Roland/ Arthur knocks him out and places him in the wind tunnel. Scully and Mulder arrive, and at Scully's desperate urging, Roland stops the machine before Nollette is killed. Roland will be held for psychiatric evaluation, and may or may not be charged with a crime – while at Grable's capsule, the temperature reading hits 150°, followed by a long, ominous beep.

CAST

Zeljko Ivanek	Roland Fuller
Micole Mercurio	Mrs. Stodie
Kerry Sandomirsky	Tracy
James Sloyan	Dr. Frank Nollette
Garry Davey	Dr. Keats
Matthew Walker	[Dr. Ron] Surnow
Dave Hurtubise	[Dr. Larry] Barrington
Sue Mathew	[Agent] Lisa Dole [graphologist; unnamed in episode]

X-actitude

Scully reveals she has one older and one younger brother (in addition to sister Melissa, first mentioned and seen in the second-season episode "One Breath")

Roland's IQ: "barely 70," according to Scully

Roland's electronic-door code number: 315

Number of stars Roland says is on Scully's blouse: 147

Mahan Propulsion Laboratory building number: 214

Office number of wind-tunnel lab: MP-7001

Heritage Halfway House address: 591 Broadway, Colson, WA

Grable's cryogenic capsule: #18

Journal in which Nollette mentions he was published: *Nature*

extra

• The female video-technician agent and a male police detective at the Keats murder scene are both uncredited.

The Cast: Zeljko Ivanek has appeared in *The Sender* (UK 1982), as well as. *Mass Appeal* (1984) and *School Ties* (1992). He's not, however, in the credited cast of *Agnes of God* (1985), as the Lowry book asserts. Ivanek's TV-movies and miniseries include *Ernest Hemingway's "The Sun Also Rises"* (1984), *Echoes in the Darkness* (1987), *Truman* (1995) and *My Brother's Keeper* (1995).

James Sloyan co-starred in the doctor series *Westside Medical* (ABC 1977), and in the sitcom *Oh Madeline* (ABC 1983-84) as Madeline Kahn's husband. He was also the voice of the unseen "Interrogator" who surreally questioned cops, crooks and victims in mid-action on the short-lived *Crime & Punishment* (NBC 1993), and played in an episode of *Murder, She Wrote* (CBS 1984-). His long, long list of TV and film roles includes the part of Ma'bor Jetrel in a May, 1995 episode of *Star Trek: Voyager*.

Micole Mercurio made her film debut with *Mystique* (1981) and has since appeared in *Flashdance* (1983), *Mask* (1985), *Colors* (1988), *The Grifters* (1990), *The Client* (1994) and *While You Were Sleeping* (1995), among other films; her episodic-TV credits include *Hill Street Blues*, *Life Goes On*, *Northern Exposure*, *Grace Under Fire* and *NYPD Blue*.

The Repertory: The remarkable, Vancouver-based Kerry Sandomirsky, who would be featured even more prominently in episode 3.06, "2SHY," played the recurring role of Angela Tessio in an arc of *Wiseguy* (CBS 1987-90). Garry Davey played a truck-stop Good Samaritan in episode 1.11, "Eve," and a paranoid principal in 3.13, "Syzygy."

The computer-file directory Mulder accesses – last six files:

Name	Size (bytes)	Date last used	Time closed
VEM-MGR.HLP	1854	03-11-94	15:43
FFRPL.EXE	7547	03-21-94	05.19
RS.DOC	468013	04-23-94	16:42
NOL.DOC	765021	04-25-94	20:50
KMAN.DOC	335844	04-23-94	00:31
ARTHUR.DOC	609258	04-25-94	05:23

X-File case: Classified

1.24 "THE ERLEN-MEYER FLASK"

May 13, 1994
Writer: Chris Carter
Director: R.W. Goodwin

The opening credo this episode: Trust No One. This is the first of three episodes to date with a different credo than The Truth Is Out There.

Ardis, MD: A police cruiser chases a car westbound to the waterfront. A fugitive flees – and after two cops beat him with nightsticks and another fires a taser (to no apparent effect), he leaps into the harbor, leaving a trail of green blood.

Early morning, May 8, 1994: Mulder is awakened by a call from Deep Throat, telling him to watch Channel 8. On a live newscast, Ardis Police Capt. Roy Lacerio talks about the manhunt. Mulder videotapes it, and later prints out a frame-grab, while he and Scully try to figure out what Deep Throat wants.

The harbor, nearly 18 hours later: The body still hasn't been recovered. At the pound, the agents learn the car was rented at Gaithersburg, MD. Yet from the TV-news frame, Mulder sees the impounded car is not the one on TV, which had a caduceus medical symbol. After checking plates, concentrating on doctors, Mulder visits Dr. Terrence Allen Berube at the Emgen

Corporation in Gaithersburg. He claims he didn't realize his car was stolen since his housekeeper uses it.

That night, Deep Throat approaches Mulder and reassures the disgusted agent. At Berube's lab, a crew-cut man demands to know if the fugitive, Dr. William Secare, has contacted him; then he kills Berube. At the harbor, Secare rises from the water to escape.

Mulder doubts the official ruling that Berube committed suicide. At Emgen, he finds a liquid-filled flask labeled Purity Control; Scully takes it to the Georgetown University Microbiology Department for analysis. By 6:30 p.m., Mulder breaks into Berube's house looking for clues. Georgetown scientist Dr. Carpenter tells Scully she thinks the liquid is a bacteria specimen – though bacteria unlike any she's ever seen. Berube's house, 7:45 p.m.: Mulder finds a phone number, which Danny eventually traces to a Zeus Storage. While Mulder waits for Danny to call back, Secare phones, and, assuming it's Berube, asks for help – but collapses before he can give an address. Outside Berube's, the Crew-Cut Man in a surveillance van monitors the call.

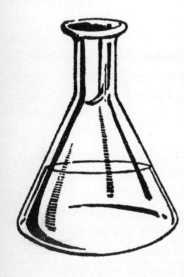

At the public phone where Secare collapsed, EMS workers try to save him. But when they attempt to do a thoracotomy, Secare's body releases a gas that disables the medics. He again escapes. Scully calls Mulder's car phone to report that the lab found bacteria that each contained a virus – Berube was cloning them. The organisms contain chloroplasts – plant cells [N] – which Scully believes is for gene therapy. Mulder enters Berube's storage warehouse to find five people each suspended in a watery tank. 11:45 p.m.: Carpenter shows Scully a sequence of genes from the bacteria sample. DNA has only four nucleotides – yet these show a fifth and a sixth. What the flask contains exists

X-otica

This episode was nominated for an Edgar Award by the Mystery Writers of America, for Best Episode and Television Series.

The disabling fumes emitted from Secare are based on two similar, widely reported incidents – at California's Riverside General Hospital on Feb. 19, 1994, and at Bakersfield, CA's Mercy Hospital a week later – in which sickening, ammonia-like fumes rose from two patients' needle-punctures, causing exposed people to collapse from the toxin.

An Erlenmeyer flask is a conical laboratory container with a flat bottom and a short, straight neck, named after the German chemist Richard August Carl Emil Erlenmeyer (1825–1909).

nowhere in nature, says Carpenter. Outside Zeus, Mulder is chased by three men, but he escapes.

7:30 a.m.: Mulder brings Scully to Zeus – but finds nothing. Deep Throat says the evidence has probably been destroyed by one of the covert organizations within the intelligence community. They weren't after Mulder, since they didn't kill him. Mulder deduces Berube was conducting human experiments with extraterrestrial viruses. Deep Throat says that it has been going on for years – they've had the tissue, if not the technology, since 1947 – and claims Roswell was a smokescreen – that they've had a half-dozen better salvage ops. He says this was the site of the first human-alien hybrids, using six terminally ill volunteers – including Berube's friend Secare. All six began recovering, and Secare gained superhuman strength and the ability to breathe underwater. Yet the government only wanted feasible technology, not survivors who posed a threat of exposure or toxicity. Berube was killed, and now the "clean-up's" moving so quickly, soon the only evidence will be Secare himself.

Scully learns Carpenter and her family all perished in an auto accident, and her evidence is gone. Mulder finds Secare hiding at Berube's home – as does a gas-masked Crew-Cut Man, who had followed Mulder and now beats him and kills Secare.

6:10 a.m.: Deep Throat surprises Scully outside the missing Mulder's apartment; Mulder won't be killed since he's too high-profile, but they'll need something to trade for him [N]. Deep Throat conspires to get Scully into the High-Containment Facility at Fort Marlene, MD, where original alien tissue is kept. On the seventh floor, a guard asks for the password; guessing, she says "Purity Control." [N] Scully logs in, and opens a cabinet marked "P.C." to find a liquid nitrogen barrel – containing an apparent alien the size and dimensions of a human fetus.

Night: Scully meets Deep Throat on a deserted bridge. She doesn't turn over the apparent alien until he heatedly convinces her how ruthless the covert community can be: They once had schoolchildren injected with experimental organisms under the pretense of vaccinations. Crew-Cut Man arrives – and after taking the box from Deep Throat, shoots him through the heart while an accomplice throws a battered Mulder from their van. The killers roar away; Deep Throat dies, gurgling to Scully, to trust no one.

Washington, D.C., 13 days later: As Scully's clock slips from 11:21 to 11:22 p.m., Mulder phones her that the X-Files unit is being closed, and they're being reassigned. Skinner claims word has come from the top of the executive branch. And Smoking Man nonchalantly puts away the apparent alien – or alien/human? – deep in the Pentagon basement.

CAST

Jerry Hardin	Deep Throat
Lindsey Ginter	Crew-Cut Man
Anne DeSalvo	Dr. Carpenter
Simon Webb	Dr. Secare
Ken Kramer	Dr. Berube
Jim Leard	Captain Roy Lacerio
Phillip MacKenzie	Medic
William B. Davis	Cigarette Smoking Man
Jaylene Hamilton	[WDT *Newscan*] Reporter

Mike Mitchell

John Payne

First Uniformed Cop

Guard [at Fort Marlene]

extra

- The official Fox *X-Files* website erroneously lists the character Dr. Carpenter as Dr. Simon.

X-act Location: The waterfront of fictional Ardis, MD is in reality Versatile Shipyards, of North Vancouver.

The Cast: Anne DeSalvo appeared in several episodes of *Wiseguy*; Amy Fisher's mom in the TV-movie *Casualties of Love: The "Long Island Lolita" Story* (1993); and the pregnant fiancee of boxer Tony Banta on two pivotal episodes of *Taxi*. She co-starred as Ray Sharkey's sister in his sitcom *The Man in the Family* (ABC 1991), and appeared in *Starting Over* (1979), *Stardust Memories* (1980), *Arthur* (1981), and *Radioland Murders* (1994), among other films.

Lindsey Ginter returns in episode 2.10, "Red Museum" as the unnamed, shadow-government assassin end-credited as Crew-Cut Man. He was in *Beverly Hills Cop 3* (1994) along with future *X-Files* antagonist Timothy Carhart. Simon Webb has been seen on *The Commish* and *MacGyver*; among his film credits is the live-action children's short *Rainbow War*, produced for Vancouver Expo 86.

The Repertory: John Payne would go on to play Alligator Man Jerald Glazebrook in

Last names of some of Mulder's neighbors (per their mailboxes): Glaniceanu; Pao/Hu; Dommann

episode 2.20, "Humbug." Ken Kramer would play a more bemused doctor as the L.A. pathologist in 2.07, "3." Jim Leard went from police captain here to police sergeant in 2.16, "Colony."

X-File case: Classified

2.01 "LITTLE GREEN MEN"

Sept. 16, 1994
Writers: Glen Morgan & James Wong
Director: David Nutter

Mulder, narrating over spacescapes, describes the NASA Voyager probes and the High-Resolution Microwave Survey, both seeking alien contact. At the shuttered Arecibo Ionospheric Observatory in Puerto Rico, electronic equipment mysteriously springs to life.

Washington, D.C., outside the Longstreet Motel: Mulder has been assigned to dull electronic surveillance of white-collar criminals. Scully's back at the Academy, teaching autopsy techniques. When Mulder returns to his desk (now on some main floor with other agents), he picks up a downturned photo of his sister – a signal to meet Scully at the Watergate Hotel and Office Complex, in a deserted staff-parking lot. Mulder tells her he "attended" Deep Throat's funeral, using eight-power binoculars from 1,000 feet away. And he has begun to believe all the "little green men" he thinks he has seen are merely in his mind.

Flashback to Nov. 27, 1973, Chilmark, MA, 6:53 p.m.: Over TV news of Rose Mary Woods' partial Nixon-tape erasure, a young Mulder plays Stratego with kid sister Samantha; he's planning to watch *The Magician* at nine. Suddenly, the house shakes, and amid eerie lights stands a thin silhouetted figure. Fox breaks open a locked gun box, but then seems paralyzed as Samantha floats away. Mulder wakes up – and finds a messenger at his door to take him to Senator Matheson [whose first name, Richard, isn't given this episode, but in 2.06, "Ascension"]. The visionary Senator is a supporter who urges Mulder to investigate Arecibo, and says for 24 hours he'll try to hold off the Blue Beret UFO Retrieval Team, which is authorized to use terminal force.

FBI headquarters, next day: Skinner, with the Smoking Man in his office, discovers that Mulder has gone. Mulder, in Puerto Rico, has hitched a ride to the Arecibo gate, from where he hikes to the control room. Scully, seeking clues at Mulder's apartment, unsuccessfully tries the passwords "Spooky" and "Samantha" on his computer before succeeding with "Trustno1"; she prints a list of numbers. Another agent, staking out the place, demands to know why she's here. Just feeding the fish, she assures him, pocketing the list. Arecibo: Mulder finds a terrified Jorge Concepcion in the lavatory, jabbering in Spanish about what sounds like alien contact.

SETI INSTITUTE

U.S. Naval Observatory: A scientist tells Scully the numbers are a record of space signals 30 times stronger than galactic-background noise, and on the "21-centimeter" frequency satellites aren't allowed to use. He gives Scully a list of SETI (Search for Extraterrestrial Activity) research locales; Scully, cross-checking with airline passenger lists, finds Mulder on a July 7 flight from Washington to San Juan with a stop in Miami. (He'd used the pseudonym George E. Hale, founder of the landmark Palomar Observatory.)

Arecibo: Mulder finds that a signal recorded at 6:30 a.m. Tuesday July 5 shows an intelligence pattern. Jorge, fearful of a sudden noise, runs into the storm outside,

X-otica

Chris Carter and writers Morgan and Wong originally wanted to send Mulder on-location to Moscow, Russia. When the logistics proved impractical, they settled for faux Puerto Rico.

The Fox website's capsule synopsis lists the young Mulder as age 12 and Samantha as age 8. This agrees with the ages evident in episode 1.04, "Conduit," in which Scully is shown an FBI file on Samantha. The flashback itself contradicts Mulder's previous description of Samantha's abduction, but that can be chalked up to the vagaries of time and memory.

Jorge's Spanish dialog, paraphrased in translation: He had gone to investigate some strange lights in where he dies of fright. Miami International Airport, circa 5:45 p.m.: Scully suspects she's being tailed by a touristy couple. She phones a message to Mulder's answering machine: "CA 519, 705, 950." She slips away, but the "tourists" "know" she's taking Caribbean Air flight 519, leaving at 7:05 for St. Croix. Yet at 6:30, Scully buys a ticket to San Juan.

Arecibo, 10:30 p.m.: As Mulder tape-records medical observations of Jorge's corpse, the room shakes, printouts spew, and he hears a distorted repetition of his own tape recording – as a familiar bright light panics him. His gun doesn't work, and he sees that same silhouette as on the day Samantha disappeared. When Scully finds him later, Mulder excitedly tells her he finally has proof of aliens, in the form of the tapes and printouts. But outside, the Blue Berets are arriving. The agents rocket out in Scully's sports-utility vehicle, literally down the side of a hill, as the Blue Berets fire. Mulder's salvaged but a single tape-reel.

Later the next day: Skinner tells Mulder that leaving his surveillance post "has four-bagger all over it . . . censure, transfer, suspension, probation." Smoking Man watches. Mulder tells Skinner he'll accept his discipline, but also notes he had enough wiretap evidence after three days to nail the suspects on 40 counts of bank fraud – yet Skinner kept him there needlessly . . . *and* someone illegally wiretapped his phone. Skinner, acknowledging all this, throws Smoking Man out – and while he won't censure Mulder, he *will* keep him on

the sky, when men like animals grabbed him and put him here.

The Magician (NBC Oct. 2, 1973–May 20, 1974) starred Bill Bixby as prestidigitator Tony Blake, who after being wrongly imprisoned vowed to use his talents to fight injustice. The Milton Bradley board game *Stratego* (introduced 1961) is probably best remembered for its commercials, which were spoofed on *Mystery Science Theater 3000*; the TV spots made it look as if the game's only purpose was to move a piece then bellow lyrically, "Stra-*teeeee*-go-oooooo . . .!"

The Arecibo observatory, affiliated with Cornell University's National Astronomy and Ionosphere Center, is a real and operational research facility, with the world's largest radio-telescope.

electronic surveillance. Later, Mulder find his entire Arecibo reel blank; Scully thinks a power surge during the storm may have erased it. And Mulder, back on surveillance, listens long into the night.

CAST

Mitch Pileggi	Assistant Director Walter S. Skinner
Mike Gomez	Jorge Concepcion
Raymond J. Barry	Senator Richard Matheson
William B. Davis	Smoking Man
Les Carlson	Dr. Troisky [unnamed in episode]
Marcus Turner	Young Mulder
Vennessa Morley	Young Samantha
Fulvio Cecere	Aide [to Sen. Matheson]
Deryl Hayes	Agent Morris [unnamed in episode]
Dwight McFee	[Blue Beret] Commander
Lisa Anne Beley	Student [FBI cadet]

Gary Hetherington   Lewin [agent staking-out Mulder's apartment; unnamed in episode]

Bob Wilde   Rand

extra

X-actitude

The airline manifest includes the names of prominent X-Philes Paulette Alves, Sylvia Bartle, T.C. Carstensen and Pat Gonzales, and of *X-Files* novelist Charles Grant.

Longstreet Motel wiretap #: 5A21147

Mulder's basketball shirt in flashback: KING 30.

• The official Fox *X-Files* website erroneously gives the alien contact site as Mexico.

The Cast: Raymond J. Barry's films include *Sudden Death* (1995), *Dead Man Walking* (1995), *Cool Runnings* (1993), *Born on the Fourth of July* (1989) and *An Unmarried Woman* (1978). On Broadway he's appeared in *Happy End*, *Zoot Suit*, and *The Leaf People*, and won Dramalogue Awards for L.A. productions of Sam Shepard's *Buried Child* (1987), and as both author and star of *Once in Doubt* (1990). He also appeared in a fledgling Gillian Anderson's unreleased film *Home Fires Burning* a.k.a. *The Turning* (shot 1991).

Mike Gomez's film work includes his 1978 debut *Uncle Joe Shannon*, *The Border* (1981) *El Norte* (1983) *Heartbreak Ridge* (1986), and *The Milagro Beanfield War* (1988).

The Repertory: Lisa Ann Beley had played the nurse in episode 1.18, "Miracle Man." Les Carlson, billed as Leslie Carlson, played the hypno-regression psychiatrist in 1.22, "Born Again." Deryl Hayes played one of two mysterious officials tracking illegally sold high-tech in 1.06, "Shadows." Gary Hetherington had a bit part in 1.03, "Squeeze." And while Dwight McFee, making the second of his three *X-Files* appearances, is here a Blue Beret Commander, he played a lawyer in 1.19, Shapes.

X-File case: Classified

2.02 "THE HOST"

Sept. 23, 1994
Writer: Chris Carter
Director: Daniel Sackheim

A Russian freighter, two miles off the New Jersey coast:
when crewman Dmitri tries to fix the ship's backed-up
toilets he is violently pulled into the septic system –
and washes up dead, with one side eaten away, in the
sewers of Newark, NJ.

Washington, D.C.: After being relieved of his
surveillance work Mulder flies from National Airport to
Newark, where his contact is Detective Norman. Mulder,
uniformed officer Kenny, and others descend into the
sewer to find the unidentified body. Back in D.C., Mulder
angrily demands to meet with Skinner about this simple –
and smelly – local homicide. Skinner is outraged that
Mulder regards this assignment as punishment.

That night, Mulder tells Scully he's thinking of leaving
the Bureau. Scully suggests he request a transfer to the
Behavioral Science Unit at the FBI Academy in
Quantico, but Mulder says the FBI doesn't want them
working together – and their partnership is his only
reason to stay. As Scully performs the victim's autopsy
she finds a tattoo of indecipherable markings, and a
slug-like creature emerging from the liver.

Newark: two sewer workers are fixing a hole in a
screen when one of them, Craig, is pulled under. The
other man saves him; later, at the Middlesex County
Hospital in Sayreville, Mulder observes as Craig

complains of a bad taste in his mouth. Craig suspects he was grabbed by a python – except that his wound has four points. Mulder gets an odd, anonymous call in which an assumedly African-American voice tells him he has a friend at the FBI, and hangs up. FBI Academy lab: Scully shows Mulder the turbellaria, a.k.a. fluke or flatworm she found. Its scolex (sucker with four spikes) matches the wound on Craig's back. That night, Craig gorily coughs up a flatworm, which disappears down the bathtub drain.

Newark County Sewage Processing Plant: Foreman Ray explains the system to Mulder. An old-timer, Charlie, hears splashing in a sewer reservoir, and when he backflushes the system, the three men all look inside a clear examination tube at what appears to be a hairless, mottled human with a sucker mouth. Scully's lab: Someone slips a supermarket tabloid under the door, with an article about a

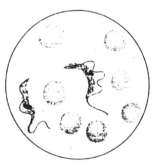

Russian ship's similar sewage death. Scully now realizes the tattoo is of Russian Cyrillic letters, and eventually IDs the John Doe.

Middlesex County Psychiatric Hospital: Mulder and Scully observe the sewer-creature. Skinner, at his office, is nonchalant, having told the local prosecutor the Justice Department wants to institutionalize the suspect for psychiatric evaluation. Mulder argues it's not a man but a monster. Then Skinner says Craig was found dead – a possibly preventable tragedy.

Night: EMS workers load the creature into a U.S. Marshal's van. When he later notices the flukeman missing, he radios for backup and parks outside the Lake Betty campsite/recreation area. The creature kills the marshal [having evidently hidden beneath the stretcher] and slithers down a campsite toilet which at 5:27 a.m., a tanker truck cleans out – with something momentarily clogging the vacuum tube. About 6:37 a.m., at the murder scene,

X-otica

The flukeman and Mulder's reaction on first seeing it were filmed separately. "I knew it was a big worm, but I hadn't seen it," Duchovny says. "So, not wanting to overplay it, I kinda went like, 'Mmm-hmmm.'" And so in the combined shot, "There's me going, 'Uh-huh. It's a six-foot worm. With human features. Uh-huh. Hmmmm, well, what do you think of that? . . . Hey, it's another one of those goddamned six-foot intestinal worms!'" he says, laughing.

Mulder gets another call from the mysterious voice, saying this case is imperative if the X-Files are to be revived. Mulder, learning dogs have tracked a scent to the toilet, traces the tank-cleaning truck to the Newark plant.

At 8:15 a.m., Ray tells Mulder if the creature's here, filters and screens should trap it. Scully calls, saying the liver fluke was an incubatory larvae – meaning the hermaphrodite creature is trying to multiply. Ray, investigating an ancient storm-overflow part of the sewer, is pulled under; Mulder rescues him, and pins the flukeman beneath a sewer gate. Back in Washington, Scully says larvae analysis indicates reproductive and physiological "cross-traiting," resulting in a quasi-vertebrate human. She says the creature came here from a decommissioned Russian freighter hauling salvage from the Chernobyl meltdown; it was born in a primordial soup of radioactive sewage. And inexplicably, somewhere, we see a flukeman opening its eyes.

CAST

Mitch Pileggi	Assistant Director Walter S. Skinner
Darin Morgan	Flukeman
Matthew Bennett	First Workman [Craig]
Freddy Andreiuci	Detective Norman
Don MacKay	Charlie
Marc Bauer	Agent Brisentine [unnamed in episode]
Gabrielle Rose	Dr. Zenzols [unnamed in episode]

Ron Sauve	Foreman [Ray]
Dmitri Boudrine	Russian Engineer
Raoul Ganee	Dmitri
William MacDonald	Federal Marshall
Uncredited:	
Steven Williams	Telephone Caller

X-actitude

The initial Newark victim: John Doe #101356, case #DP112148.

U.S. Marshall's van: #4940

Agent taking over Mulder's surveillance: Bozoff

Septic-tank service at Lake Betty: A & A Anderson Tank Cleaning Service, phone number 277-1628

X-act Location: Substituting for Newark's sewer facility was Canada's Iona Island Sewage Treatment Plant, where the poor and doubtless pungent *X-Filers* spent 12 hours filming on a hot July day.

The Cast: "Flukeman" Darin Morgan, younger brother of producer Glen Morgan, later became an *X-Files* writer and story editor. His only previous known screen credits are in an episode each of *The Commish* and *21 Jump Street*

The Repertory: Gabrielle Rose had played the prominent role of Mrs . . . Budahas in episode 1.02, "Deep Throat." Don MacKay had played the warden in 1.13, "Beyond the Sea."

X-File case: Classified

2.03 "BLOOD"

Sept. 30, 1994
Teleplay: Glen Morgan & James Wong
Story: Darin Morgan
Director: David Nutter

Franklin, PA postal center: Worker Ed Funsch gets a paper cut. After his supervisor regretfully lays him off for budget reasons, Ed then sees an electronic readout telling him to kill. In an elevator at the town's Civic Center, a claustrophobic businessman, Taber, sees a digital readout with the same message.

Later, Venango County Sheriff Spencer tells Mulder (here on routine Behavioral Science assignment, not the X-Files) that Taber murdered four people before being killed by a security guard. The town had only three murders in over 200 years – yet in six months, there have been 22 committed by seven people. No drug or alcohol traces account for it. Funsch, at a Commercial Trust ATM, sees a mother tending to her little girl's nose-bleed; then the ATM says to take his gun (referring to a security guard) and kill. Instead, he runs.

Residue on Taber's fingers, of an unidentified, non-toxic chemical compound found in plants, leads Mulder to suspect a chemical cause. The only consistent clue is the destruction of electronic devices. Evening: A mechanic tells a young, pretty Mrs. McRoberts her car needs expensive repair. She sees the word liar in the diagnostic computer, then instructions to kill. She hits him with a wrench, then stabs him to death with an oil-can spout. By 7:35 a.m., a repair order at the scene has prompted Spencer and Mulder to see McRoberts. Her microwave-oven readout tells her to kill. Berserk, she stabs Mulder until Spencer shoots her dead. At the Academy, Scully's autopsy on Mrs. McRoberts reveals anomalies the coroner missed: Adrenaline levels 200 times normal, and a high concentration of an undetermined chemical compound, similar to that found on Taber's fingers; she suspects it reacts with adrenaline to produce a substance similar to the hallucinogen LSD.

At a department store, Funsch job-hunts. He sees a blood-drive table, then violent TV images of Waco, the L.A. riots, etc. – and the words behind you (referring to the gun department), followed by do it. Mulder, jogging, notices a yard-care truck tossing insects onto a lawn; he takes one to the Lone Gunmen who say it's a Eurasian cluster fly. Mulder asks if the Gunmen are familiar with the chemical compound LSDM; Byers recognizes it as the toxic pesticide lysergic dimethrin, an unreleased synthetic botanical insecticide that, acting as a pheromone, triggers a fear response in a pest.

That night or the early morning, in Franklin, Mulder uses infrared goggles to stake out a field. He's suddenly sprayed by a crop-dusting helicopter. Later, at Franklin Community Hospital, County Supervisor Larry Winter insists no "stealth" helicopter is spraying experimental pesticides, but with pressure changes his story: Irradiated flies didn't work, crop failures would ruin lives, and this chemical was proven safe to him – though he won't say by whom. Scully, having flown in, says exposure to LSDM doesn't cause violent behavior – Mulder is proof. But Mulder suggests LSDM heightens the fear response of individuals with phobias; he suspects the read-out messages were real but subliminal.

Winter agrees to stop the spraying and to blood-test all those exposed – but only if the explanation for the tests not be linked to LSDM. With astonishing immediacy, a door-to-door "cholesterol-test drive" is launched; by around 10:30 a.m., a canvasser

X-otica

Funsch's clock-tower sniping recalls Charles Whitman's real-life Texas Tower massacre of Aug. 4, 1966, at the University of Texas. Using a high-powered rifle, Whitman killed 13 people and wounded 34.

reaches Funsch, who's afraid to let the person in. On TV, he sees the word BLOOD – and destroys the TV set. After closing his gun case, he sees BLOOD on a calculator, and KILL in his digital watch. Spencer's office: All but 25 people took the test; Scully and Mulder, canvassing, get to Funsch's home – where the door is unlocked, electronics are wrecked, and a rifle's missing.

Scully and Mulder deduce Funsch is phobic about blood, and that he's headed to shoot up the hospital. But Funsch, on a bus, sees the readouts THEY'RE WAITING and GET OFF. When the bus arrives at the hospital, the driver says the man they're looking for got off at Franklin Community College – where there's a blood fair.

There Funsch, seeing the readout UP, climbs to the top of a clock tower and begins a sniper assault. Mulder, fighting his own fear of heights, eventually disarms, and takes Funsch to the hospital. Mulder, finally pausing to take a breath, sits and makes a cell-phone call to Scully there – and in the readout sees the words, ALL DONE and BYE BYE.

CAST

William Sanderson	Ed Funsch
John Cygan	Sheriff Spencer
Kimberly Ashlyn Gere	Mrs. McRoberts
George Touliatos	County Supervisor Larry Winter
Bruce Harwood	Byers
Dean Haglund	Langly
Tom Braidwood	Frohike
Gerry Rosseau	Mechanic

Andre Daniels	Harry [Funsch's boss; unnamed in episode; last name McNally per print sources]
William MacKenzie	Bus Driver
Diana Stevan	Mrs. Adams
David Fredericks	Security Guard
Kathleen Duborg	Mother
John Harris	Taber
B.J. Harrison	Clerk

extra

X-actitude

Scully's cell-phone number: 555-3564 – area code 202, per episode 1.15, "Lazarus,"

The facts on Funsch: Age 52. High-school diploma. No driver's license. Former Navy radio operator. Wife died 10 years ago; no other family or kids.

Taber: 42-year-old real-estate agent

The Lone Gunman, April [1994]: Included an article about the CIA's new CCD-TH2138 fiber-optic-lens micro videocamera.

• The official Fox *X-Files* website erroneously gives the locale as Virginia, and truncates the name of actress Kimberly Ashlyn Gere to Ashlyn Gere. It also neglects to list front-credit guest-actor George Touliatos.

X-act Location: The University of British Columbia, with its clock tower, filled-in for Franklin Community College. X-guest Don Davis (Capt. William Scully) taught acting at UBC before becoming an actor full-time.

The Cast: William Sanderson's screen career began with *Savage Weekend* (1976 or 1980; a.k.a. *The Killer Behind the Mask* and *The Upstate Murders*). Best known as Vermont backwoodsman Larry on *Newhart* (CBS 1982–90), Sanderson also played the tragic Dr. Sebastian in *Blade Runner* (1982) as well as appearing in the miniseries *Lonesome Dove* (1989) and its 1993 sequel, *Stephen King's "Sometimes They Come Back"* (1991) and *The Rocketeer* (1991). His voiceover work includes Clem in the animated series *Santo Bugito*.

Kimberly Ashlyn Gere appeared in *Evil Laugh* (1986), *Creepozoids*, *Dreamaniac* (both 1987), *Angel III: The Final Chapter* (1988) and *Fatal Instinct* a.k.a. *To Kill For* (1991); as Kimberly Patton, she plays the recurring role of Feliciti OH 519, leader of a rebel group of A.I. beings on *Space: Above and Beyond* (Fox 1995–). Under *nom de porn* Ashlyn Gere, she has won the adult-film industry's FOXE 1991 Fan Favorite, 1992 Vixen of the Year, and 1993 Best Female Performer awards. She's appeared in at least 98 original X-rated films and clips-compilations from 1989-94, including *Shifting Gere* (1990), *Put it in Gere* (1991), and *Gerein' Up* (1992).

John Cygan played Detective Paulie Pentangeli in the cast of *The Commish* (ABC 1991-95) during the first and last seasons, and returned for at least three of the 1995-96 *Commish* TV-movies. He was also in the cast of Bob Newhart's *Bob* (CBS 1992-93), and starred in the unsold pilot *Crow's Nest* (ABC 1992).

The Repertory: Andre Daniels had played halfway-house honcho Arlan Green in episode 1.21, "Tooms." George Touliatos was an ever-so-responsible fertility doctor in 1.11, "Eve." Kathleen Duborg went from small-town mom to hooker, in 2.13, "Irresistible."

X-File case: Classified

2.04 "SLEEP-LESS"

Oct. 7, 1994
Writer: Howard Gordon
Director: Rob Bowman

Manhattan, 11:23 p.m. Dr. Saul Grissom finds a fire outside his apartment door, and calls 911. An African-American man, Preacher, leaves the high-rise, smiles enigmatically. Firefighter Lt. Regan finds no fire in the sixth-floor hallway – nor in Grissom's apartment, where Grissom is seen dead near a spent fire extinguisher.

Mulder finds an audiocassette tucked into his morning newspaper; circled is "Prominent Doctor Dies – Pioneer in Sleep Disorders." Rookie agent Alex Krycek brings Mulder a file on this "302" assignment – insisting they partner-up since he'd opened the file two hours before Mulder. Scully, teaching autopsy at the Academy, gets a call from "George Hale" (Mulder's sometime-pseudonym, used in "Little Green Men"). Mulder is at National Airport (minus Krycek), catching a shuttle to New York's LaGuardia in a half-hour; he'll have a body for her to examine by 5 p.m.

Grissom Sleep Disorder Center, Stamford, CT: A doctor describes experimental modification of brain-wave patterns by electrical stimulation, to theoretically alter dreams. Later, Mulder introduces Krycek to Scully, who says Grissom died not of the reported heart attack, but of intense heat with no external burns, as if his body simply believed it was burning.

In a run-down Brooklyn apartment, Preacher finds old acquaintance Henry Willig watching a home-shopping channel. Willig is suddenly gunned down by bloodied Vietnamese. Mulder and Krycek later find an odd scar on Willig, and learn he was with the Marines in Vietnam in 1970; Grissom was also with the Marines, though at Parris Island from 1968-71. Willig was in Special Forces & Recon Squad J-7 — one of two survivors out of 13, the other being Corporal Augustus D. Cole. Cole was discharged from the V.A. Medical Center in North Orange, NJ two days ago.

The mysterious man who called Mulder in episode 2.02, "The Host," wants to meet. He assures Mulder he doesn't want to be here. He hands Mulder data from a secret military project: Grissom was experimenting to end the need for sleep, since wakefulness dulls fear and heightens aggression. Cole hasn't slept in 24 years. The man tells Mulder there's a third living squad-member, Salvatore Matola, reported killed in action.

Someone matching Cole's description has robbed a drugstore and is holed up in a motel. NYPD Lieutenant Horton says Cole only stole some pills — and yet the SWAT team is getting antsy. Shots are fired: Two officers are down, and critical — having shot each other. Cole — a.k.a. Preacher — escapes. Mulder later tells Scully he believes years without sleep have allowed Cole to produce telepathic imagery.

The 2 Jays Cafe, Roslyn, Long Island: Matola tells Mulder and Krycek J-7 had gone AWOL, making up their own missions, killing civilians, finally wiping out a schoolful of 300 children outside Phu Bai — with no charges ever brought against them. He says Dr. Francis Girardi (now a Harvard neurosurgery professor) did the brain-stem surgery the experiment required.

At 6:15 p.m., stuck in traffic, Mulder tells Krycek the 24th anniversary of the Phu Bai killings was two days ago. Scully phones to say Girardi is coming to Grissom's funeral

X-otica

"Mr. X actually began as Ms. X," remembered co-executive producer James Wong, who confirms an actress was cast and filmed. "We shot sequences of the character in 'Sleepless,' and when we watched the dailies we said, 'Oh my God, it's not going to work.'" Partner Glen Morgan explains, "Chris [Carter] didn't like her [so] I said, 'How about Steve Williams? He's a great guy and an intense actor.' As a result, X's scene with Mulder was actually David playing against an actress, but then we went back, shot Steven Williams, and inserted the footage.

Though the surveillance tape that Mulder is transcribing has the epithet "stupid bitch" in the final shooting script, it was changed to "stupid bimbo" by airdate.

This episode netted Stephen Mark one of this season's two Emmy nominations for Editing, Single-Camera Production.

in New York, arriving at a Bronx train station at 7:30; she'll get his photo to the security desk there. Mulder and Krycek reach the station just after 7:30; Cole is there too. Cole shoots Girardi and then Mulder – or does he? Krycek rouses Mulder on the platform, saying he was waving his gun around, and that Girardi never showed.

At the station's Metropolitan Transit Authority office, Mulder has police check out security videos. A cop shows Mulder that a car parked in a restricted area at 19:38:37 isn't there at 19:43:19. This somehow leads the agents to Track 17, where Cole holds Girardi hostage. Girardi is shot by a J-7 firing squad; Mulder and Krycek find him severely wounded. Mulder goes after Cole; finding him literally and figuratively on the edge, he implores Cole to see justice by giving testimony. Krycek kills Cole when Cole raises his gun. In the car immediately afterward, Mulder finds his files missing; Scully, at headquarters later, says her office and computer were broken into. Mulder tells Scully of the new covert source [who isn't yet referred to in dialog as Mr. X].

Elsewhere, Krycek meets with a shadow cabinet of three silhouetted figures, including the Cigarette-Smoking Man. No one knows how Mulder got the files. Krycek reports Scully is a bigger problem than anticipated. Says Smoking Man, "Every problem has a solution."

CAST

Mitch Pileggi	Assistant Director Walter S. Skinner
Nicholas Lea	"Agent Alex Krycek"
Jonathan Gries	Salvatore Matola
Steven Williams	Mr. X [undesignated in episode]
Tony Todd	Corporal Augustus D. "Preacher" Cole
Don Thompson	Henry Willig
David Adams	Dr. [Francis] Girardi
Michael Puttonen	Dr. Pilsson [at V.A. hospital]
Anna Hagan	Dr. Charyn [at sleep-disorder center; unnamed in episode]
William B. Davis	Smoking Man
Mitch Kosterman	Detective [Lt.] Horton
Paul Bittante	Team Leader
Claude DeMartino	Dr. Grissom

extra

X-actitude

Dr. Grissom's address, 700 East 56th St., #606, New York, NY. could put his building smack in the East River!

Number of confirmed J-7 kills: 4,100

Cole's medical background: Treated by

• The actor who plays firefighter Lt. Regan is uncredited.

As subsequent events on the series strongly suggest, "Alex Krycek" is almost certainly a pseudonym. As a shadow-government plant – and assassin, *à la* the identity-free Crew-Cut Man – he certainly wouldn't have given the FBI his real name. Additionally, neither Smoking Man nor other shadow-government operatives have referred to him as "Krycek."

The Cast: For more on recurring guest Nicholas Lea, see his separate biography.

a Dr. Pilsson at North Orange, NJ V.A. hospital since being admitted 12 years ago. He was discharged with Pilsson's evidently forged or acquired signature.

There is no such town as North Orange, NJ.

Scully's report, based on the secret documents Mulder faxed her, describes an experimental neurological procedure to induce a permanent waking state. It included brain-stem surgery, explaining Willig's scar. The antidepressants Cole stole are consistent with drugs given to maintain high blood-levels of serotonin, produced by the body during sleep.

Tony Todd starred as the supernatural title character of *Candyman* (1992) and *Candyman: Farewell to the Flesh* (1995), and as Christopher Reeves' partner in the *Black Fox* Western TV-movie trilogy (CBS 1995). Todd got his start as one of the young ensemble cast-members of *Platoon* (1986), and has been in *Night of the Living Dead* (1990) and *The Crow* (1994). He's played the recurring role of Rhodes on *Homicide: Life On The Street*, and appeared as Lt. Worf's brother, Kurn, on *Star Trek: The Next Generation*.

Jonathan Gries played handyman Shawn on the first two season of *Martin* (Fox 1992–), and has guested on the 1980s *The Twilight Zone*, *Quantum Leap* and *Seinfeld*, among other shows. His films include *The Chicken Chronicles* (1977; his debut), *Running Scared* (1986) and *The Grifters* (1990).

The Repertory: Don Thompson had played a black-suited government thug in 1.04, "Conduit." Mitch [previously billed as Mitchell] Kosterman had played a suburban-D.C. detective also named Horton, in 1.14, "Genderbender."

X-File case: Classified

2.05 "DUANE BARRY"

Oct. 14, 1994
Writer-Director: Chris Carter
Part 1 of a 2-part episode

Pulaski, VA, June 3, 1986: At a large, gloomy home, a
man wakes and yells, encompassed by a flash of light
and the appearance of humanoid figures. A dog barks at
a spaceship hovering overhead. Memory? Or dream?
Years later, guards take the man, Duane Barry, through
a psychiatric hospital to meet with a Dr. Hakkie;
"Duane Barry" (who refers to himself in the third
person) swears he isn't crazy, and that his abductors are
coming back. He steals the guard's gun and takes
Hakkie hostage.

Washington, DC, August 7, 1994: Krycek, finding
Mulder doing laps in a pool, says four people are being
held hostage in an office building by someone claiming
to be an alien-abductee. Downtown Richmond, VA:
Police and the FBI have set up a command post across
from a storefront travel agency. The Negotiation
Commander, FBI Agent Lucy Kazdin, says Barry
demands safe passage for himself and Hakkie to the site
of his alleged abduction; unfortunately he can't quite
remember where that is, so he has stopped at this
travel agency. Kazdin had requested Mulder since she'd
heard he knows UFO jargon and could talk the perp's
language; she has no idea Mulder really believes this
stuff, and now will reevaluate his progress every three
hours to determine whether to storm the place.

When Mulder phones, Barry retorts he knows the

routine, and recites the words written on the command center's chalkboard – "Honesty, containment, conciliation" – and teases he forgets the last one, "resolution." Barry is a former FBI agent – let go in 1982, and institutionalized for a decade. Mulder demands Barry's patient records in order to understand him better. But Kazdin doesn't want to risk psychoanalyzing the guy, for fear it'll set him off. Krycek asks Kazdin what he can do to help; she sends him for coffee.

Mulder calls Scully, who is following the events on the news, to have her look up Barry's FBI background and his abduction experience. Night: At the travel agency, the lights and electricity go screwy and a panicked Barry fires five shots, inadvertently hitting hostage Bob Morris. He asks the police for a doctor [N]. Mulder, volunteering to impersonate an EMS medic, gets equipped with an

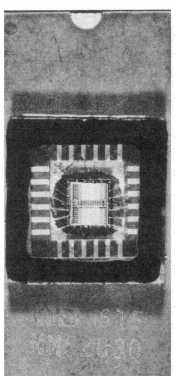

inner-ear receiver, and a microphone on top of his hidden flak jacket, and goes go in with trained medic Agent Janus. If possible, they're to get Barry near the front door so that one of three snipers can kill him. Mulder asks Barry if "they" were just here, and if time had just stopped. The questions makes Barry remember/imagine his abduction, and he exchanges Bob for Mulder – who is desperate to speak to an abductee firsthand.

As agents or police drill a hole for a covert video camera, Scully phones to tell Krycek that Barry is dangerously delusional. She later shows up to tell the hostage team in person that Barry has a rare psychosis resulting from being shot in the line of duty in 1982: The bullet destroyed the moral center of his brain, as in a [real-life] 19th-century case. Barry tells Mulder the government cooperates with the aliens, but wouldn't dare let the truth out. Mulder convinces him to let the women go; then as Barry gets enraged at

X-otica

Ah, the infamous red Speedo swimsuit scene! "Oh, that was completely gratuitous," Duchovny has said, hardly seeming unpleased at how that suit's become a female-fan icon.

This episode netted director of photography John S. Bartley a nomination for Outstanding Achievement Award for Episodic Television, by the American Society of Cinematographers. The Lowry book erroneously claims it was an Emmy nomination. It also marks Chris Carter's nicely done directing debut.

The silhouetted aliens in Barry's dream/recollection were played by several costumed kids ages 6-10.

Pulaski is a real town in rural southwest Virginia, at the foot of the Appalachian Mountains.

In-joke: With Gillian Anderson pregnant, Scully at the super-market is seen buying pickles and ice cream.

Mulder's wondering if he'd made any of this up, Mulder says Barry forgot to lock the front door. Doing so, Barry's shot.

Later, at Richmond's Jefferson Memorial, Kazdin tells Mulder Barry's critical but stable, and that his FBI career had been exemplary until he'd gotten shot with his own gun during a drug raid, and left for dead in the woods. Then she lays the bombshell: X-rays showed pieces of metal in Barry's gums, sinus cavity and abdomen, and tiny drill holes in his left and right rear molars – all as Barry had claimed. A dentist told her the drill-work couldn't have been done with available technology. Scully says it could be shrapnel from Barry's Vietnam duty. That doesn't address the gum and sinus metal – which an FBI ballistics expert says contain finely tooled or etched markings only 10 microns across. Later, at a supermarket, Scully exposes a piece of it to a cash-register scanner, which goes crazy.

At a hospital, Barry is jolted awake by white light and the images of aliens. The posted cop outside doesn't notice. Barry clubs him with a fire extinguisher and escapes. Scully leaves a message on Mulder's machine that the metal shard has numbers on it. Suddenly Barry breaks in and kidnaps Scully, as she screams on the phone for help.

CAST

Steve Railsback	Duane Barry
Nicholas Lea	"Agent Alex Krycek"
C.C.H. Pounder	Agent Lucy Kazdin
Stephen E. Miller	Tactical Commander
Frank C. Turner	Dr. Hakkie
Fred Henderson	Agent Rich
Barbara Pollard	Gwen [blond hostage]
Sarah Strange	Kimberly [brunette hostage]
Robert Lewis	Officer
Michael Dobson	2nd Marksman
Tosca Baggoo	Clerk
Tim Dixon	Bob [Morris]
Prince Maryland	Agent Janus
John Sampson	1st Marksman

extra

- The dog is uncredited.

X-actitude

Scully's office number at the FBI Academy: 555-2804

Name of travel agency: Travel Time

Barry's gun: 9mm Smith & Wesson handgun with one nine-round magazine

The Cast: Steve Railsback appeared in *The Visitors* (1972), *Helter Skelter* (1976), and as the title character of *The Stunt Man* (1980). He later starred in Tobe Hooper's *Lifeforce* (1985) and a host of small films.

Carol Christine Hilaria Pounder played the recurring role of Dr. Angela Hicks on the first season of *ER* (NBC 1994–), and previously played a head nurse on *Birdland* (ABC 1994). Pounder made her film debut with a bit part in *All That Jazz* (1979). She co-starred in *Bagdad Cafe* (W. Germany 1987; English-language), and has had prominent roles in such films as *Sliver* and

Kazdin's coffee: grande
2% cappuccino with
vanilla

Scully's supermarket
bill: $11.14; she pays
by check, aisle 1

Size of entire magnified
square showing part of
etched shard: 10
microns

Barry's heart monitor:
Life Force 9; his pulse
is 80

Receiver in Mulder's
ear: IntraAudio Mid
Aural Implant Receiver
model JD-111471

The aliens, per Barry:
Unspeaking, they can
read minds; Mulder
says abductees call this
telepathy a
"mindscan."

RoboCop 3 (both 1993) and telefilms like
Common Ground and *Murder in Mississippi*
(both 1990). Pounder also co-starred in the
sitcom *Women in Prison* (Fox 1987-88).

The Repertory: Fred Henderson had
appeared as an unnamed agent in episode
1.13, "Beyond the Sea." Stephen E. Miller
had played a key role as coroner Truitt in
the pilot. Robert Lewis and Frank C.
Turner had bit parts in, respectively, 1.11,
"Eve," and 1.21, "Tooms."

X-File case: Classified

2.06 "ASCENSION"

Oct. 21, 1994
Writer: Paul Brown
Director: Michael Lange
Part 2 of a 2-part episode

Opening credo: Deny Everything.

Washington, D.C., 11:23 p.m.: Mulder hears Scully's desperate message. At the police-filled crime scene, he speaks with Scully's mother, Margaret. By 11:40, Mulder's finished checking around [N]. FBI headquarters, 8:03 a.m.: Skinner meets with Mulder, Krycek, a silver-haired male agent, and a woman agent. Cigarette-Smoking Man observes. Skinner says Mulder's too close to the case, and has Krycek escort him home.

Route 229, Rixeyville, VA, 11:23 a.m.: Barry kills a cop who'd pulled over his speeding car (stolen from Scully, who is in the trunk). By 3:11 p.m. the FBI has the police-car video of the scene. Mulder, having gotten no sleep at home, has a video technician enhance the image – revealing Scully. At 4:03 p.m., hearing a tape of Barry describing his abduction site with words like "a mountain" and "ascending to the stars," Mulder realizes Route 229 leads to the Blue Ridge Parkway; the yellow pages display a tram ride, Skyland Mountain – motto: "Ascend to the stars." Krycek, in a car downstairs, phones Smoking Man to say he'll hold off Mulder until they locate her.

Route 211, Warrenton, VA, 5:43 p.m.: Krycek and Mulder, not alerting Skinner, are on the road to Skyland. There the tram-operator says that 45 minutes ago, he'd sent the man they're looking for up a one-hour back road, since the tram's had its cable refitted and is still untested. Mulder forces the operator to send him up anyway. Watching Mulder via video, Krycek knocks the tram-operator unconscious, moments before Mulder reaches the summit. He makes a cell call saying he'll leave Mulder hanging.

Mulder, getting no radio response, goes through a hatch to the roof. Seeing this, Krycek turns the tram back on, intending to kill Mulder and have it appear accidental. Yet Mulder goes hand over hand on the cable until he reaches ground. He finds Scully's empty car, with her gold-cross necklace in the trunk. A helicopter appears overhead, and Mulder hears Barry howling that the aliens took Scully instead. 8:46 p.m.: Search-and-rescue operations are underway, explaining the helicopter (though not who called for it and when).

At the summit, Mulder questions Barry, who says the black-suited men outside the office know all about Scully's abduction – but when Mulder turns to see them, they're gone. Mulder, losing it, starts to choke Barry, then leaves to calm down. He returns to find Krycek with Barry, claiming Barry was gagging. Skinner arrives, to see Barry collapse and die – from Mulder's choking? Or did Krycek poison him? Later, at the Academy, a pathologist shows Mulder evidence of asphyxiation – but she won't send toxicological results unless he goes through military channels. Quantico, she explains, is under military jurisdiction, and she claims there wasn't an FBI pathologist available that morning.

FBI headquarters: Krycek meets Smoking Man in the garage to ask how he should write the field report. Smoking Man instructs him to write the truth – Krycek's earned Mulder's trust, and now must preserve it. Krycek pointedly wonders if Mulder's such a threat, why not eliminate

X-otica

Scully's apartment
number remains 35,
but Barry's break-in
makes particularly
clear she's on a ground-
floor and not third-floor
apartment. (Eugene
Tooms had broken in
also, in episode 1.03,
"Squeeze," but his
mutant shape-
stretching abilities
would have allowed him
to reach hand-holds
and pull himself up
along a building's outer
wall to a third floor.)

Virginia State Road 229
does, indeed, pass by
Rixeyville, and Route
211, through
Warrenton.

him? Not policy, says Smoking Man: He
claims killing Mulder risks turning him into
a martyr. As for Scully, he says, "We've
taken care of that" – and implies Krycek
better not overstep his bounds. Conference
room, 10:36 a.m.: Skinner holds a meeting
that includes Mulder, the silver-haired man
and the female agent seen before, plus an
African-American man [who is not Mr. X].
Krycek backs up Mulder's testimony;
Skinner orders both to take polygraph
tests at OPC.

Outside the office of Sen. Richard
Matheson, 11:45 a.m., Mr. X informs
Mulder the Senator can't help him
anymore: "They have something on
everyone, Mr. Mulder." He suggests the
government wouldn't have killed Barry
unless it had something to hide regarding
Scully. Afterward, Mulder notices cigarette
butts in the car Krycek was driving even
though Krycek doesn't smoke. Mulder later
gives Skinner a document accusing Krycek
of impeding his investigation, and of
possibly murdering both a suspect and the
vanished tram operator (the first mention
of the latter's death). Skinner calls for
Krycek, and with a look as if to say events have taken a turn even
this company man can't accept, he tells Mulder he can protect him
only to a certain point. When they learn Krycek has disappeared,
Skinner declares he's re-opening the X-Files. Outside later, a hopeful
Margaret hands Mulder back Dana's necklace – he can give it to her
when he finds her.

CAST

Steve Railsback	Duane Barry
Nicolas Lea	"Agent Alex Krycek"
Mitch Pileggi	Assistant Director Walter S. Skinner
Sheila Larken	Margaret (Maggie) Scully
Steven Williams	Mr. X [undesignated in episode]
Meredith Bain Woodward	Dr. Ruth Slaughter [pathologist; unnamed in episode]
William B. Davis	Smoking Man
Michael David Simms	FBI Agent
Peter LaCroix	Dwight [tram operator; unnamed in episode]
Steve Makaj	Patrolman
Peter Lapres	Video Technician
Bobby L. Stewart	Deputy

extra

X-actitude

Barry's sweatshirt: University of Maryland

Song on car radio: "Red Right Hand" by Nick Cave and the Bad Seeds

Barry's official cause of death: hypoxemia secondary to asphyxiation

• Within the episode itself, the mysterious contact played by Steven Williams is still not called "Mr. X" in dialog. By episode 2.08, however, when Mulder tapes an "X" on his window in order to contact him, we can infer this is how Mulder himself designates the man.

X-act Location: Duchovny, dangling from the suspended tram, did his own stuntwork, by all accounts, not on a studio set but at an actual location above actual ground. Two Vancouver-area ski sites were used for these and related scenes: Grouse Mountain and Seymour Mountain.

Scully's gold-cross necklace: Given to her by her mother on her 15th birthday.

Scully's apartment-house street number: 1419; it's a brownstone with stone steps

The exterior of Mulder's apartment house is shown here as a white-clapboard row house with dark shutters.

The Cast: For more on Steve Railsback, see last episode's synopsis. For more on Sheila Larken, see 1.13, "Beyond the Sea."

The Repertory: Peter LaCroix had played the pseudonymous trucker Ranheim in episode 1.17, "E.B.E."

X-File case: Classified

2.07 "3"

X-File case #: X25693VW

Trinity Killers

Nov. 4, 1994
Writers: Chris Ruppenthal, Glen Morgan
         & James Wong
Director: David Nutter

Los Angeles, the Hollywood Hills, 12:41 a.m. In the midst of sex, the married, well-to-do Garrett Lorre is attacked by his lover, a shadowy woman he'd met at a party, and a man with a syringe. FBI headquarters: In his darkened X-Files office, Mulder flips a swimsuit calendar from May to the present November. He files his latest X-File – "Scully, Dana" – and puts Scully's glasses and badge in an evidence bag. Los Angeles: Mulder has been alerted to the vampire-like killing by news reports – he's waited three months for this M.O. to reappear. He impresses the crime-scene commander with his knowledge of the killers, whose pattern indicates they'll murder twice more by the week's end.

On a wall inside, "John 52:54" is written in the victim's blood; Mulder recites the Biblical chapter and verse about eating flesh and drinking blood for eternal life, and says the killers extract blood and store it. The cop wants to pair Mulder with a detective Gwynn, but Mulder demurs. Phoning blood banks to check on recent hires, Mulder learns the Hollywood Blood Bank has a new night watchman, "Frank." Mulder gets into the closed offices [N] and arrests a man slurping blood.

Police Interrogation Room 4: "Frank" tells Mulder he's "The Son," and he's with "The Father" and "The Unholy Spirit." He believes drinking blood prolongs life, and that only the other two can kill him. Mulder, by now convinced the man is not a real vampire, hopes

X-otica

There *is* no 52nd chapter of John – what Mulder accurately quotes is John 6:54.

This was the only episode Anderson missed because of her pregnancy.

exposure to the soon-to-rise sun will still frighten him into giving up the others. Yet after Mulder leaves, the sunlight burns the Son to death. A doctor suggests Gunther's Disease: congenital erythropoietic porphyria. Mulder – noting that the disease probably led to the creation of vampire myths in middle-ages Asia – comments that it only causes lesions and blisters.

They decipher an inkstamp on the Son's hand: "Club Tepes." There Mulder meets Kristen, who practically confesses to the murders. She take a syringe, pokes her finger, and offers Mulder her blood. When he turns her down, she leaves. With the Father watching, Mulder follows as Kristen takes a man she's picked up to a nearby closed restaurant, Ra. After the man beats up "peeping Tom" Mulder, the Father and the shadowy woman kill the man.

Later, Gwynn says the murder matches the killers' M.O. Forensic dentist Dr. Jacobs finds human bite marks from three different people. Mulder, having found Kristen's prints at the scene, pulls her license on the DMV computer – and sees she lived in the two cities where these "Trinity" murders last occurred.

Mulder and the police search her Malibu Canyon home; no one's there. Gwynn finds veterinary hypos, and a snakebite kit used to extract blood. Mulder finds blood-filled bread in an oven – but keeps it to himself and tells the cops she's skipped and won't return. Yet she does, at 2:15 a.m. – greeted by Mulder, who knows European legends about blood-baked bread as vampire protection. As she speaks with the weary and vulnerable Mulder, the kinky Kristen tells him she met John – "The Son" – in Chicago; he beat her, and in tasting each other's blood they got into "blood sports." One night John returned with two others and it all became "unnatural." They've since followed her around the country. Soon, with Mulder shirtless and shaving, they lustily kiss – while the Son, undead, watches.

At 6:47 a.m., John accosts Kristen in the hallway. He tells her he loves her and wants to atone for all eternity for beating her. He says to kill Mulder and drink the blood of his spirit – that of a believer. Brandishing a knife, she approaches Mulder in the bedroom, but instead stabs the hiding Father. The Son attacks Mulder in the hall, but Mulder binds him with electrical cord. In the garage, the female Unholy Spirit attacks Mulder, but Kristen guns the car to knock her down. As the vampiress tells Mulder something in Romanian, Kristen backs up and impales her on a wooden peg.

Kristen tricks Mulder away from the house, which she douses with gasoline. Having tasted the blood of a believer, she tells John she'll now complete the ritual by taking a human life – her own. She'll become one of them – and thus, can kill them in the fire. Firefighters later find four sets of ashes and bones – as a shattered Mulder stares at Scully's cross.

CAST

Justina Vail	The Unholy Spirit
Perrey Reeves	Kristen Kilar
Frank Military	John/The Son
Tom McBeath	Detective Gwynn
Malcolm Stewart	Commander Carver [uniformed cop; unnamed in episode]
Frank Ferrucci	Detective Nettles [glasses-wearing detective; unnamed in episode]
Ken Kramer	Dr. Browning [unnamed in episode]

Roger Allford	Garrett Lorre
Richard Yee	David Yung [Ra victim; unnamed in episode]
Brad Lorre	Fireman
Gustavo Moreno	[The] Father
John Tierney	Dr. Jacobs
David Livingstone	Guard [at blood bank]

Also, per Lowry (uncredited onscreen):

Guyle Frazier	Officer

extra

X-actitude

In addition to the X-File case number for the Trinity Killers case itself, this episode also reveals an X-File labeled "Scully, Dana: Bureau File #73317"; the unexplained number #650657 is in the lower-right corner.

The previous six victims:

In Memphis, TN: James Ellis; Linda Sun; and a Jesuit theologian.

In Portland, OR: a priest; the only son in a family of six children; and the owner of a New

• The official Fox *X-Files* website erroneously leaves Chris Ruppenthal off the writing credits. Both it and the Lowry book erroneously list the character of Detective Gwynn as Detective Munson. Lowry spells the character name "Lore," though the closed-captioning spells it "Lorre."

The Cast: Perrey Reeves was, at the time, the actress-girlfriend of David Duchovny. Based in L.A., she has worked steadily in television since 1989, appearing on *The Flash, Doogie Howser, M.D.* and *Murder, She Wrote* as well as other series and a half dozen TV-movies.

Frank Military is both an actor and a Las Vegas private investigator. As an actor, his films include *Last Exit to Brooklyn, Dead Bang* (both 1989) and *The Doors* (1991). Justina Vail's limited work includes the TV-movie *Journey to the Center of the Earth* (1993). Gustavo Moreno appears to have no other screen credits.

Age bookstore, "The Holy Spirit."

Club Tepes address: 8115 Hollywood Blvd., Los Angeles, CA

Ra address: 8428 Melrose Ave., Los Angeles, CA

The Repertory: Tom McBeath had appeared as a scientist in episode 1.09, "Space." Guyle Frazier, who's not immediately evident as a cop onscreen, would get more tube time as a Richmond police officer in 2.23, "Soft Light."

X-File case #: X256933VW

2.08 "ONE BREATH"

Nov. II, 1994
Writers: Glen Morgan & James Wong
Director: R.W. Goodwin

X-File case: Classified
Government denies all knowledge

Scully's mom, Margaret, reminisces with Mulder about tomboy Dana using a BB-gun given as a birthday present from her two brothers (one of whom is named Bill, Jr.). Then, a young man brings out a gravestone:

DANA KATHERINE SCULLY
1964–1994
LOVING DAUGHTER & FRIEND
"The Spirit is the Truth" I John 5:07

Later, however, Mulder barges into intensive care at Northeast Georgetown Medical Center, Washington, D.C. – where Scully lies unconscious, on a respirator, her mother at her bedside. When Mulder heatedly demands answers from a Dr. Daly, two security guards throw him out. Later, Daly tells Mulder and Margaret that Scully is in a critical condition and in a coma. Daly claims no one knows how Scully arrived or was admitted or administered to – and after every possible test, they still also don't know what's wrong. Moreover, Scully has a living will, specifying ending life-support once her Glasgow Outcome Scale reaches a certain level.

At Scully's bedside, Mulder meets Scully's New Agey sister, Melissa. On some other plane, Scully sits passively in a rowboat tied to shore, where Mulder and Melissa wait.

Back home, Mulder tapes an "X" to his window above his desk but hears nothing from Mr. X. At the hospital, a somber Frohike notices something odd on Scully's chart, abnormal protein chains in her blood, with an amino-acid sequence in an unknown combination. Byers says these protein chains are byproducts of branched DNA. It might be an "ID card" – or the result of grafting a human to something non-human. This DNA branch is now inactive – with poisonous waste products compromising Scully's immune system.

As a Nurse Wilkins takes blood, a man in an overcoat surreptitiously watches. Scully flatlines, causing a medical scramble – during which someone swipes Scully's blood sample. Mulder chases the Overcoat Man to an underground parking garage – where Mr. X puts a gun to Mulder's head, ordering him to stop. He says Mulder won't get *him* killed like his predecessor – "You're *my* tool, you

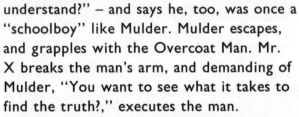

understand?" – and says he, too, was once a "schoolboy" like Mulder. Mulder escapes, and grapples with the Overcoat Man. Mr. X breaks the man's arm, and demanding of Mulder, "You want to see what it takes to find the truth?," executes the man.

Skinner's office: Smoking Man subtly threatens Skinner about the troublesome Mulder. Mulder, called in about the hospital incident, denies and obfuscates, accusing "Cancer Man" as the one responsible for what happened to Scully.

In an ethereal room, Scully lies on a table, listening as her ghostly father confirms his love and pride. In the hospital cafeteria, a woman chattily tells Mulder and Melissa someone left a pack of Morleys in the cigarette machine; too bad it's not her brand. Mulder, his antennae up, retrieves it to find an address inside.

At a shabby hotel, he bursts into Smoking Man's room. Smoking Man won't be threatened. Mulder demands, "Why her and not me?" "I like you," Smoking Man

X-otica

The episode title refers to William Scully's soliloquy to Dana, where he compares the length of a lifetime to "one breath, one heartbeat,".

For this episode, director of photography John S. Bartley was Emmy-nominated in the category of Cinematography for a Series. The Lowry book erroneously cites this nomination as for episode 2.05, "Duane Barry."

The character name "The Thinker" was inspired by the America Online *nom de plume* "DuhThinker," used by the highly knowledgeable online X-Phile Yung Jun Kim.

In 1.13, "Beyond the Sea," Scully confirms her father's Naval rank as Captain. In Scully's mind during this episode, however, she sees him with Admiral stars.

scornfully answers. "I like her, too. That's why she was returned to you." Talking Mulder down, the Smoking Man describes himself as having "no wife, no family, some power. I'm in the game because I believe what I'm doing is right . . . If people were to know of the things I know, it would all fall apart." He adds that if Mulder kills him, Mulder will never know the truth.

FBI headquarters: Mulder resigns. Skinner drops by Mulder's office, which he notes used to be a copier room. Mulder – facing his own obsessive nearness to murdering Smoking Man – confesses, "I've hate what I've become." Skinner sorrowfully relates how as a Marine in Vietnam, he'd killed a 10-year-old boy who'd entered his camp covered with grenades; later, he'd had a near-death, out-of-body experience. Now, "I'm afraid to look any further beyond that experience. You – you're not." Mulder, still quitting, carries an armload of files through the FBI garage – where he's startled by Mr. X, who tells him to wait for men who will search his apartment for Scully's file at 8:17 p.m. "You will defend yourself with terminal intensity," he says, offering Mulder ready-made revenge.

Mulder's apartment, 7:30 p.m: Melissa's come to tell him Scully's weakening. He says he can't go; they argue and she leaves. Yet Mulder, with a change of heart, is at Scully's bedside by 8:17. When he returns, his apartment is ransacked.

Mulder, breaking down, cries.

In intensive care, Nurse Wilkins notices Scully's eyelids fluttering. Someone phones

Mulder, who rushes to the private room to which Scully's been transferred. In good spirits, she remembers nothing after her kidnapping by Duane Barry. A relieved and grateful Mulder hands her back her cross. Later, Scully asks Nurse Wilkins for Nurse Owens, who kept speaking to her and encouraging her during her coma – but Wilkins says she's worked here 10 years, and there's never been any Nurse Owens.

CAST

Sheila Larken	Margaret (Maggie) Scully
Melinda McGraw	Melissa Scully
Mitch Pileggi	Assistant Director Walter S. Skinner
Steven Williams	Mr. X
William B. Davis	Smoking Man
Don Davis	Captain William Scully
Jay Brazeau	Dr. Daly
Nicola Cavendish	Nurse [G.] Owens
Lorena Gale	Nurse Williams
Bruce Harwood	Byers
Dean Haglund	Langly
Tom Braidwood	Frohike
Ryan Michael	Overcoat Man
Tegan Moss	Young Dana Scully

extra

• The children in Scully's flashback are uncredited.

The naming here of one of Scully's brothers – Bill, Jr. – marks the first time her father's name, William, can be inferred. He had not been named in his previous appearance.

X-actitude

Scully's chart: Dated 01/03/94, lab #0476.

Smoking Man's hotel: 900 W. Georgia St.

Mulder's waking-up gift to Scully: The videotape *Superstars of the Super Bowls.*

The skinny on Skinner: Enlisted in Marine Corps at 18. Served in Vietnam; when his entire patrol was killed by enemy fire, and he'd already been placed in a body bag, a corpsman noticed he was barely alive; two weeks later, he awoke in a Saigon hospital.

Continuity error: The previous episode had confirmed this episode takes place in November 1994 at the earliest; the following episode takes place Nov. 11–13, 1994. These facts together contradict the January 1994 date on Scully's chart.

The Cast: Sheila Larken, For Information see episode 1.13, "Beyond the Sea".
  Melinda McGraw appeared on *The Commish* (ABC 1991-95) for the middle two seasons. She also co-starred in the short-lived sitcom *Pursuit of Happiness* (NBC 1995).

The Repertory: Jay Brazeau had played a biologist in episode 1.15, "Lazarus"; Lorena Gale was an M.E. in 1.06, "Shadows."

X-File case: Classified

2.09 "FIRE-WALKER"

Nov. 18, 1994
Writer: Howard Gordon
Director: David Nutter

X-File case: Classified
Government denies all knowledge

Mount Avalon, Washington State – Volcano Research Team Data Room. Dr. Adam Pierce, watching the video feed of the otherwise disabled volcanic-exploration robot "Firewalker," sees chief seismologist Erikson dead, and a shadow moving in the 130°F temperature where nothing should exist [N]. FBI headquarters: Pierce tells Mulder and Scully he left the project six weeks previously after disagreements with visionary volcanologist Daniel Trepkos. Mulder worries about Scully going back into the field so soon after her abduction ordeal.

Back at Mount Avalon the agents enter the heavily damaged project office while Pierce inspects the satellite dishes and other outdoor equipment. Inside the darkened office, Mulder subdues an attacker, robotics engineer Jason Ludwig, who nervously claims he'd thought Mulder was Trepkos, whom he says has gone mad. Ludwig introduces systems analyst Peter Tanaka and Jesse O'Neil, both students of Trepkos.

In the woods, Pierce is garrotted by a soot-covered Trepkos. Later, Tanaka finds the body and brings it to the office. Mulder discovers references in Trepkos' work to an unknown subterranean organism. Scully argues that volcanic heat and toxic gases make that impossible. Mulder suggests that this might be a silicon-based lifeform. Mulder wants to search for physical evidence.

X-otica

The shooting script cited the inner-volcano temperature as 400° Celsius rather than 130° Fahrenheit. Good thing they changed it – the Celsius reading translates to nearly 752°F!

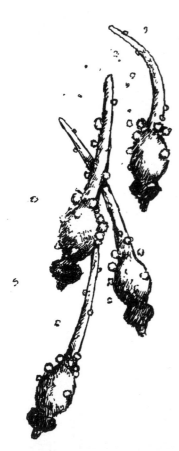

Jesse tells Scully that Trepkos became paranoid and stopped taking his medication, and that she's been here eight months and wants desperately to go home. Tanaka coughs, collapses, and turns feverish. Mulder and Ludwig carry him out on a stretcher while Scully radios for medevac – but Tanaka bolts for the woods, where a tentacle bursts through his throat. Scully analyzes it as a fungus of probably unknown genus; she believes a spore grew inside Tanaka, and eventually outgrew its host. Mulder notes that Tanaka's lungs contained sand – silicon dioxide, the theoretical waste product of a silicon-based lifeform. They need to find the means of transmission before they risk exposing the outside world; Mulder radios Search & Rescue to notify the FBI office in Spokane, and to have the CDC set up an evacuation unit on high alert.

Mulder, with the insistent Ludwig as guide, searches in the volcano for Trepkos – who kills Ludwig with a flare gun and sets him ablaze as Ludwig's throat begins to pulse. Topside, Scully has made seven unsuccessful attempts at culturing the spore, using temperatures ranging from human basal to volcanic, and nutrients of human tissue, blood, saliva, and even sulfur. She believes that unless ingested immediately upon release, the spore dies. Inside the volcano, Trepkos – saying he realizes now that the Earth holds some truths best left buried – tells Mulder that the robot Firewalker brought back a porous, obsidian rock Erikson pulverized for analysis. Trepkos then shut himself in his lab for three days, until he heard screaming: The team-members had been exposed to the spore, which grew in each until it *became* them. Trepkos destroyed his notes, and killed Pierce to prevent contagion. Mulder realizes that with Jesse exposed, Scully may soon be as well.

Indeed, with Jesse's throat about to burst – and with no other potential hosts available – the spore-enthralled Jesse handcuffs Scully and herself together. Scully desperately manages to shove Jesse into a lockable room, putting a door between them. Jesse's throat bursts, and splatters the window with spores.

Mulder, arriving with Trepkos, calls for Search and Rescue – but Army Biohazard answers. Mulder lies, stating that only he and Scully are here. Three days later: Mulder writes that they're in a month-long quarantine, undergoing Level 4 decontamination. The military confiscated all specimens and field notes, and sealed off access to Avalon. The robot was recovered, but too damaged to yield any data. While Trepkos and O'Neil are considered unaccounted for, we see Trepkos carry Jesse's body deep into the cave.

CAST

Bradley Whitford	Dr. Daniel Trepkos
Leland Orser	Jason Ludwig
Shawnee Smith	Jesse O'Neil
Tuck Milligan	Dr. Adam Pierce
David Lewis	Vosberg [opening-scene projection-member; unnamed in episode]
David Kaye	(TV) Reporter (Eric)
Hiro Kanagawa	Peter Tanaka
Torren Rolfsen	Technician

extra

- The official Fox *X-Files* website neglects to list front-credit performers Leland Orser and Shawnee Smith.

X-actitude

Date of the events, per Mulder's report: Nov. 11–13, 1994.

Volcano Research Team Data Room office number: 105

Cost of Firewalker project: Over $20 million

Real-life mountain range containing the fictional Mount Avalon: Cascade Mountains

Helicopter bringing the agents and Pierce from the Seattle airport: Cascade Search and Rescue. N-9747-P

Trepkos' medication: lithium carbonate

The Cast: Bradley Whitford had starred as private eye Dave Brodsky in the summer sitcom *Black Tie Affair* (NBC 1993). His films include *Adventures in Babysitting* (1987), *Awakenings* (1990), *Scent of a Woman* (1992), and *A Perfect World*, *Philadelphia* and *Robocop 3* (all 1993), the latter with fellow *X*-guest C.C.H. Pounder.

Shawnee Smith got her screen start as a dancer in *Annie* (1982). She played Bess Armstrong and Terence Knox's daughter on the sitcom *All is Forgiven* (NBC 1986). Chris Carter worked with her in his pre-*X-Files* series *Brand New Life* (NBC 1989–90). Her films include *Iron Eagle* (1986), *The Blob* (1988), and *Leaving Las Vegas* (1995), and the miniseries *Stephen King's "The Stand"* (1994).

The Repertory: David Lewis had a small role in episode 1.05, "The Jersey Devil."

X-File case: Classified

2.10 "RED MUSEUM"

Dec. 9, 1994
Writer: Chris Carter
Director: Win Phelps

X-File case #: XWC060361
Government denies all knowledge

Delta Glen, WI: Beth Kane, the single mom of young Steve and 16-year-old Gary, undresses to shower as someone watches through a peephole. The next morning, two deputy sheriffs find Gary wandering in the road, wearing only underwear – and with a red-marker notation on his back, HE IS ONE.

Sometime later, Sheriff Mazeroski drives Mulder and Scully to the Church of the Red Museum, which he suspects of cult-oriented activity. The Church occupies a ranch, where followers of Californian vegetarianism guru Richard Odin settled three years ago. At a mass, Mulder, hearing talk of second souls and the New Kingdom, says these are "walk-ins": believers in soul transference, in which enlightened beings take control of one's body.

Gary remembers little except a possibly animal spirit enter him. Later, as Mulder and Scully have dinner at Clay's BBQ, four teenagers including the sheriff's son Rick harass a Church member until Mulder intervenes. The next morning, clad only in underwear, Rick's girlfriend Katie stumbles through the woods, hallucinating. On her back is written: SHE IS ONE.

Scully learns Katie's blood contained traces of an alkaloid, possibly an opiate derivative, plus the controlled substance scopolamine, which in quantities above 2mg changes from motion-sickness remedy to

X-otica

Plans were afoot to make "Red Museum" cross over to an episode of CBS' *Picket Fences*, until CBS quashed that idea.

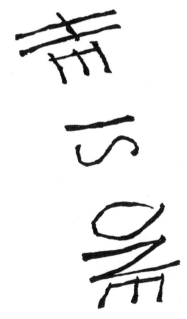

hallucinogenic anaesthetic. Odin, a.k.a. Dr. Doug Herman, was thrown out of the AMA in 1986. Graham County Sheriff's Station: While questioning Odin, the agents learn of a Red Museum demonstration at Clay's BBQ. There an older man in a red pickup asks to show the FBI agents something.

At a pasture, he points out two men injecting cattle with, he believes, BST (bovine somatropin) – a (real-life) genetically engineered growth hormone. One of them is the peeping-Tom, Gird Thomas. Later that night a local doctor Jerrold Larson is killed in a small plane crash. Investigating the wreck, Mazeroski and the agents find an empty chemical vial, a suitcase of money, and printouts of shipping orders listing credit-card numbers for families of the abducted teenagers.

At the pasture, Thomas leaves for the day. The crew-cut man who assassinated Deep Throat (episode 1.24, "The Erlenmeyer Flask") kills the other man, who was Thomas' boss. The agents learn Gary and the other abducted teenager had regularly gone to Dr. Larson for "vitamin shots." Mulder, noticing the peephole, finds a videocamera and tapes. Night: Thomas kidnaps Rick, whom deputies the next day find dead in the woods, with HE IS ONE on his back. Crew-Cut Man, gun in hand, leaves the woods. The agents pass Crew-Cut Man's car turning onto the road; Scully thinks she knows that face.

Thomas – the Kanes' peeping landlord – says he didn't murder Rick, but admits that he was the abductor. He wrote on their backs because Larson and "the tests" had made the kids "monsters." Larson conducted secret chemical experiments on them, and inoculated cattle with the same drug; after seven rapes in the small town, Larson had told Thomas' boss he felt responsible for the kids' behavior. Scully suddenly remembers where she's seen Crew-Cut Man before (possibly because some of Deep Throat's last words mentioned another secret inoculation experiment on kids).

The residual substance left in the plane-crash vial had been treated with synthetic corticosteroids containing unidentified amino acids. Scully suspects it involves Purity Control, the project from which she'd taken the alien/alien-human hybrid (in "The Erlenmeyer Flask"). Are they injecting kids with antibodies derived from alien DNA?

When Thomas' boss is found dead, Scully is convinced that Crew-Cut Man is responsible. Mulder has Mazeroski pack up every family on the credit-card list; Odin opens up the Church as their sanctuary. At J.A.S.D. Beef, where the injected cows are processed, Mulder finds Crew-Cut Man pouring gasoline around. Crew-Cut Man then locks Mulder in a meat locker. Just as Crew-Cut Man flicks his lighter, Scully, Mazeroski and deputies arrive and Mazeroski empties his gun into his son's killer.

Scully's report says the nameless man had no identity record, and his fingerprints weren't on file with either the FBI or the National System of Records. The inoculant was found to be an unstable, probably synthetic antibody of unknown origin; after three weeks of study, the components couldn't be analyzed further. The inoculated kids and some of their families developed a flu-like illness; the Red Museum members remained healthy, leading Scully to theorize they were the experiment's unwitting control group.

CAST

Paul Sand
Gird Thomas
[The spelling "Gird" agrees with both the closed captioning and other print sources; the Lowry book, however, spells it "Gerd."]

Steve Eastin	Sheriff Mazeroski
	[A deputy, leading the sheriff away at the end, addresses the sheriff in an indistinct mumble which the closed captioning records as "Bill."]
Mark Rolston	Richard Odin a.k.a. Dr. Doug Herman
Lindsey Ginter	Crew-Cut Man
Gillian Barber	Beth Kane
Bob Frazer	Gary Kane
Robert Clothier	Old Man (in red pickup)
Elisabeth Rosen	Katie
Crystal Verge	Woman Reading Words (at mass)
Cameron Labine	Rick Mazeroski
Tony Sampson	Brad
	(Rick's friend; unnamed in episode)
Gerry Nairn	1st Man
Brian McGugan	1st Officer

extra

• The actors playing the pilot, Dr. Larson, and Steve Kane are unidentified.

The official Fox *X–Files* website neglects to list front-credit actor Paul Sand.

The Cast: Paul Sand was the star of the James L. Brooks' creation of *Paul Sand in Friends and Lovers* (CBS 1973–74) which, though hammocked between hits *Mary Tyler Moore* and *All in the Family*, nonetheless bombed. Sand went on to a guest-star career in everything from *The Love Boat* to *Taxi* and *L.A. Law*. He played Dr. Michael Ridley

all likelihood, it's an assumed-name rental.

Number of shots the sheriff fires into Crew-Cut Man: Five. Since he kept pulling the empty gun's trigger, this means for some unexplained reason he didn't have a full six-bullet cartridge. Where did the other bullet go?

Famous "walk-ins," per Mulder: Abraham Lincoln, Mikhail Gorbachev, Nixon advisor Charles Colson.

Katie's small, mixed-breed dog: Pupperdog

Head of cattle at the Red Museum sanctuary ranch: 500

Scully's dinner at the barbecue restaurant: ribs

the second season of *St. Elsewhere* (NBC 1982–88), was a semi-regular in the final season of *Gimme a Break* (NBC 1981–87), and had recurring roles on *Camp Wilder*, *True Colors* and *Baby Talk*. He also headlined the cast of the anthology series *Story Theatre* (syndicated 1971), based on the Broadway play which had netted him a 1971 Tony Award.

Mark Rolston played Private Drake in *Aliens* (1986), and has had roles in *Prancer*, *Lethal Weapon 2* (both 1989), *Robocop 2* (1990), *The Shawshank Redemption* (1994) and other films and telefilms. Among his episodic credits are *Sledge Hammer!*, *Wiseguy*, *Murder, She Wrote* (as several different characters), *ER* and *Lois & Clark: The New Adventures of Superman*.

The Repertory: Gillian Barber had played an FBI supervisor in episode 1.07, "Ghost in the Machine." Lindsey Ginter reprises his role as Crew-Cut Man.

X-File case #: XWC060361

2.11 "EXCELSIUS DEI"

Dec. 16, 1994
Writer: Paul Brown
Director: Stephen Surjik

Excelsis Dei Convalescent Home, Worcester, MA: Nurse Michelle Charters peremptorily shuts off the TV set of frisky Stan Phillips and Hal Arden, and sternly tells attendant Gung Bituen there is no TV after 9 p.m. Minutes later, in an empty room, Charters is raped by some invisible entity.

FBI headquarters: Charters is suing the government since she can't get Social Security Disability or Workman's Compensation, and so must return to work around her alleged rapist, old Hal Arden, who in his five years there has continually harassed her. At Excelsis Dei, Scully and Mulder question the 74-year-old, who laughs at the allegation. A worried Stan watches, later warning Hal not to "ruin it" for all of them. Stan takes a mysterious pill, having found a secret stash; when he won't let Hal have one, Hal threatens to rat on him. Mrs. Dawson, the home's director, insinuates to Scully that Charters has a history of frivolous claims.

Hal chokes to death; Dr. John Grago, who provides medical attention here three days a week, tells the agents he had been successfully treating Hal for 11 months with an experimental Alzheimer's drug, depranil, an enzyme inhibitor that increases the amount of acetylcholine in the brain. Stan ignores Gung's warning about taking too many of the special pills.

233

Day Room, 6 p.m.: Grago points out former WPA artist Leo Kreutzer, as wheelchair-bound Dorothy tries to get old-timers Ben, Eddie, Gloria and Mabel involved in some activity. At 6:53 p.m., as the agents check out of their hotel, their investigation fruitless, Scully suggests high cholonergic activity could have caused a schizophrenia-like state in Hal; Mulder reminds her the attacker was supposedly invisible. Scully suggests environmental factors, like fungal contaminants that can cause delusional or violent behavior. When Mulder suggests Charters is faking, Scully retorts that her wounds needed 13 stitches and the head-blow resulted in a subdural hematoma.

Leo tells Gung he and Dorothy need more of the pills, but Gung politely refuses. Stan protests as his daughter, Mrs. Kelly, prepares to take him home; she tells the agents her two daughters are afraid to visit this creepy place, and that Stan had needed 24-hour attention

when he came here three years ago. Stan bolts from attendant Tiernan, who chases the curiously fleet-footed oldster to the top floor. Some unseen force pushes Tiernan through the window, and pries his fingers off the edge despite Mulder's attempts to save him. Tiernan falls four stories and dies.

Mulder tells Grago that Stan has been present at two deaths in 24 hours. The wheelchair-bound Dorothy tells Scully and Dawson there are unseen people here. Mrs. Dawson attributes this to senile dementia — yet we see three ghostly old men in bathrobes huddled around Scully. They may be real or just in Dorothy's mind (although the rape and the Tiernan events were demonstrably real). Grago tells Mulder Hal's autopsy revealed poisonous ibotenic acid; Scully says the trace amount wasn't necessarily fatal, but could have caused hallucinations.

Looking for Gung, Mulder breaks through a locked basement door to find a mushroom farm — and attendant Upshaw's

X-otica

Title translation: Latin for "glory of God." The episode title is spelled differently from that of the home as seen on-screen.

Worcester, MA is a real town.

The closed captioning misspells 'epinephrine' as 'ampinephrine.''

buried body. Gung admits it is his medicinal mushroom crop, but that he didn't kill Upshaw. These mushrooms have been used for centuries in his country, Malaysia; he had wanted to help the poorly treated residents here. The mushrooms also allow contacts with dead ancestors – and this place is full of angry spirits taking revenge for their mistreatment. The agents go to confiscate the mushroom pills, but they're missing.

Mrs. Kelly sees her father taking a pill, then hears Dorothy shooing away ghosts. Then both women see Leo being dragged across the floor by some invisible entity. Mulder rushes to Charters, screaming in a bathroom, where the unseen forces lock them inside as it fills with water; Gung finds the water main stuck. As Scully runs to get help, Mrs. Kelly screams that Stan is choking and needs Scully immediately; Scully tells Grago that Stan needs atropine, in case he, too, has been poisoned. Water pressure finally bursts down the bathroom door as Scully, Mulder, Charters and director Mrs. Dawson are all engulfed by the surge. After Grago administers atropine to Stan, Dorothy says the spirits have gone.

Scully's report, much later, says the Massachusetts Department of Health took over the home; they found traces of ibotenic acid in more than half the residents. Grago was replaced and his experiment stopped; most of his patients then had relapses of Alzheimer's. Gung was remanded to the INS for illegal-medication activity, to be deported. The government settled Charters' claim out of court.

CAST

Teryl Rothery	Nurse Michelle Charters
Sab Shimono	Gung Bituen
Frances Bay	Dorothy

Eric Christmas	Stan Phillips
David Fresco	Hal Arden
Sheila Moore	Mrs. Dawson
Jerry Wasserman	Dr. John Grago
Tasha Simms	Laura
	(Kelly; first name not given in episode)
Jon Cuthbert	Tiernan
Paul Jarrett	Upshaw
Ernie Prentice	Leo (Kreutzer)

extra

X-actitude

Mulder and Scully's hotel in Worcester: Hotel Hartley, rooms 206 and 210.

Mrs. Kelly's husband: Jack

Upshaw's wage: $5.50 an hour

Recently deceased resident: Mrs. T. Richardson

Boxing match on TV: Mike Tyson vs. a contender named Danelle.

● The official Fox *X-Files* website neglects to list front-credit performer Frances Bay. The Lowry book omits nearly half the cast.

X-act Location: The corridor where the flood was shot is at the abandoned Riverview Mental Institution in Coquitlam, B.C.

The Cast: Eric Christmas is best known as Sam Malone's parish priest, Father Barry, on *Cheers*, and the much more apoplectic priest in *Harold and Maude* (1971). He's also been in *Attack of the Killer Tomatoes* (1978), all three *Porky*'s movies, and *Wiseguy* (CBS 1987–90). Christmas was in the cast of *The Sandy Duncan Show* (CBS 1972), and has guested on *Roseanne, Coach, The John Larroquette Show*, and many other series.
    Equally prolific Frances Bay appeared on David Lynch's *Twin Peaks*, as well as in Lynch's *Blue Velvet* (1986) and *Wild at Heart*

236

> Hour that Scully began researching Charters' case: 6 a.m.
>
> Scully's stat request when Hal begins choking to death: 75mg of lidocaine, 1 amp of epinephrine, and a crash cart (defibrillator and related gear).

(1990), as well as in the films *Twins* (1988), *Critters 3* (1991), *Single White Female* (1992) and *In the Mouth of Madness* (1995).

Sab Shimono, recently seen in *Waterworld* (1995), first came to prominence in the movie *Gung Ho* (1986) and its spinoff TV series (ABC 1986–87). A former page for *The Tonight Show Starring Johnny Carson*, he's appeared on Broadway in *Mame, Pacific Overtures*, and *Ride the Winds*; his films include *Loving* (1970), *The Wash* (1988), *Presumed Innocent* (1990), and *Teenage Mutant Ninja Turtles III* (1993).

Prolific in TV-movies since 1992, Teryl Rothery has appeared in the theatrical films *Andre* (1994) and *Magic in the Water* (1995). She did the voice of Maggie Weston on the animated series *Exosquad*.

The Repertory: Tasha Simms had played the unwitting mother of an *in vitro* bad seed in episode 1.11, "Eve." Jerry Wasserman had a small role in 1.21, "Tooms."

X-File case: Classified

2.12 "AUBREY"

Jan. 6, 1995
Writer: Sara B. Charno
Director: Rob Bowman

Police headquarters, Aubrey, MO: Detective B.J. Morrow tells married detective chief Lieutenant Brian Tillman she's pregnant. He instructs her to go to Motel Black at 8 p.m. to talk. There a painful vision leads her to a field down the road, where she digs up human remains and an FBI badge. FBI headquarters, two days later: Scully confirms the body is that of legendary agent Sam Cheney. Mulder says Cheney and partner Tim Ledbetter were investigating three serial murders in Aubrey in 1942.

At the crime scene, Scully and Mulder find discrepancies in Morrow's story; when Mulder starts asking about her premonitions, Tillman hustles her away. Coroner's office, Examining Room C: Scully performs an autopsy on Cheney. Mulder describes Cheney's last case, where three raped and murdered women had "SISTER" razored onto their chests; the killer was never found. Scully, using a digital scanner, tries to determine if there's a matching razor pattern here. Morrow comes in, has a vision upon seeing Cheney's skull, then gets sick; to a sympathetic Scully, she confirms her affair with Tillman, and describes her nightmares. Morrow, to her surprise, says Cheney's cuts spell "BROTHER."

Tillman demands to know where they got these new crime-scene photos; Scully says they're from 1942. A shocked Tillman says three days ago, a young woman was found murdered with "SISTER" carved into her

X-otica

All the towns mentioned in this episode are fictional.

chest. An aide tells Tillman there's just been another such killing. At this latest crime scene, Morrow says the victim is a woman she's seen in a recurring dream. Later, at Lincoln Park, she tells the agents about it: A woman is hurt, in an unfamiliar house; Morrow looks in a mirror and sees a man with intense eyes and a rash; she then sees a monument, which she now draws. Mulder recognizes it as the famous Trylon and Perisphere of the 1939 World's Fair.

Later, looking at 1942 mug shots, Morrow sees the man from her nightmare. Highway 377, near the Missouri–Nebraska border: The suspect is Harry Cokely, living in Gainesville, NB since his release from McCallister Penitentiary on December 5, 1993. He was

convicted in 1945 for the rape and attempted murder of Linda Thibedeaux – carving "SISTER" on her chest before she escaped. Scully suggests Morrow has cryptomnesia – consciously forgotten information; maybe her cop father had discussed the case and the information remained in her subconscious. At Cokely's rundown house, the 77-year-old defiantly says he has served his time, and convincingly insists he was right here at 8:35 p.m. two nights ago.

Morrow awakens from a nightmare covered with blood – and with "SISTER" carved on her chest. She sees a young Cokely in the mirror, and collapses with visions – including one of the floorboard at her feet, which she pulls up. Neighbors, hearing the commotion, call the police; Tillman arrives to take Morrow to the hospital. Mulder finds a sack of human remains beneath the floor.

Memorial Hospital: Morrow swears Cokely attacked her. Tillman questions the old man, who denies everything. Scully tells Mulder that tests show that the blood found under the nails of the most recent murder victim is Cokely's. They visit Linda Thibedeaux, now a widow. She describes the 1940s rape, which happened here on her stairwell landing – where Mulder notices a photo of her and her late husband Martin at the 1939 World's Fair. She admits to having Cokely's child, which she put up for adoption. Scully learns the floorboard remains were Ledbetter's, and that a razor with possible fingerprints was found beneath Morrow's house – which Cokely had rented in 1942. Danny from the FBI calls to say he's tracked down Thibedeaux's son: police officer Raymond Morrow – B.J.'s father.

Morrow attacks Mrs. Thibedeaux, stopping when "SISTER" mysteriously appears on both of their chests; later, Mulder and Scully find Mrs. Thibedeaux alive. Scully, noting the new murders began after Morrow had found herself pregnant, deduces Morrow will go after Tillman next; Mulder believes she'll go after Cokely, now that she knows the truth.

Cokely, at home watching *His Girl Friday* on TV, finds his respirator cut. Morrow attacks. Minutes later, after Mulder finds a moaning Cokely, Morrow bludgeons Mulder and puts a razor to his neck. Cokely dies just as Scully and Tillman burst in, and Morrow becomes herself again. Scully's report says tests on Morrow remain inconclusive – perhaps a mutator gene activated previously dormant cells. Shamrock Women's Prison Psychiatric Ward, High Security: a very pregnant Morrow is on suicide watch after an attempted self-abortion. The fetus shows no abnormality . . . yet. Tillman has petitioned to adopt the child.

CAST

Terry O'Quinn	Lieutenant Brian Tillman
Deborah Strang	Detective B.J. Morrow
Morgan Woodward	Harry Cokely
Joy Coghill	Linda Thibedeaux

Robyn Driscoll	Detective Joe Darnell (unnamed in episode)
Peter Fleming	1st Officer
Sarah Jane Redmond	Young Mom
Emanuel Hajek	Young Cokely

extra

X-actitude

Cheney's last case: "The Slash Killer": three young women (Antonia Bradsean, Kathy Eberhardt, Laura Van Cleef), ages 25–30, disabled with a blow to the head, the word "SISTER" carved onto their chests.

Police "Slash Killer" file: HOM, RAP 942. Case 147815

Mug-shot: State Police 958674, in Cimarron County Catalogue No. 4756 (for year) 1942

Thibedeaux's address: 238 North 54th Street, Edmond, NB

Cokely background: Only son in a family

- The official Fox *X-Files* website neglects to credit performer Joy Coghill.

The Cast: Terry O'Quinn is best known as the star of *The Stepfather* (1987) and *Stepfather 2* (1989). He's played nice-guys-with-an-edge in nearly 50 movies and TV-movies since his big-screen debut in *Heaven's Gate* (1980), including the Launch Director in *SpaceCamp* (1986), Howard Hughes in *The Rocketeer* (1991), and Mayor Clum in *Tombstone* (1993). He played Citizen Reilly on several 1994–95 episodes of NBC's *Earth 2*.

Deborah Strang has guested on such TV series as *Quantum Leap, Sisters, Night Court* and *L.A. Law*, and appeared in the movies *Ramblin' Gal* (1991) and *Things to Do in Denver When You're Dead* (1995).

Joy Coghill has appeared sporadically in films since *The Parasite Murders* (1974), and has lately been seen in *Andre* (1994) and in the TV series *Sliders* and *The Commish*.

Morgan Woodward is best known for his two outstanding performances on the original 1960s *Star Trek*: "Dagger of the Mind," and "The Omega Glory." Two decades later, he played the recurring role of Punk Anderson in *Dallas*, among countless other episodic roles. His films

with five daughters. Lived in Terrence, NB (an hour from Aubrey, MO) in 1942.

Continuity error: Mulder's unseen but ever-helpful FBI friend, Danny, has the last name Bernstow in episode 1.04, "Conduit." But it's Vallodeo or Valodeo here per dialog. (It doesn't appear in closed-captioning.) The Lowry book erroneously spells it Valodella.

include *The Wild Country* (1970), John Cassavetes' *The Killing of a Chinese Bookie* (1976), *Which Way Is Up?* (1977), *Battle Beyond the Stars* (1980) and *Girls Just Want to Have Fun* (1985).

X-File case: Classified

2.13 "IRRESIST- IBLE"

Jan. 13, 1995
Writer: Chris Carter
Director: David Nutter

X-File case: Classified
Government denies all knowledge

Minneapolis, Minn. At a memorial chapel, a young woman eulogizes her friend, Jennifer. That night, the funeral director finds his assistant, Donnie Pfaster, has cut off most of Jennifer's hair. Pfaster is fired. Another day, possibly the next; Saturday: Scully and Mulder are at a Minneapolis cemetery with local FBI agent Moe Bocks and the mutilated corpse of Katherine Ann Terle. Mulder shoots down Bocks' assertion that aliens are involved, and suggests a cast of the area will show backhoe tracks. Later, a woman named Marilyn interviews Pfaster for a delivery-person job at Fificello Frozen Foods.

FBI Minneapolis office, next day: Bocks tells Mulder and Scully they've found more desecrated bodies, bringing the total to three in the last two days. Two had hair cut off them; the third had fingernails removed. To Mulder it suggests the work of an "escalating fetishist," who may resort to murder to obtain warm corpses. A queasy Scully writes a field report on necrophiles, and examines mug shots of local offenders.

Pfaster picks up a streetwalker and takes her to his apartment; he runs a bath for her and asks that she shampoo. Marilyn calls to tell Pfaster he got the job and can start right away. The prostitute complains the water is ice-cold, then grows alarmed upon seeing a

243

X-otica

The original episode title was reportedly "Fascination."

L.C.S.W. stands for Licensed Certified Social Worker.

collection of funeral wreaths around Pfaster's bedroom. She screams, and he pursues her. Later that night, the three agents are at a muddy field waiting for a body to be identified. The M.O. matches that of the escalating fetishist; he took not only fingernails, but the fingers. A prostitute IDs the victim as one of her colleagues. Next morning: Pfaster introduces himself to a suburban housewife as the new delivery-person, and creepily contemplates teenaged Lisa, one of the woman's three daughters.

Monday, Nov. 14, 11:14 a.m., county morgue: Three plainclothes men and a uniform cop appear with Scully for the streetwalker's autopsy. At a lineup, the identifying prostitute has no luck in determining a suspect. Los Cerritos Adult Education, that night: After a class, Pfaster approaches a pretty classmate to ask about their homework assignment. When he begins to menace her, she groin-kicks him and runs for help.

Scully dreams she is preparing to do an autopsy on herself; then, through the open eyes of her live self on the table, she sees the silhouette of a peering figure with pointed ears. At 11:21 p.m., Mulder phones to announce an arrest – but it turns out to be just a businessman with an assault history, who is quickly ruled out. Pfaster is held in another cell. Unnerved, Scully tells Mulder she'd like to concentrate on the forensic evidence back in Washington. Pfaster is released, after overhearing Scully's name.

FBI Latent Fingerprint Analysis Lab,

Washington: Agent Busch awaits the prostitute's body for blood tests. Scully, who plans to return to Minneapolis tonight, meets with social worker Kosseff L.C.S.W. (whose first name and middle initial Karen F. are later noted in 2.21, "The Calusari") at the Employee Assistance Program Office. Later, Scully learns Busch lifted a print from the woman's nail polish. Busch also says someone from Minneapolis phoned for her; when Scully calls Mulder to say she's modeming the print, she discovers it was neither him nor Bocks.

Bocks (having evidently matched the print to Pfaster's local arrest record) leads a raid on Pfaster's home. They find evidence including a refrigerated finger. Meanwhile Pfaster awaits Scully at the airport, having learned her arrival time from Busch. Trailing her car, he rear-ends her and makes her crash. Bocks'

X-actitude

Donnie Addie Pfaster background: Age 28. Grew up in the Twin Cities; went away for a few years, studied cosmetology, and returned to work as a funeral-home cosmetologist and attend night school to study comparative religions.

The books on Bocks: A paranormal buff; tells Mulder and Scully, "anything slightly freakazoid, that's the drill, call Moe Bocks" – an eerie image of Mulder grown older and never having found The

office: An African-American female agent reports they've found Scully's car; Mulder, at the scene, finds white paint stains and has Bocks send this evidence to Washington to determine the car's make and model.

In a deserted house, Pfaster runs a bath for the bound-and-gagged Scully – who momentarily imagines him as the apparently alien silhouette from her dream. Mulder and Bocks, having no luck with the paint sample, run a computer check on Pfaster's mother. They learn she wintered in Boca Raton, FL until her death a year ago, and owned a late-model white sedan; they look to see if she had a Minneapolis residence.

At that residence, Scully momentarily escapes from Pfaster; he recaptures her just as Bocks and Mulder lead a raid. The bruised and scraped Scully insists she's fine – until she breaks down and sobs while Mulder comforts her. In voice-over, Mulder makes the final report.

Truth. Friend at MUFON (Mutual UFO Network) who claims to know Mulder: Andy Schneider. Years on force: 22.

Mulder's football tickets: a pair of 40-yard-line seats for the Minnesota Vikings vs. Washington Redskins game at the Hubert H. Humphrey Metrodome.

Scully's airport locales: Charles Lindbergh Terminal; Lariat Rent-a-Car.

Necrophile mug shots – names and case numbers:

John (last name unreadable)
　83610272

Wayne (last name unreadable)
　49803212

Antonio (last name unreadable)
　58801297

Vick Sepa
　30227618

CAST

Bruce Weitz
　Agent Moe Bocks
Nick Chinlund
　Donnie Addie Pfaster
Christine Willes
　Kossef
Deanna Milligan
　Satin (murdered prostitute; unnamed in episode)
Robert Thurston
　Toews (unnamed in episode)
Glynis Davies
　Ellen (housewife; unnamed in episode)
Tim Progish
　Mr. Fiebling (unnamed in episode)
Dwight McFee
　Suspect
Denalda Williams
　Marilyn
Maggie O'Hara
　Young Woman (doing eulogy)
Kathleen Duborg
　Prostitute
Mark Saunders
　Agent Busch
Clara Hunter
　Coed (adult-ed classmate)

Results of paint analysis: Color is "ivory base," a two-step enamel used by three makers of late-model mid-size cars – an estimated 60,000 of them in the Twin Cities metropolitan area.

Katherine Ann Terle's life dates: 1975–95.

Previous deliverer on Pfaster's route: Skip

Friend whom Lisa is going to visit: Steve

extra   • Neither Lisa nor the female African-American agent, who have speaking lines, are credited.

The Cast: Bruce Weitz won a 1984 Emmy Award for his supporting role as Detective Mick Belker on *Hill Street Blues* (NBC 1981–87). A regional-theater actor through the 1960s and '70s, he broke into TV with a 1978 episode of *Happy Days*. Later, an appearance on the Steven Bochco series *Paris* won him a part on *Hill St. Blues*. Weitz joined the cast of *Anything But Love* (ABC 1989–92) in early '91, and played in *Byrds of Paradise* (ABC 1994). His other notable credits include the film *The Private Files of J. Edgar Hoover* (1977), and the TV-movies *Death of a Centerfold: The Dorothy Stratten Story* (1981) and *The O.J. Simpson Story* (1995).

Nick Chinlund made his film debut in *Lethal Weapon 3* (1992); he's since worked primarily in television, including a 1994 episode of *NYPD Blue*, and in an episode of the David Duchovny-narrated *Red Shoe Diaries*, "Auto Erotica."

The Repertory: Christine Willes would reprise her psychologist role in episode 1.21, "The Calusari." Glynis Davies, who played Tooms' attorney in 1.21, "Tooms," here makes the second of her many *X-Files* appearances. Dwight McFee had played a lawyer in 1.19, "Shapes," and a Blue Beret Commander in 2.01, "Little Green Men." Kathleen Duborg had a bit part as a young mom in 2.03, "Blood," and Mark Saunders a bit part as a doctor in 1.15, "Lazarus."

X-File case: Classified

2.14 "DIE HAND DIE VERLETZT"

Jan. 27, 1995
Writers: James "Chargers" Wong & Glen "Bolts, Baby!" Morgan
Director: Kim Manners

Crowley High School, Milford Haven, NH, Night: Four members of a P.T.A.- like group, the P.T.C. – Jim Ausbury, Deborah, coach Paul, and the unnamed school psychologist – call for a group prayer. They solemnly beseech the lords of darkness.

Night: High-schoolers Jerry Stevens and Dave Duran bring high-school girls Kate/Shannon Ausbury (see notes) and Andrea to the woods. The boys plan to fake a Satanic ritual in order to scare the girls and then get them drunk. As Dave reads an incantation, spectral voices murmur and rats appear. The girls and Dave run off, while a hand clutches Jerry's throat until he dies.

Crime scene, 8.55 a.m.: Sheriff Oakes tells Scully the teenager's been dead about 12 hours, his eyes and heart removed. Scully finds a book page with a partial title; Oakes goes to track it down. Then, toads rain from the sky. Later, at the school library, Mulder looks up the book traced to the torn page: M.R. Krashewski's *Witch Hunt: A History of the Occult in America* – last borrowed Jan. 16, 1995 by Dave Duran. Scully says tornadoes in northern Massachusetts probably accounted for the toads.

Substitute teacher Mrs. Phyllis H. Paddock greets the agent in a science-lab classroom. They interview Duran, and let him go. Outside the room, Ausbury wants to know which of his compatriots killed Jerry, who was displayed in accordance with the Rites of the Azazel; the others insist it was some outside force. Mulder notices that a drinking fountain drains counterclockwise not clockwise, which defies science. Paddock files papers in a desk drawer containing two eyes and a heart.

The school psychologist dismisses Mulder's question about the large number of recent student psychological complaints. Shannon, in science class, suffers a hallucination while dissecting a fetal pig. She bolts from the psychologist's office later when told her stepdad is coming for her. Outside, she privately tells Mulder and Scully a long, graphic story about unspeakable Satanic rites Ausbury and others conducted with her and her sister, whom Ausbury murdered at eight, making it appear like an accident. The agents question the Ausburys; mom tearfully swears 15-year-old Shannon had never been pregnant, and that Teresa died of crib death at eight weeks.

Paddock, the same day, prepares a (remarkably emotionally intact) Shannon to dissect a fetal pig for her final exam. Paddock solicitously takes Shannon's bracelet – which she uses as a talisman to enchant Shannon into slashing her wrists, killing herself. A grieving Ausbury learns his compatriots' plan to blame Jerry's death on Shannon, to get the police and FBI to close the case. Scully tells Mulder the regular science teacher – who'd taken just two sick days in 15 years – had contracted the rare necrotizing fascilitis, or flesh-eating bacteria; no one at the school knows anything about Paddock or who hired her. During a power outage, Paddock steals Scully's pen.

X-otica

The title is German for "the hand that wounds."

Crowley High is named after the famous occultist, sybarite and author Aleister Crowley (1875–1947).

Ausbury mentions that his family and religion have been in this town for seven generations. In mysticism, eventful things happen to the seventh generation, in particular to the seventh son or the seventh daughter.

The producers, no doubt fearing legal or bad-press repercussions, had Shannon specify that the parent-teacher group isn't the P.T.A., but the "P.T.C."

There's a real-life Milford, NH, but no Milford Haven.

The character names "Deborah Brown" and "Paul Vitaris" are those of Internet X-fans. Other fans' names have appeared in an airline manifest in the season opener, "Little Green Men."

With a warrant, Mulder searches the empty Ausbury home – where Jim Ausbury waits in the basement. The others' attempts to frame his stepdaughter have made him renounce his dark faith. Paddock performs a ritual with Scully's pen. Ausbury admits to Mulder he forced Shannon to participate in watered-down rituals, but never hurt her, and hypnotized her to repress the memories. Scully phones Mulder for help; Mulder handcuffs Ausbury in the basement while he rushes to the school – leaving Ausbury helpless when a large Burmese python slithers towards him.

Mulder finds Scully perfectly fine, saying she never called him. They rush back to Ausbury, but find only digested meat and bones next to a snakeskin. At the school, coach Paul tells the others he heard from Sheriff Oakes that Ausbury is dead. The psychologist argues they'll have to sacrifice Mulder, or the same will befall them. Scully and Mulder arrive to find an injured Paddock blaming the P.T.C. officials for killing Ausbury and Jerry. Investigating, they are attacked and bound by Paul and the psychologist. Deborah, with a prayer, raises a knife – then she and Paul are killed by two blasts from the psychologist's rifle – as Paddock, in another room, gloats. She blows a candle out, and the psychologist shoots himself. Mulder and Scully find Paddock gone – having written on her chalkboard: Goodbye.

The idiosyncratic writer credits refer to the upcoming Super Bowl XXIX. San Diego natives Morgan and Wong's home team, the Chargers, lost to the San Francisco 49ers, 49–26.

X-actitude

Student production the P.T.C. forbids: *Jesus Christ Superstar*.

Book that Mulder skims past in the card file: Stephen King's *Four Past Midnight*.

Krashewski book's file number: 354KRA. Two other borrowings:

May 17, 1994
  J. Schwartsky
Oct. 8, 1994
  L. Lemenchik

The agent's license plate: 6987N5

Paddock official background:
  Grossmont Union High School District 1992–94 (Substitute). Los Angeles Unified District 1988–89. St. Louis Municipal High School 1974–79. Education: University of California, Los Angeles, M.A.

CAST

Dan Butler
  Jim Ausbury

Susan Blommaert
  Phyllis H. Paddock

Heather McComb
  Shannon Ausbury

Shaun Johnson
  Pete Calcagni (School psychologist; unnamed in episode)

P. Lynn Johnson
  Deborah Brown (last name not given in episode)

Travis MacDonald
  Dave Duran

Michele Goodger
  Barbara Ausbury (unnamed in episode)

Larry Musser
  Sheriff John Oakes (first name not given in episode)

Franky Czinege
  Jerry Thomas (per end-credits; last name Stevens per episode dialog; spelling per script)

Laura Harris
  Andrea

Doug Abrahams
  Paul Vitaris (last name not given in episode)

Prayer at the end (Latin):

Deborah: *Dominus Inferus vobiscum* (The Infernal Lord be with you)

Men, responding: *Et cum tuo* (And with you)

Deborah: *Sursum corda*

What Scully finds during Internet research: Article from a 1934 Nazi newspaper, *Volkischer Beobachter*, blaming Jews for the type of ritual murders often blamed today on occultists.

extra • The official Fox *X-Files* website neglects to list front-credit actress Heather McComb. The Lowry book misspells the first name of actress Michele Goodger as "Michelle."

Continuity error: In the early scene with the high school kids in the woods, the girl who is later referred to as Shannon is here called Kate – both audibly and in closed captioning.

The Cast: Fans of *Frasier* would recognize actor Dan Butler as Bob "Bulldog" Briscoe. He has appeared in films including *The Silence of the Lambs* (1991), *Captain Ron* (1992), *Dave* (1993) and *I Love Trouble* (1994). His TV work includes two episodes of *Quantum Leap*, several of *Roseanne*, and *Caroline in the City*.

Heather McComb is familiar from *Beethoven's 2nd* (1993) and as Zoe in the Francis Coppola segment of *New York Stories* (1989), "Life Without Zoe." She played "X-Men" superheroine Jubilation Lee, a.k.a. Jubilee, in the TV-movie/pilot *Generation X* (1996), as well as Belinda "Scout" Jenkins in the 1990 Fox series *The Outsiders*.

Susan (a.k.a. Susan J.) Blommaert has appeared in the films *Crossing Delancey* (1988), *Pet Sematary* (1989) and *Edward Scissorhands* (1990), among others, and in TV shows including *Grace Under Fire, Mad About You*, and *Murphy Brown* (as secretary #44).

The Repertory: P. Lynn Johnson played a developmental psychologist in episode 1.22, "Born Again." Doug Abrahams was an unnamed FBI agent in 1.14, "Genderbender"; in that same episode, Michele Goodger had a leading guest role as Sister Abby.

X-File case: Classified

2.15 "FRESH BONES"

Feb. 3, 1995
Writer: Howard Gordon
Director: Rob Bowman

Folkstone, NC: Marine Private John (Jack) McAlpin explodes in anger at his wife and their baby boy, Luke. After two horrible visions, he slams his car into a tree adorned with a strange painted symbol. The following week, County Road 10: Scully and Mulder investigate; McAlpin's is the second suicide in two weeks among men stationed at the Folkstone I.N.S. Processing Center, housing 12,000 Haitian refugees. A month earlier, a ten-year-old boy had been killed under vague circumstances. At the tree, the agents speculate the graffiti might be a Haitian voodoo symbol (called a *ve-ve* or *vever*, though the episode doesn't specify).

Mrs. McAlpin says Private Harry Dunham had told her they'd found evidence of a voodoo curse – the same evidence found on a stool a ten-year-old had used to hang himself. At Folkstone, Mulder buys a voodoo charm from a kid, Chester Bonaparte. Commander Colonel Wharton says self-proclaimed revolutionary Pierre Bauvais instigated the riot in which the boy died.

Camp morgue: Dr. Foyle tells Scully McAlpin had no cardio-respiratory function, and his head was hanging. But when he pulls out the refrigerated slab, there's only a dog. Dunham, from McAlpin's squad, tells Mulder he'd seen McAlpin's head. At the brig, Bauvais tells Mulder the tree symbol represents a *loco-miroir* ("mirror of the soul"), which makes a person confront

X-File case: Classified
Government denies all knowledge

their true self. Later, the agent's car nearly hits a dazed McAlpin.

At the psychiatric infirmary, the unresponsive McAlpin is diagnosed with amnesia. Scully says gross errors like Foyle's have been known to happen. The medical report lists trace levels of tetrodotoxin, a poison found in puffer fish; Mulder says Harvard ethnobotanist Wade Davis found that this drug – which can cause paralysis and depressed cardio-respiratory activity – is a part of zombification rituals. Folkstone Municipal Cemetery: The agents check the grave of previous "dead" marine Private Manuel Guttierez; the body is missing, and the groundskeeper says body snatchers are a local problem. They find Chester collecting frogs; at a restaurant with them later, he says, that he sticks to frogs, selling them to Bauvais for 50 cents each. Scully notes certain frog species secrete bufotoxin, similar to tetrodotoxin.

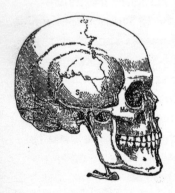

Outside, a nervous Dunham says Bauvais had told Wharton the Marines would have their souls taken one by one if the refugees weren't repatriated. Wharton responded by ordering his men to beat the refugees. Chester runs, but after the agents give chase, all they find is a cat. Next day: Wharton denies the beating allegations – yet to his horror sees blood seep from his breakfast. In the car, Scully cuts herself on a ring of thorns left there; when she drops it outside, it lands next to a *loco-miroir*. Wharton and his aide beat Bauvais, demanding to know his "secret."

Mr. X tells Mulder in 24 hours, Folkstone will be sealed from outside eyes. He says during a recent Haiti involvement, three soldiers – two of them Wharton's – committed suicide. Mulder deduces the military is letting Wharton have his revenge – which Mr. X pointedly doesn't deny.

Scully discovers Dunham's been AWOL since last night. She finds him dead in a

X-otica

Wade Davis is a real-life Harvard ethnobotanist and author of *The Serpent and the Rainbow*.

Folkstone, NC is a fictional locale.

The groundskeeper's Rottweiler is named Wong – a seemingly cutting reference to co-executive producer James Wong, who with writing partner Glen Morgan had scripted the previous episode then left *The X-Files* to create *Space: Above and Beyond*.

bloody tub; a zombie-like McAlpin holds a bloody knife. In the brig, McAlpin recalls little of the last few days, but he's signed a confession under pressure from Wharton – who tells the agents Bauvais cut his wrists with a bedspring and died, and the FBI investigation is over. Scully is growing oddly ill. Mrs McAlpin gives the agents a photo Dunham left for them – Bauvais and Wharton, chummy in Haiti.

Wharton's empty office: Wharton's aide detains the agents as they dig for evidence; they inform him Dunham and Guttierez were about to testify against Wharton, and show him both Guttierez's dog-tags, and his bones in a trunk. The aide confesses they buried Bauvais in a municipal graveyard. There, Wharton prepares Bauvais' casket for a voodoo rite. Mulder goes after Wharton as he chants an incantation, while an ill Scully waits in the car – and as liquid pours from her hand wound, a Creole-speaking man grabs her throat. Baivais appears, and downs Wharton with dusty breath. In the car, Scully desperately reaches for the protective charm; upon grabbing it, her blood and the assailant vanish – and a black cat appears. Next day: the refugees are being shipped out. Scully asks about Chester – a marine says the boy had died in that riot six weeks ago. As the groundskeeper's loud steam shovel pours dirt onto a casket, Wharton bangs and screams unheard inside.

CAST

Bruce Young	Pierre Bauvais
Daniel Benzali	Commander Wharton
Jamil Walker Smith	Chester Bonaparte
Matt Hill	Private Harry Dunham
Callum Keith Rennie	Groundskeeper
Steven Williams	Mr. X.
Kevin Conway	Private (Jack) McAlpin
Katya Gardner	Robin (McAlpin; first name not given in episode)
Roger Cross	Private Kittel (Wharton's aide; unnamed in episode)
Peter Kelamis	Lieutenant Foyle (rank not given in episode)

Uncredited:

Adrien Malebranche	Skinny man accosting Scully

extra

• The child or children playing infant Luke are uncredited.

The Cast: Daniel Benzali stars as Ted Hoffman in *Murder One* (ABC 1995–). He played James Sinclair in *NYPD Blue*, and has appeared in supporting roles in such films as *A View to a Kill* (1985, his screen debut), *The Last Days of Patton* (1986 TV-movie), *Citizen Cohn* (HBO 1992), and *The Distinguished Gentleman* (1992).

Bruce Young played Sergeant Addabbo in *21 Jump Street*, and co-starred in the parody series *Max Monroe: Loose Cannon* (CBS 1990). Young made his screen debut in *Thief*

Dunham background: In his hometown of New Orleans, he was to marry the daughter of Clyde Jessamin, an associate of Dunham's father. Jessamin's crooked business dealings enraged a voodoo practitioner, and the man's daughter died of some mysterious ailment – her autopsy revealed snakes in her belly.

(1981), and has had roles in *Risky Business* (1983), *C.A.T. Squad: Python Wolf* (1988 TV-movie), and *Lethal Weapon 2* (1989).

Matt Hill played Raphael in *Teenage Mutant Ninja Turtles III* (1993).

Jamil Walker Smith has guested on *A Whole New Ballgame* and *Hangin' With Mr. Cooper*.

The Repertory: Callum Keith Rennie had played a gun-moll's lowlife brother in episode 1.15, "Lazarus"; Peter Kelamis also had a small role in that episode. Katya Gardner had played the wheelchair-bound young woman who gets hit by a truck in the pilot; the actress was there credited as Katya Gardener.

X-File case: Classified

2.16 "COLONY"

Feb. 10, 1995
Teleplay: Chris Carter
Story: David Duchovny & Chris Carter
Director: Nick Marck
Part 1 of a 2-part episode

Mulder's voice is heard over a fierce Arctic night, as a medevac helicopter ferries him to a rescue ship. He tells himself, however, that if he dies now, it'll be knowing his belief in alien visitation has been justified. Scully bursts in, seeing Mulder on monitors and a respirator, and immersed in a tub of water. She declares he can't be warmed – the cold is all that's keeping him alive. She argues with the doctors until, in horror, she hears his heart monitor flatline.

The Beaufort Sea, the Arctic: a mysterious light has been hovering over a research vessel for 20 minutes; then it accelerates too rapidly for any helicopter, and crashes in a mushroom cloud. Two days later, Woman's Care Family Services and Clinic, Scranton, PA: The TV news calls the "UFO" a Russian aircraft; the unnamed pilot miraculously survived, but escaped his Alaska hospital. After seeing the Pilot's face, Dr. Landon Prince bolts in terror. But the Pilot stops him and demands, "Where is he?" When the doctor says he doesn't know, the Pilot stabs him with a stiletto-like weapon – drawing green "blood" from the doctor's neck. He then sets the building on fire.

FBI headquarters: Mulder has received three obits in his e-mail, all of doctors who've died in arson fires at their respective abortion clinics over the last two weeks. From their pictures, they could be triplets –

except that Mulder can't find anything about their birth or past. Scranton: A police sergeant tells Scully and Mulder he has arrested the Rev. Calvin Sistrunk, a local anti-abortion activist who has threatened Prince. The officer confirms no body was found at the fire site – just as in the last two cases. Sistrunk denies involvement, despite being arrested with a newspaper clipping of the doctor's photo in a classified ad.

The Globe and Mail, Binghamton, NY: A clerk remembers that the ad-buyer paid in cash and refused to sign anything. The agents find 24 messages in the ad-buyer's voice-mail, the latest claiming the man is Dr. Aaron Baker of Syracuse, NY.

They contact Agent Barrett Weiss (whose first name isn't given until the next episode) at the Syracuse field-office. Outside Baker's house, Weiss hears the Pilot warn Baker that his plans will not

succeed. Weiss bursts into Baker's house and to his horror sees Baker turn into green ooze; when he shoots the menacing Pilot, green "blood" harmlessly pours from the wounds. After Mulder and Scully arrive, Weiss tells them Baker's long gone. Then, out of sight, "Weiss" throws his car keys into his trunk – where the real Weiss lies dead. Morphing, the Pilot resumes his original form and leaves.

FBI headquarters: With an agent dead, an angry Skinner terminates the case. Mulder and Scully get e-mail showing yet another lookalike doctor: James Dickens, there in D.C. Outside Scully's apartment house, they are approached by a man identifying himself as Ambrose Chapel, CIA. He says the CIA has known of the identical people for 10 years; he claims that early in the Cold War, the Russians isolated genetic material in identical twins, learned to reproduce it, and eventually created human clones. The program was code-named "Gregor," the name given to each clone.

X-otica

The green liquid that the clones and the Pilot bleed appears to be the same as that spilled by Dr. Secare when he's shot by police in the opening of episode 1.24, "The Erlenmeyer Flask." Secare wasn't an alien or a clone, but a terminally ill human who underwent treatment with a synthesized extraterrestrial virus. There is likely to be some deliberate connection, since the props and makeup people could have easily come up with another eerie color.

Note: even after Scully had seen "Chapel" at the warehouse and left the scene, the man never morphed into the Pilot. Perhaps it really *is* CIA Agent Chapel who is working in tandem with the alien.

Chris Carter had originally wanted

The Gregors slowly emigrated to the U.S., obtained high-security clearances at government medical facilities, and now stand poised to contaminate the nation in event of war. In a secret agreement, he says, the U.S. is allowing the clones to be killed in exchange for Russia ending the program and sharing the science. Chapel placed the classified ad to save the Gregors, asserting he, like them, can't stomach state-sanctioned murder and wants the truth to come out.

Chapel accompanies the agents to Dickens' apartment in suburban Germantown, MD. Upon seeing Chapel, Dickens jumps three or four stories to the street and, incredibly, gets up and runs away. A woman in the apartment has kept herself hidden. Mulder and Chapel give chase; after Mulder's knocked down by a car, "Chapel" morphs into the Pilot. By the time the agents catch up, he's turned back into Chapel, saying Dickens escaped onto a roof. He leaves to go and search – as Scully notices green ooze underfoot.

Mulder's office: Scully can't believe Mulder took the CIA man at his word. Scully, upon learning Chapel's a CIA veteran of 17 years, wonders how someone so experienced could lose such an easy fugitive. She then displays an acid-like hole in one of her new shoes – evidently from the ooze she stepped in; they'll have it analyzed. Scully, doing an autopsy on Weiss, finds polycythemia, excessive production of red blood cells – Weiss' blood had curdled – yet she can find no coagulating agent. Skinner informs Mulder

Darren McGavin to play Mulder's father, but their schedules did not work out.

Scranton, PA; Binghamton and Syracuse, NY; Germantown, MD, and West Tisbury, MA, on the island of Martha's Vineyard, are all actual locales. Tilestown, VA is fictional.

of a family emergency involving his dad, William (whose name isn't given in this episode, but later in 2.25, "Anasazi"). Mulder's divorced mom answers the phone at his father's house. His mother tells Fox to rush home.

Scully, finding an address tag on the briefcase she'd collected at Dickens' apartment, tracks it to a Germantown warehouse. Inside, she finds congealed ooze on the floor, and Chapel – either the Pilot or, perhaps, the *real* Chapel – knocking over a green cylindrical chamber and squishing the organs that fall out. When he notices her, Scully tears out and hides in her apartment. [N] West Tisbury, Martha's Vineyard, MA: Mulder's enigmatic father and emotionally scarred mother introduce him to a thirtyish woman with reddish-brown hair – whom his father identifies as Fox's sister, Samantha. Fox doesn't realize it, but it's evidently the woman from Dickens' apartment.

Around 5:30 a.m., after hours of talking with her, Mulder assures his mother that it *is* Samantha; indeed, the young woman jokingly asks if Fox wants to play that game of Stratego they were about to start 22 years ago. She tells him she had returned at age nine or 10 with no memory, and was raised by adoptive parents; years later, anxiety prompted her to try regression hypnotherapy – and everything about the abduction and testing came back. She says she's in danger from a bounty hunter who had been killing "my father" and the other doctors, whom she says are aliens. Though the hunter can change his appearance, she herself can always recognize him – one reason he's coming to kill her.

Scully, on a bus, calls Mulder, saying she'll be hiding at the Vacation Village Motor Lodge off I-90 in Germantown. A few passengers away, the Pilot listens. She stops at the warehouse to examine its lab – and finds a clone/alien fetus and four grown clones, who say they're the last and ask for protection. Shortly thereafter, Scully hands them over to a federal marshal and police, for placement in maximum protective custody. The Pilot watches. Mulder phones the motel, just missing Scully as she checks in; the clerk forgets to give her the message. Mulder tries her cell-phone a few minutes later, but she's in the shower and doesn't hear. Federal Stockade, Tilestown, VA, 7:05 p.m.: The Federal Marshal appears at the clones' cells – it's the Pilot. At 11:21 p.m., Mulder arrives at Scully's room – or so it seems until her cell-phone rings . . . and it's Mulder.

CAST

Mitch Pileggi	Assistant Director Walter S. Skinner
Peter Donat	William Mulder
Brian Thompson	The Pilot
Dana Gladstone	"Dr. Landon Prince"/"Dr. James Dickens"/other duplicates
Megan Leitch	Samantha Mulder (evidently)
Tom Butler	"CIA Agent Ambrose Chapel"
Tim Henry	Federal Marshal
Andrew Johnston	Agent Barrett Weiss
Rebecca Toolan	Mulder's Mother
Ken Roberts	Motel Proprietor
Michael Rogers	1st Crewman
Oliver Becker	2nd Doctor
James Leard	Sergeant Al Dixon (unnamed in episode)
Linden Banks	Rev. (Calvin) Sistrunk
Bonnie Hay	Field Doctor
Kim Restell	Newspaper Clerk
Richard Sargeant	Captain
David L. Gordon	FBI Agent (who gets Mulder from autopsy room)

Uncredited:

Capper McIntyre   First Jailer (non-speaking role, just before end-of-shift changeover to mustached guard)

Michael McDonald   Military Policeman (not evident in episode; named in several print sources)

Continuity error: The exterior of Scully's apartment house, previously shown as a brownstone with stone steps, is here a red-brick building with a large blue front door.

X-actitude

The doctors whose obits Mulder received:

Dr. Landon Prince, of Scranton, PA
Dr. Dale Gayhart, of New York City
Dr. Harvey Buchanon, of Teaneck, NJ

Voice-mail access number for the newspaper classified ad: 236

Dr. Aaron Baker address: 737 26th St., Syracuse, NY

Tag on Dickens' briefcase, confirming his name and the warehouse address: Dr. James Dickens, 3243

The Cast: Peter Donat is the nephew of Robert Donat (1905–58), who won the Academy Award for Actor for *Goodbye, Mr. Chips* in 1939, and who starred in *The 39 Steps, The Private Life of Henry VIII* and other classics.

Donat, who here makes the first of four appearances as Mulder's cold father, has appeared in *Glory Boy* (1971), *The Godfather, Part II* (1974), *The China Syndrome* (1979), *The War of the Roses* (1989), and the baseball biopic *The Babe* (1992). On TV, he was in *Rich Man, Poor Man – Book II* (the 1976–78 TV-series) and *Flamingo Road* (NBC 1981). He also played recurring bad-guy Dr. Mordecai Sahmbi in *Time Trax* (syndicated 1992–94), and has guested on *Murder, She Wrote, The Days and Nights of Molly Dodd*, Showtime's 1990s *The Outer Limits*, and other shows.

Megan Leitch has appeared in small roles in the miniseries *Stephen King's "IT"* (1990), the TV-movies *Omen IV: The Awakening* (1991) and *Jack Reed: A Killer Amongst Us* (1996), and the films *The*

Edmonton St., Germantown, MD 21401. (The Germantown zip code is in reality 29874.)

Mulder's medical condition: severe hypothermia – basal temperature 86°F, pupils dilated, heartbeat bare.

Resurrected and *Knight Moves* (1992), among other projects. She's guested on an episode of *The Commish*, and on the CBC series *Mom, P.I.*

Dana Gladstone has appeared in films including *Beverley Hills Cop II* (1987) and *The Tie That Binds* (1995), and guested on *Amazing Stories, Beauty And The Beast, Picket Fences, Space Rangers, NYPD Blue*, and other shows.

Brian Thompson has been in *Star Trek: Generations* (1994), *Miracle Mile* (1988), *Cobra* (1986), and *The Terminator* (1984).

The Repertory: Andrew Johnston was memorable as test pilot Lt. Col. Robert Budahas in 1.02, "Deep Throat." Tom Butler had played the electrocuted CEO in episode 1.07, "Ghost in the Machine." Michael Rogers had a small role in 1.10, "Fallen Angel." James Leard, the police sergeant, had played a police captain in 1.24, "The Erlenmeyer Flask."

X-File case: Classified

2.17 "END GAME"

Feb. 17, 1995
Writer: Frank Spotnitz
Director: Rob Bowman
Part 2 of a 2-part episode

In a possible flashback, the nuclear submarine USS *Allegiance*, Beaufort Sea, cruises 87 miles north of Deadhorse, AK. Sonar detects an object, 80 meters across, emitting an apparently random pattern of radio signals from 200 meters below the ice. After the Captain informs Pacific Command of their discovery an Admiral orders them to torpedo it. Once at the site, the sub's reactor goes down, stranding them below 32 feet of ice.

The present: Vacation Village Motor Lodge: With inhuman speed, "Mulder" disarms Scully and knocks her into a wall. When she doesn't say where Mulder is, he throws her through a glass table, knocking her unconscious. When Mulder breaks in later, with Samantha, Scully's gone. Samantha says the alien bounty hunter is using Scully as bait to get her – since she knows the only way to kill him, by piercing the base of his skull. She warns Fox that human exposure to the alien's blood is fatal (à la Weiss).

Mulder's apartment: 12:38 a.m.: Samantha reveals the apparent aliens are the cloned progeny of two original visitors, and have been trying to form a colony since the 1940s. Since the clones look identical, the colony has dispersed all over the United States. They work in abortion clinics to gain access to fetal tissue, so that

X-File case: Classified
Government denies all knowledge

they can combine human and alien DNA to create non-identical progeny. The bounty hunter was sent to end this practice that dilutes the alien race. Mulder doesn't accept her story. Skinner unexpectedly arrives, asking what Mulder knows about Scully putting four men into protective custody – because they've vanished. A wounded Scully calls from a pay phone, saying her captor wants the woman who's with her. The Pilot demands that Mulder meet him at Old Memorial Bridge in Bethesda, MD in one hour.

Mulder asks Skinner for help. An hour later, near the bridge, Skinner hides with a sharpshooter. Mulder and Samantha make the exchange, and the Pilot enigmatically orders Samantha to tell him where she is. The sharpshooter, finally getting a clear shot at the one vulnerable spot, fires – and the Pilot and Samantha fall into the river. Daylight: The FBI drags the river for bodies. Scully arrives, having

been discharged from the hospital an hour ago. Mulder finally tells her that her captor was an alien; he has told Skinner as well. Later, at his apartment, Mulder breaks the news to his father, who accuses him of trading his own sister for his partner. Mulder breaks down, and his father leaves – but not before dropping an envelope from Samantha for Fox: With it is an ID access card for the Women's Health Services Clinic.

As he arrives, Scully cell-phones to say Samantha's body was found – but not the man's. After a despondent Mulder hangs up, paramedics call Scully over to see "Samantha's" body dissolving into green ooze. Mulder, inside the seemingly deserted clinic, finds a woman in surgical scrubs – another "Samantha." She beckons Mulder to a room with green cylinders – and yet another "Samantha." They knew she could be manipulated. They introduce him to the indispensable original "Samantha" (the "she" whom the Pilot

X-otica

We say the clones are "apparent" aliens since the series has already established (in episode 1.11, "Eve") that the U.S. had been involved in the "Litchfield Project" cloning experiment since the 1950s. Deep Throat truthfully admitted to the existence of psychotic Eves; he'd also said there were Adams, establishing that males were also being cloned.

What about the fact that female clones knew so much about Samantha? Doesn't *that* indicate they're aliens? Not necessarily – since Samantha may not even have *been* kidnapped by aliens. Consider that: A) we've learned in 1.02, "Deep Throat," the U.S. uses alien technology to build alien-like aircraft; B) that in 3.10, "731," Scully is perhaps truthfully told by one of the shadow-government

asked Mulder's Samantha about). Mulder, devastated, declaring he is not their savior, walks away. But the original stops him. They know where Samantha is – how else would they have known so many intimate details? A fire alarm heralds the Pilot, who has followed Mulder and now beats him up; when Mulder is rescued by firefighters later, he is informed they found no one else there.

FBI headquarters: Scully writes in her report that Mulder was treated at Samaritan Hospital and released in satisfactory condition. Many aspects of the case "defy explanation," but she states that Mulder's claim of alien involvement remains unsubstantiated. The mysterious man has now been charged with the murder of Weiss, whose body has been quarantined at the U.S. Medical Research Institute of Infectious Diseases; there warmth triggered mass production of red blood cells, which the researcher controlled by lowering the temperature five degrees.

Kennedy Center, Washington, DC: Mulder meets Mr. X, who says the aliens are all dead. Mulder replies there is still the bounty hunter, and that a nuclear sub had located his craft in the Beaufort Sea five days ago; X informs him an attack fleet is now on the way to destroy it. Mulder's apartment: Scully finds e-mail addressed to her from Mulder, asking her not to follow and risk her life. She goes to Skinner, but all he knows is that Mulder wanted time off – and warns her that Mulder's unsanctioned actions could put both his *and* her career

"elders" that she and presumably other women (and perhaps Duane Barry) were abducted not by aliens but by the government; and C) that in 3.01, "The Blessing Way," Fox's mother says Samantha's abduction was prearranged and agreed upon by William Mulder – confirming government involvement, and indicating that while Samantha may have been abducted by aliens in league with the government, it may *also* mean she was abducted by Earth forces alone, using recovered alien high-tech.

Now, the Pilot – *he* seems a genuine alien: we've seen no indication of Earth-alien hybridization technology advancing beyond the relatively crude Purity Control that created Dr. Secare – a far cry from the astonishingly morphing

and life at risk. Back at Mulder's, Scully sleeps on his couch (evidently hoping for an e-mail or some other clue to his whereabouts). Mr. X, with whom Scully isn't familiar, knocks; he unconvincingly claims he's at the wrong door, and leaves. As he gets off the elevator on the ground floor, he's accosted by Skinner, who wants to know where Mulder is. After a vicious fight, Skinner appears at Mulder's to give Scully Mulder's Arctic coordinates.

In that wasteland, Mulder finds the stranded USS *Allegiance*'s conning tower above the ice. Inside, he finds but one survivor, identifying himself as Lt. Terry Wilmer, who says a man came, sealed most of the crew below without air, and executed the rest; Wilder had survived by hiding under the Chief Petty Officer's body. Suddenly the lights go on – and Mulder handcuffs Wilmer to himself. With his gun at the base of the man's neck, he demands to know where Samantha is; in exchange, Mulder will let him get to his ship before the Navy destroys it. "Wilmer" then starts slamming Mulder around, and morphs to his Pilot form. He says he could have killed Mulder several times over, and as he prepares to do it now, tauntingly says that Samantha is alive.

Mulder retrieves his gun and fires, and is burned by the wounded Pilot's blood. Dragging Mulder out the tophatch, the Pilot breaks the handcuffs with it, then drops Mulder onto the ice. The Pilot gets back in, and the sub begins to submerge – nearly slicing Mulder with a tower fin.

Present day: Returning to last episode's

and superhuman Pilot. And there's no reason whatsoever for an Earth-created assassin to have a working, flying, attention-getting 80-meter craft crash, and to be buried deep below an Arctic icecap, especially when his mission involves assassinations in the U.S. The fact he has green "blood" like the clones and Dr. Secare seems to confirm alien physiology – and since that spacecraft indicates he's not an Earth creation, then *ipso facto* he's an alien.

Side-note: The Pilot's philosophy about Mulder and the cost of truth eerily echoes that of Smoking Man and others. He says Mulder could have been killed many times over, and wasn't; and pointedly – strangely personally – he says Mulder needs to ask himself which truths are worth dying for.

opening, Scully convinces the doctors Mulder is suffering hyperviscosity syndrome, and needs his cold-induced hypometabolic state in order to live. Eventually, she gets him stabilized.

In her report, Scully says blood tests confirmed Mulder's exposure to a mysterious retrovirus. Yet despite all these bizarre events, Scully writes she can't accept a paranormal explanation, since that means abandoning science. Later, Mulder awakens with Scully at his bedside – and a renewed faith, he says, "to keep looking."

CAST

Mitch Pileggi	Assistant Director Walter S. Skinner
Steven Williams	Mr. X
Peter Donat	William Mulder
Brian Thompson	The Pilot
Megan Leitch	"Samantha Mulder"
Colin Cunningham	Lt. Terry Wilmer
Garry Davey	Captain
Andrew Johnston	Agent Barrett Weiss
Allan Lysell	Able Gardner (unnamed in episode)

X-actitude

USS *Allegiance*: On cartography mission at cruising depth 1,000 feet. Its course heading for the unknown craft: 0.47.

Samantha's access-card number for the women's clinic: 4A

Scully's e-mail address: Dana Scully, 001013

Mulder's e-mail address: Fox Mulder, 000517

Message number of Mulder's e-mail to Scully: 238479

Mulder's Arctic journey: Commercial flight to Tacoma, WA; military flight to Deadhorse, AK; using FBI credentials, chartered a Rollagon all-terrain vehicle; drove to within 10 miles of destination, from where he hiked.

J.B. Bivens	Sharpshooter
Oliver Becker	2nd Doctor
Beatrice Zeilinger	Paramedic
Bonnie Hay	Field Doctor

Continuity error: The scene of the perplexed USS *Allegiance* finding some mysterious craft is inserted between the Pilot's arrival at Scully's hotel room, and, moments later, the Pilot's abducting Scully; by all the laws of film editing, this absolutely shows it was happening concurrently. Yet the spacecraft had crash-landed more than two weeks before the Pilot appeared at Scully's room, and was so widely reported by TV news that the *Allegiance* would *certainly* have known what they'd found. The only explanation otherwise is that the *Allegiance* scene occurred immediately after the crash, before news could be disseminated. *However*, Mr. X tells Mulder – over two weeks *after* the crash – that the *Allegiance* found the craft "five days ago." And since Mulder (and the rest of the world within TV-news earshot) knew about the craft two weeks ago, it'd be ridiculous for X to be lying now.

There's no evident way to plug these chronology holes; the best possible explanation is that the *Allegiance* events took place just over two weeks prior and was a flashback – which as a bonus helps explain how the Pilot could have been there to murder the crew. (Automatic defenses are another possibility.)

Mulder's latitude and longitude, respectively, in the Arctic, expressed in cartographic minutes and seconds.

When first we see him:
North 71'41.619"
West 146'37.287"

At submarine location:
North 71'43.010"
West 146'37.221"

X-act Location: The rusty old Canadian destroyer HMCS *Mackenzie* was scheduled to be sunk when construction coordinator Rob Maier leased it for use as the submarine interiors. The ship was then economically re-used for both the interiors and exteriors of an even rustier old ship in episode 2.19, "Dod Kalm."

For the awe-inspiring submarine conning tower, jutting from the top at the top of the world, the producers rented the larger Stage 5 at North Shore Studios and had it refrigerated to hold 140 tons of snow; the crew built a 15-foot structure with hydraulic lifts so that it would descend several feet below the stage. Chris Carter had originally wanted to shoot this at a frozen lake, but that proved impractical.

The establishing long-shot of Mr. X at Washington, D.C.'s Kennedy Center used the *real* Kennedy Center – but *not* the real Mr. X. Reportedly shot two days before the air-date, after it was realized in post-production a transition shot was needed, it required producer Paul Rabin to have a small crew of local freelancers shoot the actual place with a stand-in Mr. X: the Washington, D.C. assistant film commissioner.

The Repertory: Garry Davey, playing the submarine captain, had appeared twice before on *X-Files*, as a truck-stop Good Samaritan in episode 1.11, "Eve," and as Dr. Keats in 1.23, "Roland." He would appear again as a fanatic principal in 3.11, "Syzygy." Allan Lysell played a bullying police chief in 1.17, "E.B.E." J.B. Bivens had a small role in the pilot. Colin Cunningham returned in episode 3.10, "731," as Escalante.

X-File case: Classified

2.18 "FEARFUL SYMMETRY"

Feb. 24, 1995
Writer: Steve DeJarnatt
Director: James Whitmore, Jr.

Idaho Mutual Insurance Trust, Fairfield, Idaho: Two night janitors, Roberto and one other, watch an invisible behemoth rampage down the street and, upon reaching nearby Highway 24, trample to death a road worker on a federally funded project. The next morning, trucker Wesley Brewer barely avoids hitting an elephant. State police find the animal – 43 miles from a zoo – dying.

Same morning: Mulder and Scully investigate the road-worker's death; his spine had been crushed, and there was a circular abrasion on his chest roughly resembling an elephant's foot. They speak with Ed Meecham, operations chief of the Fairfield Zoo, who has just returned elephant Ganesha there; she apparently died of exhaustion – and her cage was found locked. Meecham's boss, Willa Ambrose, a naturalist whom the board of supervisors hired last year, confirms the cage was locked and only she and Meecham have keys. They still use cages, rather than open habitats, since this impoverished 1940s zoo is near to closing. Additional pressure comes from anti-captivity activists the Wild Again Organization (WAO).

WAO spokesperson Kyle Lang denies he let Ganesha loose. At his office, accompanied by a silent man with short-cropped blond hair, he shows the agents a tape of elephants being torturously prodded. He reveals Ambrose is being sued by the Malawi government over a gorilla she rescued there 10 years ago and raised as a child.

At Jo Jo's Copy Shop, Mulder tele-conferences with Frohike and Byers. Byers says Fairfield is known for weird animal disappearances. They add that Mountain Home Air Base, a UFO hot spot, is nearby.

Scully follows the WAO assistant into the closed zoo. She runs into Meecham, while the WAO guy videotapes some hard-to-see disturbance. A flash of light reveals a loose tigress; the man's camera records her fatal – and suddenly invisible – attack. The agents meet with Ambrose and her agitated gorilla, Sophie, who's been signing, "Light. Afraid." At Ganesha's autopsy, Scully discovers the elephant was pregnant.

Blake Towers construction site, downtown Boise, Idaho: A tigress

has two men trapped. Meecham shoots it when the animal charges Ambrose. Next day, the zoo is closed, and the board withdraws funding. The animals will be shipped to other zoos starting Monday. Mulder informs Ambrose the tigress had been pregnant; Ambrose insists she would have known about it – and laughs when he suggests alien abduction. She stops laughing when Mulder says Sophie may be pregnant, and afraid of having her baby taken away. Sophie responds to Ambrose's questions by signing, "Baby. Go. Fly. Light."

Sheriff's deputies serve a court order to release Sophie into protective custody. Ambrose seeks Lang's help to find a private reserve, but Lang says Sophie should live in the wild. Mulder, at the zoo warehouse, watches Sophie being prepped for shipping. Scully shows him a newspaper clipping.

Outside the warehouse, Lang pulls up in a truck, and goes inside looking for Ambrose. He finds Sophie's cage empty –

X-otica

The elephant's name, Ganesha, is the female form of Ganesh, the popular, Hindu household god.

The episode's title refers to the William Blake poem "The Tyger."

In-joke: Blake Towers is named after William Blake.

Fairfield, Idaho is an actual town of a few hundred people – though Highway 20, not 24, passes through.

Malawi is a real country in southeast Africa.

Inspiration alert: Congo (1995) likewise involves a naturalist raising a signing female gorilla who expresses a terrible secret in her artwork. Yet the inspiration more likely was Koko, the famous real-life signing gorilla.

and then some force throws him across the room with an odd crackling sound; a crate slams down, killing him. Scully questions Ambrose, who denies any connection to Lang – until Scully shows a note he'd left: Mulder, finding Sophie's transport-cage unlocked, tails Meecham. Scully says Lang was hit by a cattle prod, and arrests Ambrose – who declares it was an accident, that Lang had surprised Meecham, who was helping to rescue Sophie. Sophie's now at a building between there and Boise; Mulder learns Ambrose had paid Meecham for this. Sophie is hysterical in a locked room. Meecham manages to push Mulder inside with the terrified animal – though moments later, a bright light takes her away.

Scully later arrives with a police officer. Mulder says Sophie had tried to tell him something, and repeats her signing. The police radio announces a large animal on the road; the agents find Sophie has been killed by a car. Mulder's voiceover tells us Ambrose and Meecham were charged with Lang's manslaughter – and suggests alien conservationists may be involved on Earth.

CAST

Jayne Atkinson	Willa Ambrose
Lance Guest	Kyle Lang
Jack Rader	Ed Meecham
Bruce Harwood	Byers
Tom Braidwood	Frohike
Jody St. Michael	Sophie
Charles Andre	Ray Floyd (unnamed in episode)
Garvin Cross	Red Head Kid
	(apparently, the blond – strawberry-blond? – WAO person)
Tom Glass	Trucker (Wesley Brewer)

extra

X-actitude

Ganesha: a 12-year-old, female Indian elephant

Fairfield Zoo hours: 10 a.m.–5.30 p.m.

Newspaper headline appears to read: COUPLE SAVE BABY GORILLA FROM BLACK MARKET SMUGGLERS

Church sign: "Man has no preeminence above a beast: For all is vanity."

• The actors playing Roberto and the other janitor are uncredited.

The official Fox *X-Files* website erroneously includes Dean Haglund as Langley.

The Cast: Jayne Atkinson appeared in the 1986 miniseries and 1987–88 series *A Year in the Life* (NBC); and the film-spinoff series *Parenthood* (NBC 1990). Among her other film roles, she played foster-mom Annie Greenwood in *Free Willy* (1993) and its 1995 sequel.

Jack Rader has appeared in three decades of TV and such occasional films as *Black Sunday* and *Gray Lady Down* (both 1977), *The Blob* (1988), and *The Scout* (1994).

Lance Guest got his start on *Lou Grant* (CBS 1977–82); he later played on *Knots*

Landing, and *Life Goes On* (ABC 1989–93). His films include *Halloween II* (1981), *The Last Starfighter* (1984, with future X-guest Kay E. Kuter), and *The Wizard of Loneliness* (1988).

Mime Jody St. Michael, inside the gorilla suit, played a similar role in *Gorillas in the Mist* (1988) and a mime on *Father Dowling Mysteries*.

X-File case: Classified

2.19 "DOD KALM"

March 10, 1995
Teleplay: Howard Gordon & Alex Gansa
Story: Howard Gordon
Director: Rob Bowman

X-File case: Classified
Government denies all knowledge

The Norwegian Sea, 66° latitude, 8° East Longitude. Capt. Barclay of the destroyer USS *Ardent* pulls a gun on a Lt. Richard Harper, trying in vain to keep several men from abandoning ship. Eighteen hours later, lifeboat 925 is picked up by Canadian fishing vessel *The Lisette*. All on board are seemingly very old. Bethesda Naval Hospital, third floor: Scully informs Mulder the *Ardent* had apparently vanished for 42 hours. Last night, 18 crew-members were found alive, but now only Harper survives. When Scully questions a male nurse why the 28-year-old Harper looks so aged, the attending physician claims Scully's clearance code is invalid, and throws her out.

Mulder's office: Mulder says the X-Files have recorded nine ships disappearing in that 65th-parallel area. Citing the Philadelphia Experiment, he suggests "wormholes" – postulated portals where matter interfaces with time at an accelerated or decelerated rate. At 8:30 p.m., the agents leave for Norway.

Tildeskan, Norway: At a bar, Mulder and Scully, looking to hire a ship to reach the sea north of Beerenberg, roughly 10 hours away, meet willing trawler captain Henry Trondheim. He berates the other sailors for their superstition about an evil god's stone that crashed through the ice. Twelve hours later – bad weather having slowed the voyage – Mulder is seasick. Trondheim and mate Halvorson crash into a ship that's been in and out of radar – the *Ardent*, looking old and rusted though only commissioned in 1991. They find mummified-looking remains, covered with a residue. Then someone, to their horror, steals Trondheim's ship.

The *Ardent*'s radio and engines are dead. Halvorson has his skull fatally fractured. Mulder finds a terrified and aged Capt. Barclay clutching a Jack Daniels bottle. Per Barclay's log, the navigation system had failed; then crew-members saw a light in the sea and the ship began to "bleed." As Trondheim sends Halverson's body out to sea, he's attacked by a youngish man whom Mulder captures: pirate/ black-marketeer Olafsson (who speaks only Norwegian). Below Barclay is dead, and appears to be decomposing into a crystalline substance. Per his log, the ship had picked up four Norwegian sailors whose own ship had sunk, accounting for Olafsson, whom they bind, and the men who stole Trondheim's ship.

They sleep, but when Mulder wakes Scully for her turn at the watch, both agents and Trondheim have aged – though none of their hair has fallen out or grayed. Scully suspects free radicals: highly reactive chemicals with extra electrons, that attack DNA proteins and theoretically cause bodies to age. If the ship is approaching another massive metallic source, like a meteor, the two might (with the ocean as the "battery") act as terminals to electromagnetically excite free radicals.

Trondheim notices the ship "bleeding" rust; the agents follow an oddly uncorroded yellow pipe. Olafsson tells Trondheim he'll trade the secret of his youth in exchange for freedom. The agents follow the pipe to the Sewage Processing Hold, where they see the "campsite" of Olafsson's men, and what Mulder deduces is the only drinkable water on the ship; the

X-otica

"We were working on the show with John Savage where we aged to, like, 90 years old in a couple of days," Duchovny remembers. "And John Savage was playing a Norwegian guy who kept coming back to this word . . . He was yelling at a guy [Olafsson] and he said, '*bleaver!*' And for some reason, it struck Gillian and [me] as the funniest thing. You know he kept on saying, '[gibberish, gibberish] *bleaver!*' And we kept cracking up every time! We were supposed to be huddled in a corner, dying of old age at the age of 30, and every time he'd say '*bleaver!*' we'd go [desperate stifled laugh]. And so we started saying, 'Leave it to bleaver!' "

regular desalinated water must've gotten contaminated, and this recycled water may be the key. When they seek to question Olaffson (whom Trondheim has killed), Trondheim claims he escaped.

Eighteen hours, 45 minutes since the onset of symptoms, blood and urine tests show impossibly high salt levels: the contaminated water apparently catalyzes body fluids to cause rapid, massive cellular degeneration. The recycled water has slowed the aging in Trondheim and Scully, but less so in Mulder, who'd gotten dehydrated when seasick. Trondheim wants Scully to stop giving the doomed Mulder his ration of water; Scully will not, but does note Mulder's kidneys aren't secreting what she's calling "heavy salt." Hours later, Trondheim barricades the door to the sewage hold, and the last remaining water.

Later, the ship's outer hull corrodes through; as the ocean bursts into the sewage hold, Trondheim can't escape through the barricade. Fourteen hours later: Scully tells Mulder the one thing she remembers from her abduction is thinking there's nothing to fear when life is over. Later, she writes that Mulder lost consciousness at 4:30 a.m., March 12. Food and water ran out 24 hours previously. Later still: rescuers having reached them, Scully finds herself being treated by the doctor who'd thrown her out before. Thirty-six hours later: Scully is on dialysis with a high-flux filter and responding well. Based on Scully's records, Mulder is given a successful course of synthetic hormones. Scully wants to return for further research, but the doctor informs her the ship sank an hour after their rescue.

X-actitude

The Lisette registry number: CV233

Lt. Harper's hospital room: 3G

Capt. Barclay's age: 35

City where, Trondheim says, "everybody knows" Olafsson: Gildeskal

Other ship disappearances, per Mulder:

British Royal Navy battleship, on Dec. 12, 1949 between Leeds and Cape Perry

Fleet of Soviet mine-sweepers in 963, enroute to Havana

Nearest land to the area where the *Ardent* went missing: Lofoten Island

Trondheim's background: former Pensacola, FL charter-boat operator; now runs 50-ton double-hulled trawler, *The Zehar*.

Only liquids Scully can find after Trondheim barricades sewage hold:

CAST

John Savage
Henry Trondheim

David Cubitt
Captain Barclay

Vladimir Kulich
Olafsson

Mar Anderson
Halverson

John McConnach
Sailor (on *The Lisette*)

Stephen Dimopoulos
Ionesco (on *The Lisette*; unnamed in episode)

Claire Riley
Dr. Laskos (unnamed in episode)

Robert Metcalfe
Nurse

Dmitry Chepovetsky
(Lieutenant Richard) Harper

extra   ● The official Fox *X-Files* website erroneously lists the character Dr. Laskos as "Burke".

X-act Location: The HMCS *Mackenzie* was used for both the interior and exterior USS *Ardent* sets. It had previously been used for the submarine interiors of episode 2.17, "End Game."

snow-globe water, sardine-can liquid, juice of half-dozen lemons.

Mulder's take on the Philadelphia Experiment: WWII project designed to render ships invisible to radar; when the Manhattan Project kicked in, most of the scientists were ostensibly shifted to Los Alamos NM, but actually moved to Roswell, NM. Nine months after the alleged crash of a UFO there, the USS *Eldridge* vanished from a Philadelphia naval yard and reappeared minutes later in Norfolk, VA. Mulder claims the scientists were experimenting with the theory of "wormholes."

The Cast: John Savage, best known for *The Deer Hunter* (1978), made his movie debut in *Bad Company* (1972). Savage's films include *The Onion Field* (1980), *Hair* (1979), *Salvador* (1986), *Do the Right Thing* (1989) and *The Godfather, Part III* (1990).

David Cubitt has guested on *Glory Days, Booker, TekWar* and Showtime's *The Outer Limits*; his films include *K2* (1991) and *Alive* (1993).

X-File case: Classified

2.20 "HUMBUG"

March 24, 1995
Writer: Darin Morgan
Director: Kim Manners

X-File case: Classified
Government denies all knowledge

Gibsonton, FL, night: At his pool at home, Jerald Glazebrook, the circus "Alligator Man," is attacked and killed. FBI headquarters: Mulder tells Scully that Glazebrook had ichthyosis, the scale-like shedding of skin. His murder is the latest of 48 such mutilations in 28 years, occurring in nearly every state in the continental US.

Mulder, Scully and the cooperative Sheriff James Hamilton attend Glazebrook's funeral, where an armless pastor eulogizes Jerry as a renowned escape artist. Suddenly, the ground trembles and a man emerges, crazily declaring that in honor of the deceased, he'll drive a metal stake into his chest – which he does. The funeral erupts in bedlam. Phil's Diner: Mulder asks about a mermaid illustration on the menu, by local artist Hepcat Helm. Hamilton takes them to Hepcat's studio, behind the station house. Helm is offended by Hamilton's referring to his nearby "Tabernacle of Terror" as a funhouse, but he identifies the figure as a "Feejee Mermaid" – a "humbug" P.T. Barnum pulled in the 19th century, with a mummified monkey sewn onto the tail of a fish. Mulder says a trail of possibly simian tracks were found at several of the crime scenes.

Gulf Breeze trailer court: Little-person proprietor, Mr. Nutt, takes exception to Mulder's innocent question as to whether he'd worked for a circus, lecturing him about his degree in hotel management.

A slow-witted but pleasant tippler, Lanny, takes their bags to their separate trailers. Lanny used to headline, showing audiences his attached brother, Leonard, but Nutt convinced him that this lacked dignity — so now he carries people's luggage. Hepcat is killed in his studio by a tiny, crawling, bald, ape-like creature.

Next day: Mulder spots a bald man with jigsaw tattoos all over his body, catching a fish from a stream and eating it raw. At 7.15 a.m., Lanny awakens Scully to report Hepcat's murder. Mulder notices blood on the outside of one of Hepcat's small windows. The agents come across funeral disrupter Dr. Blockhead; as they chat, he taps a nail into his nose, which Mulder helpfully retrieves. Dr. Blockhead introduces his friend "The Conundrum," whom he says will eat anything; Scully wonders if that includes human flesh. Dr. Blockhead offers the agents a jar of live bugs to eat; Scully does so

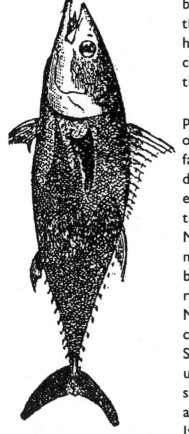

— or at least pretends to, later pulling the bug "out" of Mulder's ear and explaining that her amateur-magician uncle showed her this trick. Mulder will have the lab compare the blood on the nail to that on the window.

Gibsonton Museum of Curiosities, 3:14 p.m.: The proprietor gives Scully a tour, offers her a poster of Jim-Jim the Dog-faced Boy, and for an additional five dollars promises an authentic Barnum exhibit, "The Great Unknown" – which turns out to be an empty chest. Night: Mulder tells Scully the blood samples match, so he's running further tests. A background check on Dr. Blockhead reveals him as Jeffrey Swaim, born in Milwaukee and not Yemen (as he'd claimed); he also doesn't hold a doctorate. Scully's check on Jim-Jim reveals he grew up to become . . . Sheriff Hamilton! He'd suffered hypertrichosis, which Mulder accurately notes does not mean lycanthropy.

X-otica

Gibsonton is a real town, just south of Tampa, on Tampa Bay.

Anderson actually *did* eat a cricket, off-camera, on a dare from Jim Rose. She volunteered to do it again on film, but the producers had already spent $2,000 on edible fake crickets, and the idea kind of faded. "They spent thousands of dollars making a fake one," Anderson recalls. "But I'd seen this guy named Enigma who was in the show eat 200 right in front of us, so it seemed silly not to try one."

In-joke: The Gulf Breeze trailer court is named after the famous 1987–88 "sightings" made near Gulf Breeze, FL. For more on this, see episode 1.10, "Fallen Angel."

Inspiration Alert:

The guns-inside-the-funhouse scene recalls Orson Welles' *The Lady from Shanghai* (1948).

They spy Hamilton in his backyard, digging beneath a full moon. When they investigate, he sheepishly admits burying a potato as an old-wives' remedy for warts; he concedes he was, indeed, Jim-Jim. That same night, after the Conundrum pays his rent, a creature squeezes through Nutt's doggy door and kills Nutt. As the agents investigate, Hamilton takes a highly distraught Lanny to the drunk tank. The agents and Hamilton arrest Dr. Blockhead.

At the station house, Lanny screams in his cell. Scully and Mulder see a blood trail leading out the tiny window: Lanny's attached twin has extracted itself. Lanny pitifully says Leonard doesn't know he's hurting anyone – he's merely seeking another brother. That rejection has made Lanny miserable. The Sheriff calls for paramedics; the agents chase Leonard into the Tabernacle of Terror. Leonard escapes to attack the Conundrum, whom the agents shortly thereafter find prone but unhurt – and when they leave, he rubs his belly and burps.

Morning: Scully finds Blockhead and the Conundrum packing their yellow VW Beetle to leave. Scully informs Dr.Blockhead that Lanny died last night, of cirrhosis of the liver; his autopsy showed some offshoots of his esophagus and trachea that seemed umbilical. She inquires about the Conundrum's being so drowsy. "Probably," he suggests, "something I ate."

CAST

Jim Rose	Dr. Blockhead/Jeffrey Swaim
Wayne Grace	Sheriff James Hamilton
Michael Anderson	Nutt
The Enigma (Paul Lawrence)	
	The Conundrum
Vincent Schiavelli	Lanny
Blair Slater	Glazebrook (older)
Devin Walker	Glazebrook (younger)
John Payne	Jerald Glazebrook
Debis Simpson	Waiter
Alex Diakun	Curator
George Tipple	Hepcat Helm
Alvin Law	Reverend

extra

X-actitude

Site of first mutilation attack: Oregon. Site of last five: Florida

Glazebrook's family: Bearded-lady wife; two normal sons, approximately 8 and 10 years old.

Biblical passage read at Glazebrook's funeral: Psalm 23 ("The Lord is my Shepherd . . .")

• The deputy, who has one line, is uncredited.

The official Fox *X-Files* website erroneously refers to the Glazebrook character as a retired escape artist, and neglects to list front-credit performer The Enigma.

The Cast: Though only The Enigma and Jim Rose appear, a few words are in order about a real-life inspiration for this episode, The Jim Rose Circus Sideshow. A serious if seriously eccentric performance-art troupe started in 1991, it grew from gigs at restaurants and store openings to pack grunge-clubs in their home base of Seattle.

Gibsonton's founding:
in 1920s, when
Barnum and Bailey
performers came here
during the off-season

Copyright date of
Hepcat Helm's menu
illustration: 1992

Museum admission
charges: "Freaks Free
. . . Others please leave
donation."

Blood samples: Both
0-positive

Conundrum's rent
check: The Conundrum,
P.O. Box 6071,
Gibsonton, Florida,
180203 (sic); City trust
and Savings Bank,
Main Branch, Corner
3rd and Main.

Nutt's mutt:
Commodore

Jim-Jim the Dog-Faced
Boy background:
orphan discovered in
an Albanian forest,
1943; became sideshow
attraction, then ran
away, supported
himself, and eventually
became Gibsonton's
four-term Sheriff.

The troupe has gone on to tour three continents, and with *Lollapalooza '92*. Vancouver had some of its earliest sure-fire audiences. The troupe's first tour opened March 23, 1992 at the venue "Greg's Place" in nearby Chilliwack.

Rose, raised in Phoenix, AZ, earning a degree in political science from the University of Arizona, pursued a lifelong devotion to unusual but historic arts such as glass-eating and pounding nails into oneself; he apprenticed in France, and by 1990 was a sidewalk performer in Venice Beach, CA. After moving to Seattle, a sold-out two-night gig at a Middle-Eastern restaurant solidified his reputation and attracted a bevy of weird performers wanting to be part of a larger show. The Enigma (formerly Slug the Sword Swallower) is Paul Lawrence in his civilian mode.

Michael (a.k.a. Michael J.) Anderson became the enigmatic icon of *Twin Peaks*, in both the TV series and in the sorta-sequel film *Twin Peaks: Fire Walk With Me* (1992). Anderson's other credits include an episode of *Picket Fences*, and the surreal fable *Fool's Fire* (1992).

Vincent Schiavelli first appeared in *Taking Off* (1971). His best known parts include *One Flew Over the Cuckoo's Nest* (1975); *Fast Times at Ridgemont High* (1982) and its spinoff series *Fast Times* (CBS 1990); *Amadeus* (1984); *Ghost* (1990); *Batman Returns* (1992); he appeared in three episodes of *Taxi*. He also co-starred in the first-version cast of *The Corner Bar* (ABC 1972–73).

Wayne Grace's career stretches back to

playing a bartender in Robert Altman's classic *McCabe & Mrs. Miller* (1971); he's since played mostly police and military types in such films as *Friday the 13th – The Final Chapter* (1983), *Twins* (1988), and *Dances With Wolves* (1990), and on TV in episodes of *The Marshal* and other shows.

The Repertory: For a look at Alligator man John Payne without "ich-y" makeup, check out the guard who asks Scully for the passwords "Purity Control" in episode 1.24, "The Erlenmeyer Flask."

X-File case: Classified

2.21 "THE CALUSARI"

April 14, 1995
Writer: Sara B. Charno
Director: Michael Vejar

At a park, Steve Holvey and wife Maggie are with sons Charlie, 9, and Terry, 2. When Teddy accidentally loses his helium balloon and starts crying, dad gives him Charlie's; the older boy demands another. Minutes later, in the restroom with Maggie, Teddy mysteriously escapes his baby harness – and follows his new balloon to his death at a kiddie-railroad track. Three months later: Mulder and Scully visit Dr. Charles (Chuck) Burke at his University of Maryland lab where he uses digital-imaging software on a photo of Teddy taken seconds before the tragedy, raising an image of electromagnetic concentration seemingly pulling the balloon's string.

Arlington, VA: Maggie's old-world mother, Golda, speaks in Romanian. Mulder notices a swastika with dots painted on Charlie's hand. Golda is both protective and fearful of Charlie.

Mulder's office: Mulder says a swastika, a.k.a. a gammadion or fylfot, is an ancient good-luck symbol. Scully notes Teddy was hospitalized 10 times in two years, and suggests Golda has Munchausen Syndrome by Proxy, in which a person psychologically induces medical symptoms in their children. Holvey, at work, tells the agents he met Maggie in Romania in 1984; the highly superstitious Golda objected to the marriage. He agrees to let Scully interview Charlie with Karen F.

Kosseff, L.C.S.W., an FBI psychiatric social worker (whom Scully has consulted in 2.13, "Irresistible").

Later, Steve, with Charlie in the car, tries to undo a stuck garage door; some unseen force grabs his tie and catches it in the garage-opener mechanism – choking him to death before Charlie's tear-filled eyes. During the police investigation, Scully notices Golda speaking with men, telling them, in subtitled Romanian, that they must act quickly. It is getting stronger. Mulder finds ash all over the garage; the lab report later says it contains nothing organic *or* inorganic – technically, it doesn't exist.

Burks saw this material in India, 1979, in his hippie-trail days: *vibuti* – holy ash. He calls it an *apport* – something that materializes out of thin air. *Vibuti* is created during either the presence of spirit beings or of bi-location – wherein a person's energy is transferred to a

different place. Scully suggests someone activated the garage door by remote control.

Golda's room: As Golda and the Romanians conduct a ritual, an angry child's ghostly visage appears. Maggie and Kosseff, who has arrived to file a court report, run upstairs when Charlie screams. Golda locks Charlie into the room and raises a knife. Kosseff calls 911 and runs downstairs to alert Mulder and Scully, who are meeting her here. Something invisible attacks Golda; Charlie, chanting "*E siti din mina trup pertiti*," drops two roosters on her, and they claw and peck her to death. Scully and Mulder burst in too late to help.

Later, Charlie remembers nothing, and the room contains more holy ash and a herb called mugwort. The Romanian men say the ritual must be completed; Maggie throws them out, and explains to the agents that in Romania, such men – "Calusari" – ensure correct observance of

X-otica

Inspiration alert:

The balloon in the opening scene echoes a similarly anthropomorphic one in the classic live-action short, "The Red Balloon"/"Le Ballon Rouge" (France 1956).

rites. The white-bearded elder tells Mulder the evil here has existed throughout history under many names.

St. Matthews Medical Center, Arlington: Kosseff interviews Charlie, who denies being in Golda's room and blames it all on "Michael." Maggie says they had never told Charlie about Michael – his twin who died at birth – and Golda had wanted to perform a ritual to divide their souls. Afterward, when a Nurse Castor comes to give Charlie a shot, Michael materializes, bludgeons Castor, then wakes Maggie in the waiting room and insists they go home *now*. Mulder and Scully notice "Charlie" getting into Maggie's red station wagon – yet Charlie is still in bed, and Castor says another boy hit her. Mulder rushes to get the Calusari, and dispatches Scully to the Holveys'.

There, after Michael has taunted her, Maggie slips away to perform some ritual – but Michael, spotting her, raises a knife. At the hospital, the Calusari perform a rite that makes the walls bleed orange. At the Holveys', Michael growls in an unearthly language as a gale pitches Scully through the air. As Michael prepares to kill her, the Calusari's ritual climaxes and he disappears. Maggie rushes to the hospital, where the whitebeard-elder warns Mulder.

CAST

Helene Clarkson	Maggie Holvey
Joel Palmer	Charlie and Michael Holvey
Lilyan Chauvin	Golda
Kay E. Kuter	Calusari Elder
Ric Reid	Steve Holvey

Christine Willes	Karen (F.) Kosseff
Bill Dow	(Dr.) Chuck Burk (sic) (Closed captioning gives last name as "Burks," which appears to agree with audio pronunciation.)
Jacqueline Danieneau	Nurse Castor
Bill Croft	2nd Calusari
Campbell Lane	3rd Calusari
George Josef	4th Calusari
Oliver and Jeremy Isaac Wildsmith	Teddy Holvey

extra

X-actitude

Calusari pronunciation: "kal-u-SHARE-ee"

Kosseff's name, title, and address, per her business card: Karen F. Kosseff, L.C.S.W., Psychiatric Social Worker, J. Edgar Hoover Building, Tenth Street & Pennsylvania Ave., Washington, D.C. 205354 (sic). The address is accurate, except for that last, extra digit in the zip code.

Calusari license plate: Virginia KH7-356

• The official Fox *X-Files* website neglects to list front-credit actor Kay E. Kuter.

X-act Location: The abandoned Riverview Mental Institution, in Coquitlam, B.C.

The Cast: Joel Palmer had played the abducted teenager's young brother in episode 1.04, "Conduit." His other TV credits include episodes of *The Commish* and *The Hat Squad, Crow's Nest* (ABC 1992), and the 1995 feature *Far From Home: The Adventures of Yellow Dog.*

Helene Clarkson's known credits are the 1993 TV-movies *Ghost Mom* and *Woman on the Run: The Lawrence Bembenek Story.*

Lilyan Chauvin's film credits include Elvis Presley's *Tickle Me* (1965), *The Other Side of Midnight* (1977), *Private Benjamin* (1980), *Universal Soldier* (1992), and of course, *Pumpkinhead II: Blood Wings* (1994).

> Mulder and Scully's FBI motor-pool plate: FS4-291
>
> Guru whom Burk insists created a feast from thin air: Sai Baba

Interestingly, she appeared in both the TV-movie *Tonya and Nancy: The Inside Story* (1994) as a figure-skating judge, and in the satire *National Lampoon's Attack of the 5 Ft. 2 In. Women* (Showtime 1994) as a coach.

Classically trained for Shakespearean drama, Kay E. Kuter has long been associated with his part of *Green Acres'* Newt Kiley. Though he enjoyed his time with *Green Acres'* comic ensemble, he happily returned to such stage roles as Friar Laurence in *Romeo and Juliet*, Col. Pickering in *My Fair Lady*, and King Pellinoire in at least 18 different productions of *Camelot*. Kuter made his film debut in *Sabrina* (1954). His TV debut was a 1949 pilot, *Tales out of the Shadow*. His highly varied films include *Guys and Dolls* (1955), *Watermelon Man* (1970), *The Last Starfighter* (1984), and *Gross Anatomy* (1989). Among his recent TV appearances are *Star Trek: The Next Generation*, *Beauty and the Beast*, *Baywatch*, and *Seinfeld*; he also provide the voice of a certain children's author in the 1994 special *In Search of Dr. Seuss*.

The Repertory: Ric Reid had played a coroner in the pilot. Bill Dow was the devoured dad of 1.05, "The Jersey Devil," and Campbell Lane, an old dad in 1.18, "Miracle Man." Christine Willes reprises her role as an FBI psychological social worker.

X-File case: Classified

2.22 "F. EMASCU-LATA"

April 28, 1995
Writers: Chris Carter & Howard Gordon
Director: Rob Bowman

A Costa Rica rain forest: Dr. Robert Torrence finds a dead boar with pulsing red sores and a strange insect. As he examines a sore, using surgical gloves [N], it spurts onto his face: Night: Deathly ill, he short-waves the "R.B.P. Field Base" requesting immediate evacuation. Seven hours later, soldiers find him dead.

Cumberland State Correctional Facility, Dinwiddie County, VA. Guard Winston delivers an overnight-mail package to solitary prisoner Bobby Torrence. The original address has been blacked-out and the package readdressed. Inside is a body part with a pulsating sore. Eighteen hours later: murder convicts Paul and Steve, cleaning Bobby's empty cell, say someone named McGuire has told them the infirmary was full and all the bedsheets are to be incinerated.

Later, a Federal Marshal tells Mulder to stay out of his way during the manhunt for the escaped Paul and Steve. Mulder, noticing men in contamination suits, asks Scully to stay and investigate. At a rest stop, vacationing dad Robert is killed and the family camper stolen. Scully finds a Dr. Osborne of the CDC, who reluctantly says a "flu-like illness," invariably fatal after 36 hours, has killed 10 of 14 men infected. He is unsure if the escapees are infected; Scully cell-phones Mulder to warn him. Another man in a clean-suit demands Scully leave.

At a gas station, Paul phones Elizabeth, who has a baby boy. Station-attendant Angelo Garza discovers Steve in the rest room, splotched with sores. Paul knocks Angelo out. At the prison incinerator, Scully finds body bags – one marked "001 Torrence." She cuts it to examine the body inside; as Osborne desperately tries to close it, a pustule explodes in his face. [N]

At the gas station: Mulder informs the Marshal that the fugitives may be infectious. Mulder, figuring the men might head for a girlfriend's, has an Atlantic Bell operator tell him the last call made on the pay phone. A helicopter with no registry number – just "RESCUE" – dispatches four clean-suited persons to whisk away the terrified Garza.

The fugitives take Garza's stolen car to Elizabeth's home. Scully learns that the overnight package came from Pinck Pharmaceuticals,

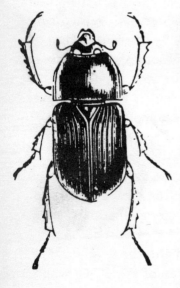

and plucks an insect from Torrence's corpse. Marshals arrest Elizabeth, just after a boil erupts onto her. Steve's dead, Paul's missing.

Osborne – infected – confides that the prison is quarantined not by the CDC but by Pinck, for whom he works. Three months ago, an entomologist seeking new species for drug applications "disappeared," though his samples were retrieved. One is the insect Scully shows him: *Faciphaga emasculata*, a parasitoid (parasite carrier) that secretes a dilating enzyme. The pustules hold its larvae, which upon eruption burrow into their new host. Since Scully was next to Osborne when the Torrence boil burst, she may be infected herself.

FBI headquarters, evening: Mulder, Skinner and the Smoking Man argue over the latter keeping information about the disease from the public. The prison: Osborne tests Scully by having her bitten by an uninfected insect, which then acts as incubator; any parasite in her blood will take 30 minutes to get into the bug, and another two hours to grow large enough to see. Dinwiddie County Hospital: Quarantined Elizabeth tells Mulder that Paul will take the 10 p.m. bus to Toronto. Scully puts Osborne in an oxygen tent. When she returns from the lab upon finding she's uninfected, he's gone.

The bus depot: A mom puts her teenage son on the Toronto bus; he gives Paul the time (9:40). At the prison incinerator, the hard-ass from earlier tells Scully they are destroying material in accordance with CDC procedure; he doesn't reply when Scully says he doesn't work for the CDC. Osborne's body gets loaded in. The depot: Mulder, having learned that Paul is infected, tries to slip on as a passenger, take Paul at gunpoint from behind, and bring him out safely as proof of the disease and cover-up. But Paul takes the boy as hostage – and after Mulder convinces him to give up and get medical treatment, a sniper shoots Paul dead.

FBI headquarters: Mulder tells Skinner that Pinck used prisoners as guinea pigs to circumvent FDA testing. Mulder plans to tell the media – but Scully arrives to report the scientist in Costa Rica was also named Robert Torrence; Pinck arranged it this way as a fail-safe, to blame "postal error." Mulder, defeated, demands to know where Skinner stands. "I stand right on the line you keep crossing," he answers . . . and adds, "as a friend – watch your back."

CAST

Mitch Pileggi	Assistant Director Walter S. Skinner
Charles Martin Smith	Dr. Osborne
Dean Norris	U.S. Marshal (Tapia, in the script; unnamed in episode)
John Pyper-Ferguson	Paul
William B. Davis	Smoking Man
Angelo Vacco	Angelo Garza
Morris Paynch	Dr. Simon Auerbach (unnamed in episode; the other doctor at the prison)

Lynda Boyd	Elizabeth
John Tench	Steve
Alvin Sanders	Bus Driver
Kim Kondrashoff	Bobby (Torrence)
Chilton Crane	Mother (at bus station)
Bill Rowat	Dr. (Robert) Torrence
Jude Zachary	Winston

extra

X-actitude

Mulder's badge number: JTT047101111

The Federal Marshal is named Tapia per the closed captioning, but not episode dialog.

Name listed on Dr. Torrence's locked case: Bio Diversity. Section he wants evacuation from: Z-15.

Overnight-mail package: Transcontinental Express #DDP112148, sent from Pinck Pharmaceuticals in Wichita, KS.

Number of roads within easy reach of the gas-station: 23

• The actors playing the boy on the bus; the camper dad (Robert); the camper mom, and the ticket agent are all uncredited.

The official Fox *X-Files* website erroneously lists the character Dr. Simon Auerbach as "Dr. Barber," and neglects to list front-credit performers Charles Martin Smith, Dean Morris and John Pyper-Ferguson.

The Cast: Dean Norris has appeared in *Gremlins 2: The New Batch* (1990), *Terminator 2: Judgment Day* (1991), *Barbarians at the Gate* (HBO 1933), the telefilm *Lakota Woman: Siege at Wounded Knee* (1944) (with future X-guest Floyd "Red Crow" Westerman), and *Safe* (1995).

John Pyper-Ferguson's TV credits include *The Adventures of Brisco County, Jr.*, *The Commish, MacGyver* and *21 Jump Street*, and the CBC series *Mom, P.I.* His two features to date are *Bird on a Wire* (1990) and *Killer Image* (1992).

Angelo Vacco was an *X-Files* production assistant with no prior film or TV acting credits; Chris Carter specifically wrote the

Elizabeth's address: 925 August St., somewhere in Dinwiddie County, VA; telephone 555-6936

Prisoner Bobby Torrence: neck sore measures 5cm; body temperature 103.5°; oxygen saturation 81

Bus depot: Paul in line to buy Greyhound ticket at 9:25 p.m.; Toronto bus (#943) at Gate 20; boy visiting his Uncle Jake.

part of Angelo Garza for him. Vacco's since had bit parts on *Chicago Hope* and *Married . . . With Children.*

Lynda Boyd's few credits have been in TV-movies and on an episode each of *Strange Luck* and *The Commish.*

The Repertory: Chiton Crane played a wheelchair-bound woman with MS in 1.18, "Miracle Man." Alvin Saunders, playing a Deputy Sheriff, was the first victim of an alien's attack in 1.10, "Fallen Angel."

X-File case: Classified

2.23 "SOFT LIGHT"

May 5, 1995
Writer: Vince Gilligan
Director: James Contner

Richmond, VA: In a hotel hallway, a distraught man insistently knocks on the door of a man named Morris, saying it's Chester. Across the hall, businessperson Patrick Newirth watches the commotion through his peephole until Chester's shadow slips beneath the door and evaporates him. Chester, hearing Newirth's scream, unscrews a hallway lightbulb and flees.

Next day: At the scene, Scully tells Mulder that Kelly Ryan, one of her Academy students, now with the Richmond Police, called last night asking for help with her first case. When Newirth didn't answer his wake-up call, Security came up three hours later to find him gone from a locked and chained room with no other means of exit. A blotch on the floor is similar to those at three other crime scenes, mostly carbon, with some potassium and trace minerals, which Scully says sounds like residue from burnt flesh. Mulder taps the unaccountably loosened bulb in the hallway, and when it appears to work, asks Ryan to check it for prints. He's thinking about spontaneous human combustion.

Outside the suburban-Richmond home of the last missing person, Margaret Wysnecki, Mulder finds a similar loose bulb. [N] Scully notes that the first victim, Gail Anne Lambert, was an engineer with Polarity Magnetics, Inc. Mulder finds a round-trip train ticket with a return date of the day she disappeared;

Newirth had also arrived by train. Ryan sends cops to check the station, where at 11:50 p.m., Chester accidentally evaporates two officers.

Morning: Ryan tells the agents the lightbulb prints didn't match those of any hotel employee or guest [N] – but two scorch marks in the alley indicate the killer was here. The agents examine security-camera tapes, noticing a man "always" sitting in the terminal. A blow-up reveals the Polarity Magnetics logo. Mulder and Scully find Polarity Magnetics closed. Dr. Christopher Davey finally answers, and says the man in the March 22 security-video print is former business partner Dr. Chester Ray Banton. Davey thought he'd died after an accident there five weeks earlier: Chester had gotten locked inside their particle generator, receiving a quanta bombardment equal to a 2 billion megaWatt X-ray.

Train station, 11:14 a.m.: Mulder notices that the diffused, soft light casts no shadows. He and Scully find and capture Chester. Yaloff Psychiatric Hospital, Piedmont, VA: They question a devastated Chester, who has insisted on soft light rather than darkness. He says his shadow is like a black hole that splits molecules into component atoms; Lambert had died by his just standing in her doorway. He's convinced the government wants to subject him to a "brain suck" to steal his ideas and commandeer the shadow. Ryan officiously tells the agents to stop; her superior, Detective Barron, wants to know why they're here. Scully lies for the scheming, manipulative Ryan. Barron says he's transferring Chester to county jail – and compliments Ryan on *her* good work.

At 2:19 a.m., Mulder meets with Mr. X, who has never heard of Chester and won't help Mulder appropriate him from the Richmond PD; he says not to contact him

X-otica

Morley Tobacco, the company for which Newirth worked, makes the cigarette brand Morley – a take-off of Marlboro. A box of Morleys is a key element in episode 2.08, "One Breath," and it may be Morley, not Marlboro, that Smoking Man lights up in 2.01, "Little Green Men."

Hampton, not Hampton Roads, is a small city on the Virginia coast where Langley Air Force Base is located.

In-joke: When the agents are confounded by how Newirth vanished from a locked room, Scully glances at the tiny heating vent. "You never know," Mulder cracks – a reference to mutant Eugene Tooms' desired method of entrance in episode 1.03, "Squeeze."

again unless absolutely necessary. At 3:24 a.m., amid a power outage, Mr. X tells a nurse they're here for Chester. Two associates start to bind and gag him – but when the lights return, they're killed. Chester escapes.

Next day: The agents learn power was selectively disconnected at a substation two blocks away by someone posing as a city engineer. Mulder, convinced Chester only wants to control his power, deduces he has fled to his lab [N]. There Ryan, ignoring Chester's pleas, evaporates in the shadow. Chester has Davey lock him in the accelerator to try and rid himself of the dark matter – and discovers Davey is working for "them." As Davey phones someone to report Chester's been caught, Mr. X kills him. Mulder and Scully arrive to see a man in the accelerator disappearing and leaving behind a dark outline.

Later, Mulder confronts Mr. X, whose description the nurse gave; he had lied about not knowing Chester. Mr. X says that despite being loyal to his predecessors, he's never made Mulder any promises. He adds he didn't kill Chester. Later, Mulder says Dr. Morris West, a physicist affiliated with Polarity, had filed a missing-person report on Davey; Mulder suggests it wasn't Chester in the accelerator. Elsewhere, a scientist tells Mr. X Davey's expertise would have been helpful. A strapped and brain-monitored Chester sits wide-eyed in terror.

X-actitude

Patrick Newirth background: age 52; a top executive with Morley Tobacco of Raleigh-Durham, NC; in Richmond for meetings. His hotel room: 606. His wakeup call: 6 a.m. Date of disappearance: March 31

Margaret Wysnecki background: age 66; retired production-line worker with Laramie Tobacco, where she worked approximately 36 years. Train destination: Hampton Roads, VA. Date of disappearance: March 17

First police-car license-plate:#48 (police-dept. symbol) 759

Second police-car license-plate:#26 (police-dept. symbol) 578

Polarity Magnetics' particle accelerator:

CAST

Tony Shalhoub	Dr. Chester Ray Banton
Kate Twa	Detective Kelly Ryan
Kevin McNulty	Dr. Christopher Davey
Steven Williams	Mr. X
Nathaniel Deveaux	Detective Barron
Robert Rozen	Doctor
Donna Yamamoto	Night Nurse
Forbes Angus	Government Scientist
Guyle Frazier	Officer #1 (Barney)
Steve Bacic	Officer #2
Craig Brunanski	Security Guard

The Cast: Tony Shalhoub's 1991 guest appearance as an Italian waiter on *Wings* led to his Antonio Scarpacci character joining the series that fall as a cabbie. His film credits include *Quick Change* (1990), *Barton Fink* (1991), *Honeymoon in Vegas* (1992), *Addams Family Values, Searching for Bobby Fischer* (both 1993), and *I.Q.* (1994).

The Repertory: Kate Twa played the female version of shape-changer Marty in

one-fifth the power of the Texas Supercollider.

Code to unlock the particle-accelerator target chamber: 8292

Colleague nurse calls to check about the outage: Frank

episode 1.14, "Genderbender"; her other known roles to date have been in the film *Devotion* (1994) and the TV-movie *The Commish: Father Image* (1995). Kevin McNulty had a small role in 1.03, "Squeeze."

X-File case: Classified

2.24 "OUR TOWN"

May 12, 1995
Writer: Frank Spotnitz
Director: Rob Bowman

Dudley, Ark., County Road A7. Lovely young Paula
Gray leads lusty middle-aged George Kearns to a
woody, torch-lit site – where a figure in a carved mask
slays him. FBI headquarters, 10 weeks later: Federal
poultry inspector Kearns is listed as missing. Mulder
and Scully go to Dudley, home of Chaco Chicken.
Mulder says a woman driving on I-40 that night saw
what she called a foxfire spirit in a field. The agents
find a 12-foot-diameter burn and a witch's peg, used to
ward off evil spirits. Sheriff Arens tells the agents
there's no body and no evidence of a crime, that the
fields are full of witch's pegs, and the fire was an illegal
trash burning.

Doris Kearns says her adulterous husband probably
ran off. Mulder, who gives her his card, notices a report
Kearns was going to file with the Department of
Agriculture, recommending that Chaco be closed for
health violations. At Chaco, floor manager Jess Harold
tells the agents and Arens that Kearns was always
trying to shut them down. Suddenly Paula, a Chaco
worker, grabs Harold and puts a blade to his head.
Arens shoots her dead, and she falls into a grinder. Staff
physician Dr. Randolph tells the agents that Paula had
complained last week of headaches and irritability.
Kearns had similar symptoms. Scully wants to do an
autopsy on Paula, and obtains permission from company

X-otica

While I-40 does run
east–west through
Arkansas, there's no
town of Dudley in the
state.

owner Walter Chaco – Paula's grandfather
and legal guardian.

Seth County Morgue: Paula, born Jan. 6,
1948, suffered from the rare, hereditary,
and non-communicable Creutzfeldt-Jacob
Disease, in which brain tissue develops
sponge-like holes, causing dementia and
death. The agents, on their way to check
against courthouse records, are run off
road by a Chaco Chicken truck that
swerves into a small lake; they learn the
driver exhibited the same symptoms as
Paula and Kearns. Arens resists Mulder's
request to drag the lake, but acquiesces
when Mulder suggests the FBI do it. [N]
The dragging produces a pile of human
bones. Scully IDs nine skeletal remains,
including Kearns'; some may be 20–30 years
old. There are no skulls, and the bones are
all smooth at the ends. At the Chaco plant,
Randolph and Harold discuss the bones,
and say a Clayton Walsh has become the
fourth to exhibit symptoms. Randolph says
Chaco's doing nothing about it.

Danny at the FBI faxes a list showing that
in the last 50 years, 87 people have
disappeared within a 200-mile radius.
Scully, who walked into the Sheriff's
station house with a bucket of fried
chicken [N], suggests a cult. Mulder thinks
cannibals, since the polished bone-ends
suggest boiling – as, he claims,
anthropologists found in studying the
(allegedly) cannibalistic Anasazi tribe of
New Mexico.

At Chaco's home, Chaco warns Harold
the townsfolk are losing their faith. Doris
arrives, saying she can't lie anymore, but

Chaco reassures her. Harold doesn't trust her, but Chaco reminds him it's the FBI who are the problem. The courthouse, after dark: The birth records have been burned – recently. Doris calls Mulder on his cell-phone, fearful Chaco will kill her. Mulder goes to arrest him, while Scully leaves to help Doris – whom a masked figure kills.

While a maid goes to get Chaco, Mulder looks at memorabilia: pictures of Chaco in WWII flying regalia (including a shot of him posing with spear-wielding South Pacific aborigines), and a human skull labeled "Jale Tribe, New Guinea, 1944." When the maid says Chaco's unavailable, and that she has no key to a memorabilia cabinet, Mulder breaks into it to find shrunken heads. The maid and Chaco vanish; Mulder calls Scully at Doris', but after a moment on the phone, she's knocked unconscious.

A bonfire-lit field: The townsfolk line up for ladles of soup. Chaco arrives, enraged at what they've done to Doris. He's brought Scully, bound and gagged. Harold accuses Chaco of bringing in the outsider [Kearns] who made them all sick, then brings out the masked man, who beheads Chaco. Mulder, driving by, sees the fire – and Scully on the chopping block. He kills the masked man with two gunshots; panic ensues, allowing Mulder to free Scully. The masked man is Arens; Harold has been trampled to death.

Morning: State Police raid the Chaco plant; Scully's report says the USDA then closed it. Twenty-seven townsfolk have died of Creutzfeldt-Jacob. Yet the remains of Chaco, who'd spent time with the supposedly cannibalistic Jale tribe, are missing.

CAST

Caroline Kava	Doris Kearns
John Milford	Walter "Chic" Chaco
Gary Grubbs	Sheriff Arens [print sources, though not the episode, give his first name as "Tom"]
Timothy Webber	Jess Harold
John MacLaren	George Kearns

Robin Mossley	Dr. Vance Randolph (first name not given in episode)
Gabrielle Miller	Paula (Gray)
Hrothgar Mathews	Mental Patient (Creighton Jones)
Robert Moloney	Worker
Carrie Cain Sparks	Maid

X-actitude

Chaco Chicken motto: "Good People, Good Food!" Indeed.

Walter "Chic" Chaco's background: born 1902; during WWII, transport plane carrying him was shot down over New Guinea (1944). The only survivor, he spent six months with the Jale tribe.

Paul Gray's background: born Jan. 6, 1948; high-school graduate; phone 555-7265.

The agents' rental-car license plate: R89 495

Foxfire spirit: associated with massacred Indians in

extra • The official Fox *X-Files* website erroneously gives actor Timothy Webber's name as "Weber."

The Cast: Gary Grubbs appeared in *For Love and Honor* (NBC 1983); *Half Nelson* (NBC 1985); in the 1988–89 *Davy Crockett* wheel of *The Magical World of Disney* (NBC 1988–90); and *Hull High* (NBC 1990). His large body of work includes the 1987 TV-movie *Foxfire*; *The Burning Bed* (1984 TV-movie) and *Without Warning: The James Brady Story* (HBO 1991).

Timothy Webber, who had a small role in episode 1.21, "Tooms," has played in films and telefilms including *Ticket to Heaven* (1981), *The Grey Fox* (1982), and *Leaving Normal* (1992).

Caroline Kava's credits include *Max Headroom*, *Quantum Leap* and *Tribeca*. Among her films are *Heaven's Gate* (1980), *Year of the Dragon* (1985) and *Born on the Fourth of July* (1989).

John Milford played LAPD Captain Dempsey in the *Dukes of Hazzard* spinoff,

19th-century Ozark folk tales, and of people taken away by fireballs.

Person whom Arens goes to speak with at Chaco plant: Logan

How Scully IDs Kearns' bones: his medical records indicate a metal pin in his femur from a bone break four years ago.

Enos (CBS 1980–81). His TV credits include episodes of *Sledge Hammer!*, *Homefront* and *Picket Fences*, and the telefilm *Spider-Man: The Dragon's Challenge* (1980). Gabrielle Miller has had guest roles on *Sliders* and *M.A.N.T.I.S.*, and appeared in a half-dozen TV-movies to date.

The Repertory: Robin Mossley, here the in-house Chaco physician, played repentant scientist Dr. Joe Ridley in episode 1.16, "Young at Heart." Hrothgar Mathews played a vagrant in 1.05, "The Jersey Devil."

X-File case: Classified

2.25 "ANASAZI"

May 19, 1995
Teleplay: Chris Carter
Story: David Duchovny & Chris Carter
Director: R.W. Goodwin
Part 1 of a 3-part episode

The opening credo this episode: Ei Aaniigoo 'Ahoot'e.
(Navajo for "The Truth Is Out There."]

Navajo Reservation, Two Grey Hills, NM, April 9:
A 5.6 earthquake hits, waking teenager Eric Hosteen.
In the morning, his grandfather, Albert Hosteen,
tells his father the Earth has a secret it needs to
tell. A motorcycling Eric spies metal oddly visible
from a quarry floor. He later shows his family
and neighbors the skeletal, barely fleshy remains of
some humanoid creature. Albert says it should be
returned.

    Dover, DE, April 10. Day. Kenneth Soona's
computer, going through key sequences, beeps "Access
Granted." United Nations Building, New York City,
April 10, night. A worried-looking Antonio tells an
Italian diplomat someone's broken into the "MJ Files."
Soon, word spreads through shadowy power echelons
of Japan, Germany, and the U.S. – including the
German-speaking Smoking Man. Masked assassins burst
into Soona's empty apartment.

    Washington, D.C., April 11. The Lone Gunmen
appear at Mulder's apartment. He's not happy to see
them here, particularly since he hadn't slept last night.
They tell Mulder about a multinational "black ops" unit
known as Garnet – "School of the Americas" alumni –

X-otica

Farmington is a real-
life small city just
outside the Navaho
Reservation.

which is after Soona, a.k.a. The Thinker
(who had helped Mulder in episode 2.08,
"One Breath"). Soona had hacked into the
Department of Defense (DOD) computer
net; now everyone including Customs &
Immigration is seeking to block his escape.
In his last communique, Soona named a
place and a three-hour window in which to meet Mulder. A gunshot
sounds, and the men race to see that a woman in another apartment
has gone crazy and shot her husband.

U.S. Botanic Garden, Washington, D.C., night: Soona (a possible
pseudonym) tells Mulder that killers are tracking him – and that he
believes he has the DOD's UFO intelligence files, with information
about Roswell, MJ-12, and everything from the 1940s on. He gives

Mulder a digital audiotape (DAT) of the
files, which he didn't have time to copy
before high-tailing it. FBI headquarters,
April 12: Mulder tells Scully he finally has
the Holy Grail: proof the government's
known of extraterrestrial existence for 50
years. They find it marked "DOD Top
Secret" – and written in code Scully
recognizes as Navajo, which her military
father had told her was a language Japanese
couldn't break during WWII. She'll try to
find a Navajo speaker. Mulder meets with
Skinner, who is investigating rumors of
Mulder receiving secret files. Mulder denies
it and turns to leave; when Skinner reaches
for him, Mulder hits him and they briefly
brawl.

Next day: Scully meets with Skinner and
four of the usual mysterious higher-ups: the
silver-haired man from her first meeting
with Blevins (in the pilot episode;
identified in the credits as 2nd Senior
Agent); a sharp-featured man with tall,
blown-dry charcoal hair (identified in the

series as Senior FBI Agent); a silver/brown-haired man (series creator Chris Carter, in an uncredited cameo); and a silent, red-haired woman. Scully can't explain Mulder's behavior. The 3rd Senior Agent makes clear that Scully had been originally assigned to debunk Mulder's work. Skinner sends her off, warning her that Mulder has been told of a disciplinary hearing, and if there's anything she's not telling them, she faces the same summary fate: dismissal without chance of reinstatement.

West Tisbury, Martha's Vineyard, MA: Smoking Man visits Mulder's father, greeting him as Bill. Mulder's dad is surprised and disturbed; over Scotch, they discuss the files. Smoking Man claims the hacker "has come forward" and fingered Fox. Bill's agitated since his *own* name is in those files, which Smoking Man assures him are encrypted. "You wouldn't harm *him?*" Bill asks. "I've protected him this long, haven't I?" Smoking Man replies, not entirely convincingly.

Mulder's apartment: Scully tells a strangely snappish Mulder she's meeting with a Navajo speaker in an hour; after she leaves, Mulder tapes an X to his window. Office of the Navajo Nation, Washington, D.C.: A woman there can only make out bits and pieces of the sample Scully's given her, and says Scully needs an actual "code-talker"; she'll ask one to contact Scully. The words she does recognize, she says, are those for "goods, merchandise" and "vaccination." Mulder's dad summons Fox; when Scully returns to Mulder's apartment, he's already gone – and a bullet pierces the window and grazes her.

Martha's Vineyard: A seemingly repentant William tries to tell Fox about "the choices that needed to be made." He warns that the meaning of words like "the merchandise" will become horribly clear. William excuses himself to use the bathroom – where the shadow-government assassin Mulder knew as "Krycek" hides in the shower; he kills William with a single shot and escapes unseen. William's dying words to a tearful Fox: "Forgive me." Mulder calls Scully with the news. They're both afraid he'll be blamed; Scully tells him to run, since a shot has been fired through *his* window, and his life may be in immediate danger. A feverish Mulder agrees to rest at her place while they plan how to find the assassin.

Next morning: Mulder awakens to find Scully's taken his gun to the FBI Firearms Unit for comparison with the bullets [N] removed from William. Scully later removes the bullet from Fox's wall – and notices a workman outside loading a tank into an unmarked van. She finds a row of water-softener tanks in the basement; one, with new valves, is unmarked. Night: Mulder, arriving home, sees a figure running around the corner of his building. Taking a shortcut, he sees an armed "Krycek" approaching. Mulder surprises him, takes his gun, and – certain "Krycek" killed his father – angrily assures "Krycek" he's going to kill him anyway, and to just give up the truth. Scully (apparently having heard the angry screams) rushes to the scene – and after warning Mulder not to kill the "Krycek," shoots Mulder in the shoulder before he can commit vigilante murder. "Krycek" escapes.

Farmington, NM, April 16. The two agents are at a hotel; Scully has driven non-stop for two days, and says Mulder has been out for 36 hours. She's tended to the bullet wound and now gives him water, saying he hasn't had any in all this time – and then shows him a valve from the unmarked tank. She says the tank was probably used to put drugs into his drinking water, explaining his erratic behavior.

Scully introduces him to Albert – a WWII Navajo code-taker who claims an omen had told him Mulder was coming. Albert had told Scully that while most of the files are in jargon, they do refer to an international conspiracy dating to the 1940s; he will take Mulder to where evidence of this conspiracy lies. Scully must return to Washington; she skipped a meeting with Skinner two days ago, certain that Mulder would've been killed if she hadn't gotten him away. She says her *own* name is in those files – in the latest entries, along with references to Duane Barry (who had been instrumental in her seemingly alien abduction in episode 2.06, "Ascension"), and to some "test."

Navajo Nation Reservation: Albert tells Mulder about a tribe who lived here 600 years ago – the Anasazi, whose name, he says, meant "the ancient aliens." Historians believe they disappeared without a trace. And the truth, Mulder asks? Nothing disappears without a trace. Albert believes they were abducted by "visitors" who come here still. Mulder rides with Eric to the quarry; as they climb down toward the exposed metal, Smoking Man calls Mulder on his cellular. He tells Mulder not to listen to everything his father said – that Mulder's father had actually authorized the project, and couldn't live with the guilt. Smoking Man says he wasn't involved; Mulder doesn't believe him. By the time he's hung up, a soldier tells Smoking Man they've gotten a coordinate on Mulder; they enter a waiting black helicopter.

Mulder dusts off a plaque showing this is a railroad car – evidently, a refrigeration car. Mulder calls Scully from inside – where bodies like the one Eric has retrieved are stacked floor to ceiling. Scully tells Mulder the coded documents refer to U.S. experiments conducted by Axis scientists granted amnesty after WWII – tests on humans referred to as "the merchandise." Yet Mulder sees these remains look *in*human – and one has what appears to be a vaccination scar. Eric slams down the hatch, as a black helicopter descends and soldiers emerge. Eric won't talk, and a soldier checking out the boxcar says Mulder's not inside – he's vanished without a trace. Smoking Man yells, in ironic counterpoint to Albert, that nothing vanishes without a trace! Then he tersely orders, "Burn it!" Taking Eric, the chopper ascends – as fire explodes from the hole.

CAST

Mitch Pileggi	Assistant Director Walter S. Skinner
Peter Donat	William Mulder
Floyd "Red Crow" Westerman	Albert Hosteen
Nicholas Lea	"Alex Krycek"
William B. Davis	Smoking Man
Bruce Harwood	Byers
Dean Haglund	Langly
Tom Braidwood	Frohike
Michael David Simms	Senior FBI Agent
Renae Morriseau	Josephine Doane (woman at Navajo Nation office; unnamed in episode)

Ken Camroux	2nd Senior Agent
Dakota House	Eric (Hosteen)
Bernie Coulson	The Thinker (Kenneth Soona)
Mitchell Davies	Stealth Man
Paul McLean	Agent Kautz (unnamed in episode; evidently the Firearms Unit agent)

Uncredited:

Aurelio Dinunzios	Antonio
Chris Carter	3rd Senior Agent
Byron Chief Moon	Father

extra

X-actitude

Buried boxcar plaque: Sierra Pacific Railroad RTC-567490

Taxi that Mulder took home from Scully's apartment: Capitol Cab; phone 555-4987

Book Soona is reading: *The 50 Greatest Conspiracies of All Time* by Jonathan Watkin and John Whalen.

• Note: Tim Michael is listed as "Albert's son" – Eric's father – in the subsequent two parts.

The official Fox *X-Files* website erroneously lists the character played by Renae Morriseau as Joseph, rather than Josephine, Doane.

The Cast: Floyd "Red Crow" Westerman spent a season-and-a-half as Uncle Ray Firewalker in *Walker, Texas Ranger* (CBS 1993–). He appeared twice on *Northern Exposure* as the spirit guide One Who Waits, and was the glimpsed-at shaman in *The Doors* (1991). He also appeared in *Dances With Wolves* (1990), *Son of the Morning Star* (1991), and *Buffalo Girls* (1995), among other roles. He appeared in the TV-movie *Lakota Woman: Siege at Wounded Knee* (1994).

The Repertory: Ken Camroux, the "2nd Senior Agent" at Scully's meeting in Skinner's office, is none other than the mysterious third man in Division Chief Blevins' office in the pilot. From all indications, he's playing the same yet-unnamed, enigmatic character – who's certainly at least as familiar with Smoking Man as Skinner, probably more so, and who seemed perfectly at ease in the room with him in the pilot. Paul McLean and Renae Morriseau had both appeared in episode 1.19, "Shapes."

X-File case: Classified

3.01 "THE BLESSING WAY"

Sept. 22, 1995
Writer: Chris Carter
Director: R.W. Goodwin
Part 2 of a 3-part episode

Albert Hosteen reflects on history being controlled by eliminating witnesses and their memories. The Smoking Man and camouflaged soldiers burst in, having seen Mulder's car outside, and beat up Albert and his son and grandson, vainly seeking Mulder and the MJ Files. After the soldiers leave, the bloodied Hosteens direct Scully to the smoldering boxcar. No sign of Mulder. That night, driving across the Navajo Reservation northwest of Los Alamos, NM, Scully is menaced by a helicopter; soldiers take her paper files, and leave when she tells them Mulder has the DAT version.

Skinner's office: At the Office of Professional Conduct four of the usual higher-ups put Scully on mandatory leave. She turns in her badge and gun, and complains to Skinner about being railroaded. Then, in Mulder's office, she finds that the DAT is missing.

New York City, (East) 46th Street: Smoking Man meets with a cabal of mysterious power-brokers, including Elder #1, #2, and #3; and the Well-Manicured Man. Elder #2 wants assurance that 40 years of work haven't been compromised. Smoking Man half-truthfully assures the files have been recovered, and the pilferers

X-File case: Classified
Government denies all knowledge

– including Mulder – "removed." The heavyset man says all pertinent parties should be informed. At her mom's house, Scully breaks down.

Next day: Albert finds a barely living Mulder beneath some rocks at the quarry, where he'd somehow hidden underground. [N] He transfers the unconscious agent to a hogan, and brings in Navajo holy men to perform the healing, days-long Blessing Way Chant. Scully's apartment: A saddened Frohike arrives, having heard of Mulder's apparent death. He shows Scully a newspaper article from two days ago, about the execution-style slaying of Kenneth J. Soona, a.k.a. The Thinker, who'd hacked into the DOD's MJ files and given Mulder the DAT.

Mulder hovers between life and death in a spectral starfield, where Deep Throat tells him, that truth without justice or judgment is hollow. Mulder's father, William, laments the lies that poisoned his soul. They urge Fox to keep his memory – and thus the truth – alive.

At the front entrance of FBI headquarters, Scully sets off a metal detector; the friendly guard, who knows her, figures it's just some stray pin. Scully shows Skinner the Soona obit, and asks to compare the Trenton PD ballistic record against that of Mulder's father. Skinner replies any match would have been noted already, and he won't doublecheck; he also tells her he's executed a warrant to search her apartment for the DAT. As she leaves Scully and the guard narrow the source of the alarm to something imbedded in her neck. (A doctor later extracts what he at first suspects is buckshot.)

Navajo Reservation: On the third day of the ritual, Mulder awakes and asks for water; and recuperates. Scully's doctor now tells her that the metal object is a computer chip. At her sister Melissa's urging, Scully sees a regression-hypnosis special, psychotherapist Dr. Mark

X-otica

Since Scully walks to her mother's house we must assume they live close by, almost certainly in the same town.

The division usually referred to as the Office of Professional Responsibility is here called the Office of Professional Conduct.

Pomerantz. She hazily recalls her "lost" abduction time: A man took her, there were other men, a light, and distorted sounds – including that of an alarm and of someone wondering if she were all right. Panicked, she cuts the session short. Later, she sees Skinner leaving her apartment house and driving away.

Albert tells Mulder that as part of the ritual, he cannot bathe or change clothes for four days, and explains Mulder had gone to the "origin place" in each of us – it was all a dream. Scully phones Skinner, who, with Smoking Man in his office, denies being at her apartment. That night, Scully dreams Mulder is alive and speaking to her. Garden of Reflection, Parkway Cemetery, Boston: At William Mulder's funeral, Scully tells Fox's mother she believes her son is alive. Afterward, the Well-Manicured Man approaches Scully; he is from a consortium representing global interests that would be extremely threatened by the DAT being leaked. He tells her that Mulder is dead and she herself is next. He warns her only because her murder will draw problematic attention to his group. Its business? They predict the future.

Greenwich, CT: Mrs. Mulder is ecstatic to see Fox alive. Yet she only reluctantly takes him to the attic to find artifacts of his father – and unconvincingly swears she doesn't recognize any of the other seven men in a photo taken in 1972 (per Mulder this episode) or "about 1973" (per Mulder next episode), though we can clearly see one of them is Smoking Man. Mulder pulls a gun from a trunk and leaves. Scully's apartment: A worried Melissa phones that she is coming over; Scully agrees, but then, recalling the warning, decides to go to Melissa's instead – with an automatic pistol. Yet as she leaves, Skinner pulls up, claiming he needs to speak with her immediately in private; warily, she takes him to Mulder's apartment – and at gunpoint demands to know who sent him.

At Scully's, assassin Luis Cardinal (identified only as "Hispanic

Man" until episode 3.16, "Apocrypha") shoots Melissa in the head; his partner, the man known as Alex Krycek, realizes their horrible error and the two quickly vanish. Back at Mulder's, Skinner says it was he who had taken the DAT from Mulder's desk – and insists he, too, wants justice done. Suddenly, Scully hears footsteps outside the door – and in that split-second of distraction, Skinner draws *his* gun on *her*. They stare down each other's barrels in a standoff.

"In Memoriam LARRY WELLS 1946–1995"

CAST

Mitch Pileggi	Assistant Director Walter S. Skinner
Peter Donat	William Mulder
Floyd "Red Crow"	
Westerman	Albert Hosteen
Melinda McGraw	Melissa Scully
Sheila Larken	Margaret (Maggie) Scully
Nicholas Lea	"Alex Krycek"
William B. Davis	Smoking Man
John Neville	Well-Manicured Man
Tom Braidwood	Frohike
Jerry Hardin	Deep Throat
Alf Humphreys	Dr. (Mark) Pomerantz
Dakota House	Eric (Hosteen)
Michael David Simms	Senior FBI Agent
Rebecca Toolan	Mrs. Mulder
Don S. Williams	Elder #1 (Heavyset man)
Forbes Angus	(Scully's) MD

Mitchell Davies	Camouflage Man
Benita Ha	Tour Guide
Victor Ian	Minister
Ernie Foort	Security Guard
Lenno Britos	Hispanic Man (Luis Cardinal)

Uncredited:

Stanley Walsh	Elder #2
John Moore	Elder #3
Martin Evans	Major Domo (goateed man)*

extra

X-actitude

Men in the old photo, from statements and evidence in this and the following episode, left to right:

Smoking Man, William Mulder, Victor Klemper, unknown, unknown, Deep Throat, unknown, Well-Manicured Man

Apartment across from Scully's: #3. Since Scully's apartment is #35, it's likely that a digit is missing from the door across the hall.

● * Actor name and character designation given in episode 3.16, "Apocrypha."

Note: The Lowry book lists Tim Michael as playing Albert's son (Eric's father) this episode – yet for the previous episode, Lowry lists Byron Chief Moon in the role. Neither are credited onscreen, but Moon, who appears in *White Fang 2: Myth of the White Wolf* (1944), appears to be correct.

The Cast: John Neville is probably best known as the acerbic butler Desmond on *Grand* (NBC 1990) and as the title character in Terry Gilliam's *The Adventures of Baron Munchausen* (1988). He made his film debut with *Oscar Wilde* (UK 1960). His more recent movies include *Little Women* (1994) and *Dangerous Minds* (1995).

Rebecca Toolan also appeared in *Little Women* (1994). She has appeared in *MacGyver* and *The Commish*, and films including *The Accused* (1988) and *Hideaway*

License plate on Scully's personal car: 2N9-521 (state indecipherable). Since Scully is on mandatory leave with no access to motor-pool vehicles, this two-door car must be her own.

Melissa's family nickname: Missy

Newspaper article: (paper) *The Examiner*; (headline) Homicide Victim Body Discovered at City Dump; (article highlights) body of Kenneth J. Soona discovered April 16 in the Trenton Landfill by longtime landfill worker Sparky Sinclair; Soona had spent his early childhood in Youngstown, PA, and went to college on an academic scholarship; survived by mother Jane, sisters Isabel and Elsbeth, and brother Mike.

(1995), and most recently playing a teacher in *Big Bully* (1996).

Dakota House has to date appeared in *The Diviners* (1993).

The Repertory: Michael David Simms appears a third time as a nameless senior agent who takes delight in ordering sanctions against Mulder and Scully. His TV credits, from 1986 on, include *Matlock, NYPD Blue* and *The Marshal.* His sole movie credit to date is *Alien Nation* (1988). Forbes Angus, who's guested all over the Vancouver TV circuit, had a small role as a scientist in 2.23, "Soft Light." Don S. Williams – separated at birth from British comedian Robbie Coltrane? – would reprise his role as one of the covert-cabal "elders" next episode and in 3.10, "731" (a.k.a. "Nisei, Part 2"). Mitchell Davies, the camouflaged lead soldier who needlessly batters an old man and two other civilians, plays evidently the same soldier in the previous installment, credited as "Stealth Man."

X-File case: Classified

3.02 "PAPER CLIP"

Sept. 29, 1995
Writer: Chris Carter
Director: Rob Bowman
Part 3 of a 3-part episode

In a voiceover, Albert Hosteen describes Mulder's recuperation, and gives news from Native Americans in the Great Plains of white buffalo's birth – a major omen of change. Mulder's apartment: Mulder, gun drawn, bursts into the standoff and forces Skinner to hand Scully his gun.

Scully complains about her death threat; Skinner asks Mulder what is in the DAT. After telling Skinner that "your cigarette-smoking friend" killed his dad and tried to kill him, Mulder explains that the tape holds the secret DOD documents confirming the existence of alien life on Earth. They let Skinner hold onto it for safekeeping when he insists it is their only leverage to bring the conspirators to justice.

D.C. General Hospital: A doctor tells a frantic Margaret Scully that her daughter just out of surgery for a cranial gunshot wound isn't Dana, but Melissa. Office of *The Lone Gunman*: The agents show Langly and Byers the 1972 photo of Mulder's dad and others. They discuss Project Paper Clip, in which Nazi scientists were granted immunity in the U.S. after World War II. Langly recognizes one such war criminal in the photo: Victor Klemper, who conducted inhuman experimentation on Jews. Frohike gently breaks the news (gleaned from a police scanner) about Melissa;

Scully bolts to go, but Mulder convinces her that whoever's responsible will be gunning for *her* there.

New York City, (East) 46th Street, 7:09 a.m. At the covert cabal's suite, the heavyset man cautions Smoking Man about the repercussions of an innocent woman being shot; another "elder" confirms the assassins work for Smoking Man. The Well-Manicured Man wants the DAT, which Smoking Man, lying, says he has in safekeeping and will bring tomorrow. At a greenhouse, the agents speak with Klemper, who says only that the photo was taken at the Strughold Mining Company in West Virginia, and then asks if they know the formula of Napier's Constant. After they leave, Klemper phones the Well-Manicured Man to taunt him that he's been visited by the son of one of his old colleagues. The Well-Manicured Man, now aware that Mulder is alive despite Smoking Man's assertions, arranges for more satisfactory killers.

As an ominous man in a blue suit paces outside Melissa's room, Albert arrives to tell Margaret that Dana's fine but can't come; he stays to pray over the comatose Melissa. West Virginia: Inside an abandoned coal-mining facility, Scully and Mulder find an incongruous set of security doors with numeric-keypad locks. They punch in the first five digits of Napier's Constant (see below), until Scully gets one door open.

FBI headquarters: Skinner tells Smoking Man he may have the DAT, and wants to keep it from the wrong hands. Smoking Man hisses he doesn't make deals and insinuates that Skinner's own assassination is possible. At the mine, Scully and Mulder find countless rows of file cabinets containing medical files – each including a smallpox vaccination record and a tissue sample. They find records both for Scully and for Mulder's sister, Samantha – the latter originally earmarked for Mulder himself. A rumbling brings Mulder upstairs,

X-otica

Scottish mathematician John Napier (1550–1617), who invented logarithms and introduced the decimal point in math, devised a base number for all natural logarithms. This Napier's Constant is 2.71828 – yet, somehow, the agents opened the five-digit coded door by entering not 27182, but 27828.

Klemper calls the Well-Manicured Man "the most venal" he has ever met – which is really saying something, considering Klemper's a World War II Nazi scientist.

Mario Mark Kennedy was a prominent on-line X-Phile.

where he sees a majestic spacecraft slowly moving overhead. Inside the mine, small apparent aliens scurry past an astonished Scully. Suddenly, unmarked cars arrive. Gun-toting men chase Mulder downstairs but the agents slip out a back door [N].

Morning: Charlotte's Diner, Route 320A, Craiger, MD. Meeting with Skinner, the agents reveal their find. Skinner wants to turn over the DAT in exchange for their own safety; Mulder objects, but Scully says the truth won't do them any good if they're fugitives. Skinner – who confirms that whoever downloaded the files (e.g., Soona) copy-protected them against either digital or hard copies [N] – assures them the conspirators will honor the deal, or else he will turn State's evidence and they'd have to kill him, too. The agents agree to the trade, and Skinner gives them a lift (to, ostensibly, their hidden car).

Melissa's hospital room: Albert has been praying for two days. Skinner, arriving, introduces himself to Albert and Margaret. The blue-suited man still hovers ominously; a suspicious Skinner chases him into a stairwell, where he's ambushed and beaten by Blue Suit and two others – Luis Cardinal, and the man known as Alex Krycek, who takes the DAT. Southeast Washington, D.C.: Krycek and the others stop for gas and beer; after the others leave, a wary Krycek sees the clock oddly blinking, and escapes just before the car blows up.

Klemper's greenhouse: The agents find Well-Manicured Man, who tells them Klemper's dead, and doesn't deny complicity; he also admits to being in the 1972 photo, and to knowing Mulder's father. He offers three disconnected bits of information – a 1947 spaceship crash in New Mexico (e.g. Roswell); Dr. Josef Mengele's Nazi wartime super-soldier experiments, also worked on by scientists granted amnesty under Operation Paper Clip; and Kemper's orchid hybrids – and Mulder deduces Kemper was working to create an alien-human hybrid. Well-Manicured Man continues: During the Cold War, men like Mulder's father collected genetic data for, ostensibly, post-apocalyptic identification; but these medical records gave Klemper access to a DNA database of hundreds of millions of vaccinated Americans. When William Mulder learned of this misuse, he threatened to expose this eugenics project – so they took Samantha hostage.

Elsewhere, a seething Krycek phones Smoking Man at the cabal's suite, and promises exposure if Smoking Man ever threatens him again. Greenwich, CT, 2 a.m.: Mulder's mother, under pressure, painfully reveals to Fox that his father was told to make a choice between their children (confirming Well-Manicured Man's story). FBI headquarters: Skinner tells Smoking Man he'll trade the DAT (which he doesn't have) for Scully and Mulder's safety. Smoking Man knows he's bluffing, and suggests he may have Skinner killed for trying. But Skinner reveals Albert, and informs Smoking Man that Albert has memorized the MJ Files' contents, and has carried on the Navajo oral tradition by teaching it to 20 others: unless Smoking Man can have every Navajo in four states killed, he'd better leave them alone. At the hospital, Scully tells Mulder that Melissa died three hours ago – as with Mulder, they've taken away her sister. Now even the skeptical Scully admits she has heard the truth – and moreover, wants answers.

"In Memoriam MARIO MARK KENNEDY 1966–1995"

CAST

Mitch Pileggi	Assistant Director Walter S. Skinner
Walter Gotell	Victor Klemper
Melinda McGraw	Melissa Scully

Sheila Larken	Margaret (Maggie) Scully
Nicholas lea	"Alex Krycek"
William B. Davis	Smoking Man
John Neville	Well-Manicured Man
Tom Braidwood	Frohike
Dean Haglund	Langly
Bruce Harwood	Byers
Floyd "Red Crow" Westerman	Albert Hosteen
Rebecca Toolan	Mrs. Mulder
Don S. Williams	Elder #1 (Heavyset man)
Robert Lewis	ER Doctor
Lenno Britos	Hispanic Man (Luis Cardinal)

Uncredited:

Stanley Walsh	Elder #2
Peta Brookstone	ICU Nurse
Martin Evans	Major Domo*

X-actitude

Scully's birth year: 1964

Scully's childhood home the year she received her smallpox vaccination: 3170 W. 53rd Road, Annapolis, MD

Scully's vaccination certificate number: 29510

extra   •   * Actor name and character designation given in episode 3.16, "Apocrypha."

The official Fox *X-Files* website misspells Langly as "Langely," and neglects to list front-credit performer Floyd "Red Crow" Westerman.

The Cast: Walter Gotell has played memorable *mittel-Europeans*, including Colonel Riaf in *Black Sunday* (1977), Mundt in *The Boys From Brazil* (1978), Ambassador

Mulder's birthdate, per medical-record file: Oct. 13, 1961

Mulder's vaccination certificate number: 378671

The scoop on Samantha, per medical-record file: Samantha Ann Mulder, born Nov. 21, 1965. The police report, in the pilot episode, gives her middle initial as "T.," but then, the report also showed a typo in the spelling of her hometown. Her medical records here seem more credible.

License plate on the assassins' car: 3CB-502

Dr. Josef Mengele's genetic-experimentation center: Institute of Hereditary Biology and Racial Hygiene

Gotell in *Basic Training* (1985), Max Klizer in an episode of *Miami Vice*, and Max Klaus in an episode of *Spenser: For Hire*. He's probably best known as the KGB chief, General Anatol Gogol, in six James Bond movies.

X-File case: Classified

3.03 "D.P.O."

Oct. 6, 1995
Writer: Howard Gordon
Director: Kim Manners

Connerville, OK, Sept. 12. Night: At a strip-mall video arcade, off-duty pizza deliverer Jack Hammond declines to let Darren Oswald have back the "Virtua Fighter 2" game which Darren had left for a minute. A fight brews, as Darren's arcade-clerk friend Zero watches. But then Jack, seemingly not in control of his body, leaves and gets into his car – where he's killed by a strange electrical surge.

Lloyd P. Wharton County Building, next morning: Scully examines Hammond's body as Stan, the county coroner, and Johnston County Sheriff Teller watch. This latest in a pattern of odd electrocution deaths shows, curiously, no contact point; the coroner doesn't remember if the previous bodies had them, and defensively insists it's just lightning – though admitting the five recent Connerville strikes (four fatal) are statistically "improbable." Teller asserts there's nothing unusual: The nearby Astadourian Lightning Observatory on Route 4 has 100 ionized rods designed specifically to stimulate lightning. Later, Mulder wonders why the lightning only strikes 17- to 21-year-old males.

Checking the only shop open after Jack quit work, they question Zero; he noticed nothing, he says, what with the noise and flashing lights here. An onscreen display alerts Mulder that the 10-game record-holder on "Virtua Fighter 2" is initialed D.P.O. – as in Darren Peter Oswald, the only survivor of the lightning strikes. The notations place D.P.O. here at the time of the incident. Kiveat Auto Body: Darren, working there, nervously greets Sharon Kiveat, the beautiful wife of garage owner Frank. He has a crush on her, which makes her uneasy. Frank returns from a towing job, soon followed by Mulder and Scully. As the agents fruitlessly question Darren, Mulder's cell-phone mysteriously heats and starts melting.

Night: At the dilapidated Oswald house, Darren's couch-potato mother belittles him, and doesn't bat an eye when he changes channels from across the room without the remote. When Zero comes by, Darren goes to a pasture next door to "barbecue" some cows. Zero begs him not to – but Darren calls lightning down to hit him, and the next morning Teller is there as three dead cows are towed away. He shows the agents a fulgarite – a place where lightning strikes sandy soil to form glass – and declares their

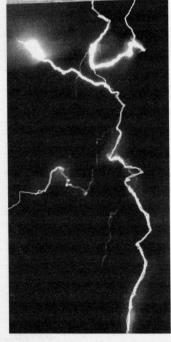

investigation over. Yet after he leaves, Mulder finds a partial footprint incongruously in the fulgarite. Forensic Lab, Johnston County Sheriff's Office: Scully finds it is from a size 8½ standard military boot; she also finds traces of antifreeze. They go to find auto mechanic Darren.

County Road A-7: Darren manipulates traffic lights, hoping to cause an accident. Zero suggests he stop all this, and use his power to make a killing in Vegas. But Darren won't go anywhere without Mrs. Kiveat. Oswald house: the agents find an 8½ shoe and a clipped picture that fits the cut-out yearbook space for Mrs. Kiveat. Accident scene: Darren causes tow-trucker Frank to have an apparent heart attack; when the two EMS workers find their portable defibrillator unaccountably chargeless, Darren "heroically" rescues Frank by defibrillating him by hand while EMS is preoccupied with the spare unit.

Community Hospital, Felton, OK, 10:25 a.m.: As Frank recuperates, the agents learn Darren was admitted here five months ago in cardiac arrest after his lightning-strike – and that he has acute hypokalemia, an electrolyte imbalance of high sodium and low potassium, which, Mulder theorizes, somehow explains his ability to generate electricity. They question Darren at the Johnston County Jail, but he admits nothing, and thinks Zero squealed on him. With 72 hours to hold him, they try to get Mrs. Kiveat to press harassment charges. She had been afraid to, but the agents say they can hold him 72 hours on suspicion of murder, so she and Frank will be safe.

At the jail, Teller has decided the feds have a weak case, and lets Darren go. The agents rush to the hospital, but Darren has stopped at the arcade first to kill Zero. Darren eludes Mulder to get to Frank's room, where Scully draws her gun – but Sharon, wanting no danger near Frank, agrees to walk out with Darren. Outside, she runs away when Teller pulls up. Darren, over the edge, kills Teller before Mulder can fire; then Darren falls in a lightning-crumpled heap himself. Oklahoma State Psychiatric Hospital: Scully tells Mulder the coroner has ruled Teller's death accidental, by lightning, and the D.A. can't fathom how to prosecute for murder. And Darren, inside his cell, stares blankly at a TV screen that may or may not be channel-changing according to his whim.

X-actitude

Darren's "Virtua Fighter 2" records (rank/initials/date/time):

1.	D.P.O.	09-12-95	11:41 PM
2.	D.P.O.	09-11-95	11:35 PM
3.	D.P.O.	09-11-95	10:50 PM
4.	D.P.O.	09-11-95	10:30 PM
5.	D.P.O.	09-10-95	10:15 PM
6.	D.P.O.	09-10-95	11:04 PM
7.	D.P.O.	09-10-95	11:18 PM
8.	D.P.O.	09-10-95	11:33 PM
9.	D.P.O.	09-08-95	10:37 PM
10.	D.P.O.	09-08-95	10:56 PM

Hammond's body found: 12:17 AM (Sept. 13)

CAST

Jack Black
   Zero*

Giovanni Ribisi
   Darren Peter Oswald

Ernie Lively
   Sheriff Teller

Karen Witter
   Sharon Kiveat

Steve Makaj
   Frank Kiveat

Darren's other three victims: Corey Huffar, Burke Roberts, Billy (no last name given)

Mrs. Oswald's TV shows: A talk show with a heavily tattooed man discussing rebellion and S&M and a (fictional) music video Darren switches to – The Rosemarys, "Mary Beth Clark I Love You," J. Hartling Records, Director: Deb Brown. The latter is an X-Phile also referred to in episode 2.14, "Die Hand Die Verletz."

Radio frequency of lightning, per Mulder: 8Hz; called the Schuman Resonance

Lettering on Frank Kiveat's tow truck: Kiveat 24 Hr. Towing Auto Service

Sharon Kiveat: Remedial reading teacher at Gravenhurst High School; Darren failed her class

Peter Anderson
  Stan Buxton (last name not given in episode)
Kate Robbins
  Mrs. Oswald
Mar Andersons
  Jack Hammond
Brent Chapman
  Traffic Cop
Jason Anthony Griffith
  Paramedic #1
Uncredited, each with one or more speaking lines:
Cavan Cunningham
  Paramedic #2
Bonnie Hay
  Night Nurse

extra   ● * Character's full name (given in print sources but not in the episode) is Bart Liquori.

The Cast: Giovanni Ribisi played the recurring role of Jeff Billings in the final season of *The Wonder Years* (1988–93), and co-starred as 18-year-old Elvis DeMattis in the Peter Scolari–Pamela Reed ensemble sitcom *Family Album* (CBS 1993). He's guested on series including *NYPD Blue*, *Chicago Hope*, and *These Friends Of Mine* (*Ellen*). He debuted in a 1987 episode of *My Two Dads*.
  Jack Black appeared in *Dead Man Walking*

Frank's hospital room: 404

Darren's t-shirt when he's taken in for questioning: Vandals (front); Nitro records (back)

Specified charge level of the portable defibrillator: 300 joules

(1995) as one of Sean Penn's younger brothers. Other films include *Bob Roberts* (1992), *Demolition Man* (1993), *Waterworld* (1995), and *Bio-Dome* (1996). He's played "Randy" on a couple of episodes of *The Single Guy*, and guested on *Picket Fences*, *Life Goes On*, *Northern Exposure* and elsewhere.

Ernie Lively's credits include *Shocker* (1989), *Turner and Hooch* (1989), *Hard to Kill* (1990), *Passenger 57* (1992) and *My Family, Mi Familia* (1995). He's been a *Murder, She Wrote* utility player since 1990, and has also appeared in *Beauty And The Beast*, *Newhart*, *Quantum Leap*, *Sisters*, and *Seinfeld*.

Karen Witter played Ms. February in the TV-movie *I Married a Centerfold* (1984). Her movies include Chuck Norris' *Hero and the Terror* (1988), *Popcorn* (1991), and *Ratboy* (1986). Her screen start was as a challenger on *Star Search* in 1983.

X-File case: Classified

X-File case: Classified
Government denies all knowledge

3.04 "CLYDE BRUCKMAN'S FINAL REPOSE"

Oct. 13, 1995
Writer: Darin Morgan
Director: Rob Bowman

St Paul, MN, Sept. 16. Insurance salesman Clyde Bruckman buys a Lotto ticket in a liquor store. Outside, he passes a thin, balding, redheaded man going to see palm reader Madame Zelma. The man (later identified as "Puppet") asks Zelma why he envisions and then carries out terrible things. Then he murders her.

North Minneapolis, three days later: A doll collector and amateur tasseographer (tea-leaf reader) is the latest in a string of prognosticating serial-murders. Detective Cline tells Detective Havez he has asked for the help of Mulder and Scully, who have arrived to investigate.

Elsewhere, Bruckman tries to sell a life-insurance policy to young marrieds the Gordons – before envisioning Gordon, two years from now, suffering a fatal head-on collision with a drunk in a blue 1987 Mustang. Later, Bruckman helps senile apartment-house neighbor Mrs. Lowell with her garbage. He has a momentary vision of her Pomeranian eating entrails; moments before, he'd envisioned a human head in a bag of lettuce. At the dumpster, he finds Madame Zelma's body.

Scully and Mulder question him since he knows details the police hadn't divulged. Mulder suspects he may be psychic, and they take him to the tea-reader's apartment. The reluctant Bruckman says the killer feels his life is so out-of-control he's like a puppet – and he states they'll find the victim's body tomorrow morning at a specific spot in Glenview Lake. After the agents do so, Mulder returns to Bruckman (who's just lost at Lotto) and convinces him to be tested for psychic ability – which they discover is limited to foretelling death.

Scully arrives with one of three identical keychains found on the victims; it has a logo she has traced to Uranus Unlimited, which sells astrology-based marketing advice. Bruckman says Uranus owner Claude Dukenfield has been murdered; they find his body near some woods to which Bruckman directs them. On the way, Bruckman has shut up the inquisitive Mulder by suggesting there are worse, if more

dignified, ways to die than autoerotic asphyxiation. Why are you telling *me*, Mulder worriedly asks. Later, Bruckman says the killer is a psychic himself, and Bruckman sees what *he* sees: Mulder being stalked in a kitchen, getting his throat slashed after stepping in a banana-cream pie. Just a madman's ravings, Bruckman insists. He explains the vision came after touching a letter from the killer, in which he vows to kill Bruckman – and though postmarked the day before the agents met him, the letter says to tell the feds hi.

Le Damfino Hotel, Sept. 21: Scully guards Bruckman in protective custody and asks him about her own death. Midnight: Mulder, relieves Scully and gets an earful from Bruckman about his recurring dream of being dead and decomposing. Morning: Detective Havez relieves Mulder. He accompanies Scully to the murder site of yet another tarot-reader. While Havez uses the bathroom, Bruckman lets in a bellhop who'd just bumped into Scully and Mulder. It's the killer, who is astonished to find Bruckman here. Coincidence or destiny? Brandishing a steak knife, the killer asks why he does what he does. Bruckman says simply it's because he's a homicidal maniac. He adds, "You don't kill me now." Havez isn't so lucky.

At the tarot-reader's, Scully concludes that the bellhop did it. At the hotel she finds Havez dead and Bruckman gone. Mulder grapples with the bellhop in the kitchen, and though the prediction's specifics are a bit off, the killer *is* about to knife Mulder when Scully kills the man with a single shot. They find Bruckman in his apartment, dead or about to die of autoerotic asphyxiation; Scully holds his hand compassionately while a tear rolls down his cheek. He's left a note asking Scully to care for Mrs. Lowell's remains and maybe adopt her dog. Later, at home, Scully watches a late-night Laurel & Hardy short with the pooch – and when a Yappi infomercial comes on, throws her phone at the screen.

X-actitude

Bruckman's apartment: 503; Mrs. Lowell's is 504

Doll-collector's apartment: 66

Minneapolis police APB, based on Yappi's very general "psychic reading": White male, 17–34, with or without facial hair, with or without a tattoo.

Value of life-insurance policy Bruckman wants to sell the Gordons:

CAST

Peter Boyle	Clyde Bruckman
Stu Charno	The Killer ("Puppet")
Frank Cassini	(Detective) Cline
Dwight McFee	(Detective) Havez
Alex Diakun	Tarot Dealer
Karin Konoval	Madame Zelma
Ken Roberts	(Liquor-store) Clerk
Jaap Broeker	The Stupendous Yappi
David McKay	Young Husband (Mr. Gordon)
Greg Anderson	(Police) Photographer

Uncredited (no lines, but prominent presence):

Doris Rands	Mrs. Lowell

$200,000, for $2,400 net annual cost.

Bruckman's Scotch: J&P

Claude Dukenfield data: 43 years old, divorced with two kids, lives at 316 Roundview Lane, non-smoker, makes about $87,000 a year.

Winning Lotto numbers: 8, 12, 36 (by extrapolation), 38, 40, 44. Bruckman's numbers: 9, 13, 37, 39, 41, 45.

extra   • Yappi's lovely assistant (who has no lines but appears in Yappi's scenes and in his infomercial) is uncredited, as is the animal-performer.

Continuity error: Bruckman's Lotto ticket is dated Monday, Oct. 9, 1995 (which is probably the date of the drawing and not of the purchase). Since this is the only onscreen artifact relating to the date, it holds more credence than the date-and-place subtitles, which place the events in mid-September.

The Cast: Peter Boyle made his movie debut as the title character of *Joe* (1970). He was Robert Redford's campaign manager in *The Candidate* (1972), the sympathetic monster in *Young Frankenstein* (1974), the cabbie-guru Wizard in *Taxi Driver* (1976), Chief Orman in *Honeymoon in Vegas* (1992) and George in *Bulletproof Heart* (1995). On TV, he starred in *Joe Bash* (ABC 1986) and has played recurring characters on *NYPD Blue, Lois & Clark: The New Adventures Of Superman, Flying Blind*, and *Midnight Caller*.

Stu Charno, billed as Stuart Charno until 1991, has guested on *Perfect Strangers, Newhart, Chicago Hope* and elsewhere.

Frank Cassini has appeared in *The Commish* and *M.A.N.T.I.S.*, as well as the feature *Timecop*.

The Repertory: Dwight McFee's many films and telefilms include *The Journey of Natty Gann* (1985), *Malone* (1987), *Knight Moves* (1992), *Dead Ahead: The Exxon Valdez Disaster* (HBO 1992), and *Unforgettable* (1996). Vancouver-based Alex Diakun, who'd appeared in episode 2.20, "Humbug," has been in films and telefilms including the first three above with McFee.

X-File case: Classified

3.05 "THE LIST"

Oct. 20, 1995
Writer-Director: Chris Carter

Night: On a remote road, a car picks up a waiting man. Eastpoint State Penitentiary, Leon County, FL, 5 p.m.: Warden Leo Brodeur begins the execution of Napoleon "Neech" Manley. Manley's wife Danielle swears that she'll never love again. The waiting man appears inside the electric-chair chamber – wearing a black hood.

As Manley dies he swears he'll be reincarnated, and that five men will die to pay for his mistreatment. FBI headquarters, three days later: Mulder tells Scully Manley was convicted in 1984 for driving the getaway car in a Florida liquor-store double-murder. Mulder has discovered that Manley appears to be making good on his threat. The guard who had led him to the chair was found dead of suffocation in Manley's cell.

At the prison, Brodeur figures Manley had help from confederates. As he, Mulder and Scully approach the guard's body they find it covered with maggots. Mulder questions convict John Speranza, who'd known Manley well. Speranza is convinced that Manley has returned. The whole prison is nervous. A guard, Fornier, takes Scully to examine Manley's cell, and leaves her alone there. She is then pulled into the shadows by guard Vincent Parmelly, who tells her a con named Roque has Manley's hit list.

7:03 a.m.: Fornier's maggoty head is found inside a paint can. The state coroner explains to Scully that *Lucilia Cuprina*, or the green bottle fly, can lay eggs within a minute after death occurs, and hot, humid environments promote rapid growth. Roque privately tells Mulder he'd overheard Manley giving Speranza the names; now Roque will exchange them for transfer to another prison. But Brodeur, later, tells Mulder he won't deal – and moments afterwards, walks into his office to find Fornier's headless body in his chair. Manley's cell, 3:45 p.m.: Scully and Mulder find evidence of Manley's obsession with soul-transmigration, and a letter from his wife. They visit Danielle at her home; she's genuinely terrified that Manley has returned. At the prison, the Warden beats Roque to death while demanding he read who's on the list. All Roque will say is that Brodeur is number five.

Danielle's lover, Parmelly, assures her that Manley is not coming back. At the prison, Mulder pressures Brodeur into revealing the executioner's name – Perry Simon – to save him from becoming one of the next victims. But the agents find him dead in his attic, covered

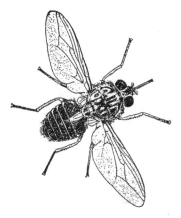

with maggots. Speranza refuses to give Mulder the list, but reveals that Roque was not on it. Two more will die. Scully alerts Mulder that in that last two months, Manley made 30 calls to a Danny Charez – who's been to see Speranza three times since the first murder. Questioning Charez, the agents learn that he was Manley's 26-year-old court-appointed lawyer who Manley always blamed for his conviction. Charez hopes to get Speranza a retrial, and avoid Manley's supernatural wrath. He had even sought Danielle's help, but her boyfriend Parmelly had threatened him with a gun. At the prison, Speranza agrees to Brodeur's deal: Stop the murders, and Brodeur will pull strings with the governor. That night, Charez brushes away a large fly, just before some blurry African-American man – Manley? Or Parmelly? – smothers him with a pillow.

The agents then stake out Danielle's place and, later, pick Parmelly out of a prison-guard mug book. When Brodeur tells them Charez has been murdered, they go to arrest Parmelly. Danielle, at home, wakes to see Manley in her room; she follows him to the living room, but sees only Parmelly. Convinced he's actually Manley, she kills him with two shots as the agents and cops burst in. At the prison, the sadistic Brodeur beats a bound Speranza as he had beaten Roque.

As the agents drive away, aspects of the "closed" case still bother Mulder – there are too many unanswered questions about how and why Parmelly could have been the killer. Brodeur drives by in the opposite direction, calmly swatting a large fly. To his horror, he sees Manley in the back seat – reaching over to wrestle with the wheel until the car smashes into a tree, killing Brodeur. The back seat's already infested with maggots.

CAST

J.T. Walsh	Warden Leo Brodeur
Bokeem Woodbine	Roque (print sources, but not the episode, give his first name as Sammon)
Badja Djola	Napoleon "Neech" Manley
John Toles-Bey	John Speranza
Ken Foree	Vincent Parmelly
April Grace	Danielle Manley
Greg Rogers	Daniel Charez
Mitch Kosterman	Fornier
Paul Raskin	Ullrich (coroner; name not given in episode)
Denny Arnold	Key Guard
Craig Brunanski	Guard
Joseph Patrick Finn	Chaplain

Uncredited:

Bruce Pinard　　　　　Executioner Perry Simon

Listed in print sources, but not evident in episode:

Don McKay　　　　　Oates

Michael Andaluz　　　Tattooed Prisoner

The Cast: J.T. Walsh earned a 1984 Drama Desk award and a Tony in David Mamet's Pulitzer Prize-winning *Glengarry Glen Ross*. He made his telefilm debut in *Little Gloria . . . Happy at Last* (1982) and his movie debut with *Hard Choices* (1984). Later movies include *Hannah and Her Sisters* (1986), *Tin Men* (1987), *Good Morning, Vietnam* (1987), *Tequila Sunrise* (1988), *Hoffa* (1992), *The Last Seduction* (HBO 1993, theatrical 1994), *The Client* (1994), and *Nixon* (1995). His TV includes episodes of *The Equalizer, L.A. Law* and *Lois & Clark: The New Adventures of Superman*.

X-actitude

Manley's mug shot/ arrest number: 50416.

Prison time: 11 years, 56 days. His wife was allowed only three visits in that time. Two stays of execution.

Death-row cell-block: Q

Agents' Lariat rental-car license plate: Florida plate OKE 46J

Guards visible in mug-shot book: Sgt. S. Gold #4151; Guard V. Parmelly #4310

Badja Djola played a heavyweight boxer in *The Main Event* and a con named "Half-Dead" Johnson in *Penitentiary* (both 1979). His movies include *Night Shift* (1982), *The Serpent and the Rainbow* (1988, with fellow X-guest Dey Young), *Mississippi Burning* (1988), *A Rage in Harlem, The Last Boy Scout* (both 1991), and *The Waterdance* (1992).

John Toles-Bay wrote the screenplay for *A Rage in Harlem*, and has appeared in films, including *Midnight Run* (1988), *Trespass* (1992), *Angie* (1994) and *Waterworld* (1995); his extensive TV work includes recurring roles on *The Watcher* and *The Flash*.

Bokeem Woodbine, who appears to be making his network-series debut here, was one of the ensemble stars of *Dead Presidents* (1995), and appeared in *Jason's Lyric*, Spike Lee's *Crooklyn* (both 1994) and *Panther* (1995).

Ken Foree has appeared in some 30 films and telefilms since his debut in *The Bingo*

Long Traveling All-Stars and Motor Kings (1976), and his countless TV credits include the 1980s *Alfred Hitchcock Presents, The Tracey Ullman Show, Quantum Leap, Cheers*, and *M.A.N.T.I.S.*

April Grace recently appeared in *Headless Body in Topless Bar* (1996), starring recurring X-guest Raymond J. Barry, and in the movies *Angie* (1994) and *Safe* (1995); on TV, she's guested on *China Beach, NYPD Blue*, and *Empty Nest*.

Joseph Patrick Finn is one of the series' producers.

The Repertory: Vancouver-based Mitch a.k.a. Mitchell Kosterman broke into network TV guesting on *Wiseguy* in 1989. He's twice played a police detective named Lt. Horton on *The X-Files*.

X-File case: Classified

3.06 "2SHY"

Nov. 3, 1995
Writer: Jeffrey Vlaming
Director: David Nutter

Cleveland, OH. Night. A man and woman talk in a car, against a romantic skyline. Lauren MacKalvey is a plain-looking, somewhat overweight woman; her date is an attractive, charming man she met online three months earlier. When he kisses her, she gags up a gelatinous substance. Morning: A cop finds a grotesque, goo-covered skeleton in the car. Detective Alan Cross contacts Mulder and Scully, recommended as FBI experts in the unusual. A few months earlier in Aberdeen, Mississippi, four women who'd answered personal ads had disappeared in less than a month. The sole body found was too decomposed for an autopsy.

The killer, going by the alias Virgil Incanto, chats online with overweight Ellen Kaminsky, whose computer handle is "Huggs." His is "Timid," and he wants to meet. Incanto is interrupted by his landlady, who, thinking him a novelist or editor, asks him to critique her poems sometime. Cuyahoga County Morgue, same day (Aug. 29; see X-actitude, page 343), 4:15 p.m. [N]: Scully discovers Lauren's remains have decayed into a skeleton and a pool of red glop. Mulder, meantime, learns the man Lauren had dated last night had been communicating with her online, handled "2Shy"; Lauren's roommate gives Mulder copies of the romantic letters 2Shy had sent Lauren. Mulder calls Scully to say 2Shy's their serial killer – he'd opened his online account with one of the Aberdeen victims' credit cards.

Morgue: Scully tells Mulder the crime-scene goo is mostly hydrochloric acid, similar to stomach acid; it also contains traces of the digestive enzyme pepsin. The red glop is composed of normal body chemicals, except for extremely low amounts of adipose – fatty-tissue. Night: Ellen is nervous about meeting "Timid" – all the more so when her friend Joanne reminds her about the general warning the FBI has just issued. Ellen rationalizes that she's been chatting with Timid every day for a month – but ultimately doesn't show up at a French restaurant where he waits. Incanto finds a chunky streetwalker, Holly McClain – who scratches him savagely before he kills her in an alley. Incanto runs when another hooker and her john come by.

Morning: Scully finds all air passages in McClain's body blocked with the viscous hydrochloric goo. Mulder tells Cross that 2Shy's

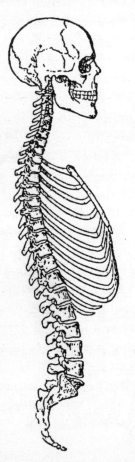

e-mail to Lauren quoted from obscure 16th-century Italian poems found only in controlled-circulation academic libraries; he asks Cross to compile a list of literary professors and such. Incanto – a translator of Italian literature – signs for a package at his apartment house, running across the landlady and her blind pre-teen daughter, Jesse.

Cleveland P.D., 1st District, 10:13 a.m.: Mulder arrives with an FBI analysis of the killer's skin, found under McClain's nails. There's no match in the DNA database of known offenders – but the report does note the samples contained no oils or essential fatty acids. Mulder thinks the killer is (in Scully's sardonic words) "a fat-sucking vampire." Cross arrives with a list of 38 names. Ellen e-mails Incanto asking for another chance. Cross, canvassing, questions Incanto. Night: Ellen gives Incanto a lift home after dinner. The landlady, with her poems, has let herself into Incanto's apartment – where she finds

342

X-actitude

Scully, tape-recording her autopsy notes, gives the date as Aug. 29. This episode, then, would have to have taken place before episode 3.03, "D.P.O.," which demonstrably takes place Sept. 12–14, 1995.

Incanto's apartment: #27

Online chat-room where Timid and Huggs meet: "Big and Beautiful"

Two unseen people to whom Det. Cross refers: Wendy Sparks, the Cleveland PD's liaison with the FBI; and Dr. Kramer, the county coroner. Unseen social worker in whose care Scully places Jesse: Mrs. Shepherd

Restaurant where Incanto is stood up: Les Trois Etoiles ("The Three Stars")

Cross' body. Incanto, seeing the light on, leaves Ellen to investigate. Later, Jesse comes by, looking for her mom; Incanto lies, saying he hasn't seen her. But Jesse, who's smelled her mother's perfume, calls 911.

When the agents and police burst in they find Incanto gone, and Cross and the landlady dead. FBI Regional Office, Computer Crime Section: An agent restores the erased files on Incanto's hard drive, and breaks the password and encryption to retrieve a list of Incanto's online chat-room women. Incanto, meantime, talks his way into Ellen's apartment. The agents e-mail a warning and a sketch to everyone on Oncanto's list, then go to check on two women unreachable by phone – including Ellen, who's excused herself to excitedly e-mail Joanne. Doing so, she finds the FBI sketch in her bin; Incanto sees it, too, and attacks.

The agents break in when Ellen doesn't answer, and neighbor Joanne confirms she's home. Ellen's injured but alive; Mulder chases a man he sees fleeing down the street – who turns out to be just a graffiti-tagger. Incanto, hidden, attacks Scully in the bathroom – but Ellen shoots him with Scully's gun, left behind in the bedroom [N]. Cuyahoga County Jail, one week later: Incanto, his skin mottled and curdling, confesses to 47 murders in five states. He insists he's no monster, that he gave them what they wanted and they gave him what he needed. In Italian he adds, "The dead are no longer lonely."

Lauren's weight on driver's license: 165; at death: 122. Lab container with the acid found on Lauren: #43978

Ellen's address: 658 South Hudson Ave., #23; her license plate: DUF 274

Numbers on cover of FBI DNA-report folder (top-to-bottom): 458790; 477998; 45879V

FBI hotline number: 800-555-0132

Per Mulder, the poems Incanto quotes from include: Guinzelle's "Lavitanova"; Casteona's "Il Courtagiano." Poem Incanto says he'll read to Ellen: "E Cazzone." Book Incanto receives from Strautcher Publishing, via the FedEx-like Transcontinental Express (seen in

CAST

James Handy	Detective Alan Cross
Timothy Carhart	"Virgil Incanto"
Catherine Paolone	Ellen Kaminsky
Kerry Sandomirsky	Joanne [(Jo) Steffen]
Aloka McLean	Jesse
Suzy Joachim	Jennifer (Lauren's roommate; unnamed in episode)
Glynis Davies	Monica (landlady; unnamed in episode)
Randi Lynne	Lauren (MacKalvey)
William MacDonald	Agent Kazanjian (unnamed in episode)

Uncredited:

Brad Wattum	Patrolman
P.J. Prinsloo	(Graffiti) Tagger
Jan Bailey Mattia	Second Hooker
Lindsay Bourne	Second Hooker's John

episode 2.22, "F. Emasculata"): *Poeti Italiani Del Novecento*.

Church where landlady takes a poetry class: St. Frank's

Man whom a canvassing Scully questions: Mr. Brennan

Computer-handles of woman on Incanto's list (ostensibly all in the "Big and Beautiful" chat room) include: Big Heart, Opera-Girl, Jenni, KSmithe, louise, Delphine, Friend, Jeannie, Marsha, LoriG, Badgrrr, Riosha, Care Bear, Huggs, NightenGail, Gina L., BarDoe. Real names include: Rhonda Jahnitz, Tara Jarrette, Alison Pritchard.

Dean McKenzie   Lt. Blaine (African-American detective; unnamed in episode)

The man playing Brennan (no lines) is uncredited.

Listed on the official *X-Files* website, but not evident in episode:
Beverly Elliot   Raven

extra   • The official Fox *X–Files* website neglects to list antagonist Timothy Carhart.

Continuity error: Though Ellen's handle is Huggs, Mulder tells Scully and the computer tech it's Friend.
   Three of the 47 women Incanto has killed: Jennifer Flackett, Kathy Miller, Hillary Turk

X-act Location: The Cleveland police station is the First District Police Headquarters Building in Washington, D.C., close to the Capitol Building, on Virginia Avenue.

The Cast: Timothy Carhart played the guy who tried to rape Geena Davis' character in *Thelma and Louise* (1991). After making his film debut in the teen sex comedy *The Party Animal* (1984), he did off-Broadway and episodic TV work before playing Dr. Tony Metzger in the cast of the Richard Chamberlain series *Island Son* (CBS 1989–90). He also appeared on *thirtysomething* and on *John Grisham's The Client*. Carhart's movies include *Desperately Seeking Susan* (1985), *Working Girl*

(1988, with Duchovny), *The Hunt For Red October* (1990), *Red Rock West* (1993), *Beverly Hills Cop III* (1994, as the villain), and *Black Sheep* (1996). On Broadway, he appeared with Jessica Lange and Alec Baldwin in *A Streetcar Named Desire*.

James Handy is best known for his recurring role of Borough Commander Haverill on *NYPD Blue*. Among his nearly 40 films and telefilms are *The Verdict* (1982), *Brighton Beach Memoirs* (1986), *The Preppie Murder* (1989 TV-movie), *The Rocketeer* (1991), *Jumanji* (1995) and, as Detective Vannatter, *The O.J. Simpson Story* (1995 TV-movie). His other series work includes *Melrose Place, Picket Fences, L.A. Law, Midnight Caller*, and *Walker, Texas Ranger*.

Catherine Paolone played the recurring role of Rose on early episodes of comedian John Mendoza's 1993–94 sitcom, *The Second Half*. Her other TV credits include *Cagney & Lacey*, the 1980s' *The Twilight Zone, Perfect Strangers, Hard Time on Planet Earth*, and *Chicago Hope*. Among her films are *Heart Like a Wheel* (1983), *Project X* (1987) and *Unlawful Entry* (1992).

Suzy Joachim made her film debut with the direct-to-video *Ultimate Desires* (1992), and has appeared in *Hideaway* (1995) and *Unforgettable* (1996).

The Repertory: Glynis Davies makes her fourth and most prominent appearance; her other work includes the miniseries *Evergreen* (1985), the telefilms *One Police Plaza* (1986) and *For the Love of Nancy* (1994), and the feature *Stella* (1990).

X-File case: Classified

3.07 "THE WALK"

Nov. 10, 1995
Writer: John Shiban
Director: Rob Bowman

Army Hospital Psychiatric Ward, Fort Evanston, MD: Lieutenant Colonel Victor Stans has tried to commit suicide three times in three weeks, and tells a doctor some phantom figure won't let him die. Stans goes alone to the hydrotherapy room, where he sets a whirlpool to almost 200°, then jumps in, holding weights. An alarm goes off – and a manually bolted door somehow unlocks by itself. He's rescued, horribly burned. Three weeks later, he tells investigators Mulder and Scully about the phantom, who appears to be a soldier, and had burned alive his wife and children three months ago. Captain Janet Draper informs the agents that General Thomas Callahan is quashing their inquiry. A take-charge Scully threatens to have Callahan investigated for obstruction. Mail clerk Quinton "Roach" Freely watches suspiciously. At a therapy session for wheelchair-bound veterans, bitterly obnoxious quadruple amputee Leonard "Rappo" Trimble berates a single amputee for describing "The Walk," an apparently common recurring dream about having working legs; Roach, Trimble's flunky, wheels him away. Roach – a fellow combat vet whom Leonard blames for a mistake that cost him his limbs – is worried about the FBI.

Callahan tells the agents he has reported their "gross misconduct" to Justice; the agents fire back with questions about germane facts strangely missing from Stans' file, plus the lackadaisical Army investigation of the family's house fire. Scully notes similar under-reported circumstances in the case of a Staff Sergeant Kevin Aiklen six months ago; both served under Callahan in the Gulf War. Investigating the hydrotherapy room, Mulder suspects some Gulf War biological weapon as the root cause, and Scully suspects the general is protecting the men who murdered their families.

Night: The phantom soldier momentarily materializes in Callahan's office, then leaves a garbled message on the answering machine – even though Callahan turns it off. Minutes later (10:32 p.m.), Draper, swimming at the officers' gym, is murdered by some invisible force; the agents later find bruises consistent with a struggle. Callahan tells them about the phantom, who'd left two previous garbled messages

on his home answering machine. Rosslyn, VA: Eight-year-old Trevor Callahan screams to his mom, Frances, that a stranger is in the house; Roach surreptitiously leaves. The agents arrive with Callahan, who plays them the one phone microcassette he's saved of the phantom voice. They see a man fleeing through the yard, and later find fingerprints that direct them to Roach at his apartment; there they find mail addressed to Aiklen, Draper, Stans, and Callahan. And at the Callahan home, while a uniformed guard sneaks a smoke, something kills young Trevor in his sandbox – burying him alive.

Roach, under questioning, says he's only a "mailman" for Trimble, whom the agents discover is a quadruple amputee. Later, Roach in his cell cries in terror to a guard that Rappo's going to kill him; about an hour later, the guard and Scully find Roach suffocated to death with a bedsheet. Mulder shows Scully dental plates he's been

carrying; each reveal radiation exposure –

from, Mulder theorizes, astral projections, which supposedly have psychokinetic capabilities. He is convinced it is Trimble; Freely's mail-gathering may have provided a necessary connection to people and places to which he could project. As for the tapes, they're backwards-masked, saying his time has come. The agents confront Trimble, who laughs in their faces.

That night, Callahan sees the phantom in combat uniform – and follows bloody bootprints upstairs to find Frances dead. Callahan loads his .45 and goes to Stans; admitting Stans was right, Callahan puts the gun to his own head but gets only clicks. Stans tells him Trimble is the phantom killer – and indeed, the unspeakably evil Rappo gleefully admits killing Frances and the boy, too. He urges Callahan to kill him, but the general lets him live, to suffer like the rest. After the agents arrive and take Callaghan's gun, the general rides an elevator that deposits him against his will in the sub-basement. There the phantom traps him amid bursting steam-pipes. Mulder tries to help, but the phantom tosses him away. Trimble goes into cardiac arrest, and as Scully goes to fetch a crash cart, Stans suffocates Trimble. The hell downstairs abruptly stops. Later, Mulder's report says the murders remain officially unsolved. The disfigured Stans, now a mail clerk, brings letters to the tragedy-stricken Callahan's desk.

CAST

Thomas Kopache	Gen. Thomas Callahan
Willie Garson	Quinton "Roach" Freely
Don Thompson	Lt. Col. Victor Stans
Nancy Sorel	Capt. Janet Draper
Ian Tracey	Leonard "Rappo" Trimble
Paula Shaw	Ward Nurse
Deryl Hayes	Army Doctor
Rob Lee	Amputee

Andrea Barclay	Mrs. (Frances) Callahan
Beatrice Zeilinger	Burly Nurse

Uncredited (each with speaking lines):

Pat Bermel	Therapist in group session
Brennan Kotowich	Trevor Callahan
Paul Dickson	Uniformed Guard
D. Harlan Cutshall	Guard

X-actitude

Agents' license plate: Virginia ND4-729

Roach's fingerprints: two matching index fingers and a thumb, on the mailbox and on the backyard door.

Trimble's remains: cremated and ashes interred at Tannersville, PA cemetery; the Army refused him burial at Arlington.

Type of bugs in Roach's drawer: ant

Continuity error: Callahan (who from the way he checks outside the door has never encountered the phantom before) tells the agents that the phantom knows his name. Yet the phantom never uttered Callahan's name, calling him only "Killer."

The Cast: Ian Tracey had the recurring role of John Hibbs on *The Commish*; he also co-starred in the final season of *Sweating Bullets* (CBS; new episodes 1991–93). He made his film debut as a child, in the obscure 1975 Canadian film *The Keeper*, and most often appears in TV-movies, including *Conspiracy of Silence* (1992), *The Comrades of Summer* (HBO 1992), and *Incident at Deception Ridge* (1994). Among his films are *The Journey of Natty Gann* (1985), *Stakeout* (1987), and *Timecop* (1994).

Thomas (a.k.a. Tom) Kopache made his movie debut with *Strange Invaders* (1983). Recent films and telefilms include *This Boy's Life* (1993), *And the Band Played On* (HBO 1993), *Star Trek: Generations* (1994), and *Leaving Las Vegas* (1995). On TV he's guested on *Spenser: For Hire, Law & Order, The John Larroquette Show, Murder One*, and other series.

Nancy Sorel went from *Generations* (NBC 1989–91) to *Down the Shore* (Fox mid-1992 to 1993). She played Roxanne Rawlins in two

1992 episodes of *Doogie Howser, M.D.*, and most recently co-starred as Sarah Johnson in the *Black Fox* Western TV-movie trilogy (CBS 1995).

Willie Garson has played Lee Harvey Oswald *twice* (in *Ruby* and in an episode of *Quantum Leap*, both in 1992). Among Garson's other work is *Groundhog Day, Untamed Heart* (both 1993), *Speechless* (1994), *The Tie That Binds* (1995), and the occasional role of Carl in some 1980s episodes of *Mr Belvedere*. More recent guest-spots include on *Mad About You, Boy Meets World*, and *L.A. Law*.

The Repertory: Don Thompson, in his most extensive role to date, had played a black-suited government thug in episode 1.04, "Conduit," and an experimented-on Vietnam vet in 2.04, "Speechless." His work includes *And the Sea Will Tell* (1991 TV-movie), *Knight Moves* (1992), and *The Program* (1993). Deryl Hayes, as the African-American doc, had played a mysterious investigator in episode 1.06, "Shadows," and an FBI agent in 2.01, "Little Green Men." Beatrice Zeilinger had played a paramedic in 2.17, "End Game."

X-File case: Classified

3.08 "OUBLIETTE"

Nov 17, 1995
Writer: Charles Grant Craig
Director: Kim Manners

Valley Woods High School, Seattle, WA: Amy Jacobs, 15, has her class picture taken. The photographer, Larken, berates his creepy assistant, Carl Wade, for fixating on the girl. That night at 10:05 p.m., Wade abducts Amy from her room, as her sister calls out for mom. That same moment, at a fast-food restaurant 20 miles away, 30-year-old counter-woman Lucy Householder starts bleeding inexplicably, and collapses – repeating exactly what Wade had told Amy: that nobody was going to spoil them.

Jabobs house, next day: Special Agent in Charge Walt Eubanks tells Mulder he will be happy to have him interview Lucy and explore this vague connection. University Medical Center, Seattle, 10:31 a.m.: Mulder meets Scully, who has flown in separately. The doctors say Lucy has glossolalia, or incoherent speech. Mulder notes that when Lucy was eight, she, too, was kidnapped; she spent five years locked in a basement before escaping. Now the troubled Lucy – who has a criminal record of prostitution and narcotics, and whose boyfriend is doing time for assault and child endangerment – is belligerent and unhelpful to the agents. Elsewhere, with his car disabled on a rainy two-lane road, a tire-iron-wielding Wade threatens a tow-truck driver who stopped to help.

FBI Regional Field Office, Seattle, 1:53 p.m.: Lucy's blood is O-positive, yet Forensics found both that and B-positive – Amy's blood-type – on her clothes; Scully will run a P.C.R. to see if that blood's DNA matches

X-otica

An oubliette (from the French *oublier*, "to forget") is a dungeon with a trap door on top as the only way in or out.

Amy's. Bright Angel Halfway House, 7:19 p.m.: Lucy's shivering, has fresh scars on her face, and tells housemate Henry it's dark and she can't see. Amy, at that moment, in a basement cell, shivers in the dark, with the same scars. Bright Angel, 8:03 p.m.: A paramedic pronounces Lucy fine, yet a sympathetic Mulder – who sees his sister Samantha's plight in Lucy – still can't get her to talk. FBI Seattle office: Scully and Mulder see a tape of 13-year-old Lucy, shot a week after she was found in 1978; like Amy, she'd been kept in the dark by a largely unspeaking captor. Scully finds that school photos taken by Larken Scholastic had been sent to all students except Amy; Larken himself had checked out, but Wade – whom he had fired the next day – had spent most of the last 15 years institutionalized with a bipolar condition.

Day: When Wade drives away, Amy escapes. Wade returns and gives chase. Amy runs – as does Lucy the moment Mulder shows her Wade's photo. When Amy stumbles and hurts her wrist, so does Lucy. After Mulder returns to her room, Scully, Eubanks and another agent arrive to arrest her: The blood on her uniform matched Amy's DNA. But Lucy has fled. Eubanks, though acknowledging Lucy was 20 miles from Amy, thinks she and Wade are in league. FBI Seattle office, 5:35 p.m.: The tow-truck driver, responding to a police-bulletin photo of Wade, shows on a map where he'd encountered Wade; Mulder, checking his direction and the available roads, spots nearby Easton, WA –

where Lucy had been taken 15 years ago [N]. Soon, three unmarked cars speed through the small town; Mulder and Scully check Bilton Photo to see if Wade has an account – and an address. Soon, about ten agents storm Wade's house; he's gone, but Lucy is in the cell, sobbing; no one knows why she came back to her place of imprisonment.

Lucy starts shivering, and says Amy is cold and wet. With most of the agents heading north, to where Wade's car has been spotted, Mulder and Scully head east, toward the river; they leave Lucy with a young Agent Kreski. In the river, Wade hears distant police sirens and starts to drown Amy. Lucy, simultaneously, starts vomiting water and stops breathing; Kreski calls EMS. At the river, after Wade ignores Mulder's demand to stop, Mulder shoots him dead. Scully and Mulder try to resuscitate Amy, to no avail. Yet moments after Scully convinces an obsessed Mulder that it's futile, Amy starts to breathe – as Lucy, at that moment, dies. Bright Angel, next day: Scully tells Mulder Amy hasn't even a cut on her – and the state pathologist found five liters of water in Lucy's lungs. Even skeptic Scully says that Lucy died for Amy. And a brokenhearted Mulder suspects also this was Lucy's way of putting her past to rest.

CAST

Tracey Ellis	Lucy Householder
Michael Chieffo	Carl Wade
Jewel Staite	Amy Jacobs
Ken Ryan	Eubanks
Dean Wray	Tow Truck Driver
Jaques LaLonde	Henry
David Fredericks	Larken
Sidonie Boll	Myra Jacobs (first name not given in episode)
Robert Underwood	Paramedic

Dolly Scarr   Fast Food Supervisor

Bonnie Hay   Woman

David Lewis   Young Agent (Kreski)

Uncredited:

Alexa Mardon   Sadie Jacobs

(Amy's sister; name not given in episode)

X-actitude

Roads near where tow-truck driver found the west-bound Wade: Interstate 12; County Road 15 North; Route 903

Amy's birthday: Upcoming this Tuesday, per Mrs. Jacobs the morning after Amy's abduction.

Name of driver who'd called for tow-truck: Gary Mosier

Tow-truck driver's call to Eubanks: Line 3

extra   • The African-American cop, who has a line, is uncredited.

The official Fox *X–Files* website erroneously lists the character Carl Wade as John Wade, and Eubanks as Banks.

The Cast: Tracey Ellis made her film debut with 1992's *The Last of the Mohicans*, and broke into TV the same year with an episode of *Law & Order*. Her other films to date are *This Boy's Life, The Age of Innocence* (both 1993), and *The Neverending Story III* (1994). On TV she's been seen in *Grace Under Fire, ER*, and other shows.

Jewel Staite, making her network-episodic debut, has appeared in the TV-movies *Posing: Inspired By Three Real Stories* (1991) (TV-movie), and *Liar, Liar* and *The Only Way Out* (both 1993), plus the feature *Gold Diggers: The Secret of Bear Mountain* (1995).

Michael Chieffo had previously guested as a photographer on another Chris Carter-produced series, *Rags to Riches*. His other TV credits include *Cagney & Lacey, Picket Fences* and *These Friends of Mine*; among his films are *The Last American Virgin* (1982), his movie debut, and *I Love You to Death* (1990), *Last Action Hero* (1993), *Cobb* (1994), and *Crimson Tide* (1995).

Ken Ryan appeared in the films *Astonished* (1988) and *Popcorn* (1991), and was announcer on the Toronto-shot game shows *Bumper Stumpers* (USA Network 1987–90) and *Jackpot* (USA Network 1985–88).

The Repertory: Bonnie Hay had played a field doctor in the two-parter "Colony" and "End Game" (2.16–2.17), and was uncredited as the night nurse in 3.03, "D.P.O." David Lewis, in his third and most prominent appearance, was briefly in 1.05, "The Jersey Devil," and 2.09, "Firewalker." David Fredericks had played a security guard in 2.03, "Blood."

X-File case: Classified

3.09 "NISEI"

Nov. 24, 1995
Writers: Chris Carter, Howard Gordon,
            Frank Spotnitz
Director: David Nutter
Part 1 of a 2-part episode

Knoxville, TN: At a railroad yard, an older Japanese man steps out of a train car uncoupled there that day, as four other Japanese men go inside to a surgical suite – where a videocamera records them operating on someone receiving transfusions of green "blood." Gas-masked soldiers brandishing automatic weapons slaughter the unarmed men, and body-bag an apparent alien or alien-human hybrid. FBI headquarters, days or weeks later: Mulder plays Scully an "alien autopsy" video he ordered from a magazine; someone in Allentown, PA had recorded it off a satellite dish at 2 a.m. It shows the scene we've just witnessed, up to the soldiers' arrival.

Allentown. Day: Scully and Mulder find Steven Zinnszer bound and executed in his bedroom, his body still warm. Mulder captures a fleeing Japanese man, Kazuo Sakurai, taking his briefcase. Police Substation C, Allentown. Night: Skinner unexpectedly arrives with a federal attorney, to free Sakurai – a high-ranking Japanese official with diplomatic immunity. Outside, the briefcase Mulder "forgot" to turn in contains satellite photos of a ship, and a list of local members of the UFO-buff group MUFON, headed by Zinnszer. Scully goes to the home of the circled Betsy Hagopian, while Mulder takes the photos to the Lone Gunmen. Washington: Byers, Frohike and Langly say the ship in these probably Japanese photos is the *Talapus*, a salvage vessel out of San Diego. It has supposedly been

357

searching for a Japanese ship sunk during WWII. Nothing was reported found – yet the ship returned not home, but to a Naval yard in Newport News, VA. Night: A well-dressed, hawk-like man kills Sakurai in his limo as Sakurai's driver remains impassive.

Day: At Hagopian's, Scully is greeted with eerie recognition by two women who tell each other, she is one of them. She later meets several "alien-abductee" women each taken repeatedly to what they call "the bright, white place." Coast Guard headquarters, Newport News: An official tells Mulder the DEA wouldn't let the *Talapus* into port, and the ship put out to sea next morning. Mulder finds an unmarked ship with a *Talapus* jacket inside; when a squadron of black ops storm aboard, he dives to safety. The women show Scully they have, like her, neck scars where a computer-chip was extracted. They take her to the Allentown Medical Center's Oncology

Department, where a tumor-filled Hagopian is dying – as a result, the women contend, of repeated abduction and testing since her teens. They say it's their and Scully's fate.

Night: Mulder looks inside a shipyard building guarded by black ops; inside is an obscured, blimp-shaped vessel surrounded by scientists and soldiers. At home, Mulder finds his apartment ransacked; Skinner, who arrived afterwards, demands the briefcase, citing pressure from higher-ups. Mulder says Scully has it, and he doesn't know where she is; Skinner leaves, seeing that Mulder's on his own. Office of Senator Richard Matheson: Mulder's benefactor provides the names of the four murdered doctors – and hints of monsters begetting monsters. Mulder matches the names to a World War II photo of a (real-life) Japanese medical corps code-named 731, which performed heinous human experimentation. One member is Dr. Takeo Ishimaru, reported dead in 1965 – whom Scully

X-otica

Scully recognizes Ishimaru as one of the doctors in the autopsy video, and Senator Matheson confirms to Mulder the doctors were killed, not wounded. Yet *Ishimaru is alive to catch the train*. What's going on? The answer – neglectfully unaddressed in the episode itself – is that Mulder's autopsy video began *before* the operation, and that Ishimaru is the man leaving the train car when the other four doctors arrive. (While it's true that Ishimaru's name isn't among those of the four dead doctors, that's no indication Ishimaru hadn't been one of them, since we know he uses aliases.)

Dialog: When Scully first sees the alien-autopsy video, she comments humorously that this is even

insists she's seen. Mulder is certain this all involves the alien-human hybrid project Deep Throat spoke of (in episode 1.24, "The Erlenmeyer Flask") and the Well-Manicured Man hinted at (in 3.02, "Paper Clip"). Mulder receives a fax (evidently but not definitively from Matheson) showing car 82517 of a secret government railroad.

An FBI scientist tells Scully her mysterious computer chip has state-of-the-art microlithography and an unknown purpose; he'll keep checking. Quinnimont, WV: As Mulder watches, several Japanese men place into the train car a living, alien-like figure in an anticontamination suit. The train pulls away before Mulder can catch it. Washington: Scully, reviewing the "autopsy" video, recognizes Ishimaru – and envisions him peering over her in the bright, white place. Mulder calls to say the surgical car will connect with a Canadian passenger train outside Cincinnati; Scully apprises him of Ishimaru.

Edwards Terminal, Queensgate, OH: One of the men who ushered the "alien" into the train car is killed by the hawk-like assassin. A distinguished Japanese man (Dr. Shiro Zama, a.k.a. Dr. Takeo Ishimaru, per next episode) arrives for the Vancouver-bound train – which Mulder, arriving minutes later, just misses. Scully, arriving at her or a friend's apartment door, finds Mr. X outside in the hall, saying Mulder's in danger if he boards that train. Scully cell-phones Mulder with the warning; disregarding her, he jumps from an overpass onto the train's roof, losing his phone.

hokier than the one they ran on the Fox network!

Quinnimont, WV is a fictional town; the other towns and cities are real.

The Japanese word "nisei" translates literally to "second generation," and refers to the U.S./Canadian-born and -educated children of immigrant Japanese ("issei"); those born here of immigrants and educated in Japan are "kibei." Metaphorically, the title apparently refers to the second generation of Japanese-conducted human (and by extension human/alien) experimentation.

X-actitude

Allentown MUFON (Mutual UFO Network) members noted here:

Steven Zinnzser (deceased)

CAST

Mitch Pileggi
  Assistant Director Walter S. Skinner
Stephen McHattie
  Assassin*
Steven Williams
  Mr. X
Raymond J. Barry
  Senator Richard Matheson
Robert Ito
  "Dr. Shiro Zama"/Dr. Takeo Ishimaru
Tom Braidwood
  Frohike
Dean Haglund
  Langly
Bruce Harwood
  Byers
Gillian Barber
  Penny (last name Northern per Fox *X-Files* website, but not per end-credits or dialog)
Corrine Koslo
  Lottie Holloway (name not given in episode; first name given in closed-caption only)
Liri Triolo
  Diane (name not given in episode)
Paul McLean
  Coast Guard officer

Betsy Hagopian
(hospitalized, terminal)

Edna Cooper

Doug St——— (rest of
name obscured on list)

Penny

Cathy (woman whom
Penny phones)

unnamed woman
("Lottie" per closed-
caption) who opens
door

Doctors murdered in
surgical train car:
Naofomi Sakaguchi,
Shigeru Takeuchi,
Matanaru Shimizu,
Daisuke Nishigaba.

Senate Committee of
which Matheson is a
member: Intelligence

Agents' Lariat Rental
Car license plate:
Washington, D.C. 4S7
573

"Alien-autopsy" train
car: 82594; second

Brendan Beiser
Agent Pendrell (name not given in this
episode, but in next)
Yasuo Sakurai
Kazuo Sakurai

Uncredited (with speaking lines or notable
presence):
Carrie Cain Sparks
Train station clerk
Warren Takeuchi
Man killed at train station
Bob Wilde
Limo driver

Listed in print sources, but not evident in
episode:
Roger Allford
Harbormaster

extra   • The official Fox
X–Files website erroneously gives the
character name of Agent Pendrell as Agent
Comox, and the character Kazuo Sakurai as
Kazeo Takeo.

 * Print sources refer to the character as
"Red-Haired Man," but McHattie
demonstrably does not have red hair;
compare his brown locks with Scully's or
Agent Pendrell's red hair.

surgical car: 82517; train engine that uncouples the former: 756

"Alien-autopsy" tape: $29.95 plus shipping, from Rat Tail Productions, Allentown, PA

Where Sakurai was found dead: C&O (Chesapeake & Ohio Railroad) Canal

Announcement at Queensgate station: "Your attention, please: All passengers for Canadian Northwest Express to Vancouver, prepare for boarding on track four."

Apartment Scully has keys to: #5, off a traditional-looking apartment-house hallway. Apparently, she's no longer in the subdivided house with a private entrance to her apartment (#35). But why did she move to a smaller, much less elegant place?

The Cast: For backgrounds on Pileggi, Williams and the Lone Gunmen, see their separate biographies; for Stephen McHattie, see next episode; for Raymond J. Barry, see 2.01, "Little Green Men."

Robert Ito is best known as Jack Klugman's assistant coroner, Dr. Sam Fujiyama, on *Quincy, M.E.* (NBC 1976–83). Ito made his screen debut in two 1966 B-pictures, *Women of the Prehistoric Planet*, a.k.a. *Prehistoric Planet Women*, and *Dimension 5*, a sci-fi/secret-agent flick. Among his early TV work is the voice of son Henry Chan in *The Amazing Chan and the Chan Clan* (CBS 1972–74); Ito would join fellow cast-member Keye Luke (who voiced Charlie Chan) in the hit TV-movie *Kung Fu* (1972).

Brendan Beiser, Yasuo Sakurai, and Corrine (a.k.a. Corrine L.) Koslo appear to be making their network-episodic debuts.

The Repertory: Gillian Barber had played a tough FBI supervisor in episode 1.07, "Ghost in the Machine," and a single mom in 2.10, "Red Museum." She'd made her film debut playing the Yellow Queen in the 1986 children's short *Rainbow War*, produced for Vancouver Expo 86; recent work includes *Jumanji, Gold Diggers: The Secret of Bear Mountain* (both 1995) and the TV-movies *The Commish: In the Shadow of the Gallows* (1995) and *Maternal Instincts* (1966).

X-File case: Classified

3.10 "731" a.k.a. "NISEI (PART 2)"

December 9, 1995
Writer: Frank Spotnitz
Director: Rob Bowman
Part 2 of a 2-part episode

Opening credo this episode: Apology is Policy

Perkey, WV: At the seemingly abandoned Hansen's Disease Research Facility, soldiers roust several frightened, alien-looking figures in concentration-camp attire, brutally shoot them in the backs and dump their bodies into a mass grave.

Scully confronts Mr. X at gunpoint for answers, but he snatches her weapon away and tells her cryptically that her extracted microchip-implant holds more than he could ever tell her. Night: Mulder finds the surgical train car locked, with a quarantine sign. The conductor can't open it; the railroad picks up such cars sporadically without knowing what's inside. The conductor does say a Dr. Shiro Zama, who'd come aboard at Queensgate, was checking it earlier. At Zama's compartment, there's only a briefcase with handwritten Japanese journals; Mulder gives it to the conductor for safekeeping, along with an empty .45 pistol with which to bluffingly restrain Zama till Mulder returns.

FBI headquarters, 8:25 p.m.: Agent Pendrell informs Scully that the incredibly state-of-the-art microchip's neural network appears capable of storing biological information traveling to and from a person's nervous system – and mimicking memory formation, so that it could, theoretically, reproduce a person's mental processes. Studying the chip effectively destroyed it (though it is outwardly physically intact), but the good news is that a manufacturer's name was printed on the silicon matrix. Pendrell's thorough search through U.S. and Japanese records turned up only one hit: a courier mailing-label to a Dr. Zama in Perkey, WV.

The hawk-like assassin from the previous episode garrotes Zama in a restroom; Mulder later finds him there. At the Hansen's facility there, Scully finds terrified leprosy victims hiding beneath a trapdoor. Their spokesman says they've lived here most of their lives – they're among the last to contract Hansen's before treatment was developed. He says Zama and his medical staff haven't been here for a long time, and that death squads have killed hundreds of people

who began arriving several years ago, and were kept segregated from the lepers. The spokesman shows Scully an open mass grave, saying others have been filled. Suddenly, a helicopter death squad arrives. Scully and the man dart for the woods; captured, Scully hears two shots close by.

Mulder instructs the conductor not to stop the train until he captures Zama's killer. The surgical car is now open – and behind a second locked door at its end is a frightened apparent alien. Then the hawk-like assassin loops a garrote around Mulder's neck, nearly killing him before the conductor, at gunpoint, orders him to stop. The assassin does so, and asserts he's a law-enforcement agent; the nervous conductor runs and closes the door, locking the two men in. Mulder gets the drop on the assassin, who has National Security Agency (NSA) ID; Mulder, knowing garrotes aren't standard-issue, doesn't believe it. The assassin says there's a bomb on the train.

Perkey: Scully is brought to the heavyset, shadow-government "elder" last seen in episode 3.02, "Paper Clip." He claims the (evidently liquidated) lepers had been exposed to something vague from an inhuman project by Dr. Zama – a.k.a. Ishimaru – who'd begun working on his own, behind the elders' backs. Mulder, on the train, tries the assassin's key-card on the door, risking that the entry code, when used to try exiting, won't detonate the bomb. As he's about to press the last number, the assassin's cell-phone rings – it's the elder, who puts Scully on with Mulder.

She declares the being in the car with them isn't alien, and that the leper colony was a front for Ishimaru's disease and radiation experiments on the homeless and the insane. Scully believes the man, she says, because she's in a train car like the one in the "alien-autopsy" video – the very room in which *she* was tested during her disappearance. The elder's eyes flicker impatiently. Following some momentary phone static, a skeptical Mulder asks if Zama/Ishimaru abducted the women. Scully, sidestepping, saying alien abduction is a smokescreen to cover the doctor's experiments, and that the "UFO" he saw in Newport News was part of a Russian nuclear sub. Scully says the president, two weeks ago, even apologized for the tests, which supposedly ended in 1974. Finally, she says, if the bomb explodes, then thousands might contract hemorrhagic fever, which the being has been exposed to. She tells Mulder precisely where the bomb is; the timer counts down from 01:42:00.4.

They want him to stop the train at the next station – but Mulder pretends the call's staticky again, and hangs up. He tells the conductor to route the train to an unpopulated area, and uncouple it. At dawn (5:59 a.m., per Mulder's watch), they do so; time to detonation is now 01:11:06.3. Mulder calls Scully, driving back to D.C., telling her he's sure the train car is on satellite surveillance; if the being here is important, someone will rescue them. By 00:38:16.1, however. Mulder is convinced no one's coming. Threatening to make the assassin's last half-hour excruciating, Mulder compels the man to admit the creature is "a weapon"; Mulder takes his hints to mean it's a prototype for soldiers immune to the effects of laser, nuclear, or biological arms. Mulder suggests it is an alien-human hybrid; the assassin suggests if that were true, someone would have rescued them by now.

Mulder's apartment: Scully, reviewing the "autopsy" tape, sees Ishimaru punching the exit code; she calls it in to Mulder. It works – distracting Mulder so that the assassin bloodily beats him. He exits, knowing the explosion's only seconds away – and is shot by Mr. X, who steps over the still-living killer. With 59.3 seconds left, X looks in on the creature (who may or may not still be alive). He carries out only Mulder, as the car explodes.

FBI headquarters, one week later: Mulder can find no trace of the train car; Matheson is ostensibly out of the country and not returning calls. Scully has the briefcase from the train – but it's a fake. In some darkened room, a white-bearded Japanese man translates the real journals, as the Smoking Man lights up.

CAST

Stephen McHattie	Assassin
Steven Williams	Mr. X
William B. Davis	Smoking Man
Michael Puttonen	Conductor
Robert Ito	"Dr. Shiro Zama"/Dr. Takeo Ishimaru
Colin Cunningham	Escalante (name not given in episode, except in closed-caption)
Don S. Williams	Elder
Brenden Beiser	Agent Pendrell

The Cast: Stephen McHattie is best known to TV audiences as the ruthless crime lord Gabriel in the final season of *Beauty and the Beast* (CBS 1987–90); he's also been in episodes of *Seinfeld*, and an episode of *Northern Exposure*. McHattie got his start in films with *The People Next Door* and *Von Richthofen and Brown* (both 1970), and went on to play the title role in *James Dean* (1976 TV-movie), and Judah in *Mary and Joseph: A Story of Faith* (1979 TV-movie). His films include *Gray Lady Down* (1978), *Belizaire the Cajun* (1985), *Bloodhounds of Broadway* (1989),

X-actitude

Mulder's phone
number: 555-0199

Railroad car door
codes: entry –
1111471; exit –
101331

Mailing label (name of
courier service n.a.):

From: (label obscured)
a company on
(Constitution Way,
Washington, D.C.
20005

To: Dr. Shiro Zama,
R.R. 214, Perkey, WV
26301; (304) 555-
0103

Location of train when
Mulder tells conductor
to find unpopulated
area: Twenty minutes
past Murray Station,
Iowa.

Location of train when it
blows up: Near the town
of Blue Earth, Iowa.

and *Beverly Hills Cop III* (1994).

The Repertory: Michael Puttonen played the motel manager in episode 1.02,"Deep Throat," and a V.A. doctor in 2.04, "Sleepless." He's done Vancouver film and network TV since 1991, starting with the movie *Pure Luck* and an episode of *MacGyver*; among his other work is *Look Who's Talking Now* (1993), and the TV-movie *The Commish: In the Shadow of the Gallows* (1995).

Colin Cunningham played "Lt. Terry Wilmer" – actually, an alien in morphed disguise – in 2.17, "End Game." He's appeared on *The Commish* and *The Marshal*, a couple of TV-movies, and the film *The Bawdy Adventures of Tom Jones* (1976).

X-File case: Classified

3.11 "REVELATIONS"

Dec. 15, 1995
Writer: Kim Newton
Director: David Nutter

A demonic industrialist (Kenneth Welsh) who's murdered 11 false prophets now stalks an Ohio boy (Kevin Zegers) who may be a genuine stigmatic. While Mulder proves skeptical of the case's religious apparent-miracles, the Catholic-reared Scully finds her faith both tested and renewed.

Kenneth Welsh is well-known to *Twin Peaks* fans as the evil mad-genius Windom Earle, Agent Cooper's old partner. Michael Berryman is a cult-favorite horror-movie figure (*The Hills Have Eyes*, etc.). R. Lee Ermey is a former military man and now an actor (*Dead Man Walking*) and TV/film military consultant; he also did the voice of the toy soldier Sarge in *Toy Story*.

CAST

Kevin Zegers	Kevin Kryder
Sam Bottoms	Mr. Kryder
Kenneth Welsh	Millennium Man
Michael Berryman	Owen Jarvis
Hayley Tyson	Susan Kryder
R. Lee Ermey	Reverend Findley
Lesley Swan	Carina Maywald
Fulvio Cecere	Priest

Nicole Robert   Mrs. Tynes

Uncredited:

Selina Williams   School Nurse

X-File case: Classified

3.12 "WAR OF THE COPROPHAGES"

Jan. 5, 1996
Writer: Darin Morgan
Director: Kim Manners

In a seeming self-parody — written by the scripter of the tongue-in-cheek "Humbug" and the often blackly comic "Clyde Bruckman's Final Repose" — the agents try to counter a *War of the Worlds*-like panic brought on by possibly extraterrestrial insects — specifically, coprophages (dung-eaters), which in this case are cockroaches. Among the surreal touches: a Dr. Strangelovian scientist, and a town called Miller's Grove (a play on *WOTW*'s Grover's Mill).

CAST

Bobbie Phillips	Dr. Bambi Berenbaum
Raye Birk	Dr. Jeff Eckerle
Dion Anderson	Sheriff Frass
Bill Dow	Dr. Newton
Alex Bruhanski	Dr. Bugger (exterminator)
Ken Kramer	Dr. (Alexander) Inavov
Nicole Parker	Chick
Alan Buckley	Dude
Tyler Labine	Stoner

Maria Herrera	Customer #1
Shaw Allan	Customer #2
Norma Wick	Reporter
Wren Robertz	Orderly
Tom Heaton	Resident #1
Bobby L. Stewart	Resident #2
Dawn Stofer	Customer #4
Fiona Robertz	Customer #5

Uncredited:

Tony Marr	Motel Manager

Note: No role is listed as "Customer #3"

X-File case: Classified

3.13 "SYZYGY"

Jan. 26, 1996
Writer: Chris Carter
Director: Rob Bowman

When a planetary alignment causes demonic changes in two small-town high-school girls – turning them into powerful, witch-like harpies – Scully and Mulder find panicked townsfolk marching on supposed Satanists, and that even they are acting out-of-character: Scully gets angry at Mulder's supposed flirting with police detective White, and teetotaller Mulder gets tipsy on vodka and almost succumbs to a close encounter with the comely cop. *In-joke:* The cross-dressing local doctor is named R.W. Godfrey – close to R.W. Goodwin, the co-executive producer.

CAST

Dana Wheeler-Robinson

Detective White

Wendy Benson	Margi Kleinjan
Lisa Robin Kelly	Terri Roberts
Garry Davey	Principal Bob Spitz
Denalda Williams	Zirinka
Gabrielle Miller	Brenda (J. Summerfield)
Ryan Reynolds	Jay ("Boom") De Boom
Tim Dixon	Dr. R.W. (Richard) Godfrey
Ryk Brown	Minister
Jeremy Radock	Young Man
Russell Porter	Scott Simmons

3.14 "GROTESQUE"

Feb. 2, 1996
Writer: Howard Gordon
Director: Kim Manners

The mean-spirited Behavioral Sciences agent who literally wrote the book on the field brings Mulder in to help solve the apparent copycat crimes following the arrest of an artist/serial-killer – and he won't stand for Mulder's agreeing with the suspect that demonic possession is involved.

Kurtwood Smith is a cult-favorite film actor, perhaps best known as bad-guy Clarence in *RoboCop* (1987).

CAST

Mitch Pileggi	Assistant Director Walter S. Skinner
Kurtwood Smith	Agent Bill Patterson
Levani (Outchaneichvili]	
	John Mostow
Greg Thirloway	Agent (Greg) Nemhauser
Susan Bain	Agent Sheherlis
Kasper Michaels	Young Agent
Zoran Vukelic	Model

Uncredited:

John Milton Brandon	Aguirre
James McDonnell	Glass Blower
Paul J. Anderson	Paramedic
Amanda O'Leary	Doctor

3.15 "PIPER MARU"

Feb. 9, 1996
Writers: Frank Spotnitz & Chris Carter
Director: Rob Bowman
Part 1 of a 2-part episode

In a "mythos" episode, members of a secret French mission to salvage a sunken World War II plane in the Pacific Ocean meet slow radiation-burn death after an unknowing encounter with a demonstrably alien lifeform – one that exists in an oil medium, and can take over human bodies. Mulder's investigation discovers an export firm trading in government secrets – with the help, in Hong Kong, of a desperate "Alex Krycek," who still possessed the DAT of the government's UFO files, (stolen from Skinner in episode 3.02, "Paper Clip,") Skinner – who's kept up an unofficial investigation into Melissa Scully's death after higher-ups mysteriously ordered the case closed – is gunned down in a restaurant. Mulder, meantime, prepares to escort traitor Krycek back to the U.S. – unaware he's been possessed by the alien. *Background*: We discover Dana and Melissa spent part of their early childhoods living on a San Diego Naval Base. This is in addition to their Annapolis home, where they were living when Dana got her childhood smallpox vaccine.

The episode title is the first and middle names of Gillian Anderson's daughter. Bit-player Robbie L. Maier is the series' construction coordinator.

X-File case: Classified
Government denies all knowledge

CAST

Mitch Pileggi	Assistant Director Walter S. Skinner
Nicholas Lea	"Alex Krycek"
Robert Clothier	Chris Johansen
Jo Bates	Jeraldine Kallenchuk
Morris Panych	Gray-Haired Man
Stephen E. Miller	Wayne Morgan
Ari Solomon	Gauthier
Paul Batten	Dr Seizer
Russell Ferrier	Medic
Lenno Britos	Hispanic Man (Luis Cardinal)
Kimberly Unger	Joan Gauthier
Rochelle Greenwood	Waitress
Joel Silverstone	Engineer #1
David Neale	Navy Base Guard
Tom Scholte	Young (Chris) Johansen
Robbie L. Maier	WWII Pilot
Young Dana Scully	Tegan Moss

Uncredited:

Darcy Laurie	Engineer #2
Richard Hersley	Capt. Kyle Sanford
Peter Scoular	Sick Crewman
Christine Viner	Young Melissa Scully

X-File case: Classified

3.16 "APOCRYPHA"

Feb. 16, 1996
Writers: Frank Spotnitz & Chris Carter
Director: Kim Manners
Part 2 of a 2-part episode

Skinner barely survives the shooting, and only Scully's fortunate intervention during his transfer to a new hospital saves him from a second attempt – both made by the Hispanic assassin who killed Scully's sister Melissa, and who is himself killed in jail. Mulder himself is nearly killed by agents ambushing him and Krycek – who, possessed by the alien, eventually reaches Smoking Man, who calmly promises to give him what he wants. That proves to be a spacecraft, hidden deep within an abandoned nuclear-missile silo – where Mulder and Scully nearly find their hard proof of alien life, before being captured by the Smoking Man's soldiers. Krycek is left locked and forgotten in an underground vault – after having painfully spewed out the alien through his mouth, nose and eyes. *In-joke:* The vault number is 1013, like the name of Chris Carter's production company, which alludes to Carter's 10/13 (Oct. 13) birthday.

CAST

Mitch Pileggi	Assistnt Director Walter S. Skinner
John Neville	Well-Manicured Man
William B. Davis	Smoking Man

(left margin) X-File case: Classified
Government denies all knowledge

Tom Braidwood	Frohike
Dean Haglund	Langly
Bruce Harwood	Byers
Nicholas Lea	"Alex Krycek"
Kevin McNulty	Agent Fuller
Barry Levy	Navy Doctor
Dmitry Chepovetsky	1st Government Man (Young William Mulder)
Sue Mathew	Agent Caleca
Don S. Williams	Elder #1
Lenno Britos	Hispanic Man (Luis Cardinal)
Frances Flanagan	Nurse
Brenden Beiser	Agent Pendrell
Peter Scoular	Sick Crewman
Jeff Chivers	Armed Man
Martin Evans	Major Domo

Uncredited:

Eric Breker	Ambulance Driver
Harrison R. Coe	3rd Government Man
Richard Hersley	Capt. Kyle Sanford
David Kaye	Doctor
Stanley Walsh	Elder #2
Craig Warkentin	Young Smoking Man

X-File case: Classified

3.17 "PUSHER"

Feb. 23, 1996
Writer: Vince Gilligan
Director: Rob Bowman

A brain tumor has apparently given a cold-blooded killer psychic powers, allowing him to induce his "perfect-crime" victims to commit suicide or otherwise bring on their own deaths. Calling himself "Pusher," he chooses Mulder for a cat-and-mouse game leading to a game of Russian roulette across a hospital table.

Scully and Mulder hold hands at the end, in what seems not particularly a hail-fellow-well-met manner. Whether caused by relief that Mulder wasn't killed or by something else is unclear.

CAST

Mitch Pileggi	Assistant Director Walter S. Skinner
Robert Wisden	Robert Modell/"Pusher"
Vic Polizos	Agent Frank Burst
Julia Arkos	Holly
Steve Bacic	Agent Collins
Meredith Bain-Woodward	Defense Attorney
Roger R. Cross	SWAT Lieutenant
Ernie Foort	Lobby Guard
Janyse Jaud	Nurse

X-File case: Classified
Government denies all knowledge

Darren Lucas	Lead SWAT cop
Don MacKay	Judge
D. Neil Mark	Deputy Scott Kerber
Brent J.D. Sheppard	Prosecutor
Henry Watson	Bailiff

X-File case: Classified

3.18 "TESO DOS BICHOS"

March 8, 1996
Writer: John Shiban
Director: Kim Manners

After a recently unearthed, Ecuadoran female-shaman mummy (an *amaru*) is shipped to a Boston museum despite warnings from the native Secona Indians, strange deaths occur. A jaguar-spirit curse at work? Or political terrorism to force the return of the artifacts? Mulder and Scully suspect expedition-member Dr. Bilac, who returned from the site – called Teso Dos Bichos – a strangely changed man.

CAST

Vic Trevino	Dr. Alonzo Bilac
Janne Mortil	Mona Wustner
Gordon Tootoosis	Shaman
Garrison Chrisjohn	Dr. Winters
Tom McBeath	Dr. Lewton
Ron Sauve	[Security Guard Tim]
	Decker
Alan Robertson	[Dr.] Carl Roosevelt
Frank Welker	Special Vocal Effects

3.19 "HELL MONEY"

March 29, 1996
Writer: Jeffrey Vlaming
Director: Tucker Gates

During the Chinese Festival of the Hungry Ghosts, Mulder and Scully investigate the burning alive of an immigrant whose death is linked to a mysterious Chinatown lottery where betters risk losing their organs to vicious black marketeers. A Chinese-American police officer, Detective Chao, is caught between ancient traditions and modern law, while a desperate Chinese father hopes a lottery jackpot will help him pay for his daughter's needed medical care. This is one of the rare *X-Files* episodes without paranormal components.

CAST

B.D. Wong	Detective Chao
James Hong	Hard-Faced Man
Michael Yama	Hsin
Lucy Liu	Kim
Doug Abrahams	Lt. Neary
Diana Ha	Dr. Wu
Stephen Chang	Large Man

X-File case: Classified
Government denies all knowledge

Donald Fong	Vase Man
Ed Hong-Louie	Money Man
Graham Shiels	Night Watchman
Paul Wong	Wiry Man

X-File case: Classified

3.20 "JOSE CHUNG'S FROM OUTER SPACE"

Working title: "ETH SNAFU"
April 12, 1996
Writer: Darin Morgan
Director: Rob Bowman

In a surreal take on *Rashomon*, best-selling author Jose Chung interviews Scully and other, wackier participants who claim to have seen or been involved in an alien abduction of two small-town teens – and abduction of one of the apparent aliens by the monstrous Lord Kinboat of the Earth's Core. An Air Force cover-up and mysterious men in black also figure, as the interviewees' stories conflict and the details grow ever more ludicrous. It all culminates in a book: Jose Chung's *From Outer Space*.

CAST

Charles Nelson Reilly Jose Chung
William Lucking Roky

Jason Gaffney	Harold
Sarah Sawatsky	Chrissy
Jesse Ventura	1st Man in Black
Larry Musser	Detective Manners
Alex Diakun	Dr. Fingers
Terry Arrowsmith	Air Force Man
Andrew Turner	CIA Man
Mina Mina	Dr. Hand
Allan Zinyk	Blaine
Michael Dobson	Lt. Schaeffer
Jaap Broeker	The Stupendous Yappi

extra

● The official Fox *X–Files* website erroneously lists professional wrestler-guest Jesse Ventura as "Jesse Venture."

X-File case: Classified

3.21 "AVATAR"

April 26, 1996
Story: David Duchovny & Howard Gordon
Teleplay: Howard Gordon
Director: James Charleston

His 17-year marriage dissolving, Assistant Director Skinner picks up a woman in a bar and later wakes up with her dead beside him. Mulder and Scully must investigate not only the crime, but Skinner's claim that he is being haunted by an apparition of an old woman – who'd first appeared to him in Vietnam. When the agents delve into the dead woman's past in an effort to clear Skinner, they find a call-girl ring that she'd belonged to – and are then targeted by mysterious assassins.

CAST

Mitch Pileggi	Assistant Director Walter S. Skinner
William B. Davis	Smoking Man
Tasha Simms	Jay Cassal
Amanda Tapping	Carina Sayles
Bethoe Shirkoff	Old Woman
Tom Mason	Detective Waltos
Cal Traversy	Young Detective
Stacy Grant	Judy Fairly

X-File case: Classified
Government denies all knowledge

Janie Woods-Morris	Lorraine Kelleher
Jennifer Hetrick	Sharon Skinner
Malcolm Stewart	Agent Bonnecaze
Brenden Beiser	Dr. Rick Newton
Michael David Simms	Senior Agent
Morris Paynch	Gray-Haired Man

X-File case: Classified

3.22 "QUAGMIRE"

May 3, 1996
Writer: Kim Newton
Director: Kim Manners

X-File case: Classified

Government denies all knowledge

Following a rash of deaths at Rigdon, GA's Heuvelmans Lake – a tourist site famed for a supposed Loch Ness Monster-type beast named Big Blue – Mulder explores the nature and limits of his Ahab-like obsession with truth, while Scully's pet Pomeranian, Queegqueg, gets eaten by a mysterious something. As human deaths mount, the agents' boat is sunk by some powerful lake creature, stranding Mulder and Scully on a rock where they spend time examining their lives. Onshore later, Mulder comes face to face with the flesh-eating leviathan – which turns out to be a very large 'gator. Yet there is still, it seems, something in the lake. . . .

The name "Queegqueg" is that of the cannibalistic crewman in *Moby Dick*.

Guest cast includes:

Chris Ellis, Timothy Webber

3.23 "WETWIRED"

May 10, 1996
Writer: Mat Beck
Director: Rob Bowman

April: 29: A shadowy new source lures Mulder to investigate small-town murders with no apparent pattern. Mulder and Scully discover each of the killers was subjected to subliminal messages transmitted covertly through their TV sets. Scully finds herself victim to this cathode-ray coercion, and believes Mulder is out to get her – and that she has to kill him first. After Mulder tracks a cable installer and a psychiatrist to a rural house, the two conspirators are killed by Mr. X. He was the one who'd sent the shadowy source to Mulder, in hopes that Mulder might uncover the conspiracy before X had to kill the two men – under orders from the Cigarette-Smoking Man, to whom X, it is revealed, reports.

CAST

Mitch Pileggi	Assistant Director Walter S. Skinner
Sheila Larken	Margaret (Maggie) Scully
William B. Davis	Smoking Man
Tom Braidwood	Frohike
Dean Haglund	Langly
Bruce Harwood	Byers
Steven Williams	Mr. X

Also in guest cast:
Colin Cunningham, Tim Henry, others

X-File case: Classified
Government denies all knowledge

3.24 "TALITHA CUMI"

May 17, 1996
Story: David Duchovny & Chris Carter
Teleplay: Chris Carter
Director: R.W. Goodwin
Part 1 of 2

After a shooting at a fast-food restaurant, a mysterious Jeremiah Smith miraculously heals the wounds of the shooter and his three victims – then disappears. Mulder and Scully discover that identical "Jeremiah Smiths" exist all over the country, working for the Social Security Administration. At the abandoned Quonochontaug, RI summer home of Mulder's parents, the Cigarette-Smoking Man argues with Mulder's mother over the whereabouts of some mysterious object – while alluding to an intimate relationship with her since before Mulder was born. Shortly thereafter, she suffers a stroke – yet still gives Mulder a clue to find a weapon like that used by the Pilot to kill the clones in episodes 2.16–2.17, "Colony" and "End Game." Cigarette-Smoking Man captures the Jeremiah Smith who appeared at the restaurant, with plans to have the Pilot execute him for drawing unwanted attention that may threaten "The Project": alien colonization of Earth, for which a date has already been set. Mr. X battles Mulder for the weapon – the only thing that can kill the clones – yet retreats empty-handed. Smith, who'd rattled the Smoking Man by morphing into Deep Throat and Mulder's father,

X-File case: Classified

Government denies all knowledge

escapes or is let free; he goes to Mulder and Scully to reveal all about The Project – just as the Pilot appears, his weapon in hand.

CAST

Mitch Pileggi	Assistant Director Walter S. Skinner
Roy Thinnes	Jeremiah Smith
William B. Davis	Smoking Man
Peter Donat	"William Mulder"
Jerry Hardin	"Deep Throat"
Brian Thompson	The Pilot
Angelo Vacco	Man Shot at Restaurant Door
Steven Williams	Mr. X
Hrothgar Mathews	Galen Muntz [first name not given in episode]
Rebecca Toolan	Mrs. Mulder
Stephen Dimopoulos	Detective
John MacLaren	Doctor
Cam Cronin	Paramedic
Bonnie Hay	Night Nurse

Uncredited onscreen; listed in Fox *X-Files* website:

Brian Barry	Last Man
Ross Clarke	Pleasant Man

X-File case: Classified

X-tras
Biographies, Dates, Equipment, Case Numbers and more

One of the best things about narrative series, be they Sherlock Holmes or the *X-Files*, is how characters are revealed, bit by bit, by the story-line evolving. With *The X-Files*, however, the facts given in the episodes themselves – the authoritative source, however contradictory – have gotten muddied by companion novels, fanzines, and even an "official" book all making claims unsubstantiated within the show itself.

Keeping that in mind, here are dossiers on Mulder and Scully, as well as a timeline, a list of X-File case numbers, and other such data – all based only on evidence revealed on-screen. Some of this, undoubtedly, will have changed between the time of publication and the continuing parade of episodes. But as of now, this is most accurate information anywhere.

DOSSIER: THE MULDER FILE

Address: Street address and city unknown, Apartment #42
Phone: (Area code n.a.) 555-0199
E-mail address: Fox Mulder, 000517
Apartment-house neighbors include (family names): Glaniceanu; Pao/Hu; Dommann

Born: Oct. 13, 1961, probably Chilmark, MA (Martha's Vineyard),
Raised: 2790 Vine Street, Chilmark, MA
Religion: n.a.

Family (parents divorced):
Mother: name n.a., Greenwich, CT
Father: William Mulder (d. April 1995, West Tisbury, MA)
Sibling: Samantha Ann Mulder, b. Nov. 21, 1965, Chilmark, MA; abducted Nov. 27, 1973

Education:
High school: n.a.
College: Oxford University, Oxford, England; degree in psychology (whether graduate or undergraduate degree uncertain); attended c. 1983

FBI Academy, Quantico, VA
  Wrote monograph on topic of serial killers and the occult, 1988
  Academy nickname: "Spooky"

FBI: Joined age 28
Current status: Special Agent
Partner: Dana Scully (as of 3/21/92)
Badge number: JTT047101111
Office: Basement, former copier room
Prior assignments:
  Briefly in Violent Crimes, partnered with Jerry Lamana. First case:
    under ASAC Reggie Purdue, helped to capture John Barnett
  Behavioral Science unit, profiling serial killers (1989–92)

Blood type: O-negative
Smallpox vaccination certificate number: 378671
Misc. Personal Data:
  Wears glasses for reading and close-up work
  Used pseudonym "M.F. Luder" on *Omni* article
Recreational pursuits include: Washington Redskins;
  pornography; basketball; running; pet fish
  Enjoys eating sunflower seeds

THE SCULLY FILE

Dana Katherine Scully
Address: 107 E. Cordova, Apartment #35* Washington, D.C.
Phone: (202) 555-6431 (home); (202) 555-3564 (cellular)
  * per police report; per visual examination, house number is 1419;
  multiple-dwelling residence with possible entrances on two
  perpendicular streets (if a corner building) or on parallel streets (if
  building is one-block deep).

Born: Feb. 23, 1964
Raised: 3170 W. 53rd Road, Annapolis, MD; San Diego, CA, and
  possibly elsewhere.
Religion: Catholic

Family:
  Mother: Margaret (Maggie) Scully
  Father: Captain William Scully, USN (d. December 1993)
  Siblings:
    Older brother: William Jr.
    Older sister: Melissa
    Younger brother: name n.a.

Pets:
  Queeg-Queg (Pomeranian; adopted October 1995; killed by alligator attack, spring 1996)

Education:
  University of Maryland (B.S. Physics)
  Senior thesis: "Einstein's Twin Paradox: A New Interpretation."
  Medical school: n.a.; M.D., specialty n.a.
  FBI Academy, Quantico, VA
    Recruited immediately after medical school
    Class included: Tom Colton, Marty Neil

FBI: Joined 1990
  Current status: Special Agent
  Partner: Fox Mulder (as of 3/21/92)
  ID#: 2317-616 (badge number n.a.)

Prior FBI assignment:
  Instructor, FBI Academy, Quantico, VA (1990-92)
  Office phone during assignment there: (703) 555-2804

Smallpox vaccination certificate number: 29510
Misc. Personal Data:
  Wears gold-cross necklace given by mother on 15th birthday
  Wears glasses for reading and close-up work
  While instructor at Academy, had year-long relationship with
    Agent Jack Willis; gave him engraved watch Feb. 23, 1992.

X-FILE CASE NUMBERS

Unlike zip codes and *Star Trek* stardates, the case numbers of the actual, paper-in-manilla-folder X-files have no set pattern. Sometimes they're labeled "X" and followed by five digits; sometimes by four. Sometimes they begin with other letters; sometimes they don't begin with letters at all. Sometimes they're hyphenated, sometimes the name of file is incorporated, and occasionally, they're whimsical: The Cecil L'Ively case (episode 1.12, "Fire") is X-file 11214893, which starts with the birthdate of Chris Carter's wife – 11/21, a number that pops up often on the show. Whether "48" is her birth year is uncertain, though '93 *is* the year this episode aired (though not on 4/8).

The following X-file case numbers are taken directly from dialog (mostly the narration of field reports) or from actual onscreen artifacts, such as file folders or computer monitors. No assumptions have been made, and only verifiable X-file case numbers have been included. Note: The case number for 1.03, "Squeeze," was given in the sequel, "Tooms."

Episode	Case #
1.02 "Deep Throat"	DF101364
1.03 "Squeeze" and 1.21 "Tooms"	X 129202
1.12 "Fire"	11214893
1.22 "Born Again"	X-40271
2.07 "3"	X256933VW
	Trinity Killers
2.10 "Red Museum"	XWC060361

Additionally:

File labeled Visionary Encounters w/ The Dead (seen in "Beyond the Sea")	X-167512
File labeled Scully, Dana (following her disappearance; seen in "3")	73317 / 650657

TODAY'S CLASS: NUMEROLOGY 1121

November 21, the birthdate of Chris Carter's wife, Dori Pierson, has made a cameo appearance in a multitude of episodes, from case numbers to clocks; sometimes it's even preceded by her initials. And Mulder, for some reason, seems to really like phoning Scully at 11:21. Surprisingly, the missile-silo vault containing an alien spacecraft in 3.16, "Apocrypha," was numbered 1013, after Carter's *own* birthdate.

Episode	Instance
1.01 "Pilot: The X-Files"	Mulder phones Scully at 11:21 p.m.
1.12 "Fire"	X-File case #: 11214893
1.18 "Miracle Man"	Scully begins autopsy at 11:21 p.m.
1.24 "The Erlenmeyer Flask"	Mulder phones Scully at 11:21 p.m.
2.02 "The Host"	Newark Police Dept. case #DP112148.
2.22 "F. Emasculata"	overnight-mail package #DDP112148
2.13 "Irresistible"	Mulder phones Scully at 11:21 p.m.
2.16 "Colony"	Mulder phones Scully at 11:21 p.m.

NOVELS

Goblins
By Charles L. Grant
HarperPrism ISBN 0-06-105414-3

Near Fort Dix, NJ, while babysitting rookie agents Hank Webber and Licia Andrews, Scully and Mulder investigate the throat-slashing murders of a young soldier and an old drunk. An old woman claims it's the work of goblins, but the agents uncover a military experiment to create a breed of "stealth humans."

Whirlwind
By Charles L. Grant
HarperPrism ISBN 0-06-105415-1

Mulder and Scully try to discover what split-second force is skinning cattle and people near a Konochine Indian community in New Mexico. Note: Grant is Indian-ritual expert "Geoffrey Marsh" in the acknowledgments.

Ground Zero
By Kevin J. Anderson
HarperCollins (hardcover)

The ghosts of atomic-bomb victims are stalking nuclear-weapons researchers.

YOUNG ADULT NOVELS

Episode adaptations, by Les Martin
HarperCollins
X Marks the Spot (adaptation of the pilot)

Squeeze
Darkness Falls
Tyger, Tyger (adaptation of "Fearful Symmetry")
Humbug

COMIC BOOKS

Topps Comics
Writer: Stefan Petrucha
Artist: Charles Adlard
Cover Artist: Miran Kim
Editors: Jim Salicrup, Dwight Jon Zimmerman

#1: January 1995
"Not To Be Opened until Xmas" (25 pages)
When the final Fatima Prophecy is stolen from the Vatican, and the U.S. military agrees to retrieve it and return it only after reading it for themselves, Scully and Mulder investigate a murder and the possibility that angels are in reality aliens. A black-and-white "ashcan" release of the first half appeared in *Star Wars Galaxy* #2.
Reprinted in *The X-Files Special Edition* #1, June 1995

#2: February 1995
"The Dismemberance of Things Past" (24 pages)
A general guarding the UFO secrets of a small Kansas town begins murdering witnesses when a memory-destroying gas used since 1948 stops working effectively. Part 1 of 2.
Reprinted in *The X-Files Special Edition* #1, June 1995

#3: March 1995
"A Little Dream of Me" (24 pages)
Following the general's suicide, and the agents' gradual recovery of their memory, the Lone Gunmen help Mulder find a covert conspirator and double-agent who appears to have access to Samantha – and needs Mulder to break into the Pentagon. Part two of two.
Reprinted in *The X-Files Special Edition* #1, June 1995

#4: April 1995
"Firebird Part One: Khobka's Lament"
Mulder and Scully find the skull of a modern-day scientist
researching the Tunguska, Siberia meteorite – a skull which
carbon-dating pegs as millions of years old – as an atomic energy-
draining creature tries to build up energy enough to go home. Part
one of three.

#5: May 1995
"Firebird Part Two: Crescit Eundo"
The "Firebird" is loose in the White Sands Missile Range near
Alamagordo, NM, as military scientists try to uncover the secret of
its cold fusion. Scully, Mulder, and a Siberian shaman, Khobka, face
both the creature and the covert-government forces. Part two of
three.

#6: June 1995
"Firebird Part Three: A Brief Authority"
The captured Mulder is pressed to obtain from Khobka any
information on how to stop the "Firebird" from devastating New
Mexico, as the cabal prepares both its cover story in case of failure,
and its eradication of witness Mulder. Part three of three.

The series continues.

Other Topps "X-Files" Comics Work includes
"Trick of the Light" (10 pages)
Insert done for the magazine *Hero Illustrated* #22, April 1995
    Writer: Stefan Petrucha
    Artist: Charles Adlard
    Cover Artist: Jim Salicrup
    An artist's models are mysteriously disappearing.

"Circle Game" (5 pages)
Insert done for *TV Guide* July 15-21, 1995
    Writer: Stefan Petrucha
    Artist: Charles Adlard
    Editors: Jim Salicrup, Dwight Jon Zimmerman, Charles S. Novinskie
    A series of crop circles help uncover a murder.

All times relative to their time zone. Primary sources are onscreen timestamps, clocks, and dated printed matter such as tickets, newspapers, and police reports. An additional factor used in assessing whether a day has passed is a clearly visible change (or not) of clothing.

1992
1.01 *Pilot: "The X-Files"*

Agents meet	March 6 (Sat.)
Agents fly to Oregon	March 7, 8 a.m.
Scully begins autopsy on exhumed body	March 7, 10:56 p.m.
Scully writes report in hotel room	March 8, 4:37 a.m.
Agents speak with doctor at Raymon County State Psychiatric Hospital	March 8, day
Blinding light; Mulder checks watch	March 8, 9:03 p.m.
Agents at cemetary decide to see Billy	March 9, 5:07 a.m.
Agents see Billy, speak with woman orderly	March 9, day
Billy interviewed at FBI headquarters	March 22
Mulder calls Scully date n.a., probably	March 22; 11:21–22 p.m.

1993
1.03 *"Squeeze"*

Tooms arrested (per police report in 1.21)	July 23

1.04 *"Conduit"*

Pre-episode:	Greg killed Approx. 3 weeks ago; probably before Aug. 7

Note: Episode probably occurs late August, after episode 1.05

1.05 *"The Jersey Devil"*

Dead vagrant Roger Crockett found	Aug. 9, 1993 (Mon.)
Agents meet with Atlantic City coroner	Friday (probably Aug. 13, possibly a later Fri.)
Mulder released from jail	Following Monday
Scully's date with Rob	Monday, 7:30 p.m.
Brouillet calls Mulder	Monday, 7:55 p.m.
Agents, Brouillet, Diamond at coroner's	Day; evidently Tuesday
Autopsy reports on beast-people arrive	One week later

1.06 *"Shadows"*

Lauren Kyte ATM mugging on security video	Sept. 22 (Wed.), 9:45 p.m.
Agents at coroner's	Sept. 23, approx. 4 a.m.

Note: Per headstone, Graves died Oct. 5; this is a continuity error, as it was established he died approximately two weeks before Sept. 22.

1.07 *"Ghost in the Machine"*

Scully writes in field journal, night of the day agents question Wilczek	Oct. 24 (Sun.)

1.08 *"Ice"*

Ice-Core transmission sent	Nov. 5 (Fri.)
Agents arrive in Nome	Wed. (possibly Nov. 10)

1.13 *"Beyond the Sea"*

Scully has dinner with parents	c. Dec. 15-25
William Scully suffers fatal coronary	hours later, c. 12:45 a.m.
Boggs execution	one week after Capt. Scully's ashes-scattering

1994
1.18 *"Miracle Man"*
Scully begins autopsy	March 7 (Mon.), 11:21 p.m.
Scully gives Mulder preliminary results	March 8, 12:29 a.m.

1.22 *"Born Again"*
Barbala killed; agents arrive in Buffalo	March 28 (Mon.)
Fiore takes out Morris homicide file	March 29, 2–2:15 p.m.
Felder killed	March 29, evening
Charlie/Michelle attacks Fiore at home	March 30, night
Post-episode: Fiore pleads guilty	April 18

Note: When Mrs. Bishop on March 28 speaks of her fourth nanny this year and it being only April, she's speaking casually and alluding to March being nearly over.

1.23 *"Roland"*
Pre-episode: Grable car accident	November 1993
Dr. Surnow killed in wind tunnel	April 23, 1994 (Sun.)
Agents arrive at crime scene	April 24
Dr. Keats killed	April 25, 12:31 a.m.
Roland/Arthur closes Grable file	April 25, 5:23 a.m.

1.24 *"The Erlenmeyer Flask"*
Dr. Secare leaps into harbor	May 7 (Sat.), day
Deep Throat phones sleeping Mulder	May 8, very early a.m.
Agents speak with police at harbor	18 hours after Secare leap
Mulder interviews Dr. Berube	May 8, 5 p.m.
Mulder breaks into Berube's house	May 8, 6:30 p.m.
Secare phones Mulder at Berube's house	May 8, 7:45 p.m.
Carpenter shows Scully her DNA analysis	May 8, 11:45 p.m.
Agents finds Zeus Storage empty	May 9, 7:30 a.m.
Crew-Cut Man abducts Mulder, kills Secare	May 9, night or May 10, early a.m.
Deep Throat meets Scully at Mulder's apt.	May 10, 6:30 a.m.

Deep Throat killed	May 10, night or
	May 11, early a.m.
Mulder phones Scully X-Files shut down	13 days later,
	11:21–22 p.m.

2.01 *"Little Green Men"*

Pre-episode: Arecibo receives signals	July 5 (Tues.),
	6:30 a.m.
Matheson meets with Mulder, promises to	
delay the Blue Berets for 24 hours	July 6
Mulder flies to San Juan	July 7
Scully being followed at Miami Intern'l	July 7, 5:45 p.m.
Scully buys ticket to San Juan	July 7, 6:30 p.m.
Bright light (aliens?) at Arecibo	July 7, 10:30 p.m.
Scully finds Mulder; Blue Berets arrive	July 8, day (probably
	early a.m.)

2.05 *"Duane Barry"*

Mulder and Krycek go to hostage scene	Aug. 7 (Sun.), day
Duane Barry shot	Aug. 7, night, or
	Aug. 8, early a.m.
Kazdin speaks with Mulder at hospital	Aug. 8

Note: Barry's escape from the hospital, and his kidnapping of Scully, took place anywhere from one to several days following his shooting, surgery and at least partial recuperation. Scully is wearing different clothes the night of her kidnapping than at either the previous office scene, or at the hostage site.

2.06 *"Ascension"*

Mulder hears Scully's message	date n.a., 11:23 p.m.
Mulder finishes examining crime scene	same night,
	11:40 p.m.
Skinner takes Mulder off case	next day, 8:03 a.m.
Barry kills VA police officer	same day, 11:23 a.m.
Mulder views police-car video of scene	same day, 3:11 p.m.
Mulder listens to tape of Barry	same day, 4:03 p.m.
Mulder and Krycek drive to Skyland	same day, 5:43 p.m.
Mulder reaches summit	night of the same day

Barry being questioned at summit   same night,
8:46 p.m.

Barry autopsy performed   next day, morning

Skinner meetings; Krycek backs up Mulder   same day, 10:36 a.m.

Mr. X meets Mulder near Matheson's office   same day, 11:45 a.m.

Skinner meets Mulder, reopens X-Files   next day, 8:11 a.m.

2.07 "3"
X-files reactivated; Mulder flips calendar from
May to present   November 1994

2.08 "One Breath"
Note: The date of Scully's return is not specified in episode;
though her hospital chart is dated Jan. 3, 1994, this is a continuity
error, based on the time-stamps of the previous and following
episodes. She was evidently missing from August to November
1994.

2.09 "Firewalker"
Date of events, per Mulder's report   Nov. 11-13

Post-episode: In quarantine for next month   Nov. 13–c. Dec. 13

2.13 "Irresistible"
Agents meet Moe Bocks at cemetery   Nov. 12 (Sat.)

Agents meet Bocks in his office   Nov. 13

Scully performs autopsy on streetwalker   Nov. 14, 11:14 a.m.

Mulder phones Scully to announce arrest   Nov. 14, 11:21 p.m.

Note: These dates are continuity errors, since per Mulder's report
last episode, the agents were still in Washington State on the "Fire
walker" case from Nov. 12-13, and were in quarantine immediately
afterward until mid-December. The previous episode's time-stamps
are the more reliable, since much dialog concerns the nearness of
Scully's recent, November return. These episodes most likely take
place December.

1995

2.14 *"Die Hand Die Verletzt"*
Pre-episode, possibly by only hours: Dave
Duran checks out occult library book   Jan. 16 (Mon.)

2.16 *"Colony"* (events below are flashbacks)
Mysterious aircraft appears in Arctic	date n.a.
Pilot kills Dr. Prince in Scranton	two days later
Mulder tells Scully of murdered doctors	two weeks from first death

2.17 *"End Game"* (events below are flashbacks)
Samantha speaks to Mulder before Skinner arrives and Scully phones	date n.a., 12:38 a.m.
Exchange on Old Memorial Bridge	approx. one hour later
FBI drags water for bodies	next day
Mulder breaks news to father; drives to Rockville clinic	same day

2.19 *"Dod Kalm"*
Food and water depleted	March 11 (Sat.), approx. 4:30 a.m.
Rapidly aged Mulder loses consciousness	March 12, 4:30 a.m.

2.23 *"Soft Light"*
Pre-episode: Wysnecki disappearance	March 17
Newirth disappearance at hotel	March 31 (Fri.), night
Agents meet with Ryan at hotel	April 1, morning
Police confront Banton at train station	April 1, 11:50 p.m.
Agents and Ryan at train station	April 2, morning
Agents interview Dr. Davey	same morning
Agents find Banton at train station	same morning, 11:14 a.m.
Mulder meets with Mr. X	April 3 (Mon.), 2:19 a.m.
Mr. X tries to abduct Banton	April 3, 3:24 a.m.
Agents captured by Dr. Davey, whom X kills	April 3, day

2.25 *"Anasazi"*

Earthquake; Eric Hosteen finds boxcar	April 9 (Sun.), day
The Thinker hacks into gov't E.T. files	April 10, day
Multinational cabal learns of break-in	April 10, night
Lone Gunmen go to Mulder's apartment	April 11, day
Mulder meets the Thinker, Botanic Gardens	April 11, night
Mulder shows Scully files, brawls w/Skinner	April 12
Scully meets w/Skinner and senior agents	April 13, day *
Smoking Man visits William Mulder	same day
Mulder visits William, whom Krycek kills	night of April 13 or early a.m. April 14
Mulder awakens in Scully's apartment	April 14, day
Mulder confronts Krycek, is shot by Scully	April 14, night
Agents in New Mexico after "two-day" drive	April 16 (Sun.)
Albert Hosteen brings Mulder to reservation; Smoking Man orders boxcar afire	same day

* A senior agent asks Scully, "Weren't you originally assigned to agent Mulder to debunk his work?" Scully replies, "Yes, sir, a year-and-a-half ago," even though she was teamed with Mulder March 21, 1992, over three years ago. Blame it on the stress of the moment.

3.01 *"The Blessing Way"*

Soldiers brutalize Hosteen family	April 16 (Sun.)
Kenneth Soona's body discovered	same day
Soldiers take Scully's hard copy	April 16, night
OPC meeting	April 17
Scully walks to mother's	April 17, night
Albert finds Mulder buried beneath rocks	April 18, morning
Frohike shows Scully newspaper article	April 18
Scully sees Skinner, sets off metal alarm	April 19
Third day of Blessing Way ritual	April 19
Scully dreams Mulder's alive	April 19, night
William Mulder funeral	April 20
Mulder recuperates; does not change clothes	For four days following end of ritual

3.06 "2SHY" [episode out of order in continuity]

Incanto kills Lauren	Aug. 28 (Mon.), night
Cop finds Lauren's remains	Aug. 29, morning
Scully attempts autopsy	Aug. 29, 4:15 p.m.
Incanto kills streetwalker	Aug. 29, night
Mulder arrives with FBI skin analysis	Aug. 30, 10:13 a.m.
Incanto kills canvassing Cross	same day
Incanto has dinner with Ellen; kills landlady; is captured	that night
Incanto confesses to 47 murders	one week later

3.03 "D.P.O."

Darren gets high score on arcade game	Sept. 12 (Tues.), 11:41 p.m.
Hammond's body found	Sept. 13, 12:17 a.m.
Darren electrocutes cows	Sept. 13, night
Teller and agents find cows and fulgarite	Sept. 14, morning
Frank Kiveat admitted to hospital	Sept. 14, 10:25 a.m.
Darren kills Teller; is captured	Sept. 14, night, or Sept. 15, early a.m.

3.04 "Clyde Bruckman's Final Repose"

Note: Sept. 16 and Sept. 21 subtitles directly contradicted by onscreen artifact (Lotto ticket with Oct. date)

"Puppet" kills Madame Zelma	Oct. 4, night
Agents, police and Yappi at doll-collector crime scene	Oct. 7
Agents question Bruckman, bring him to doll-collector crime scene	Oct. 8
Agents find body in lake	Oct. 9, morning
Lotto drawing	Oct. 9 (Mon.)
Agents and Bruckman find Dukenfield	Oct. 9
Havez killed	Oct. 10, morning

Mad #335 (May 1995)
"The Ecch-Files"
Writer: Dick DeBartolo
Artist: Angelo Torres
Five-page parody, featuring agents Moldy and Skulky

Weird Science (fantasy-sitcom based on the 1985 film)
"Fly Boy" (USA Network 7/22/95)
Writer: Jeff Vlaming
Director: David Grossman
FBI agents Molly (Jamie Rose) and Scolder (Larry Poindexter) arrive in Catsworthy County, NB, where an old man has seen a mysterious small object fall from a "shooting star" in the daytime sky. It turns out to have been a swizzle stick dropped by Gary Wallace (co-star John Mallory Asher), who with his friend Wyatt (co-star Michael Manasseri) have the computer-created a genie-like "perfect woman," Lisa (Vanessa Angel); Gary's flying sneakers make him sought-out by the menacing Smoker (Bill Bolender).

"Robotman" (comic strip)
Writer-artist: Jim Meddick (some strips beginning 6/19/95)
Agents Mulder and Scully question Robotman's roommate, Mr. Montahue, about Robotman.

ReBoot (computer-animated Saturday-morning series)
"Trust No One" (ABC 12/30/95; YTV [Canada] 1/18/96)
Teleplay: Mark Leiren-Young
Story: Gavin Blair, Mark Leiren-Young, Phil Mitchell, Ian Pearson, Susan Turner
CGI agents Data Nully (voiced by guest-star Gillian Anderson) and Fax Modem — who specialize in the ASCII Files — join guardian Bob in seeking a mysterious "web creature" who's abducting the citizens of Mainframe. (Anderson's husband, Clyde Klotz, has worked on the series.)
    Computer puns here: CGI is computer-generated

imagery; fax modem is, of course, a combination device for sending faxes as well as data transmission via computer; and ASCII (pronounced ASK-ee) files are computer files written in a raw, plain-vanilla computer language.

The Axed Files #1
Parody Press comic book, published mid-1995
(Parody Press, P.O. Box 1546, Chesapeake, VA 23327)

Mad TV
"The XXX Files'" (Feb. 10, 1996)
Six-minute segment with Mulder and Scully investigating the alien abduction of (fictional) porn star Wynonna Juggs.

While *The X-Files'* writers and producers do an exceptionally good job of avoiding glaring lapses in logic, fans nonetheless love to nitpick. And since *X-Files* presents so much evidence it is a rich lode for obsessives and nit-pickers. This is a list of the most glaring bloopers and inconsistencies.

1.01 *Pilot: "The X-Files"*
Scully can't accept that they "lost" nine minutes; time, she says, is a universal invariant, to which Mulder replies negatively. As an undergraduate physics-major Scully should know that only the speed of light is a universal invariant, or constant.

And if Mulder, Scully and the car lost nine minutes, why didn't Mulder's watch?

1.07 *"Ghost in the Machine"*

The COS computer had Scully's home phone number with which to call up her home computer. But how did it switch-on Scully's turned-off computer?

1.08 *"Ice"*
After Bear dies, the others discover that though all the victims have had the worm-like organism, only Bear's remains alive. But later, Scully places an ammonia jar with one live "worm" next to a jar with another live "worm," to see them each respond aggressively. Where did the second worm come from?

1.10 *"Fallen Angel"*
Scully agrees with Mulder that there are no railroad tracks near the town on which a train-car of "toxic cargo" could've derailed. So how come the local reporters didn't discover this, but just blithely reported on *an entire railroad line* nobody had ever heard of in the area? That government claim would've been ridiculously easy to check. Anyone ever hear of maps?

X-Humation
The Nitpick File

409

1.11 "Eve"
After her father's homicide, would eight-year-old Cindy really be
allowed to open the front door by herself when someone – perhaps
the homicidal maniac – rings?

1.12 "Fire"
At Boston Mercy Hospital, Bob/Cecil is in a hyperbaric chamber with
fifth- and sixth-degree burns? The rating only goes up to fourth-
degree, in which flesh is burned down to the bone.

1.17 "E.B.E."
How is it trained UFOlogist Mulder can't tell that Deep Throat's
photo is a fake, and Scully gets it just by a quick visual examination?

1.20 "Darkness Falls"
The sun has just recently risen when Spinney returns with the Jeep,
and it's only a four-hour drive down the mountain. So since they
leave right away, how is it night already on the drive back down? Did
they stop for a long picnic?

1.21 "Tooms"
Why would Tooms defy his animalistic genetic instincts to *frame*
Mulder rather than just eat his liver?

1.22 "Born Again"
Mulder, an Oxford-trained psychologist, confuses Multiple Personality
Syndrome with schizophrenia.

1.24 "The Erlenmeyer Flask"
How did Scully just pick up an apparent alien fetus – which looked
too large for a briefcase – and walk off with it? They're willing to
kill, but not to check inside your bag?

2.01 "Little Green Men"
The pay phones at Miami International Airport require more than 20
cents.

2.02 "The Host"
EMS workers load the strapped-in creature to a U.S. Marshall's van,

with a single Marshall and no one else. It's extremely unlikely that this scientific marvel would be treated so casually, but let's give benefit of doubt and say the Justice Dept. genuinely believed it was a normal man, self-mutilated.

2.04 *"Sleepless"*
Girardi is coming to Grissom's funeral in New York, and arriving at a Bronx station on the 7:30 train. *A Bronx station?*

2.05 *"Duane Barry"*
After Barry accidentally shoots hostage Bob, he asks the police for a doctor. But he's already *got* a medical doctor there – Dr. Hakkie.

2.07 *"3"*
How does Mulder get into the closed Hollywood Blood Bank at night, in a presumably legal way that won't get the case thrown out of court?

2.08 *"One Breath"*
Byers misspeaks when he says he "downloaded" Scully's chart to The Thinker. Actually, he "uploaded" it – to download is to receive, and to upload is to send.

2.09 *"Firewalker"*
If 130°F temperature is so hot that Pierce says nothing can long survive, there, how did Trepkos do so?

2.16 *"Colony"*
Scully runs to escape from "Chapel" at the warehouse, and then goes hide in her apartment – where "Chapel" knows the address!

2.22 *"F. Emasculata"*
If Dr. Torrence was worried enough about contagion to put on surgical gloves, why not also a surgical mask? Plotwise, he *still* could have been spurted on and infected.

2.23 *"Soft Light"*
RE: The light-bulb prints not matching those of any hotel employee or guest. Since hotels don't keep fingerprints of guests on file – and

not usually employees either, for that matter – we have to assume the Richmond P.D. had simply gotten a list of names and then run them through the national fingerprint database. But there's no way that every person in the hotel would have a criminal, immigration or other sort of record requiring fingerprinting.

2.24 "Our Town" 5/12/95
Sheriff Arens has to drag the lake since he doesn't want the FBI to do it. So why didn't he conveniently not find anything?

3.02 "Paper Clip"
Skinner confirms that "whoever downloaded the files (e.g., Soona) copyprotected them against either digital or hard copies. So how did they print out a hard copy in the first place for Scully to have the Navajo woman in Washington look at, and which the soldiers retrieved?

3.05 "The List"
Would a prison guard *really* leave a woman alone in a maximum-security, death-row cell block?

3.06 "2SHY"
Scully says it's 4:15 p.m. when she's about to do the autopsy – yet the morgue clock, while blurry, definitely doesn't read 4:15: It's either 11:05 or 1:55. Of course, it's possible the clock's broken. . . .

Trained FBI agent Scully leaves her gun behind in the bedroom when going to get first-aid stuff from the bathroom?

3.08 "Oubliette"
Mulder, spotting Easton on the map, says Lucy was taken 15 years ago. Yet earlier he'd said she's 30 now, was kidnapped at 8 – that's 22 years ago.

3.10 "731" a.k.a. "Nisei (Part 2")
Medical doctor Scully, believing the being is human, contends "thousands" will be exposed to hemorrhagic fever if the train explodes in a populated area. Yet no human body could have survived the eventual explosion and fire – the steel train car didn't survive it!

Waltz, Lisa 1.06
Wasserman, Jerry 1.21, 2.11
Webb, Simon 1.24
Webber, Tim a.k.a. Timothy 1.21, 2.24
Weitz, Bruce 2.13
Welliver, Titus 1.20
Westerman, Floyd Red Crow 2.25–3.02
Wheeler, Maggie 1.22
Whitford, Bradley 2.09
Wick, Norma 1.09
Wilde, Bob 2.01
Wildsmith, Jeremy Isaac 2.21
Wildsmith, Oliver 2.21
Willes, Christine 2.13, 2.21
Williams, Denalda 2.13
Williams, Dick Anthony 1.16
Williams, Don S. 3.01–3.02, 3.10
Williams, Steven 2.04, 2.06, 2.08, 2.15, 2.17, 2.23, 3.09–3.10 (see also "Uncredited")
Willett, Chad 1.13
Winton, Colleen 1.03
Witter, Karen 3.03
Woodbine, Bokeem 3.05
Woods–Morris, Jamie 1.06
Woodward, Meredith Bain 2.06
Woodward, Morgan 2.12
Wray, Dean 3.08

Yamamoto, Donna 2.23
Yee, Richard 2.07
Young, Bruce 2.15
Young, Dey 1.22

Zachary, Jude 2.22
Zeilinger, Beatrice 2.17, 3.07

UNCREDITED ONSCREEN:
Andaluz, Michael 3.05 *
Bermel, Pat 3.07
Carter, Chris 2.25
Cunningham, Cavan 3.03
Cutshall, D. Harlan 3.07
Dickson, Paul 3.07
Dinunzios, Aurelio 2.25
Frazier, Guyle 2.07 *
Hay, Bonnie 3.03
Kotowich, Brennan 3.07
Malebranche, Adrien 2.15
Mardon, Alexa 3.08
McDonald, Michael 2.16 *
McIntyre, Capper 2.16
McKay, Don 3.05 *
Michael, Tim 3.01 **
Moon, Byron Chief 2.25 **
Moore, John 3.01
Pinard, Bruce 3.05
Rands, Doris 3.04
Sparks, Carrie Cain 3.09
Takeuchi, Warren 3.09
Walsh, Stanley 3.01–3.02
Wilde, Bob 3.09
Williams, Steven 2.02 (voice only)
* No speaking lines or prominent presence onscreen, but listed in print sources, with scene(s) likely cut in editing
** Role credited in print sources to Tim Michael in 3.01–3.02, though performer is the same in all three episodes.

Writers

Barber, Larry & Barber, Paul 1.14
Biller, Kenneth & Brancato, Chris 1.11
Brown, Paul 2.06, 2.11
Carter, Chris 1.01–1.02, 1.05, 1.09, 1.12, 1.20, 1.24, 2.02, 2.05, 2.10, 2.13, 2.16 (teleeplay), 2.25 (teleplay), 3.01–3.02, 3.05, 3.13
Carter, Chris & Gordon, Howard: SEE under "Gordon"
Carter, Chris; Gordon, Howard; Spotnitz, Frank 3.09
Charno, Sara B. 2.12, 2.21
Craig, Charles Grant 3.08
DeJarnatt, Steve 2.18
Duchovny, David & Carter, Chris 2.16 (story), 2.25 (story)
Gansa, Alex & Gordon, Howard 1.04, 1.07, 1.10, 1.15, 1.22, 2.19 (teleplay)
Gilligan, Vince 2.23, 3.17
Gordon, Howard 2.04, 2.09, 2.15, 2.19 (story), 3.03, 3.14
Gordon, Howard & Carter, Chris 1.18, 2.22
Gordon, Howard & Gansa, Alex: SEE under "Gansa"
Kaufer, Scott and Carter, Chris 1.16
Morgan, Darin 2.03 (story only), 2.20, 3.04, 3.12, 3.20
Morgan, Glen & Wong, James 1.03, 1.06, 1.08, 1.13, 1.17, 1.21, 2.01, 2.03 (teleplay only), 2.08, 2.14
Newton, Kim 3.11
Osborn, Marilyn 1.19
Ruppenthal, Chris and Morgan, Glen & Wong, James 2.07
Shiban, John 3.07, 3.18
Spotnitz, Frank 2.17, 2.24, 3.10
Spotnitz, Frank & Carter, Chris 3.15–3.16
Vlaming, Jeffrey 3.06, 3.19
Wong, James & Morgan, Glen: SEE under "Morgan"

Directors

Bowman, Rob 1.14, 2.04, 2.12, 2.15, 2.17, 2.19, 2.22, 2.24, 3.02, 3.04, 3.07, 3.10, 3.13, 3.15, 3.17, 3.20
Carter, Chris 2.05, 3.05
Contner, James 2.23
Freedman, Jerrold 1.07, 1.12
Gates, Tucker 3.19
Gerber, Fred 1.11
Goodwin, R.W. 1.24, 2.08, 2.25, 3.01
Graham, William 1.09, 1.17
Katleman, Michael 1.06
Lange, Michael 1.16, 1.18, 2.06
Longstreet, Harry 1.03
Mandel, Robert 1.01
Manners, Kim 2.14, 2.20, 3.03, 3.08, 3.12, 3.14, 3.16, 3.18
Marck, Nick 2.16
Napolitano, Joe 1.05, 1.20
Nutter, David 1.08, 1.13, 1.15, 1.19, 1.21, 1.23, 2.01, 2.03, 2.07, 2.09, 2.13, 3.06, 3.09, 3.11
Phelps, Win 2.10
Ruppenthal, Chris 1.23
Sackheim, Daniel 1.02, 1.04, 2.02
Shaw, Larry 1.10, 1.12
Surjik, Stephen 2.11
Vejar, Michael 2.21
Whitmore, Jr., James 2.18